Apalachicola Valley Archaeology

A Dan Josselyn Memorial Publication

APALACHICOLA VALLEY
ARCHAEOLOGY
Prehistory through the Middle Woodland Period

VOLUME I

NANCY MARIE WHITE

The University of Alabama Press   Tuscaloosa

The University of Alabama Press
Tuscaloosa, Alabama 35487–0380
uapress.ua.edu

Copyright © 2024 by the University of Alabama Press
All rights reserved.

Inquiries about reproducing material from this work should be
addressed to the University of Alabama Press.

Typeface: Adobe Caslon

Cover image: *Above,* Middle Chipola River; *below* (left to right), Weeden Island bird-effigy jar, Late Archaic disc bead, and Weeden Island Incised vessel; photographs by William D. Tyler (above) and Nancy Marie White
Cover design: Michele Myatt Quinn

Cataloging-in-Publication data is available from the Library of Congress.
ISBN: 978-0-8173-2180-2 (cloth)
ISBN: 978-0-8173-6130-3 (paper)
E-ISBN: 978-0-8173-9481-3

To the people of Jackson, Calhoun, Liberty, Gadsden,
Gulf, and Franklin Counties, Florida;
Seminole, Decatur, and Early Counties, Georgia;
and Henry and Houston Counties, Alabama,
whose sharing of archaeological knowledge and wonderful hospitality
have made the research possible

Contents

Preface	ix
Acknowledgments	xiii
Abbreviations	xvii
Introduction: Archaeological Background	1
1 Environments in the Region	23
2 Resources and People	44
3 Paleoindian Period, ca. 15,000 to 10,000 BP (13,000 to 8000 BC), the First People	89
4 Early and Middle Archaic Periods, 10,000 to ca. 5500 BP (8,000 to 3,500 BC)	137
5 Late Archaic Period, ca. 3,500 to 800 BC	162
6 Early Woodland Period, 800 BC to AD 300	194
7 Middle Woodland Period, AD 300 to 700	218
References Cited	273
Index	313

Plates follow page 126.

Preface

Arriving in northwest Florida's Apalachicola–lower Chattahoochee valley in 1973 as a student, I was instantly immersed in public archaeology, lush environments, and great research. We students came from Case Western Reserve University (CWRU) in Cleveland, Ohio, with our anthropology professor David Brose, to work in a warm region during a January session. Florida State University (FSU) professionals arranged it, and Calhoun County residents helped us urban college kids learn the cultural heritage. I was entranced with the region, returned for surveys and graduate research, and then established a continuing program with my own students. Over the years I have traversed 300 river miles through this valley in Alabama, Georgia, and Florida, recording sites and collections and conducting excavations. However, this book has taken a long time, first requiring many projects to be finished and details organized.

Positive aspects of taking so long are that I have a greater understanding of landscapes and the big picture, better results from newer methods, and far more field experience in the eastern United States and abroad. Living in Mexico for a year initiated me to the wonders of archaeology, and later visits included a road trip researching my *Gulf Coast Archaeology* book and survey in Yucatán with Mayanist Tony Andrews. A semester in Italy showed me how Native American chiefdoms in the southeastern United States were similar to complex Iron-Age Etruscan societies (except Etruscans had iron and wine). Touring mounds, megalithic structures, and other sites in Europe, the Middle East, and East Asia, as well as high-Andes South American stoneworks (challenging for an acrophobic) brought me more appreciation of the incredible skills of past peoples. Visiting Lascaux and other European Paleolithic sites and learning from professionals in southwest France made me think more about the lifestyles and artistry of foragers. A southern Africa trip with game walks raised my awareness of big, dangerous beasts similar to what Paleoindians experienced. Two semesters in Borneo, with a visit to breathtaking Niah Cave and field excavations in jungle highlands, broadened my knowledge of tropical-forest and wetlands archaeology and fisher-gatherer-hunter and farming cultures in Malaysia, Brunei, and Indonesia.

Archaeology must be shared. I began holding archaeology day programs in 1978 throughout the Apalachicola–lower Chattahoochee research region, learning of its amazing research potential and immense community enthusiasm and knowledge. No synthesis of the cultural record existed, and the valley was often ignored for the lack of published work. Beyond a small booklet, *Apalachicola Valley Archaeology* (White et al. 1992, reprinted 1998), much more was needed. Thus, I present this two-volume work. This volume covers the time from the first people in the region, probably at least 15,000 years ago, through the Middle Woodland period, which ended around AD 700, and Volume 2 covers the last millennium, from the Late Woodland period through the present. The drawings at the top of this preface and the acknowledgments are from a design on a Weeden Island Incised pot from Pierce Mounds in Apalachicola (Moore 1902:223); they are my greetings and thanks to readers, with hopes that you will enjoy this book or at least find it useful. I love archaeology, and I love the Apalachicola–lower Chattahoochee–lower Flint River valley and its forests, swamps, bluffs, creeks, marshes, sinks, springs, bays, and beaches. Humorist Dave Barry says you should not confuse your career with your life, but it is impossible not to when you do fascinating things in beautiful places with great people. Archaeologist Ian Brown gave me a copy of his narrative of field research in the Mobile delta (Brown 2012), which he inscribed with this line: "Swamp archaeologists like yourself know both the beauty and perils of an environment that will get into your soul at the same time as it is eating you up." He is right; it becomes a life passion that you want to share. Even more important is that the incredible multicultural human record here demands documentation and interpretation.

A Note on Data

The region of concern for this book encompasses the entire valley of the Apalachicola River and the lowest 50 river miles of the Chattahoochee River. Descriptions and interpretations are supported by considerable amounts of archaeological data that are summarized in these pages but too unwieldy to present in complete detail. Readers can find all this information through the University of South Florida Digital Commons website for the Apalachicola

Valley Archaeology Supporting Data. Included there are tables listing the research chronology, documented watercraft sites, steatite artifacts, plant and animal remains, county populations, reported human remains, Paleoindian sites and isolated finds, Early and Middle Woodland mounds, Fort Walton mounds and cemetery sites, ceramic mushrooms, protohistoric sites, Creek/Seminole sites, and radiocarbon dates as well as a summary of my field and lab methods and an artifact sorting/classification guide. In addition, in the book, private collection sources list the collectors' initials only.

A Note on Terminology

The past peoples discussed in this book were Native Americans of prehistoric times, meaning simply that they lived earlier than any written records about them, so we do not know their names. Their historic descendants went by many names, including those given to them by outsiders, which were often inaccurate or insulting. As a group, their descendants have been called Indians, though that word originally meant South Asians, and even "America" is a foreign name, from an Italian mapmaker. Indigenous or aboriginal or native are words that simply mean they were the original or first peoples of this land, and current experts disagree on which terms are most appropriate and least biased or demeaning (e.g., National Museum of the American Indian website; Canadian usage is better: "First Nations"). I use all of these terms. My goal is respectful reconstruction of their diverse cultures using the material evidence they left, to bring greater knowledge of their fascinating past lifeways within the landscapes that we continue to appreciate today.

Acknowledgments

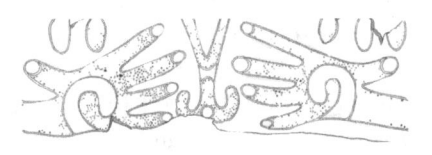

In this work I have been honored to receive help and hospitality from fellow professionals and from the people of northwest Florida, southeast Alabama, and southwest Georgia. I have been educated in areas ranging from catfish fries and peanut boils to forest and wetland life to site formation processes by the generous folks of this ten-county research region. Though I cannot possibly name all who have made my investigations possible, some merit special thanks. In the upper Apalachicola–lower Chattahoochee area, the Cox family of Sneads provided great support. Park ranger Ralph Cox often rescued us when vehicles failed. Dale Cox, interested in archaeology as a teen, became a journalist and historian and has helped for decades, sending me old maps and other valuable information. On the lower Flint River, outdoorsman Jack Wingate showcased artifacts on the walls of his Lunker Lodge, shared site data, and saved me from a rattlesnake. Botanist Angus Gholson, Jim Woodruff Dam manager, provided logistical support and plant knowledge. I remain grateful to residents Nathan Arnold, Coleman Bevis, Scott Evans, Hub Chason, Homer Hirt, Ron Hunt, O. Y. Ingram, Bill and Neil and Jason Keene, John McKinnie, Terry Mercer, D. D. Miles, Eddie Nesmith, and their families. Leon Perry donated his Curlee site collection (thirty boxes!), and Georgia archaeologist Frankie Snow facilitated that transfer and has given much additional advice over the years.

In the middle valley, Suella McMillan, artist and former director of the W. T. Neal Civic Center, has been a guardian angel, supplying funds, facilities, child care, and killer parties with "liquid research materials." Forest expert Phil McMillan aided with knowledge, permissions, and other help. Finlay and Donna Corbin, Dan Brymer, Calvin Foran, and others around Blountstown provided much assistance. Avocational archaeologist and flintknapper Jeff

Whitfield has shared artifacts, sites, guide services, archaeology-day presentations, and introductions to collectors. He contributed greatly on a 5,000-mile research trip around the Gulf of Mexico, valiantly reviewed the original (huge) draft of this book, and helps me expand my still-limited forest-survival skills.

In the lower valley, the Apalachicola National Estuarine Research Reserve and St. Joseph Bay State Buffer Preserve agencies enabled work in the delta swamps and estuaries. Their citizen-support groups led by Lisa Johnston, Marie Romanelli, Denise Williams, and others have made a huge difference. Former director Woody Miley supplied resources, rescues, and laughs. Bonnie Holub, education coordinator, was a constant source of help. Rebecca Bernard, Sandra Chafin, Lee Edmiston, Jean Huffman, Neil Jones, Erik Lovestrand, Roy Ogles, Dylan Shoemaker, Jenna Wanat, Kim Wren, and all the other admirable staff have cared for my students and facilitated research. Extraordinary efforts have been put forth by Pat Millender and Jimmy Moses and their families. Jimmy and Pat have sustained crews in rough conditions, such as waist-deep swamps while carrying heavy equipment in a lightning storm, or hauling the pregnant archaeologist into the boat from alligator-infested waters, in the dark. They also contributed on the trip around the Gulf and often save projects from disaster or boredom.

People around Howard Creek Fish Camp offered ample hospitality (two of them marrying students on my crews). Max Fleming provided a crew house, where adoptive godparents Arthur and Eletha Nixon cooked us swamp cabbage (palm heart) stew. Also in Gulf and Franklin Counties Kristin Anderson, Doug Birmingham, Wayne Childers, Bill Herring, Kate Johnson, Lisa Johnston, Charlotte Pierce, Tim Nelson, Tom Semmes, Janie Shealy, and Roy Whitfield and his family shared artifacts and information. Herman, Pam, and Trip Jones have generously contributed knowledge, materials, and funds for analyses. Jerry Cauthen shared artifact and site data and donated his entire collection (thirty boxes with computer database!). Mark and Ken Elliott first brought me to Pierce Mounds, where landowner George Mahr later supported the work. Troy Deal III shared his materials and knowledge of St. Joseph Bay. The Apalachicola Maritime Museum, Apalachicola Main Street, and Carrabelle History Museum help heritage conservation. Dianne and Ed Mellon invited and supported the Dog Island survey. Librarians in all the counties are phenomenal resource persons.

Enormous thanks are due to many colleagues. Professor David Brose introduced us students to the marvels of Ohio archaeology and inspired my field forays into western New York and elsewhere before bringing us to learn of the archaeology (and virulent poison ivy) in the South. He influenced my career especially with his broad perspectives on the whole eastern United States. George Percy, Florida State University (FSU) professor and later State

Historic Preservation Officer, was always encouraging. Historic preservation grants from the Florida Division of Historical Resources have been the major support for this research. Their site file, research, and historic preservation specialists are knowledgeable and amiable. Marie Prentice and other collections staff have supplied expertise and patience. Calvin Jones trekked into remote sites with me from my student days onward. Louis Tesar volunteered on my field projects, donating refreshments and flintknapping skills. Kathy Jones computerized the Florida site file in the 1980s and made site distribution maps (though we had to go to another building to get printouts). Fellow students Stephanie Belovich, Eloise Gadus, Rusty Weisman, and others worked on the Lakes Seminole and Andrews surveys, struggling with the boat, finding the whole pot on a day I was home writing the monthly report, and bringing much labor and friendship.

Assistance has been provided in Alabama by archaeologists Rick Fuller, Eugene Futato, Ned Jenkins, Jason Mann, Betsy and Craig Sheldon, and Greg Waselkov, and in Georgia by Frank and Gail Schnell, Marvin Smith, and Mark Williams and his staff. In Florida, Jerry Milanich was encouraging since I first showed up at the Florida Museum of Natural History (FLMNH) as a hopeful student. Ethnobotanical identifications were done by Michelle Alexander, Donna Ruhl, Mallory Melton, and Betsy Sheldon. Zooarchaeology was done by Elizabeth Wing and her FLMNH team, including Karen Jo Walker, Irv Quitmyer, Arlene Fradkin, and Bruce Shockey, and also Judith Fandrich and malacologist James Williams. For considerable research assistance I also thank archaeologists Keith Ashley, Bob Austin, Dennis Blanton, John Blitz, Sam Brookes, Craig Dengel, Tom Foster, Jerry Lee, John O'Hear, Dan Penton, Mike Russo, Karen Smith, Roger Smith, Keith Stephenson, Rosie Bongiovanni Tullos, Rob Tykot, Rich Weinstein, and personnel at the Smithsonian National Museum of the American Indian and National Museum of Natural History collections, especially James Krakker. Penton, also a Traditional Chief of the Muscogee Nation of Florida, graciously reviewed the book manuscript. Stephenson provided radiocarbon dates. At FSU, Jessi Halligan reviewed the Paleoindian chapter, and Rochelle Marrinan has contributed hugely in everything from zooarchaeology to theory. She improved my recitation of the line in Flannery's (1982) "Golden Marshalltown" parable, that "archaeology is the most fun you can have with your pants on," by saying that archaeology is the most fun you can have in life!

I am indebted to Gordon Willey, gracious "big man" of archaeology, for encouragement, stories, a symposium contribution (Willey 1985), and copies of his mystery novels. Roy Larick, specialist in southeast Asia, French Paleolithic, East African ethnoarchaeology, and Ohio geoarchaeology, provided fresh perspectives and took me to Paleoindian sites out West when we were students.

Geologist Joe Donoghue visited sites, provided references, data, and reviews, and explained how rivers move and seas rise. Soils specialist Bob Brinkmann, geologist Frank Stapor, and cultural anthropologist Roberta Hammond also furnished support. I appreciate all the efforts of anonymous reviewers and of University of Alabama Press editor Wendi Schnaufer.

Former University of South Florida students who gave more beyond field, lab, and thesis research are Jeff Du Vernay, Maggie Goetze, Ryan Harke, Susan (Henefield) Harp, Chris Hunt, Kerri Klein, Karen Mayo, Erin McKendry, Bart McLeod, and Brian Parker. Mayo, an incomparable organizer who also assisted on the Gulf trip, did the index. Alumna Dorothy Ward often donated funding for student work. Over two dozen students wrote theses involving research in the region, as cited in the chapters. Stimulus for beginning the writing of this book in earnest came during my 2014 visiting professorship at the University of Malaysia Sarawak. I thank colleagues there, especially Cheng Sim Hew and her family, who made everything possible, and Nicholas Gani, Yuen Kok Leong, Elena Gregoria Chai, Juna Liau, Sharifah Sophia Wan Ahmad, and Neilson Ilan Mersat. Gani and Lindsay Lloyd-Smith invited me and the new archaeology students to do fieldwork in the Borneo highlands. Archaeologist Lee Hutchinson, a true-blue pal, also cheerfully reviewed the early gigantic draft of this book and has provided food, spirits, folding shovel, flowers, research data, and laughs. Musician Dawn Lovins suggested the idea of a Middle Woodland burial planner. Neighbors Sandra and Greg Haxton always look out for me. Offspring Tony White, engineer and honorary archaeologist, has done fieldwork, mapmaking, drone videos, and computer assistance.

Abbreviations

ANERR	Apalachicola National Estuarine Research Reserve
BAR	Florida Bureau of Archaeological Research (within the DHR, Department of State)
CMNH	Cleveland Museum of Natural History
CWRU	Case Western Reserve University
DHR	Division of Historical Resources, Florida Department of State, Tallahassee
FLMNH	Florida Museum of Natural History
FSU	Florida State University
GIS	Geographic information systems (computer mapping and layering data)
NOAA	National Oceanic and Atmospheric Administration, US Deptartment of Commerce
pXRF	Portable X-ray fluorescence
UGA	University of Georgia
USDA	United States Department of Agriculture
USF	University of South Florida, Tampa
USGS	United States Geological Survey

Apalachicola Valley Archaeology

Introduction

Archaeological Background

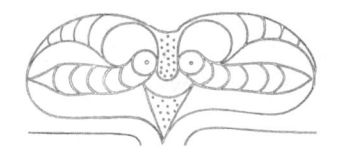

In a fast boat, one could start at the top of the Apalachicola River, at the Georgia-Florida border, and go all the way down to the Gulf of Mexico, about 110 river (navigation) miles, in a good day. Or the trip could take two days (or go fast) and begin another 50 miles upriver at Omussee Creek, by Columbia, Alabama, scooting down past the higher bluffs of the lowest part of the lower Chattahoochee River. One would see few buildings on the banks (two power plants, occasional cabins, houseboats), few bridges, two dams, farmlands, pastures, people fishing. But mostly there are vast forests in the bottomlands and up the valley sides and terraces, all connected in a watery network, vibrating with calls of birds, frogs, insects, splashes of jumping fish, and rustles of scurrying animals. At the end of the day, at the river's mouth, there would be a seafood dinner in the picturesque town of Apalachicola and a view of the wide bay. The archaeology of this valley is astoundingly rich: no prehistoric stone monuments or gold, but in the plowed fields, dirt roads, and stream banks, stone tools, potsherds, and food remains testify to a long record of human residence. Earthen mounds along waterways entomb the sacred ancient dead, and hundreds of shell midden ridges reflect the continuing bounty of the waters. Remnants of prehistoric communities are shrouded in jungle foliage.

People first arrived by probably at least 15,000 years ago and harvested now-extinct large animals. They persisted through the first global warming humans experienced, when the Pleistocene (Ice Age) ended about 10,000 years ago, and thrived for another ten millennia. Collecting wild foods, they moved with the seasons, repeatedly camping on higher ground. By AD 300, they were making and importing ornate artifacts and developing elaborate funerary rituals to bury their dead in mounds. The archaeological record of this long human sequence is related in this book. (Volume 2 takes up with the origins of farming societies by AD 1000, the invasion and colonization by European peoples, the surviving Native Americans, Europeans, and Africans, and the developing American nation in the region.) The natural and cultural processes that form the landscape leave physical evidence that tells the stories far deeper into the past than written records ever could. Anthropological archaeology, studying the material remains of human existence, is the major way to reconstruct the past(s) of the "people without history" (Wolf 1982), those not described well or favorably, or at all, in documents. Especially important here are the Indigenous societies who inhabited the land for so many thousands of years before any written descriptions. Though Native American descendants remain, their ancient cultures do not. Archaeology helps recover their voices and explore their past lifeways.

Figure I.1. Apalachicola–lower Chattahoochee valley research region outlined within the US Southeast. (Nancy Marie White)

The specific research region for this book (Figures I.1 and I.2), nearly 160 river (navigation) miles long, overlaps modern boundaries of three states and individually named rivers, but is distinctive archaeologically and environmentally. The basin of the upper Apalachicola and lower Chattahoochee has hardwood bottomland forests, wide pasturelands dotted with fat, old oaks and magnolias, tall straight pines, sinkhole ponds, and cypress domes. On the east side of the Flint River and the upper Apalachicola are high, steep ravines with seeping springs and rare plants and animals. The valley widens downstream into vast cypress and tupelo wetlands, where the "watery wilderness

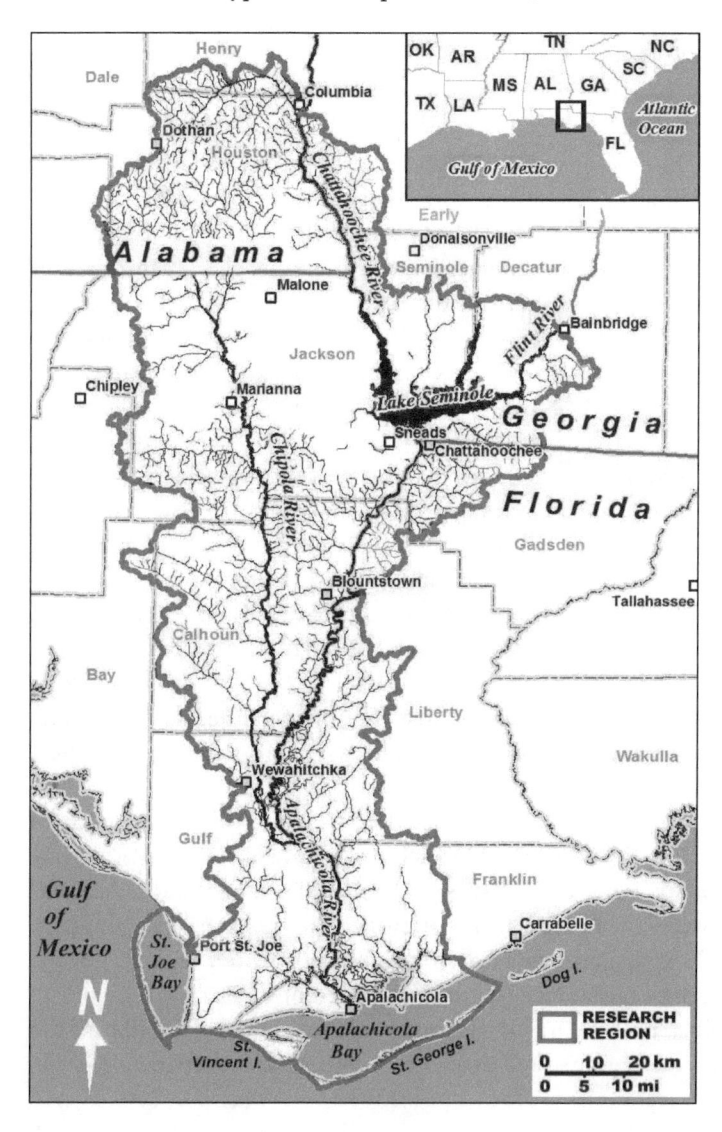

Figure I.2. Apalachicola–lower Chattahoochee valley research region in Florida, Alabama, and Georgia (Nancy Marie White)

of Apalach" (Watts 1975) is deep and dark. It gives way to estuarine marshes with tall rough grasses, scrawny oaks, cedars, and cabbage palms. The Apalachicola delta is some of the wildest land left in Florida, with immense wet hammocks and marshlands that sustain one of the nation's most productive fisheries (Byers and Willson 1988:22). The south edge of the mainland is the north shore of Apalachicola Bay. Opposite shores are on white-sand barrier islands, with scrubby dune vegetation and gorgeous Gulf beaches. These diverse but connected ecosystems of the fluvial network have notable continuity in geography and material culture. I have worked well beyond these boundaries but have found that both environments and past material cultures are markedly different outside this region.

Goals of This Book

This preview gives some background on the early prehistory of the research region. After summarizing here the work by those who came before me and my investigations, theoretical orientations, and methods, I describe in Chapters 1 and 2 the natural environments, resources, and peoples. Then I present the archaeology from the first humans through the Middle Woodland period, ending about AD 700 (Volume 2 begins with the Late Woodland period and continues through recent history). Tables with the original supporting data and descriptions of methods and artifact classifications are available online (White 2023).

Archaeological knowledge is more than just fascinating science. Past humans used and manipulated species and ecosystems, succeeded despite disasters, transformed from lesser to greater sociopolitical complexity or vice versa, made handy artifacts and beautiful art, and affected their own health and biology. Understanding all this is applied anthropology, with potential practical applications today for resource managers, architects, biologists, policy makers, and others. In addition, all archaeology is, or should be, public archaeology, part of exploring the enormous complexity of human cultures and expanding our ability to understand, even tolerate, peoples whose lives are or were different from ours (Barrett 2021:7).

In 1980 the premier book on Florida archaeology noted that much of northwest Florida was unknown (Milanich and Fairbanks 1980:24). Milanich (1994) later updated the prehistory of the whole state, though peninsular Florida (closer to universities) has often been more examined. Similarly, Alabama and Georgia archaeology mostly emphasize central regions, not the remote corners. But my summary here of one coherent valley region is not just an attempt to fill gaps. I tie in related data from throughout the Southeast and beyond to place the region's archaeological record within the larger context, before the cultural resources are lost.

Modern American Indians in the region, as well as local historians and genealogists, now strive to recover their heritage before the historic documents and memories of old ways are gone (e.g., Penton 2001; Toner 2016a, 2016b). Often the cultural adaptations of many millennia before them have disappeared except for their archaeological traces, which themselves are hugely biased, due to differential preservation of materials and accidents of exposure and destruction. In addition, sites keep disappearing at an alarming rate because of human and natural action, from sea-level rise to construction. Florida, Georgia, and Alabama continue the political battle over water rights in the Apalachicola–Chattahoochee–Flint Rivers (ACF) "water wars," the longest fight over water in US history. Amid these disputes, little attention is paid to preserve cultural resources. Dams, dredging, and land alteration enlarge the losses. Now in this region, development of new communities and retirement complexes is shifting areas from agricultural to residential, often without study of archaeological impacts (Elliott and Dean 2006:60). Of course, past peoples, probably since the time of their first arrival, manipulated landscapes themselves and greatly affected natural systems, but not on the scale that we see today. The positive view is that archaeological resources are so fabulously abundant here that there has still been a lot to find.

Early Interest and Investigation

Descriptions of archaeological remains in the Apalachicola–lower Chattahoochee valley come from early Euro-American settlers who amused themselves by digging in Indian mounds, as a passage from a Florida woman's 1835 letter shows (Denham and Huneycutt 2004:17). More charming evidence is in a poem discovered by director of Apalachicola Main Street Augusta West in the January 1, 1844, edition (Vol. 2, No. 1, p. 3) of the *Commercial Advertiser*, an Apalachicola newspaper. The first verse is reproduced here as in the original; the author is given as "LUCY":

> *TO A SOLITARY FLOWER,*
> Plucked from an Indian Mound, near Apalachi-
> cola, 22nd December, 1843.
> Sweet, simple flower! and thou didst wave
> Above the mound:—the Indian's grave?—
> I found thee there to-day;
> Where Chattahoochee's waters lave,
> Thou bloomed;—where sleeps many a brave
> Whose souls have fled away. . . .

Four more verses follow, in the same romantic style, speculating on Native American history.

Other early documentation exists because the city of Apalachicola was commercially connected with New York. Artifacts at the New York Historical Society were described by geographer/ethnographer Henry Schoolcraft. He was especially interested in materials given by James R. Hitchcock of Florida, who had obtained much pottery in 1841, from "one of the minor species of mounds on the Appalachicola [sic] bay" (Schoolcraft 1847:127). These mounds were "generally from thirty to fifty feet in diameter and from twelve to eighteen feet in height" and contained burials. Schoolcraft thought that the Florida pots were aesthetically superior to those from elsewhere in the United States. The source of this collection was probably the Pierce Mounds complex (8Fr14; see Chapters 6 and 7 herein), with burial and temple mounds and shell ridges lining the old riverbank.

The British tradition of nineteenth-century naturalists and the monumental institution of the British Museum ironically resulted in more early documentation of the same Pierce Mounds (White 2013). In London I studied the artifacts sent to this museum by antiquities dealers. A clay pipe and four ground-stone items were obtained in 1869 from Pierce, and stone and shell tools and pottery from a mound or mounds near or at "Appalachicola" were acquired in 1875. Another collection from Pierce, dated 1888, was accumulated by Apalachicola resident H. L. Grady and donated to the Florida State Museum (now Florida Museum of Natural History [FLMNH]) in Gainesville. The Grady materials include a pipe, shell beads, and a sketch map. These recorded activities were probably a small part of the artifact hunting that was going on in this bustling city. The ancient Native Americans' major mound center here was the same place later settlers chose as a base for international commerce, a strategic location at the river mouth.

Another place in the valley where early American settlers uncovered artifacts is at the top of the Apalachicola River near the town of Chattahoochee, where the Chattahoochee Landing Mound complex (8Gd4) is the only other multimound center in the region (White 2021). Sitting just below the Chattahoochee–Flint River confluence or forks, it was an important travel and commerce hub, with a ferry and an inn (on top of Mound 2) in 1837 (Castelnau 1843). The Smithsonian National Museum of Natural History collections contain chert and pottery pieces from "near Chattahoochee Landing in Gadsden County, Florida," and one stemmed chert scraper from "near Bainbridge in Decatur County, Georgia," collected by W. H. Dall in the 1890s. Beyond these examples, farmers probably plowed up millions of artifacts annually. I have seen cherished collections that have been in families for up to four generations.

Archaeology in the Apalachicola–lower Chattahoochee valley region became more visible with Clarence Bloomfield Moore in the early 1900s. He was a wealthy Philadelphian, president of a paper company, world traveler, and big-game hunter. When an accident resulted in a serious eye injury, he began (supposedly) less dangerous archaeological work in the South. With his specially outfitted steamboat, the *Gopher*, he traveled along rivers to dig mounds, sending artifacts home to the Academy of Natural Sciences in Philadelphia. He worked in the winter months, usually with an African American crew from the northwest Florida town of Sopchoppy. Though his methods were not modern, he kept notes and published in the Academy's journal. Moore (1902, 1903, 1907, 1918) came early to the Apalachicola–lower Chattahoochee valley region and returned for four seasons because he was so impressed with the pottery (Brose and White 1999). Discussion of sites here, as elsewhere in the South, often begins with what he found. After moving around several times (Peck and Stroud 2012; Wardle 1929) his collections are now at the Smithsonian's National Museum of the American Indian (NMAI).

Early Professional Archaeology

American archaeology became professionalized during the Great Depression, with economic relief programs established by the federal government to make jobs for the unemployed. Researchers recorded American peoples and cultures, including those of prehistoric times. Gordon R. Willey, while excavating in Georgia in the 1930s with A. R. Kelly, visited the Florida panhandle and saw its huge archaeological potential. He began his survey along the Gulf with Richard Woodbury in 1940, relocating some of Moore's sites (Willey and Woodbury 1942). He tied ceramic-based time periods to sequences in Georgia and the Lower Mississippi valley, and his *Archeology of the Florida Gulf Coast* (1949) is still the major reference for the region, refined by later radiocarbon dating. Willey moved on to archaeology in Mesoamerica and Peru, but he was always fond of northwest Florida. After retiring from Harvard, he wrote mystery novels including *Selena* (Figure I.3), a story of a retired, elderly archaeologist amid murder and intrigue in the Florida panhandle (Willey 1993; White 1994a). He fictionalized town names, and he called the Pierce site "Bull mounds."

Archaeologists came next to the Apalachicola–lower Chattahoochee valley for projects in the Smithsonian's River Basin Surveys (RBS) program, in advance of dam construction. The US Army Corps of Engineers built the Jim Woodruff Dam at the confluence of the Chattahoochee and Flint Rivers, creating the Jim Woodruff Reservoir (Lake Seminole) that extends 25 river miles up the Chattahoochee to the Alabama line and a similar distance up the Flint (see Figure I.2). Table I.1 gives distances. Another dam, at Chattahoochee Mile 46.5 near Columbia, Alabama, is named George W. Andrews. It backs up 29 river miles but does not form a wide reservoir. Farther up the Chattahoochee at Mile 75, the Walter F. George Dam created a reservoir (Lake

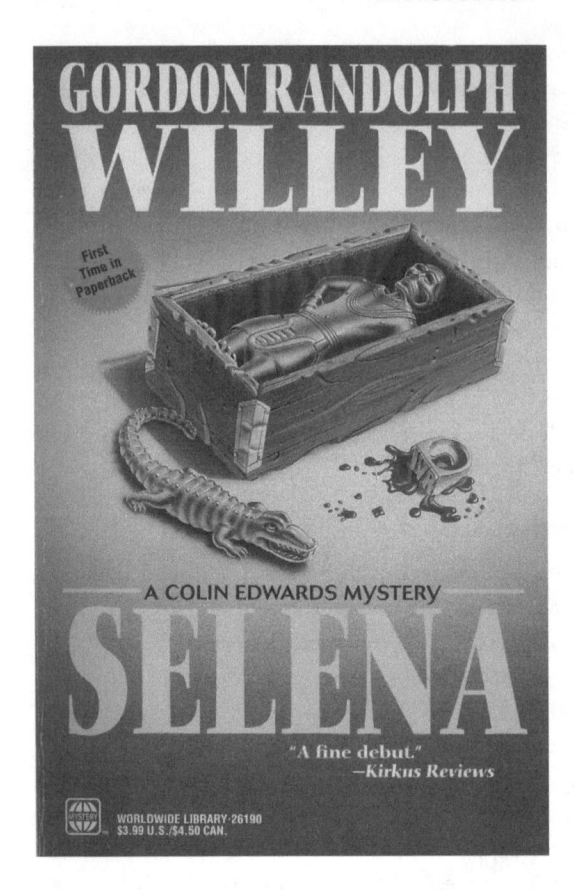

Figure I.3. Cover of *Selena*, 1993 mystery novel by Gordon Willey set in northwest Florida. (Nancy Marie White)

Eufaula) just above Fort Gaines, Georgia. Up to this dam is the farthest north I have surveyed. The research area for this book does not reach that far north, but the archaeology up there is instructive to compare. Combining distances on the Chattahoochee, Flint, Chipola, and Apalachicola gives me over 300 river miles (485 km) of boat, truck, and pedestrian survey, plus thousands more miles along tributary and distributary creeks.

Beginning in 1948, archaeological surveys were performed around the proposed Woodruff Reservoir by Ripley P. Bullen (1950) for the Florida Park Service, and A. R. Kelly (1950a, 1950b, 1950c) and Joseph R. Caldwell for the University of Georgia (UGA). Most pre-reservoir survey was surface collection, driving around talking with collectors, and inspecting plowed fields, as shovel-testing was not done then. Later, the extensive clearing operations for reservoir construction opened large areas. In the early 1950s salvage excavations were carried out at selected sites by these archaeologists and also Carl Miller, Clemens DeBaillou, and others. A letter from Frank H. H. Roberts Jr., the

TABLE I.1. GEOGRAPHIC LOCATIONS ALONG THE APALACHICOLA–LOWER CHATTAHOOCHEE VALLEY REGION

Place	River (Navigation) Mile	Total mi. inland by water (km)
North of Research Region		
Origin of Chattahoochee River in north GA mountains	—	436 (702)
Columbus, GA, at Fall Line	Chattahoochee 156	266 (428)
Walter F. George Dam, Fort Gaines, GA	Chattahoochee 75.1	185 (298)
Within Research Region		
Columbia, AL	Chattahoochee 49.5	159.5 (257)
Omussee Creek, AL	Chattahoochee 47.7	158 (254)
Andrews Dam	Chattahoochee 46.8	157 (252)
Farley Nuclear Plant, AL	Chattahoochee 44.2	154 (248)
Confluence of Cowart's and Marshall Creeks, origin of Chipola River, 6 mi. (10 km) S of AL-FL border	Chipola 92.5	120 (194)
Bainbridge, GA	Flint 28	138 (222)
Confluence of Flint and Chattahoochee Rivers, forming the Apalachicola River	Apalachicola 110* Chattahoochee 0, Flint 0	110 (177)
Aspalaga Landing, Interstate 10 bridge	Apalachicola 100	100 (161)
Blountstown and Bristol, FL, Highway 20 bridge	Apalachicola 79.4	79.4 (128)
Chipola Cutoff (making Cutoff Island 15 to 20 mi. [25–30 km] long)	Apalachicola 41.6	41.6 (67)
Mouth of Chipola River into Apalachicola River	Apalachicola 28	28 (45)
Mouth of Jackson River into Apalachicola River	Apalachicola 6	6 (10)
Mouth of Apalachicola River into Apalachicola Bay; then 8 to 20 mi. (13–30 km) across bay out to Gulf of Mexico	Apalachicola 0	0

*Variously reported as 106.3 (Brown and Smith 1994:197–198); 106.7 (US Army Corps of Engineers 1978); 110 (Helen Light, personal communication 2000); 112 (Wikipedia). For this book a standard 110 is used.

Smithsonian's RBS director, to Miller (April 28, 1953, in Carl Miller Papers, National Anthropological Archives) notes how the work about to get underway was the first for which the Corps of Engineers had issued an actual archaeological permit. Smithsonian and UGA archives include letters in which these archaeologists lamented how working for institutions in the different states made it difficult to be consistent in their interpretations, a lingering problem.

Reports from these investigations were published by Bullen (1958) for Florida and Kelly (1953) for Georgia. Caldwell's manuscript on the Fairchild's Landing and Hare's Landing Sites (9Se14 and 9Se33) on the lower Chattahoochee, unfinished at his death, was edited by Betty A. Smith (1978) for the National Park Service, then redone with more information (Caldwell et al. 2014). I reviewed Miller's work at Montgomery Fields (9Dr10) on the Flint (White 2019). Before construction farther up the Chattahoochee at Columbia and Walter F. George dams, survey and testing were done by Hurt (1947) and Hushcher (1959a, 1959b). Other documentation by these archaeologists was in field notes, survey forms, maps, and proveniences on artifact bags and boxes at the various repositories. Much of the research was never written up because the archaeologists were sent from project to project for fieldwork, with no time even to inventory materials, let alone analyze anything.

Then the dams were finished, the basins somewhat cleared, and the water filled these artificial lakes, drowning some sites, making islands out of others that had been on hilltops, or cutting into those on the original riverbanks. The dams were for flood control, power generation, and recreation. Water levels fluctuated and archaeological sites began washing out of the shores. Picnic areas, parking lots, and boat ramps were also built. No universities with professional archaeologists were close to the region, and the plentiful prehistoric sites went unrecognized. Frank T. Schnell Jr., of the Columbus Museum, soon commented on the need for resurvey of reservoirs on the Chattahoochee (Schnell 1969), then did preliminary work at the Walter F. George reservoir (Schnell 1973). Knight and Mistovich (1984) were resurveying Walter F. George at about the same time as I was leading similar resurvey at the next two reservoirs downriver.

From the 1950s onward, the closest professional archaeologists to the Apalachicola–lower Chattahoochee region, at Florida State University (FSU), became involved when collectors brought their artifacts to Tallahassee to get information. Little of this work was reported. The FSU site numbers were later not coordinated with current official numbers, so it is difficult to tell even from where the bags of curated artifacts actually came. When the State Historic Preservation Office renumbered Florida sites, even published ones, it did not always keep them in the same numerical order, producing confusion. One FSU graduate student, Glenn T. Allen (1954), tested some coastal sites and another, Bennie Keel, dug at Yon Mound (8Li2) in the middle Apalachicola. William Gardner, a student at both FSU and the University of Florida (UF), surveyed in Jackson County. He dug at the Waddell's Mill Pond site (8Ja65), important for caves, mounds, Middle Woodland and later cultural deposits (Gardner 1966; also see Volume 2). This site was tested again in the 1970s by the Bureau of Archaeological Research (BAR) (Tesar and Jones 2009). My pursuit of clues from other professional work has shown me that many other archaeologists visited sites in this rich valley, collecting artifacts and data, which are now often lost. William Sears (1959), on a survey funded by the National Science Foundation, picked up artifacts at several sites, but they cannot be located. He mentioned collections that I have tried to trace, such as one from Yon Mound at Louisiana State University (LSU). Louisiana colleagues Steve Fullen, David Beriss, and Rick Shenkel (personal communication 2007) were unable to find any such collections there or at the University of New Orleans or Tulane. They also said that many earlier archaeologists moved around the South a lot and stopped at famous sites. As old collections are mined for new research, perhaps some of these materials will turn up.

By the 1970s more professionals from Tallahassee were in the region, notably BAR staff Dan Penton, Louis Tesar, and Calvin Jones, and FSU professor George Percy and his students (Jones 1974; Percy 1971; Percy and Jones 1976). Jerald Milanich (1974) of the FLMNH excavated the Sycamore site on the upper Apalachicola in the path of Interstate 10 construction. Aided by Percy, David Brose, of Case Western Reserve University (CWRU) and the Cleveland Museum of Natural History (CMNH), came with his students to Florida for fieldwork. Ned Jenkins (1978) surveyed on the lower Chattahoochee in Alabama. The investigations of all these archaeologists are cited in the appropriate chapters. It is satisfying to become familiar with the literature and how one's predecessors worked and thought, decipher their handwriting on old notes and bags, see their maps and artifacts, even talk with some of the same collectors or their descendants—doing the history and archaeology of the archaeologists.

Latest Work

I came with the Cleveland group to Blountstown, Florida, in the middle Apalachicola valley, to work on the FSU projects and salvage excavations in the path of the interstate bridge. Later Brose sent me to lead shoreline resurveys at Lakes Seminole and Andrews on the lower Chattahoochee and Flint. We stayed in Sneads, where people were so devoted to the outdoors that they closed the post office Thursday afternoons so they could go fishing. I learned the material culture of all time periods for the whole 180-river-mile stretch from Fort Gaines, Georgia, to the Gulf. Real differences were clear in the material record above the lowest 50 navigation miles of the Chattahoochee. Here the valley environments also change, with higher bluffs, perched streams falling into the river, more clayey than sandy soils, and cooler temperatures approaching the fall line, the northern edge of the Coastal Plain, where it meets the Piedmont near the city of Columbus. Below Chattahoochee Mile 50, a coherent archaeological area is recognizable, possibly reflecting some Native American cultural boundaries.

Very important for this book is that its research valley region is therefore that lowest 160 river miles on the big river (Chattahoochee-Apalachicola), the lowest 25 river miles of the Flint River, and all 92 river miles of the Chipola (see Table I.1). A crucial issue arose as I integrated survey results with the known record of "the lower Chattahoochee" and saw that much depends on how one defines this phrase. Most of what is known about an area named in this way concerns the archaeology within the Walter F. George reservoir, around Columbus, the fall line, and the Kolomoki Mounds. Those areas are 20 to 100 miles upriver from the Chattahoochee's lowest 50 river miles, which the literature seldom includes. Above this very lowest valley segment I was seeing significant differences during survey. Regular visits to the Kolomoki site and museum to compare materials, soils, and environments also convinced me that I was moving between two geographical and cultural territories.

At the Georgia site file in Athens, Alabama files at Moundville, FLMNH in Gainesville, and Florida site file in Tallahassee, site records were often confusing, with different names and numbers. For example, a Georgia site near the common border of three counties had been issued six different site numbers with three different county prefixes. Bullen's 54 Florida sites were originally numbered J-1, J-2, and so on, for Jackson County and G-1, G-2, and so on, for Gadsden County. A later system used the abbreviations "Ja" and "Gd," but often sites did not keep the old number, getting new numbers apparently based on their presumed importance. For example, Bullen's famous Chattahoochee River 1 site J-5 was renumbered 8Ja8. But boxes of artifacts from his survey mostly just had the new county prefix confusingly added to the old number. Another past practice was that none of the prehistoric lithic debitage Bullen listed for his sites was in the FLMNH drawers, because in those days chert flakes were recorded then discarded in the field (personal communication, Jerald Milanich, 1979); thus I may have been picking up the same flakes Bullen had counted and thrown back down. Months spent resolving these problems helped correct records somewhat (Belovich et al. 1982; White 1981).

State border issues were other cans of worms. Science and management are so often state-based that they create research impediments for anyone working in natural ecosystems that are cut by modern political boundaries. Terminology and administration are inconsistent from state to state. The creation of Lake Seminole straddling the Florida-Georgia border meant that boaters see a sign in the middle of this lake saying "Georgia Fishing License Required Beyond This Point." Aerial images of southwest Georgia show agribusinesses with circular farm fields from using center-pivot irrigation, while Florida fields to the west across the Chattahoochee are rectangular. The research complications extend to archaeology, as analyses have often not crossed state boundaries. Indigenous peoples doubtless saw the river as a connecting hub, not a dividing line. However, the region has been either unnaturally segmented for investigative purposes or somewhat neglected due to its location at the states' edges. Artifact-type names and time-period names also differed by state. My artifact sorting criteria standardize existing typologies in order to classify specimens into nonoverlapping categories; thus, even those who disagree with a type name can at least see what it means.

As for site formation processes, I learned that backed-up water in reservoirs made hilltops into islands with artifacts eroding out of their sides. Other islands with surface artifacts turned out to be artificial, made of dredging spoils. Seasonal inundation of some remains caused deterioration. At Lake Blackshear, north of the research region on the Flint, submersion in the reservoir obliterated surfaces of prehistoric ceramics (Schnell 1975). Further, roads everywhere, dirt and paved, were made of prehistoric midden materials—shell, sand, or clay. I had thought that artifacts on the roadside far enough away from the pavement or up the sides of the road-cut face were eroding out of the top, until I saw how they instead were dumped there in fill dirt. Artifacts in dirt roads were often put there when holes were filled with soil from borrow pits miles away.

More survey and then test excavations expanded my explorations in the Apalachicola valley, and a website on the region's archaeology was developed (Prendergast and White 2017). From the beginning, I did public archaeology day programs almost yearly and studied private collections constantly. Terry Simpson's 1996 thesis compiled the first regional database, including FLMNH materials that were acquired by J. Clarence Simpson of the Florida Geological Survey between 1930 and 1952. Adam Schieffer's (2013) thesis was the next GIS synthesis, and this book expands on all that work. The research is data heavy, driven by a need to go back to primary sources, run down original site and artifact information, and include other professional work (e.g., Elliott 2004; Elliott and Dean 2006). I spent decades traversing portions of a six-county area of Florida's panhandle, three counties in south Georgia, and two in south Alabama. It was hard to pause when so many quests and questions remain, but a synthesis became necessary. Though our databases pale before those of regions such as the Tennessee valley, there is enough to pull together and, I hope, interest southeastern US archaeologists and set jump-off points for future study. Going doggedly after early records, I corrected mistakes and interpretations for many sites. Of course I hope any who come after me will fix my mistakes too.

Work continues, aiming for all projects' data to be scanned and available for research (a Herculean task, but with less poison ivy than fieldwork).

Research Questions and Theory

Frameworks, methods, and biases in interpreting the archaeological record in the Apalachicola–lower Chattahoochee research region must be clear so future work can address problems and compare alternative explanations. Science is self-correcting, though often prejudiced, and correction may take time. But reconstructing the past must be based on foundational knowledge, which is my goal to establish here. Willey (1999:202) noted that failure to publish is the greatest weakness in archaeology, and also that anthropologist Alfred Kroeber said "what isn't published doesn't exist" (Willey 1988:129). Therefore the objectives of this book are archaeological description (culture history), with patterns and anomalies interpreted in the context of the greater Southeast, combined with scientific methods to explore cultural processes, and some humanistic speculation to visualize some of what past human life would have been like. Assembling details for this volume over the years has made trends and gaps in the record jump out and demand explanation. Research questions are numerous: When did the first people arrive and how and where did they live? How did they survive global warming? How did social and economic differences arise? Was there prehistoric warfare? How early are burial mounds and how did they relate to social/ceremonial networks throughout the eastern United States? How have humans interacted with environments over the millennia?

Wrestling with incomplete or scant information means possibly being grandly wrong, even ridiculous. I welcome scrutiny and testing of models with new data as they become available. All archaeology is biased in that it uses analogy, reference to what we do know, to understand the distant past, where things might have been hugely different. Another bias favors areas where more investigations have been done, with outlying places often excluded from discussions. Archaeology in the Southeast is too often colored by the information from just a few significant mound sites (Willey 1999:203). The Apalachicola–lower Chattahoochee valley region as defined here has often been ignored within the bigger picture.

Because we have direct material knowledge, most archaeologists reconstruct past human societies using information on their technological, environmental, and physical conditions and constraints. The fieldworker out in the forest, on the river, mucking through the swamp, eating the fresh fish or venison, might understand slightly better how ecosystems help shape cultures. Subsistence methods and economies are easier to infer, while social organization and beliefs are more obscure. Stories that attribute intention, factionalism, struggle, or other motivations and relationships to past peoples, especially in prehistoric times, need supporting evidence or else they are just imaginative. Archaeologists laughingly explain puzzling finds by saying they "must be ceremonial." Yet among many peoples worldwide, including Native American groups, spiritual concerns—deities, ancestors, nonhuman beings—do fill daily life (e.g., Sahlins 2022), for example, with the connectedness of landscapes as a major ideological principle (though there have also been cultures that were not religious, e.g., Whitmarsh 2015). Symbolism and ceremony represented in material objects can be interpreted using ethnographic and ethnohistoric description (e.g., Hall 1997), but radical change has happened between prehistoric times and the recording of historic peoples' beliefs. Besides religion, ideologies include magic, family or team associations and hopes, ancestor veneration, or just nonreligious appreciation for nonmaterial beings. We are a long way from interpreting much of the prehistoric evidence, like the puzzling design drawn at the top of this chapter on a pot from Green Point Mound (probably Middle Woodland; Moore 1902:257) that looks to us moderns like a happy face but may symbolize anything or be just decorative.

Some postprocessual/postmodern archaeologists advocate understanding the minds and intentions of past peoples. But we are in shaky territory with fantasy ungrounded in solid evidence (White 2008, 2014a). Furthermore, archaeological "stories" may have biases that reflect the views of those telling them. To counteract standard western economic models, for example, we cannot assume past societies did the least amount of effort for the greatest return in actual resources when they might also have acted for social prestige, spiritual gain, or just fun. Equally undesirable are sexist reconstructions, such as associating hard stone tools and animals with men and plants with women. Material culture seldom gives information about gender, which is a sociocultural, not a natural role. Further, few activities worldwide (even hunting or childcare) are limited to one gender, and the only actions universally restricted by a person's biological sex "are insemination and conception" (Bruhns 1991:427–428). Historic southeastern Native Americans had matrilineal societies, yet archaeological reconstructions seldom explore the implications of this (or even have the word "matrilineal" in book indexes). In addition, all societies have age-based divisions of labor, but rarely are children's roles examined archaeologically. My interpretations respect postprocessual theory but emphasize empirical data and environments, a resilient anthropological archaeology grounded in science and ethnography (Flannery 2006). Brose (2002:25) noted that cutting-edge theory may not last, but carefully collected and curated data and materials do.

This book presents the archaeology by traditional time periods (Table I.2; Volume 2 has the remainder of the time sequence). These temporal categories are semiartificial devices to organize the long record of the past. I avoid finer divisions such as "phases" that are hard to pin down, and I recognize that artifacts

TABLE I.2. ARCHAEOLOGICAL TIME PERIODS/CULTURES OF THE APALACHICOLA–LOWER CHATTAHOOCHEE REGION DISCUSSED IN THIS BOOK

Period	Dates	Diagnostics	Cultures, Environments
Paleoindian	ca. 15,000–10,000 BP (13,000–8000 BC)	Clovis, Suwanee, Simpson points, Waller knife	hunter-gatherer small groups, cold Pleistocene environments
Early Archaic	10,000–ca. 8000 BP (8000–6000 BC)	Bolen Beveled and Plain, Kirk, other corner-notched and side-notched points, bola stone	hunter-gatherer small groups in warming environments; fishers?
Middle Archaic	6000–ca. 3500 BC	various stemmed points, bannerstone	hunter-gatherer-fisher small groups
Late Archaic	ca. 3500–800 BC	preceramic portion? fiber-tempered ceramics, chert microtools, Poverty-Point-related artifacts	seasonal fishing-gathering-hunting; small groups; near-modern environments
Early Woodland	800 BC–AD 300	Deptford, early Swift Creek ceramics, early mounds, some exotics	seasonal foraging? larger groups? social ranking?
Middle Woodland	AD 300–700	Swift Creek, early Weeden Island ceramics, Baker's Creek points, exotics, burial mounds	seasonal foraging? larger groups? social ranking

Note: See Volume 2 for remainder of sequence.

never behave well enough to fit cleanly in the established categories. However, detailed description will at least allow for scientific evaluation. Good science is necessary for daily life and even for democracy to function well (Staedter 2017). For archaeology, where cultural deposits are destroyed as they are excavated, the same experiment cannot be repeated. But data can be reanalyzed to verify results, and similar sites or other parts of the same site can be compared.

METHODS

Field and lab work have followed standard methods; I am always in the field and lab with students and other workers to insure consistency. A few details of equipment and techniques are mentioned here to explain the nature of the data. For archaeological survey, USGS paper maps in the USF archaeology lab show site locations and cross-hatching where nothing was found. When free online aerial photos became available in the 1990s (e.g., on the Terraserve website), much of the research region was blank, not imaged because too few people lived there. Similarly, USDA soil surveys of each county were old or nonexistent, though some were being updated as I worked. The first soil book for Franklin County (Mooney and Patrick 1915) actually showed "Indian mound" locations. Now soil surveys are online, and other imagery aids site discovery. Lidar (Light Detection and Ranging) uses laser light to measure distances from air to ground to see elevations such as mounds hidden under forest cover. But it can be deceptive: one lidar image of a small "mound" turned out on the ground to be a newly installed septic tank covered in sod (White 2013:37).

The most valuable survey resource is local residents who know the land. Now locational coordinates for sites are available using cell phones (though signals are often not reliable or obtainable in this region). Collectors often keep records of their finds and have artifact-identification apps. Another major survey strategy has been to target gaps on the maps where no sites are known. Surface inspection is always combined with shovel-testing, including in lower-probability zones. Rarely, I have also surveyed transects across a wide area, such as a straight 29 km line across Lake Seminole (White 1981:122–124); this is usually less productive. Shovel tests, judgmentally placed, are always 50 cm square and a meter deep unless we hit hardpan, the water table, or roots too thick to chop; a quick-connect 10-cm (4-in.) bucket-auger corer can reach additional depths up to five meters. Screening has always been done except on the lower Chattahoochee surveys of the late 1970s, when carrying a screen over many kilometers per day was difficult and not yet required, but careful troweling allowed good artifact recovery.

Survey has not been statistically rigorous, and results are of course biased in favor of large or disturbed sites. There are still wide swaths of land in the region that have not been examined because of time, difficulty of access, or, in Georgia and Alabama, because survey was mostly confined to the immediate riverbanks. These biases are obvious on the site distribution maps in each chapter (which only have sites of known time periods; indeterminate-culture prehistoric sites number over a thousand more). The lowest site density is in the lower valley away from the coast, where the fewest people live today, the water table is the highest, and the landscape is mostly wetlands. Here the river has dumped the most sediment, burying sites. Nonetheless, I have surveyed much of this area, targeting higher ground patches, with some success. The patterns of known site distributions in the region reflect the characteristics of traditional survey and the geological processes, not necessarily past human settlement decisions.

In reality, no survey fully covers a region. There are always inaccessible or damaged areas and tracts where permission is refused or where logistics fail. Archaeological studies claiming 100% survey coverage are done in deserts with great visibility. Even mathematically stringent survey plans end up, in the reality of field conditions, weather, and budgets, falling short. Within the Apalachicola–lower Chattahoochee valley region I cannot say I have been down every road or up every creek. However, if the acreage is added up, including the work of other researchers, it should total perhaps 10% coverage of the whole region. Deep excavation often exposes earlier components under later prehistoric materials. It has been a long struggle to show management agencies the need for deep testing here. On the heavily alluviated riverbanks and old channels, from 0.5 to 2.5 m of recent flood sands overlie prehistoric sites because of soil runoff after deforestation from nineteenth-century large-scale agriculture.

In sum, my survey methods are traditional but with more and deeper subsurface tests. I have probably done more survey on rivers and side streams by boat than most, despite having only a few small boats (none of which ever ran well). I have followed in the footsteps and jeep tracks of earlier archaeologists, looked at a million artifacts in collections over the decades, and talked with thousands of collectors and local people. Still, much remains to be discovered. For example, only in 2013 did I get to a site on a creek on the upper Apalachicola where someone had been digging for 11 years, recovering tens of thousands of artifacts from Archaic through Fort Walton in age (Prendergast 2015). The collector attended an archaeology day program, invited us to dig, and helped with the fieldwork. I had not known of this rich site but would have seen it on the map as a high probability area to check. Important sites do remain to be found.

Formal excavation is always in 1-m square or larger units, with standard dry or water screens. Though I have used five types of heavy earth-moving equipment for archaeology, none of it was in this region. When identifying soil colors with a Munsell color chart, I test all fieldworkers for color blindness. Digging is usually in arbitrary levels since real strata are often invisible in the dark forest. When strata were clear, excavation was done according to their boundaries or in arbitrary subdivisions of them. Water-screening is preferred, for better recovery of tiny things (and squirting feels good during the hot summer), with our 3-hp pump connected to the nearest water source. On the St. Joseph Bay shore, bay water is so salty that we had to haul in a 10-gallon cooler of fresh water to suck into the pump to rinse it at the end of each day so it would not seize up with salt and rust.

Placement of all test excavation units has been judgmental: on the highest, least-disturbed ground. Soil samples are taken from all levels or strata of all units. On the advice of zooarchaeologist Elizabeth Wing (personal communication 1985), samples for flotation are consistently 9 liters. They are taken from the southwest quadrant of the unit by shovel or chunked out by trowel, as recommended by ethnobotanist Betsy Sheldon (personal communication 1995), because chunking is less damaging to fragile floral remains. Many archaeologists sample shell middens by hacking bits out of columns in unit walls. But this destroys the adjacent potential unit and is no more accurate than doing it first thing from the level/stratum being dug. An additional one-liter soil sample is taken from that same southwest corner for permanent storage and future study. Sites were mapped using USF's ancient mechanical transit, or occasionally a borrowed total station. I have not done geophysical prospection such as ground-penetrating radar or mechanical coring because the terrain seldom allows access for such equipment.

All excavation has been with the permission of landowners and proper permits for public lands. Fieldwork usually involves community members and volunteers. All projects have been subject to logistics, weather, and other conditions (about which any field archaeologist has stories), meaning not all expeditions had best outcomes. My 1993 research to de-water and test mounded shell middens in the lower valley swamps had only small success. It included hauling in a heavy (465-kg) pump by helicopter and drying out blocks of cultural deposits, but only allowed excavation a few tens of cm deeper (White 2003a). However, in 1994, a summer of record rainfall and high water, it would have been impossible. During the 1998 remote-areas survey (White 1999), done after the winter El Niño climate event brought record rain, it was harder to find sites in the lower valley because the higher water table prevented shovel testing or coring deeper than about 40 cm. My excavations have usually been smaller tests, not large block units, which would be better for understanding a typical site. Given the huge research region, short summer seasons, and modest funding, I have chosen to learn a little bit about the broader picture instead of returning yearly to the same site. But much is lost with this wide-but-shallow strategy, such as not encountering structure patterns or complete site layouts.

Laboratory processing and analysis, often begun in the field, take abundant supplies and years of labor, and some things do get lost or mixed up. From seeing the work and notes of dozens of archaeologists before and after me, I think that any field project leaves at least 10% of the data and collections unstudied and/or somewhat lost. While this book synthesizes cultural chronology and geography based on the most robust information possible, it is critical to indicate potential problems. Many site records are incomplete or inaccurate; archaeologists unfamiliar with the region may misclassify or misinterpret. For example, Schieffer (2013:15) was shocked to see how many professionals labeled sites as Archaic when only a few chert flakes were found, but no diagnostics. And once something is classified, that name becomes a shorthand requiring little further investigation, so caution is needed in interpretation.

Artifact description in this book uses existing typologies. Projectile point guides are those for Alabama (Cambron and Hulse 1964; Johnson 2017), Florida (Bullen 1975a), and Georgia (Whatley 2002). Lithic debitage is labeled based on simple morphology (Odell 2004; White et al. 1963) though such categories are less than adequate (Carr et al. 2012). Ceramic typologies are those by Willey (1949; also Williams and Thompson 1999), with a few additional types in other sources as appropriate. As a "lumper," not a "splitter," I know that the "type-variety" system used elsewhere in the South divides ambiguous (if established) types into even more confusing classifications with overlapping attributes. Future work seeking to isolate subtypes or varieties should involve elemental study of clays, residue analysis, use-wear studies, and examination of design and morphology, including by machine learning or "computer vision" methods (Pawlowicz and Downum 2021; University of South Carolina 2017). Diagnostic artifacts are crucial to recognize time periods, but typologies do have multiple problems, such as obscuring variation that might be significant and including overlapping type attributes. Type definitions used here are clarified in an artifact sorting guide I developed over decades (White 2023) that gives nonoverlapping classification criteria.

For most ceramics that do not clearly fall into recognizable types, generic names are used to avoid confusion. For example "cobmarked" is better than "Alachua Cob Marked" because the Alachua region is in central peninsular Florida and that type was protohistoric, while the cobmarked pottery in the Apalachicola–lower Chattahoochee region is mostly prehistoric. Recognizing types from plain sherds is impossible unless they are vessel rims with distinctive treatment. Ceramic tempers do not indicate time period, other than fiber (Late Archaic) and shell (Mississippian, rare in the region; see Volume 2). Sand, grit (crushed quartzite), and grog (hardened or fired clay bits—perhaps smashed in a fit of temper) were used from Early Woodland times onward in the region. Quantifying proportions of tempers in assemblages of different time periods has not been done but would be useful. Some portable X-ray fluorescence (pXRF) work has shown trace elements in the clays that suggest most pottery of all time periods was made locally, as discussed in the appropriate chapters.

Floral and faunal specimens recovered by flotation are identified as far as possible, with some sent for identification by experts. Dating of sites has been done mostly by radiocarbon assay of charcoal or bone. I have not sent shell for dating because the "reservoir effect" can give dates over 400 years older, since shellfish incorporate old carbon from oceans, but a few dates on shell were done by others. Some early dates have little description of material dated or its provenience, and earlier radiocarbon methods also have larger error ranges. Measurement in this book, by scientific convention, is in metric units except for waterways, for which distances are given in official river miles up from the Gulf, as they are indicated on maps, navigation charts, and signs along the rivers.

Processing and analyses of materials and information take up to a hundred times the amount of time as did the fieldwork, and often are not completed. Even federal-standard zipper-lock 4-mil bags shred after several years. Collections management and curation require careful, constant labor and are often neglected. The memorable last scene in the movie *Raiders of the Lost Ark*, where the precious ark was boxed and stuck up on a museum shelf, is a real indictment of professional archaeology. I hope to get the USF collections properly stored and in accessible databases before I myself become part of the archaeological record.

Public Archaeology and Ethics

Public engagement and collaboration have always been crucial to this work. Permission, acceptance, involvement, and perspectives from local communities are ethical requirements, not to mention necessary for success. The professional cannot just disrespectfully barge into an area to do research. I usually learn more from those who live in the region than they learn from me. Residents of the Apalachicola–lower Chattahoochee valley have shared artifacts and sites, explained how landscapes have changed over time, and indicated where buildings and features once existed. They know archaeology is detective work, not treasure hunting or dinosaurs. They have described forest composition and shown me how fishing and hunting have changed through the years and how animals behave. For example, after finding a lot of garfish remains amid the clam and oyster shell of the estuarine middens, I learned that few eat gar today because it is too bony and hard to clean. However, local experts said that prehistoric people probably ate gar because this fish is easy to catch, lying in shallow water where it can be gigged or speared. For another example, after years of looking for Moore's Chipola Cutoff Mound (8Gu5), I saw artifacts from it in a Wewahitchka library display. Librarians contacted the collector, who immediately took us to the site's location, now underwater, where he had seen it as a boy.

The historical and archaeological richness of the region and its rural nature and emphasis on the outdoors mean that there are innumerable avocational archaeologists. Many are incredibly dedicated; Chason (1987:24) figured he spent 150 hours per year for 18 years collecting artifacts. Others have frames full of points or sherds hanging proudly in their homes (even bedrooms and bathrooms) or whole storage areas devoted to their materials. "Citizen scientists" means knowledgeable individuals who provide practical data for professional study in any field (including astronomy, bird migration research, or nesting sea turtle conservation). Avocationals have often been those who actually establish professional sciences (Peck and Stroud 2012).

Some unethical collectors do dig on public lands illegally and on private land without permission and destroy sites to grab artifacts to sell for profit; this can be a huge problem (Glowacki and Dunbar 2019). Some are obsessed by local legends of (nonexistent) treasure; some, with no connection to the region, just buy artifacts to have stuff to show off. These looters and commercial interests do not realize—or care—that they are trashing the cultural heritage of the land. If the context of an object is not recorded, the scientific value is lost. Professional archaeologists cannot ethically buy or sell artifacts or evaluate them for pricing—just as unethical as physicians buying or selling human kidneys or livers. To distinguish between ethical collecting and looting, each case must be studied carefully from the perspectives of all stakeholders (Pitblado et al. 2022). Most important, cultural resources, unlike biological resources such as endangered species, are nonrenewable; what is destroyed is gone forever.

Most people in the Apalachicola–lower Chattahoochee valley who collect do so ethically and are truly interested in the human heritage. They keep their artifacts for family and friends to enjoy and learn from, and share information with professionals; some donate collections. These are the people who have contributed to my work, and it is irresponsible and unethical not to use the data they willingly share; without the huge body of collectors' knowledge, the profession would never have made the strides it has (Keck 2021; Pitblado 2014; Pitblado and Shott 2015). One study demonstrated that projectile points found by private collectors outnumbered those found by survey archaeologists at the same site by about 32 to one (Shott 2017). Some states have amateur certification programs. The Society for American Archaeology has many nonprofessional members, and its Archaeologist-Collector Collaboration Interest Group had over 600 members in 2021. Documenting the tragic worldwide looting of archaeological sites by terrorists, the National Geographic Society called for increased collaboration between the collecting and scholarly communities as a powerful tool to protect the human past (Mueller 2016). Studying how humans have lived, shaped environments, and handcrafted artifacts is not just looking at "stuff in the ground"; archaeology explores what it is—and has been—to be human (Langlands 2018). It has been a pleasure to work with so many who share this passion for the past.

1

Environments in the Region

The Apalachicola–lower Chattahoochee valley region (see Figures I.1 and I.2, Plates I–V) lacks the stark grandeur of snow-capped mountains or red-yellow desert canyons. Its allure is complex, often subtle, from the thousands of different greens of the deep forest to the sparkle of quiet backwater sloughs, the hot-pine-scented high bluffs of the middle-valley ravines to the open-water breezes of the rivers and bays. High-energy, even dangerous environments are the Gulf shores during storms or the swift big river at flood stage. Sudden, violent winds make tall pines and sabal palms thrash around wildly, and massive live oaks suffer the brutality of broken limbs or complete toppling. The river swamps are soft, mysterious places where gray Spanish moss and tough vines hang low and dripping, met by cypress knees rising from dark waters, something like the stalactites and stalagmites of the numerous cool limestone caves. Dazzling landscapes include the sugar-white sand barrier islands in the intense green-gray sea, under brilliant blue skies. The biodiversity of this region is close to the greatest in the nation, and one of the joys of field archaeology here is experiencing these different but connected ecosystems. Past peoples also must have felt an awe, even a sense of the spiritual, amid this beauty, as well as a practical appreciation for the abundant resources.

Research Region

The Chattahoochee River flows out of a cold spring in the Blue Ridge mountains, 1,070 m high, in northeast Georgia, 30 km from the North Carolina line. Running down to the Gulf of Mexico (see Table I.1), it marks the Georgia-Alabama border for 160 river miles (260 km) of its lower portion (I use waterway/navigation miles because they are marked on maps and on signs on the riverbanks). At the Florida-Georgia border, having come 436 miles

(702 km), it joins the Flint River, which originates below Atlanta. The Flint is named after its abundant stone (Spanish: "Pedernales"; same meaning). From the Flint-Chattahoochee confluence or forks flows the Apalachicola, some 110 miles (177 km) to the Gulf. The entire river system, the eleventh largest in the United States, is nearly 540 miles (869 km) long (Cook and Cook 2000). Navigation charts (USACOE 1978) that I used for years of boat survey show the Apalachicola's length at 107.6 river miles, but now geomorphologists say modern changes have lengthened it. Columbus, Georgia, 260 river miles (420 km) inland, is at the fall line, which divides the Piedmont and Coastal Plain.

This book's research region is the lowest 50 river miles of the Chattahoochee, the lowest 25 miles of the Flint, and the entire Apalachicola, a valley system totaling about 160 river miles (260 km) long, and between 2 and 20 miles (3 to 50 km) wide. This segment of the basin has geographic and archaeological continuity and integrity as a distinct region. It includes some 65 east–west km (40 mi.) of Apalachicola Bay shore, about 56 km (35 miles) of barrier islands, and the 24-km-long (15 mi.) barrier peninsula around St. Joseph Bay. The north end of the region is at 31°16'33" north latitude, 85°6'51" west longitude (UTM coordinates zone 16R E679500, N3461700); the southernmost point is 29°35'4" north latitude, 85°3' west longitude (UTM E689060, N 3274500). The region is nearly 200 km in straight-line distance north–south. East–west width varies from under one km to nearly 80 km at the coast along the barrier islands (see Table I.1 for distances). The northernmost extent of the region in Alabama is the basin of Omussee Creek, and in Georgia, the lower basin of Spring Creek just south of Miller County. Although today St. Joseph Bay and Peninsula are strictly not within this drainage, in the past they were connected geographically and culturally. At the north end of the region, elevations of archaeological sites on the riverbanks can be over 100 m (330 ft.) above sea level, while sites at the south end, on bay shores, can be under 0.6 m (2 ft.). In fact, this valley traverses some of the highest and lowest land in Florida (Hine 2013:2). Figure 1.1 is a lidar image of the region, with higher elevations as a lighter band in the middle. At the north end Omussee Creek arcs westward away from the river; Marshall and Cowart's Creeks flow southward over the Alabama line to converge into the Chipola River, which joins the Apalachicola from the west in the lower valley.

The region comprises several watershed segments (Figure 1.2) described here. Surveying another 25 river miles (40 km) farther up the Chattahoochee beyond this research region, I have seen how the prehistoric cultural landscape changes just beyond these boundaries, with immediate contrasts in artifacts from surface survey. Years of exploring this terrain by water and land, in all seasons, have also shown me environmental differences: farther upriver means chillier weather, different vegetation, steeper riverbanks, sheer rock valley sides.

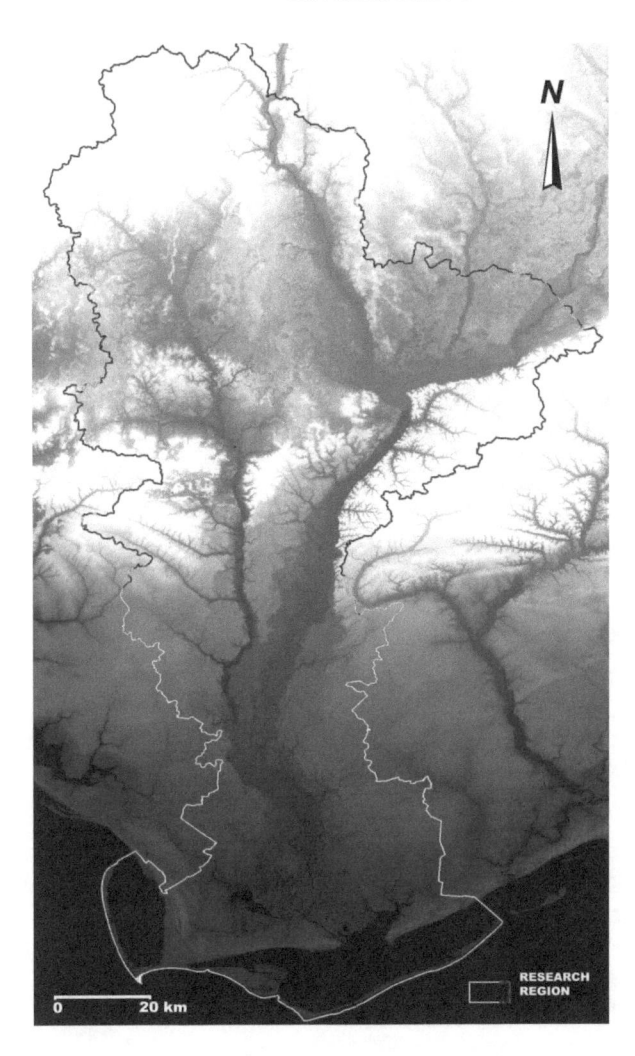

Figure 1.1. Apalachicola–lower Chattahoochee River valley research region outlined on a lidar image (compare with Figure I.2). The lighter the color the higher the elevation. (Image courtesy of Christopher N. Hunt.)

I must emphasize that archaeological descriptions given for what is called the "lower Chattahoochee" valley in much of the literature usually refer to the vicinity of Columbus, Georgia, at the fall line, 100 river miles above the northern boundary of this region, and the Walter F. George dam and reservoir near Fort Gaines, Georgia, 25 river miles above the northern boundary. This is not the same as the prehistoric cultural record on the lowest 50 miles of the lower Chattahoochee or lowest 25 river miles of the Flint, which are in the northern part of the research region described here.

The big river is wide and swift, with dangerous currents and bends, muddy, silt-laden waters, and banks of pale sand flecked with glittering mica particles brought downstream from the mountains (prehistoric ceramics have

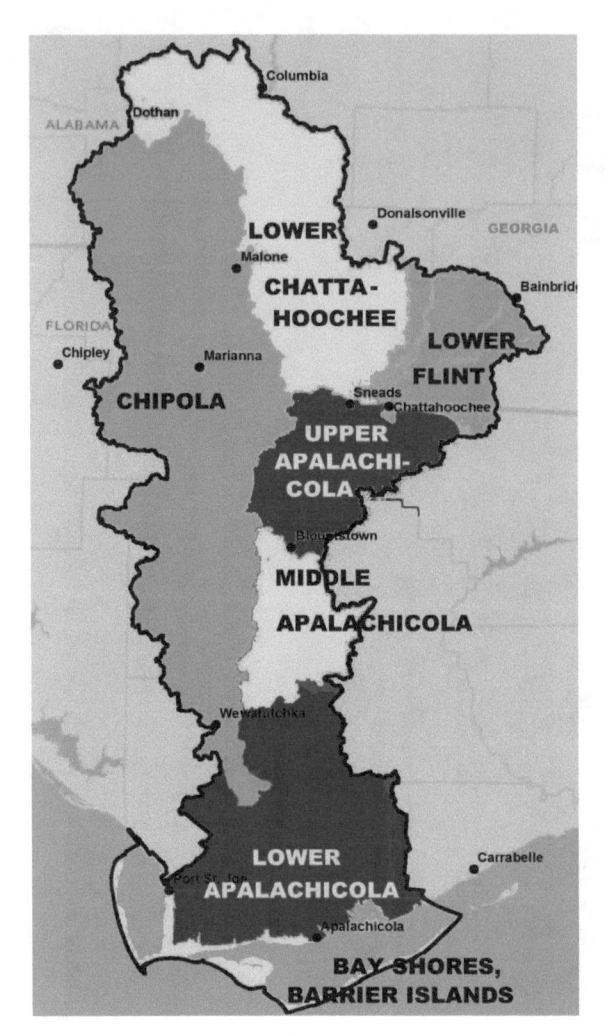

Figure 1.2. Drainage subbasins within the Apalachicola–lower Chattahoochee valley research region; complete Flint and Chattahoochee basins extend much farther north. (Adapted from Schieffer 2013:Figure 3; Nancy Marie White.)

distinctive mica flecks). Today the Chattahoochee and Apalachicola mark the boundary between Eastern and Central time zones (locally, "fast" time and "slow" time) as well as political borders. Probably in prehistory, when most important travel and interaction was along waterways, the rivers were not barriers but easily crossed and navigated daily. Much of the riverbank is natural levee, where people preferred living for millennia. Behind and paralleling levees are backswamps, replenished during winter floods, then dry bottomlands and upland terraces. The verdant bottoms harbor amazing ecological diversity, with thousands of plant species (Johnson 1993:23). Subbasins differ: the Flint River is narrower, clearer, with spring-fed tributaries. The Chattahoochee is full of sediment, runoff from agricultural fields. Before

Figure 1.3. Aerial photo (Flight 1A, Jackson County) from 1940 of the Chattahoochee-Flint confluence (forks) showing different characters of the rivers. The Chattahoochee is white with farm-runoff sediment. The Flint is spring-fed, dark, and clear even far below where the waters merge to become the Apalachicola. To the east is the town of Chattahoochee. Highway 90 bridge crosses the river. (Photo by US Department of Agriculture. Courtesy of University of Florida Digital Libraries.)

construction of the dam at the forks, the two rivers' different characters were apparent; a 1941 aerial photo (Figure 1.3) shows how they maintained their individual nature well downstream from where they merged. The Chipola River, the Apalachicola's largest tributary, is equally distinctive, also spring-fed and clear. The region's landscape has been sculpted by water, and until recently was continually traversed by water, so the geometry of past human interaction is described in terms of distances by water.

Notable ecological variability characterizes the region. The Nature Conservancy declared the Apalachicola valley to be one of six biodiversity hotspots in the nation because it is replete with rare habitats and species, has one of the country's most pristine estuaries, and retains the largest amount of longleaf pine forest left in the world (Edmiston 2008; Livingston and Joyce 1977). Native longleaf pine, live oak, and sabal palm trees are drawn at the top of this chapter. Neither archaeology nor past human lifeways can be described without understanding natural settings. The field archaeologist is in constant interaction with environments and with others (not always human) who use them. The division between nature and culture falls away in research on social ecology and landscape history, seeing how people shape their physical world and vice versa. The romanticized view of natives living in peaceful harmony with nature conflicts with data showing how humans continually modify their surroundings. Effects of prehistoric Native Americans on natural resources were probably less than those of historic times, because of technological limitations and smaller population sizes (Delcourt and Delcourt 2008; Krech 1999). Yet the Indigenous heritage here remains, not only in the archaeological record, not only in modern Native Americans, but also in names across the region. For example, in the lower valley the town name of Wewahitchka is Creek for "water view" (Simpson 1956), probably because of its two wide lakes. In the middle valley, Estiffanulga (nicknamed "Stiff and Ugly") is perhaps from isti + fani + ulga, meaning "where there are plenty of human bones" (Swanton 1934:218). In the upper Apalachicola, Aspalaga may be from "àsi-àpi-laiki," place where *Ilex vomitoria*, yaupon holly for black drink tea (asi) is found (Swanton 1934:19).

Past and present geology illuminates archaeological site formation processes. Even earthquakes occur in the region: one in 2006, centered in the Gulf, was felt far inland at Bristol. Natural regimes have changed considerably through the millennia. Humans have dealt with global warming before, at the end of the Pleistocene (Ice Age) 10,000 years ago; this and other drastic climate spells are described in appropriate chapters. However, it is sometimes hard to understand past habitats after so much recent modification. The prehistoric record is damaged by modern development along coasts and by dams, dredging, and other alterations of the river. Reservoirs trap sediment that would normally resupply the floodplain, meaning waters emerge to cut more out of the riverbanks (Isphording 1985). Comparison of the pre- and post-dam imagery shows the upper Apalachicola riverbank has eroded back almost 50 m (165 ft.) from the water.

The Lower Chattahoochee Valley

The Chattahoochee is one of the most dammed rivers of the South. I surveyed its lowest 75 river miles, beginning at the Walter F. George Dam at Fort Gaines, Georgia. Downstream from there 27 miles is the Andrews Dam, 23 miles above the Florida-Alabama border, creating Andrews "Lake," which mostly maintains the original riverbanks. The lowest 25-mile stretch of the Chattahoochee (with Florida on the west, Georgia on the east) widens as it becomes the Jim Woodruff reservoir or Lake Seminole (see Table I.1). Of this 75 river miles, the lowest two-thirds are included in the research region of concern here, encompassing portions of Henry and Houston Counties,

Alabama; Decatur and Seminole Counties, Georgia; and Jackson County, Florida. Georgia's Seminole State Park, Florida's Three Rivers State Park, and many local and federal parks have relatively protected forests but also landscapes altered by these dams. On the west side of the Chattahoochee is also the Apalachee Wildlife Management Area (though the historic Apalachee Indians actually lived farther east, in Tallahassee, probably not in the research region; see Volume 2).

The lower Chattahoochee part of the research region sits within the Southern Red Hills and Dougherty Plain geological districts, with rolling uplands from 75 to 15 m (250 to 50 feet) above sea level, some dark red clayey soils, and many sinkholes, marshes, and ponds; some streams disappear from the surface into the permeable limestone bedrock (Hubbell et al. 1956). Limestone outcrops contain usable chert (see Plate I), and on the banks are occasional quartzite cobbles, also good for tools, and fossilized oyster shell. The banks taper down to about 3 m high at the Florida end. Manipulations of this river system have been dredging, straightening, dike construction, and other actions with unexpected consequences (Heuvelmans 1974). Corps operations manuals (e.g., USACOE 2015) discuss water control effects on wildlife but not on cultural resources.

The great low area west of the lower Chattahoochee and upper Apalachicola is the Marianna Lowlands karst formation. It is scarred with curves of old river channels, sometimes still containing water as creeks or oxbow lakes, and often with prehistoric sites on the banks. People must have first settled along these old meanders when they were actual riverbanks, before the river moved eastward. The landscape here is dotted with myriad sinkhole ponds and springs that were significant during the late Pleistocene and early Holocene, when the colder, drier climate and low sea levels meant they were rare dependable water sources. So far they have not been explored by professional underwater archaeologists. Of the many dry-land caves, most are too small to offer living space for creatures larger than bats. The river bottomlands support hardwood forests with cypress wetlands, plentiful wildlife, and captivating flowering plants: spring dogwood, redbud, and wild azalea. Aquatic creatures abound (jumping fish, playing otters, riverine shellfish), though species such as sturgeon are now diminished. The land is still fairly remote, with pastures, planted pine, farm fields, and natural pine–open wiregrass uplands. The high number of sites recorded in this segment of the region is not surprising given all the cleared, plowed ground.

The Lower Flint Valley

The lowest 25 river miles of the Flint River, up to the town of Bainbridge, encompassing parts of Seminole and Decatur Counties, Georgia, are now also backed up in the reservoir, but the high bluffs of the Pelham Escarpment (Wharton 1978) on the east side still tower above the river. The Flint runs down from the Atlanta Plateau through the Tifton Uplands, also called the Tallahassee Hills and Apalachicola River Bluffs in northwest Florida and formerly the Altamaha Grit Region of Georgia (Hubbell et al. 1956); such terms demonstrate another example of name differences based on state boundaries. These bluffs, reaching 100 m above sea level and sloping down to as low as 12 m at the river, are covered in longleaf pine sandhills, flatwoods, and bottomlands (Thomas et al. 1961). They continue along the southern/eastern bank down the east side of half the Apalachicola, forming a barrier stopping the river's eastward migration. Their surfaces have been removed by erosion and human action, leaving red sandy clay subsoil.

In dry times, the Flint discharges more water into the Apalachicola than does the Chattahoochee because it is sustained by groundwater from springs. Its tributaries, especially on the west side, probably flow in its old channels, but much drainage is subterranean, and many small streams are seasonal (Hasty et al. 1939). Some 4 miles above the confluence, a major tributary is called Spring Creek, for obvious reasons (one of several Spring Creeks in the region). This stream meanders southward over 50 water miles from near the town of Blakely over the low hills of southwest Georgia and in its lower reaches is today an arm of the reservoir. A slightly smaller stream, Fishpond Drain, fed into Spring Creek near its mouth and today forms the smaller, western arm of the reservoir within the forks triangle between the two big rivers. These are the largest of the many streams created by the ubiquitous springs or "boils" of this karst area, and the most severely altered by the dam. Along their lengths were hundreds of archaeological sites that are now drowned. Today the area is graced with Seminole State Park, Silver Lake Wildlife Management Area, and other picturesque destinations.

Down from the eastern blufftops extend unusual high steephead ravines with seeping springs that create short creeks. Endemic species of plants and animals here are found nowhere else in the world. These higher-latitude relict species are Ice-Age remnants that survived in the sheltered ravines when the climate warmed. Among these rare organisms is Barbour's map turtle, with its saw-toothed shell patterned in maplike lines (Cerulean 1992; Means 1977:41), and the rare Florida yew. Another species is the torreya tree, *Torreya taxifolia*, also called stinking cedar because of its unpleasant odor when bruised. This is the rarest North American tree, with its closest relatives in California and eastern Asia. Torreya trees historically grew huge, but since the 1950s they suffer from a fungal blight that kills them at a young age. No full-grown trees remain except for dead, decaying specimens fallen long ago, though young torreyas were still growing on remote blufftops along the Flint in the 1980s (Angus Gholson, personal communication 1979). More abundant river mollusks were once found along the Flint than on the other segments of the basin (Brim Box and Williams 2000:7), and Canada geese live permanently along the banks, as they do on the upper Apalachicola.

Compared with the lower Chattahoochee, the lowest portion of the Flint has fewer known archaeological sites due to that survey bias of our having looked mostly at only the immediate riverbanks of the federal easement. Other work farther up the Flint (Elliott and Dean 2006; Worth 1988), beyond the research region, shows a different prehistoric material record. This lowest portion of the Flint takes on a distinct character as it approaches the confluence, where there was the greatest opportunity for interaction and communication, not only among people but also in movement of species between valleys. The original surveyors of the proposed reservoir noted how the Flint-Chattahoochee forks area was extremely dense with prehistoric sites, especially freshwater shell middens, around the junctions of so many streams. The visibility of white shellfish beds at the water's edge attracted the first Native Americans, and later the obvious white shell washing out of the middens brought more campers (and archaeologists). At least one submerged prehistoric mound is known within the forks (Underwater Indian Mound, 9Se27), an area with strategic importance. In a century, when Lake Seminole turns into a large mud hole—and it will, according to the Corps' own predictions—some good archaeology may be possible.

The Apalachicola Valley

The Apalachicola River, wholly within Florida, is the largest of Florida's 17,000 rivers in terms of flow (Light et al. 1998) and the only one containing snowmelt. Its 6,200 km^2 basin is naturally divisible into three segments (see Figure 1.2). The dam at its head affects the hydrology and archaeology. The bottom is sand and gravel, and shifting sandbars are typical along the banks. Some modern sandbars are made of dredged material containing prehistoric artifacts and fossils. Past natural sandbars, however, usually forming inside bends, would have offered solid ground, shallow water, perhaps access to shellfish beds, a distant view, and other advantages for prehistoric peoples. In high-water season, late winter and early spring, flood conditions connect various habitats with the river channel, making additional resources available. Dry-season loss of this connectivity is now more common because of modern manipulation, setting the stage for the continuing "water wars" (Southern Environmental Law Center 2016) as Alabama, Florida, and Georgia fight in court over control of this precious resource. Throughout the valley the changes in water regimes have resulted in loss of aquatic species and calls for dam removal to permit their restoration (Williams et al. 2014:102–103).

Upper Apalachicola
The upper valley extends almost 30 river miles (47 km) from the Flint-Chattahoochee confluence down to just above the towns of Blountstown and Bristol. It encompasses parts of Jackson and Calhoun Counties on the west, Gadsden and Liberty Counties on the east. Tributary streams run perennially across the floodplain. The river runs in gentle bends, hitting up against that same high eastern bluffs formation as on the Flint, the Beacon Slope and westernmost Tallahassee hills, with similar low-permeability clays that cause erosional runoff on ridgetops (Rupert 1990a). The soaring bluffs are nicely visible from Torreya State Park, with its panoramic view. Streams originating as seeps out of the sides of the bluffs dissect these hills to form ravines as deep as 30 m that may hold water year-round. These Torreya Ravines and Bluffs, rising above the shallow seas that once covered the rest of Florida, allowed many more northerly Appalachian species to survive in the refugia of their sheltered depths, as previously noted. The temperate hardwood forests here have the greatest plant diversity north of Mexico, and even the huge Mississippi River system does not bring as many northern plants down so near to the Gulf. The list of at least 127 globally rare and often endangered endemic species, from daisies to trees to turtles, in the Torreya Ravines includes, mysteriously, a higher proportion of plants with close relatives in eastern Asia than anywhere else in the South (Means 1985:14, 1994:20). Unfortunately, Hurricane Michael of 2018 took out 20% of the remaining endangered torreya trees and up to 90% of old-growth forest.

These are also Florida's only upland glade natural communities, and they hold the world's largest population of red-cockaded woodpeckers (Nature Conservancy 2000). The notable biodiversity in these longleaf-pine forests comes from regular burning, natural or not. The upper Apalachicola has the highest diversity and density of amphibians and reptiles north of Mexico, rare species of salamanders and crayfish (Means 1977), and the rare eastern indigo snake, the longest in North America (over 2.5 m long, now being reintroduced after near extinction). Streams running to the narrow floodplain make the branching pattern on the east side (see Figure 1.1). On the west side, broad, flat lowlands rise gradually to the Grand Ridge elevation, a stream-incised remnant (Rupert 1990b), and then drop slightly westward to the Marianna Lowlands karst plain (Clewell 1977). Continual eastward migration of the river widens the valley and leaves this west side with eroded remnants of ridges. So far, however, few archaeological differences are known between the two sides.

There were surely many shellfish beds on the upper Apalachicola, as on the lower Flint and Chattahoochee, judging by the number of shell midden sites. At one time the Apalachicola would have been nourished by countless springs, and some are still extant. Pope Lake swamp on the west side has gurgling springs into which a canoeist can stop and stick her feet. Blue Spring (see Plate II) is large and breathtakingly gorgeous. As with the lower Chattahoochee, on the Apalachicola prehistoric cultural deposits may be buried under a meter or two of historic alluvium. My survey after the 1994 record flood found that some sites were sliced away vertically by the floodwaters, others were covered with 30 cm of new alluvium, and others experienced both effects.

Middle Apalachicola
The middle valley is a smaller area, extending about 35 miles (56 km) from around Bristol and Blountstown down to the Chipola Cutoff at River Mile 42. It includes parts of Calhoun, Gulf, and Liberty Counties and has large tributaries (Light et al. 2006) amid low wetlands, as the high east-side bluffs peter out, and the Chipola River on the west side widens into Dead Lakes. The floodplain here ranges from 3 to 5 km wide, and the river runs in large loops in the northern, more elevated portion and smaller, tighter bends to the south. Elevations range from 45 m above sea level on the east side to less than 30 m on the flatter west side and south end. The dendritic trellis pattern of middle valley streams, such as Fourmile and Juniper Creeks in Calhoun County, results from the formation of ancient barrier islands and marine terraces. When the land of Florida was much smaller a couple million years ago, the river was shorter and had not yet built up its huge delta. These creeks today occupy remnant floors of lagoons between barrier islands that existed then. As the ancient river continuously dumped sediment and the delta prograded southward, it left these islands as high ridges and their land-side lagoons as low channels for streams to fill (Moore 1955). In its middle stretch, the valley's sandy floodplain is scarred with old meander loops. Sites of all time periods line these banks, but no geomorphological dating of meanders exists, as in the Mississippi Valley. Indeed, geologists have asked me if archaeological remains can date the meanders. Also, in its continual eastward migration, the river has obliterated or seriously altered and redeposited myriad older sites that we will never know about. Dissection of ridges and old banks or deep burial of them in more recent sediment must account for the paucity of evidence from earlier prehistoric times.

The east side of the middle valley still has some high ground: Alum Bluff and the Apalachicola Bluffs and Ravines Preserve are the farthest downstream of these striking formations with lovely vistas. Here is Florida's longest exposed geological section, the bluff face continually shaved open by the bending river and one of the South's most significant fossil sites (Means 1985). In local lore the bluffs were called the "Garden of Eden" because the rare torreya trees are also called gopherwood, a biblical name for the material of Noah's ark (Jahoda 1967). These bluffs hosted the rare species noted above in great stands of longleaf pine, but are now planted over with commercial slash and other fast-growing pines. While silviculture continues, some conservation areas are undergoing restoration. The Nature Conservancy (2014) purchased much of the land and hand-planted over a million longleaf-pine seedlings, though it will take 80 years for them to become habitat for red-cockaded woodpeckers. The middle valley is a distinctive setting of white sand rolling hills, hot pine-scented breezes, and trees with little undergrowth but blackened trunks from the prescribed burning that now mimics natural conditions and enhances productivity.

Lower Apalachicola
The lower valley (Figure 1.4) extends up some 42 river miles (68 km) from the river's mouth, incorporating parts of Gulf and Franklin Counties. The river is the county boundary until it meets with the large tributary Jackson River flowing in from the west, whereupon the border becomes the Jackson River up to the mouth of Lake Wimico, then it takes a southwesterly arbitrary course to the coast (dotted line on Figure 1.4) ignoring natural waterways. The lower valley, bay, and islands were designated a World Biosphere Reserve by the United Nations Educational, Scientific, and Cultural Organization (UNESCO) in 1983. Much of it all is now public lands: the Apalachicola National Estuarine Research Reserve (ANERR), the St. Joseph Bay State Buffer Preserve, the western portion of the Apalachicola National Forest (the largest national forest east of the Mississippi), and Tate's Hell State Forest. Tate's Hell Swamp is named after a late 1800s character who ventured into it, got snakebit and lost, crawled out after a week, saying it was "hell in there," then died (Jahoda 1967). However, his view of swamps must have differed from that of thousands of years of Native Americans who enjoyed the bounty of wetland resources, the equivalent of modern superstores. Tributary and distributary lakes and streams thread across the lower valley (see Plate IV), where slightly raised areas were once offshore bars. Elevations rarely reach 10 m, and much of the floodplain is seasonally waterlogged. Shallow, densely wooded swamps and poorly defined creeks called "bays" (Rupert 1991) have peat deposits across the 5- to 8-km-wide floodplain (Couch et al. 1996). Unsurprisingly, the heavily alluviated lower valley has the fewest number of known archaeological sites in the region.

The Apalachicola is tidally influenced as far as about 25 miles (40 km) upstream. Some of the riverbank has been converted to sterile sandbar habitat by dredging and dumping spoils in huge piles; walking over these in summer is like trekking the Sahara. On the west side, the wetlands have been cut with canals for large-scale agriculture (straight crisscross lines on Figure 1.4). Pine

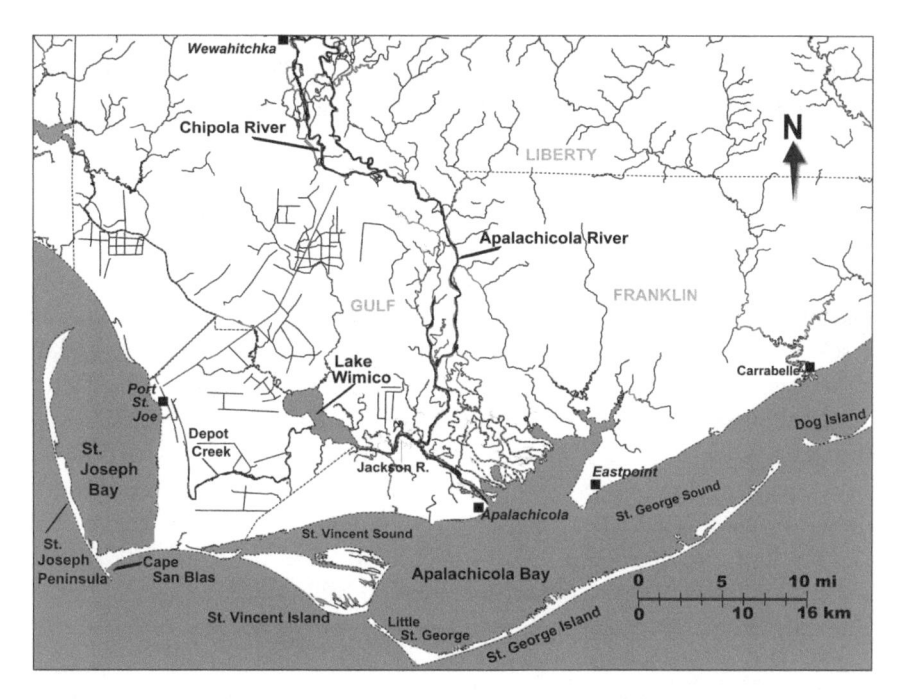

Figure 1.4. Apalachicola lower valley delta area, bays, barrier islands, and St. Joseph barrier peninsula. (Nancy Marie White)

forests stretching westward to the shores of St. Joseph Bay in the past were more like open savannah that one could ride a horse through until deliberate tree planting and fire suppression in historic times made them denser. Lake Wimico, a former river channel, is a major tributary. East-side wetlands include squishy seepage bogs with carnivorous plants such as sundew, Venus flytraps, and pitcher plants.

Prehistoric shell middens on lower-valley stream banks were often reinhabited over thousands of years, showing long-term subsistence continuity in these estuarine settings. As the river builds up its delta toward the sea, it dumps tons of alluvium, blocking or forming distributary channels perched on top of impermeable clayey sand (Sasser et al. 1994). Different delta lobes have built up as the river migrates eastward, apparently pushed by rising sea level since the end of the Pleistocene that backs up the outflow at the mouth. This shift is archaeologically visible at shell middens. Marsh clams (*Rangia* and *Polymesoda*) live in fresh to brackish water, between 0 and 25 ppt (parts per thousand or up to 2.5 percent salt by volume), with 15 ppt optimal. Oysters tolerate greater salinity, between 6 and 35 ppt, with 10–18 ppt optimal (Andrews 1951; Auil-Marchalleck et al. 2000; Puglisi 2008). Marsh clams are found in Woodland deposits of shell middens that overlie earlier Late Archaic deposits containing mostly oyster and more saltwater fishes. The only known single-component Late Archaic shell midden, Sam's Cutoff (8Fr754), the farthest northeast, is all of oyster and is today less than a meter above water, apparently abandoned after sea level rise brought the river mouth eastward and fresh water closer. Assuming people collected what was closest and easiest to get (a big assumption), the archaeology shows fluvial morphology since 4,000 years ago.

A change in salinity, rise or fall, is necessary for *Rangia* clams to spawn, and offspring survive only in salinities between 2 and 10 ppt. Stable salinity results in the dying-out of a clam population in 15 to 20 years at the end of their lifespan. Thus this species stays in favorable breeding zones with fluctuating salinities (Hopkins et al. 1973). The river mouth, emptying fresh water into the bay, where salinity also depends on tides, is ideal. Oysters need saltier bay waters and do not live today in the estuarine areas where clamshell middens exist. Near Clark Creek shell midden (8Gu60), a water sample we tested had a salinity of 3 ppt (personal communication, Joe Donoghue, 1988). But the clam middens always have a few oysters, probably reflecting ancient estuarine fluctuations. No marsh-clam middens exist upriver beyond Mile 10, or on the bay shores, which have all-oyster sites.

The vast estuary was once considered useless by those who drained, canalized, and filled some of it. But the productivity of estuaries, where rivers meet the sea, is second only to that of tropical rainforests and higher than that of croplands. Prehistoric Native Americans surely also valued this prime real estate for more than practical uses. They may have revered the sparkling, luxuriant landscapes for magical or spiritual reasons (Larson 1995:xv). Brown freshwater streams are "tea-colored" because of vegetation decay, which indicates that the water is fresh, drinkable, even useful for hair-coloring or mixing with bourbon (Watts 1975:27). White spider lilies or tall red wild hibiscus flowers as big as a hand spring up amid the marsh grasses. Terrestrial species seek higher, dryer ground, making them easier to get. Oak hammocks merely centimeters above water are good campgrounds, surrounded by cypress and tupelo living in the water. The lower Apalachicola has the largest stand of tupelo trees in the world. Apiarists bring bees in by boat to make the prized tupelo honey. The swamps and marshes full of nutrients from decaying forest vegetation provide nurseries for aquatic species including blue crabs, flounder, mullet, snapper, and grouper. Archaeological evidence is harder to find in the estuary because of the difficulty of access today, dense vegetation, lack of agricultural fields and other exposed areas, and heavy sedimentation. But where the mainland edges are visible, there are sites. Linear shell middens run along the Lake Wimico shoreline and the bay shores, especially at stream mouths. At the big river mouth, the bank edge surrounding the city of Apalachicola was a continuous shell midden ridge for several km. The first soil survey of Franklin County listed "Shell Mounds" as an official soil type (Mooney and Patrick 1915:29–30).

The Chipola River

Born of the convergence of Marshall Creek and Cowart's (or Big) Creek, which originate in southeast Alabama, the Chipola River flows 92.5 stream miles (149 km) to its mouth into the Apalachicola. It drains an area over 3,200 square km, nearly half the Apalachicola's basin (Edmiston 2008:9), and strongly boosts the bigger river's flow. The Chipola's stunning clear blue-green waters come from its abundant tributary springs, lack of sediment content, and hard limestone bottom (see Plate III). With the Flint, the Chipola is in the class of blackwater rivers, as opposed to whitewater rivers full of runoff such as the Chattahoochee. The Chipola occupies the mostly flat land west of the lower Chattahoochee and upper-middle Apalachicola, paralleling the larger river for most of its length until it turns eastward toward its mouth.

In contrast to the big river, the Chipola cuts through the stark white stone, insuring that the hundreds of springs continue to flow instead of becoming silted up. Some 63 springs are known in its basin (Barrios and Chelette 2004:3), with many smaller ones unrecorded. The upper and middle sections of the Chipola have multiple caves. At Florida Caverns State Park near Marianna the river dives underground into a solutional opening, surfacing again in a few hundred meters. This natural bridge may have been culturally significant in prehistory. The Chipola is also famous for what is under its waters: abundant Paleoindian and Archaic stone tools, Pleistocene fossils, and evidence of later prehistoric time periods. Like the Aucilla River and others to the east, the Chipola was apparently formed during the Holocene as rising sea level brought the water table up enough to connect lines of sinkhole springs. The sinks would have provided permanent water sources and attracted game during the cold dry time when the first humans got to Florida. Further, the lower Chattahoochee may once have flowed in the channel now inhabited by the Chipola until it was altered by stream capture upriver. The Apalachicola, then a small tributary to the Chattahoochee, with a steeper gradient along the southwestern edge of the Tallahassee Hills, cut back into the drainage of the Flint and Chattahoochee to divert the latter eastward and create a sharp "elbow of capture" along the lowest reaches of the Flint. Then the Apalachicola greatly increased in volume (Hendry and Yon 1958:18–20), and the smaller Chipola possibly inhabited the old Chattahoochee-Apalachicola channel (Vernon 1942:306–307).

The Chipola has abundant tributaries. Its creeks flowing northwest–southeast define a parallel series of relict beach ridges (Rupert 1990b:3). The upper and middle basin has outcrops of good chert for toolmaking. At a small rocky rapids section around Chipola Mile 47.5 (a total of 75.5 water miles inland) locally called "Look and Tremble," the river drops almost 2 m over a distance of 13 m. Though outdoors expert Jeff Whitfield (personal communication 2008) calls it a "Class II rapids for 2 seconds" it is usually labeled a Class-I rapids, but still tricky to run in a canoe, and known as a good place to spearfish. In the lower Chipola, the backup of sediment from the larger river causes blockage at the mouth to create an unusual system: the small river opens out into wide water flows that are together called Dead Lakes, a series of intermittently wet oxbow channels 9 miles (15 km) long with mirror-still water dotted with stumps and cypresses. Dams built in 1962 and 1974 for recreational purposes were meant to stabilize water levels year-round, but were removed in 1987. The Chipola flows into the Apalachicola at the big river's Mile 28 (45 km inland by water), but it also creates a cutoff channel just downstream from Dead Lakes, a meandering path 3 miles (5 km) long that draws off 25% of the Apalachicola's waters at its Mile 42 (68 km). Between this channel (at the top of Figure 1.4 near Wewahitchka) and the Chipola's mouth is the Cutoff Island, an isolated 16 km stretch of swamp forest up to 4 km wide. This inaccessible wilderness has not even been surveyed into legal property sections or had much archaeological investigation.

Bays, Coasts, Barrier Formations, and Delta Development

The great detritus load that the river washes into the bay has bacterial colonies and fungal mats composing a biomass with more protein than the original plant matter. The barrier formations enclose this nutrient-rich water, making a nursery for diverse aquatic and terrestrial life (Livingston 1983). Apalachicola Bay is one of the richest ecosystems in the northern hemisphere, benefiting from the lack of large human populations as have seriously damaged other American estuaries. As sea levels rose in the Holocene, coastal forests were drowned and thick spongy peat layers formed around the bay (Gore 1992:62). Peat strata exposed on barrier islands after storms contain fiber-tempered ceramics up to 4,000 years old. The barrier islands around the river mouth enclose the bay and estuary, buffering the mainland from surf and wind. The bayshores have some of the largest dunes in Florida, some with buried cultural deposits. Formed by winds, dunes are stark white sand, contrasting with black midden soils. Beyond the barrier formations, the open Gulf is warm, relatively benign, and easily navigated.

Apalachicola Bay

Florida's most productive estuary, Apalachicola Bay until recently supplied annually 6 million pounds of shrimp, 90% of Florida oysters, and 10% of the nation's oysters, with commercial and recreational fishing also important. Nearly every species in the bay originates in the estuary. Oyster reefs provide habitat, nurseries, and feeding grounds for dozens of marine creatures and protect shorelines, though they are now greatly diminished from what they once were. The bay averages only 2 to 4 m deep and has two tides daily. At least 84% of its fresh water comes from Georgia and Alabama. Harvesting its resources is easy. In fact, a marine ecologist asked me if humans might even have created or positioned the richest oyster bars that exist today, since they seem to be in interesting spatial alignment (Rom Lipcius, Virginia Institute of Marine Science, personal communication 2016), roughly trending north–south, perpendicular to the long axes of the bay and sounds (Twichell et al. 2010). However, such orientation may be natural, just to permit oysters to filter food from flowing water more efficiently (Baird 2020:101).

Indigenous peoples took advantage of this natural bounty. The bayshores are packed with oyster shell middens containing fish and turtle bone. Certain plants such as cedar trees and Florida soapberry trees (*Sapindus marginatus*), normally a more southerly species, thrive on shell midden soils, and a rush (*Juncus interstincta*), usually also seen in south Florida, lives in swales behind midden ridges (Clewell 1977:10). Bay sediments with microfossils of organisms that usually occur up to 5 km offshore permit inference of storm patterns over the last 4,500 years, which might be correlated with changing prehistoric cultural adaptations. As sea levels have risen and fallen through the last millennia, people altered lifeways. Further, coastal cultures may have integrated landscapes such that they did not even differentiate between land and water but saw only points along a continuum, and many might also have perceived the actions of the sea as deliberate, directly or through some supernatural force (Van de Noort 2011).

Geologists identify a dozen old river channels in the bay, buried at least 2 m below the current bottom and estimated to be up to 8,000 years old. Offshore in the Gulf other paleo-channels and ancient delta formations are up to 64 m deep and 12,000 years old. Before today's barrier formations emerged, when sea levels were lower and shorelines far out under the modern Gulf, Paleoindian and Archaic settlement was along waterways and is now probably buried up to 16 m deep (Donoghue 2011:29). Hints of such sites have now come with the recovery of very old projectile points eroding out of barrier island shores. On the west side of Cape San Blas, old Apalachicola River channels run northeast–southwest, orthogonal to today's coast. This orientation is also seen in the oldest ridge formations on the east side of St. Joseph Bay, which run northeast–southwest but are cut by the north–south ridge system and then the younger east–west ridges. All these geological features may mean that the big river once flowed to the southwest (Schnable and Goodell 1968:44). Depot Creek is good evidence of these processes. It formed from a long swale between beach ridges running north–south, flowing south until it hit the youngest east–west trending ridges, which made it swing around almost 180 degrees to run north and east into Lake Wimico (see Figure 1.4). An older configuration of southwesterly running waters may explain a few curious phenomena such as evidence of a freshwater spring on Black's Island in salty St. Joseph Bay.

During the Pleistocene, the river emptied into the Gulf within a cuspate delta, meaning its sediments were dumped on a straight shoreline and reworked by waves outward into curved shapes. The current delta is a birdfoot-lobate shape. Continual shoreline loss means that forested land is claimed by the sea, leaving tree stumps on beaches amid materials washing out of archaeological sites and peat deposits with even older sites sometimes exposed below the dunes. Correlating stages of coastal development with the archaeological record has only just begun (Donoghue and White 1995). Archaeological research on St. Vincent Island contributes to the reconstruction of sea-level fluctuation curves and helps confirm indications of a higher-than-present sea level between about 1,500 and 500 years ago (Balsillie and Donoghue 2004; White and Kimble 2017).

Barrier Islands
From west to east, the chain of barrier formations drapes around the Apalachicola's protruding delta like a sparkling white necklace, with ever-shifting dune fields and wetlands on the landward or back-barrier side. The eastern islands are thin strips with many overwash zones, narrow places that open into channels and close again periodically, especially during storm surges, creating more or fewer individual islands. On the west side, St. Joseph peninsula is a similar thin barrier spit running north–south and connected to the mainland at Cape San Blas on the south end. St. Vincent Island is triangular and wide, unlike the other barriers, a result of long-term progradation of beach ridges (Randazzo and Jones 1997). St. Vincent encompasses 4,860 ha and has sets of parallel dune ridges and swales running at different angles, from marine processes of different time periods. It is now a national wildlife refuge, only accessible by boat. Wider and much closer to the mainland, St. Vincent has greater time depth for human occupation, including sites older than the island itself that were occupied when it was mainland during the Pleistocene.

St. George Island is a 48-km-long strip running southwest–northeast, bent at the west end around a cape. That triangular western end, 15 km long, was often cut off by storms that opened and closed a passage called New Inlet. Now the passage is a permanent channel, Sikes Cut, built for easier Gulf access. This Cut insulates the triangular Cape St. George or Little St. George Island, the pendant jewel in the necklace, an uninhabited refuge. Even the northwestern tip of Little St. George has been cut off into its own island (Sand Island) at times, then stuck back on by different storms. The long remainder of St. George Island east of the Cut is full of houses at its western end, especially after construction of a bridge in 1965. The eastern end has a 9-mile-long state park, mostly unmarred and often designated as one of the best US beaches. Archaeological sites on St. George Island are numerous. Dog Island is a small strip to the east, only 11 km long, with some 100 houses and a preserve, and only accessible by boat or plane. Though it is opposite the mouth of the Carrabelle River, outside the Apalachicola drainage and beyond the research region boundaries, it is part of the whole delta formation.

The barrier islands are the most dynamic part of the region's landscape, changing continually, often radically with violent storms as well as slower erosional processes. Waves here average the highest of the entire US Gulf Coast, and between 1856 and 2013 there were 96 major storms. A storm can take off a chunk from one end of an island and deposit another chunk at the other end, changing the islands' shapes over the centuries. Shorelines can retreat up to 50 meters from one storm. Recent shoreline loss on Little St. George Island is estimated at between 4.3 m and 0.2 m per year, mostly off the southeast-facing shores, while accretion takes place on the southwest-facing shore (Donoghue et al. 1990; Sankar 2015). To be healthy, beaches must move, and the shores seen by past peoples, even recently, are not those we see today or will see tomorrow (Kaufman and Pilkey 1979:9, 13). The incredible instability of barrier formations might suggest that human habitation was rare and brief. However, multiple sites from all time periods are recorded on their shorelines. Fresh water may have been available in swales and sloughs between the beach ridges, or in intermittent streams, ponds, or old springs, or else by digging wells. Vegetation cover is rangy slash and sand pines with fire-blackened trunks, scrub oaks on the older dunes, and reindeer moss or fragrant rosemary growing underfoot. Fewer biotic species are present than on the mainland, but some (grasses and weedy plants, the occasional mangrove and manatee) do occur only there (Anderson 1988:4). Salt marsh grasses sway out to the bay waters, while flocks of shorebirds nest on the ground and ghost crabs scurry along, nearly indistinguishable in the white sand. The barrier islands sit within major seasonal flyways of millions of migrating birds, and year-round avian residents are also abundant. All this gives way to white sand beaches on the Gulf shores (see Plate V), with dunes up to 30 m high covered in protective sea oats and glittering sand that squeaks as you walk on it.

Though some evidence suggests shoals on their way to becoming barrier formations existed as early as 6400 BP, the barrier islands are at most 5,000 years old, but comprise one of the oldest such systems in the Gulf (Osterman et al. 2009; Twitchell et al. 2013; cf. Ahmad 2011). During the Pleistocene and early Holocene, before they formed, the places where they now sit were mainland and hosted ancient human settlements. These islands may have formed around Pleistocene cores of higher ground (Rizk 1991), which could have been already inhabited riverbanks or coastal dunes. On the barrier island Gulf sides, the desert-like hot sand, lack of fresh water, and remoteness from the sheltered mainland probably meant that few later prehistoric people would go there for more than fishing excursions or possibly the experience of the waves. We do not know how aboriginal cultures thought of the Gulf in spiritual or aesthetic terms. Its bounty of resources may not have been enough to attract settlement directly on the shores, since its dynamism would mean risk. Bridges, fast boats, piped-in water, and air-conditioning now make these barrier beaches some of the most expensive and desired land in the country.

St. Joseph Peninsula and Bay
The St. Joseph barrier peninsula is 24 km north–south, less than 1 km wide, and has washover areas, one of which divided it in two (again) after Hurricane Michael in 2018. At another washover, large rocks and riprap are continually piled up to prevent similar division. This peninsula is now packed with houses, but the northern end is preserved as a state park, which was named the best US beach in 2002. The peninsula curves like a left parenthesis; its south end attaches to a thin strip running 5 km east–west forming the elbow-hook of Cape San Blas. This cape is the second-most rapidly eroding—actually migrating—coastal spot in the world, losing up to 10–12 m per year, according to century-long records (Rizk 1991). A subpeninsula at the southeast end of St. Joseph peninsula, jutting out to the northeast, is Richardson's Hammock, which has the oldest beach ridges and large shell middens (Richardson's Hammock, 8Gu10) protected in the state preserve.

The peninsula encloses St. Joseph Bay, which is 8 to 13 km wide and unusually salty since it has few freshwater tributaries. This salinity means a different array of aquatic species. Most prehistoric shell middens on its shores have large gastropods, lightning whelk and horse conch, with smaller amounts of oysters and saltwater shellfish, fish, and turtles. Eroding prehistoric middens were noticed even a couple centuries ago when John Lee Williams visited in 1823 and said the shore was "paved with beautiful shells" (quoted in Porter 1975:16). Also unusual are two islands in the bay, close to the southeast shore, Conch Island (8Gu20) and Black's Island (8Gu11), which are themselves shell middens, formerly elevated shoreline sections. Black's, about 4.5 ha, is unusual because its black midden sand, packed with artifacts and animal remains, is completely indurated, rock-hard, for unknown reasons, perhaps rapid change in salinity or pH or fire effects. Our limited archaeological testing there produced bones of freshwater fish, suggesting the presence of a spring, other stream, or the river itself as recently as 1,000 years ago (Mayo 2003). Other than the saltwater seafood remains, the prehistoric material culture does not change much around St. Joseph Bay from that elsewhere in the region except to include more large-gastropod shell tools. Historic legend or hearsay has made the St. Joseph Bay and St. Vincent Sound areas famous for tales of buried treasure. Searchers dig into prehistoric sites, often trespassing, at night, with headlamps. C. B. Moore's field notes (1902, Book 22:59) mention one site, Mounds at Eleven Mile Point (8Fr10), as being "riddled with pits and trenches owing we were told to a dream revealing the existence of buried treasure."

Delta Development, Fluvial Migration, and Sea Level
Apalachicola Bay was formed during the Neogene and Quaternary periods, some 23 to 2.5 million years ago, when the paleo-Apalachicola Delta was near the present Florida-Georgia border. The delta grew southward into the Gulf over the Holocene, depositing sediments to cover the original embayment. The entire research region except for the Red Hills/Torreya Ravines was under shallow seas while marine organisms busily worked and died to deposit layers of shell and coral that formed the limestone bedrock. From the late Pleistocene onward, the time during which people arrived, the sea and ground water reached higher and lower levels than at present. At its lowest, sea level is estimated to have been at least 100 m below that of today, then rising between 1 to 4 cm per year for several thousand years until it slowed dramatically. Sea level curves for the region have in the past been of low resolution, usually depicting a smooth, slower rise in more recent times (Donoghue 1992, 1993, 2011). More finely tuned models (Balsillie and Donoghue 2004; McNabb 2012; Walker et al. 1995) often use archaeological data, along with sediment cores, ground-penetrating radar, and other methods.

Oscillations in sea level, often correlated with seawater temperature and more- or less-stormy conditions, are potentially important for interpretation of different archaeological time periods and are summarized in the appropriate chapters. The modern river's valley size and channel size relative to the amount of flow, as well as the data from seismic profiles of paleochannels in Apalachicola Bay, suggest that the river was once much larger and has moved a lot. While its lower portion was pushed eastward during the early to mid-Holocene, it still flowed through Lake Wimico and the Jackson River until about 7,500 years ago, when the upper river changed to bend sharply eastward, cutting off Lake Wimico and making the Jackson River into a relict channel (Donoghue 1993). All these substantial landscape shifts over the estimated 15 millennia of human occupation in the research region probably meant continual adaptation to changing ecosystems and waterways.

2

Resources and People

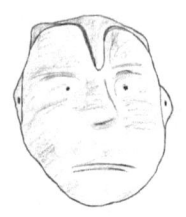

The rich Apalachicola–lower Chattahoochee valley region offers copious geological and biological resources in different but linked ecosystems that supported large prehistoric human populations. Most material culture would have been perishable, but some is reconstructible. Human-made products, in both their need for raw materials and their uses, create patterns in the landscape, while environments and human imaginations determine the nature and character of crafts and crafting (Langlands 2017:27). Things past peoples made and used are reviewed here.

Water and Transport

The region is connected by networks of water, critical in itself and for obtaining other resources and available in magnificent abundance. The river system has countless tributaries, distributaries, ponds, oxbow lakes, and wetlands. Vast underground reservoirs of the Floridan and Coastal Lowlands Aquifers send waters rising to the surface so much that this region has one of the highest concentrations of freshwater springs in the world (Scott et al. 2004:3). Often on survey I have found artifact scatters in unlikely places, only to learn later they are near now-dead springs or once-flowing channels. Divers tell me that the river bottoms have countless spring vents. Southeastern American Indians had many types of ritual bathing (Hudson 1976), which may have meant that springs and rivers were spiritually significant. In prehistoric times, these constant water sources may have been the equivalent of shopping malls with churches too. Today Florida sinkholes swallow cars and houses; prehistoric sinkhole activity, whether resulting in the disappearance or appearance of water, might have been linked to the supernatural.

Instead of being a barrier, water enhanced movement of people, goods, and ideas. It was the primary variable structuring native settlement and subsistence, the foundations for sociopolitical, economic, and probably ideological systems too. Sites of all time periods are distributed along waterways. Until Europeans arrived with horses in the 1500s, the only ways to go anywhere were to walk or take a boat. Indigenous peoples probably measured distances in travel time—how far one could move on land or water in a morning or day, with watercraft faster and easier for heavy burdens. Research on coastal and estuarine travel is pertinent. Blanchard (2000) documents a typical Native American canoe as holding about 40 times the load an adult can carry on foot. Traveling at 2–3 knots, it averages 5 miles (8 km) in 2 hours, giving a catchment area of over 300 square miles for cultures in southwest Florida estuaries. One or two paddlers in an 18-foot (5.4 m) canoe can average 3 mph (5 km per hour) and can access a wide variety of resource zones (Blanchard 2008:64). Living sites may not have been near food sources but at places with good launches, waterways, and weather patterns. Archaeologists have often noted how prehistoric peoples cached canoes at linked drainages (e.g., Byrd 2017).

For most of its human past, the Apalachicola–Chattahoochee River system was a major transportation and information artery of the South, reaching up from the Gulf vast distances into the interior, where it came close to other important rivers. Undoubtedly, tracks ran along the banks for overland travel, but voyagers would know how to follow tributaries to other streams and use tidal influences assisting paddlers up to 30 water miles (48 km) up- or downriver from/to the mouth. Important trails surely met at crossing places or portage spots for east–west movement; one of these was at the river forks. Native dugout canoes, made by burning off layers of logs to chisel out, were narrow and unstable; the early Spanish noted that they capsized frequently. Yet travelers stood to paddle and pole them and carried fires in them. Preserved dugouts and other wooden boats are more numerous in Florida than elsewhere in the Americas, eroding out of shorelines when water levels drop during dry seasons (Wheeler et al. 2003) or found underwater. However, surprisingly the Apalachicola–lower Chattahoochee research region has so far not produced any prehistoric examples. Probably ancient canoes were recovered long ago and quickly disappeared or preservation conditions were unfavorable. A late prehistoric canoe from Dog Island (White et al. 1995:67), just outside the region, may be typical of those that once existed (see Volume 2 for this and for historic watercraft known archaeologically).

Rock and Soil

Karst and Caves

Marine forces shaped the fossiliferous limestone bedrock of the Apalachicola–lower Chattahoochee region, which was then overlain with sands and sandy clays. Limestone for building material was commercially quarried through the 1950s (Moore 1955) but was not used for prehistoric construction. Rocks and shoals in the rivers were probably not worrisome for Native American travelers in smaller maneuverable watercraft.

Caves form as decaying vegetation makes an acidic solution that percolates through the soil, dissolving stone. Jackson County has the most archaeological cave sites recorded in Florida (Dunbar 2016:99), and others occur farther up the Chattahoochee. Underwater caves (see Plate I) might have attracted Paleoindian habitation during the Pleistocene when far lower water levels meant they were dry or had small streams. Most caves in the region are too small for people; those at the Florida Caverns State Park were hacked out to be big enough for visitors. Before that park was built, Bullen (1949) recorded a few sites where prehistoric people sheltered in rock overhangs. At Waddell's Mill Pond site (8Ja65; Tesar and Jones 2009) mounds and cave occupation date to Woodland and later times, with a compartmentalized cave on a large spring-fed creek. A few Chipola River rock formations have openings large enough for human activity and sometimes contain a few prehistoric sherds amid the modern debris, though conclusive evidence of rock art on walls is not known, only scratches local people have confirmed as recent. Cave fauna in the region include huge populations of bats of a dozen species. A "maternity cave" near Sneads held up to a quarter-million bats, many of which died in the record 1994 storms (*Orlando Sentinel* 1994). Bats were important in Mesoamerican native ideology and could have been also for this research region's peoples: bats only emerge at night and hang upside down during the day. Caves and rockshelters here might have been sacred places, as are many across the Southeast and worldwide (Watson 2012), with their unusual creatures, acoustics, and darkness.

Soils and Features
The sandy soils of the region have been assessed, mostly for agricultural potential, at different times for each county, and their types and units named and renamed by government soil surveys in confusing fashion. They are composed of alluvium, quartz sand grains brought down the river from the mountains or originating in ancient seas and deposited in the valley over clay subsoils, and hardpans on top of the bedrock. Inundated often during the Pleistocene, they were continually reworked on the shallow sea bottom to form marine terraces and hills. The lack of stone and ubiquity of sandy soils means that prehistoric rock-lined fire pits or pavements typical elsewhere in the eastern United States are not found in the research region. There are no stone mounds or boulders or smaller rock in mound fill, as are known farther north in Alabama and Georgia. Historic deforestation for agriculture led to soil runoff that covers prehistoric sites in thick alluvial strata.

Clay for making pottery lies below the sand, exposed in riverbank faces and eroding blufftops. It contains mica flecks that give Native American ceramics a distinctive glittery appearance. Clays are more reddish farther north in the research region; when fired they turn brown, black, or orange. Moving downstream from the lower Chattahoochee to the mouth of the Apalachicola, soil hues move from the Munsell color chart's 5YR or 7.5YR (yellow red) pages to the 10YR page as the red clayey bluffs on the east side of the upper valley give way to the pale yellowish brown sands farther downriver and also on the west, flatter side. Midden soils are darker because of human activity that produces organic waste. On the coast and barrier islands, the brilliant white dunes are pure quartz sand grains reshaped continuously by wind and waves (Hine 2013:137–138). Dark soil color can also be from natural processes, such as black swamp muck, fine clay from below the water table packed with natural decaying organics. Also, pale coloration does not necessarily indicate the absence of archaeological deposits, since charcoal bits and burned soil can be leached away. At the Sassafras site (8Gd12; Scarry 1975), on a high bluff of the upper Apalachicola, over a meter into the pale yellow-brown sand we unearthed Late Archaic fiber-tempered ceramics about 4,000 years old. The soil color did not change at all in this buried midden, but the stratum with the sherds was of coarser texture, harder to trowel.

Mound builders throughout the Southeast often chose diverse, colorful soils based on both functional/engineering and symbolic concerns (Sherwood and Kidder 2011). Bright colors were probably also important for walls and floors (see Plates VI, VII). Though prehistoric ditches, canals, walls, and other earthen constructions occur elsewhere, such as canals in coastal Alabama (Waselkov et al. 2022) and the western Florida panhandle (Wheeler 1998), in the Apalachicola–lower Chattahoochee region so far the only known human-made earthen structures are mounds, the earliest being Woodland burial mounds of sand, occasionally with some reused shell midden.

Little is known in the region of soil features indicating houses or other structures. A distinctive thin yellow-sand lens in the Clark Creek shell mound (8Gu60) could have been an Early Woodland prepared-floor fragment (see Plate VI), but postmold patterns are so far only known from later prehistoric sites, as described in Volume 2. Middens and other features such as hearths, refuse pits, or postmolds are dark stains in pale sand. An unusual feature type at the creek-bank McKinnie site (8Ja1869) in the upper Apalachicola, with soil not much darker than the surrounding matrix but specific kinds of artifacts, dated to the Middle–Late Archaic, is described in Chapter 4. Some dark pits might be latrines, especially those with shell, where the lime could have been thrown in to reduce odors (as typically in outhouses); ash-filled pits might also be toilets if ash was used to hasten decomposition of wastes (also common in outhouses). Features are rare at shell middens in the region, possibly because these sites are continuous, mingled dumps of food garbage.

Chipped Stone

Among the kinds of fine-grained silicious rock used to make chipped-stone tools (Plates VIII–X), local chert is abundant in the northern and central portions of the Apalachicola–lower Chattahoochee valley. A flint formed in limestone, it is cryptocrystalline silica, often fossiliferous (Moore 1955; University of South Alabama 2004a). It occurs in limestone outcrops, on the edges of sinks and ponds (Hasty et al. 1939; Hubble et al. 1956); in the Flint River, some rocks stick out above the water. The Creek Indian name for the Flint was "Thlonotiska" or "where flint is picked up" (Swanton 1946:542). The Ocala and Suwanee Limestone formations are the source rock, and the "quarry cluster" approach to identify this stone is useful (Upchurch et al. 1982). Upper Apalachicola and lower Chattahoochee cherts belong to the Marianna Quarry Cluster; the Citronelle formation sands and gravels also contain chippable stone. Figure 2.1 shows locations of these. A bluish chert I saw on the Aucilla River, probably from the Wacissa Cluster, is rare in the research region. Determining chert origins is based on appearance (texture, color, fossil inclusions); variability prevents geochemical sourcing (Austin et al. 2014).

Relatively few actual quarry sites are recognized in the region, but many may be drowned in the reservoirs or hidden by forest. Bullen (1950) recorded the Lime Sink (8Ja28 or J-26) and Rock Hill (8Ja21 or J-19) quarries. Kelly (1950b) noted a probable quarry site at 9Dr5 on Spring Creek, and UGA and Smithsonian field notes show unrecorded quarries along Spring Creek. Between the upper Chipola and lower Chattahoochee Rivers, avocational archaeologists documented the Two Egg Quarry (8Ja1126) south of the tiny settlement of that name (Sharon and Watson 1971:77) before it was demolished for a housing development. This name continues to be used in reports as if it indicated a specific type of stone instead of the common local material. More chert outcrops farther downriver may now be buried under heavy alluvium or rising water levels.

This local chert is naturally translucent and amber or honey-colored. Area experts differentiate between the good "honey chert," "butterscotch chert," or Flint River or Albany chert found around the forks and up the Flint River, and the more fossiliferous, whitish, lower-quality rock along the lower Chattahoochee. These two may be opposite ends of a continuum, since weathering turns the stone opaque and whitish. A point recently snapped in two may show in cross-section what looks like a white-chocolate candy bar with a caramel filling if it has not weathered all the way through. Efforts to determine age based on the thickness of the weathering rind are misguided; I have seen

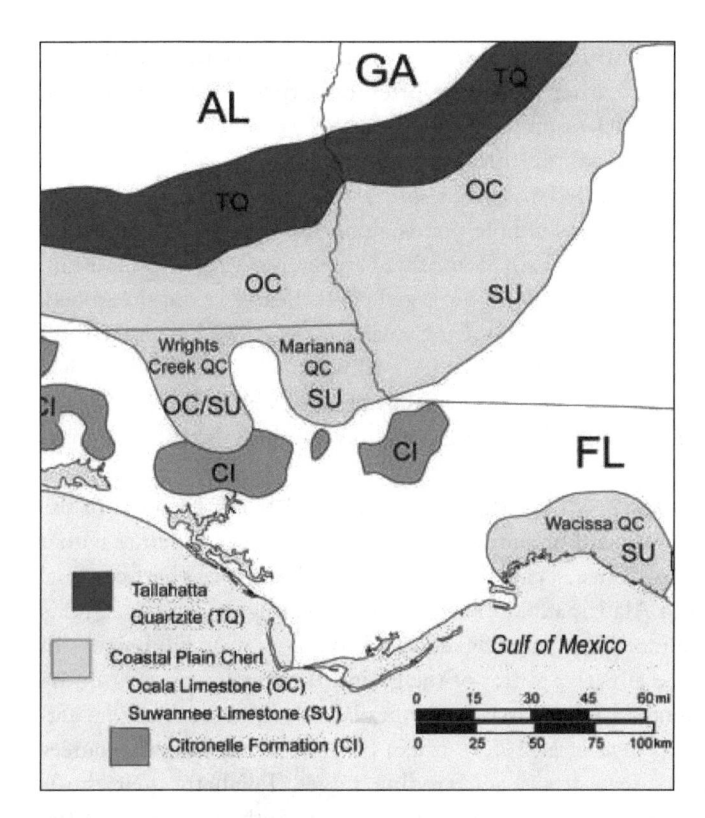

Figure 2.1. Chert outcrops in the Apalachicola–lower Chattahoochee region. (Adapted from Austin et al. 2014:Figure 10.1; Nancy Marie White.)

points in plowed fields with the side recently exposed to the sun weathered white and the side facing down still unweathered. Heavily weathered lithic materials may indicate very old sites, but care is needed to avoid the circular view that sites yielding weathered chert artifacts are automatically older. Sometimes the white chert has a pinkish or reddish cast, or, rarely, purple, blue, brick red, or brown. Even unweathered translucent pieces can be brownish, pink, yellow, multicolored, or striated. Some contain fossils, especially miniscule shells, and sometimes pretty crystalline inclusions, tiny geodes. Rosy colors and shiny or lustrous surfaces are probably due to intense thermal alteration that aids flaking. Forest fires are not hot enough to alter the chert on the ground surface, merely leaving black smudges on it. I observed flintknapper Jeff Whitfield's experiments with heat-treating local chert before toolmaking. He cooked it in an outdoor pit in the sand at about 700 degrees F for two hours and found it turned black or bluish. The appearance of chert artifacts is also affected by inundation, which makes them smooth and shiny. They may acquire distinctive colors, sometimes according to the particular river, though the causes of coloration are so far unknown. The Chipola is famous for laying on a red-violet color (see Plate IX) that can change to black or brown after the artifact dries out a while. Chert from the Apalachicola River bottom is tan, like peanut butter. Earlier tools were often resharpened by later peoples, removing some of the ancient darker patina.

Agatized (petrified) coral, the Florida state stone, was also important for toolmaking. It is available as beach rock and also far inland near the Flint-Chattahoochee forks and in sinkhole ponds along the lower Chattahoochee. At the Rozar site (9Dr91), on a small unnamed creek emptying into the Flint, a collector showed us boulder- to cobble-sized coral "heads" in the streambed. We hauled a heavy one up the side of the ravine; it is stored in the CMNH paleontology department (White 1981:597). This stone is brown, yellowish, gray, or white and recognizable by the shapes of the coral bodies in it. Seen head-on, these are star-shaped or hexagonal, but in most flaked stone they appear as little nicks.

Tallahatta sandstone or Tallahatta quartzite is another raw material in the research region. Known as "buhrstone," it is "a light gray quartz arenite with a distinct snow-flake pattern . . . caused by patchy distribution of chert cement" (University of South Alabama 2004b). It has translucent greenish-gray grains with opaque white mottling ("snowflakes") and weathers to a dull beige, still recognizable by the distinctive glitter of the grains. It outcrops most in southwest Alabama, extending into Mississippi, but also in southeast Alabama and southwest Georgia (Lloyd et al. 1983). It can be obtained at primary sources and as pieces in stream bottoms and eroding ridges. Tallahatta quartzite is the most common prehistoric lithic raw material in south Alabama and the western Florida Panhandle, though the variety from the lower Chattahoochee is less useful for knapping (Phil Carr, personal communication 2000). In the Apalachicola–lower Chattahoochee region, after colleague Ned Jenkins showed me how to recognize it, we saw it as a minority type among lithic assemblages throughout the valley down to the coast (Austin 2003; Schieffer 2013).

Other lithic raw materials are rarer in the region. Silicified wood was found on the lower Chattahoochee at the Fairchild's Landing site (9Se14), embedded in the white clay and as tool raw material (Caldwell et al. 2014:3). A large specimen of petrified wood recovered from the reservoir bank is displayed at the Three Rivers State Park. This material might be hard to recognize as it resembles agatized coral or fossiliferous chert. Also rare is chipped quartz, clear/transparent rock occasionally made into points. White, translucent or opaque quartz, more difficult to chip but common in north Georgia, where good chert is lacking, undoubtedly came downriver from the mountains. Other stone includes rare exotic or imported cherts, which can be myriad different colors, especially black, dark gray, or bluish. In the research region more different kinds and colors of stone are found at Middle Woodland sites than at any others.

Lithic assemblages in the region need much more work on relative frequencies of raw materials across space and time. Expedient, disposable tools, a sharp edge handy for a quick task, may make up more of the debitage than we recognize, and later peoples collected, recycled, and reshaped earlier artifacts. Debitage or waste flakes are the most common evidence. Though collectors usually do not pick up flakes and archaeologists now do, we may not get the very small bits. My work has only classified debitage by raw material and morphological categories: primary decortication flake, > 50% cortex; secondary decortication flake, < 50% cortex; secondary flake, thin, flat, no cortex and classic shape; tiny bifacial thinning flakes; and block shatter sometimes made by farm machinery. This typology mostly reflects the production sequence but is inadequate for good lithic analysis (Carr et al. 2012). My identifications of chipped-stone tools are based on the standard guides listed in this volume's introduction. However, many type descriptions overlap or are specific to one state and are called something else in the adjacent state. Further, less than total faith can be placed in the culturally or temporally diagnostic nature of many types, and the guides do not illustrate a range of variation within types. No analysis, measurement, or other attribute determination has been done for types within the Apalachicola–lower Chattahoochee research region. Farr (2006) and Thulman (2007) have valiantly tried to reclassify Florida points and isolate clusters, but their samples may lack specific proveniences, and few are from the research region. Much work is needed to permit agreement on type names, definitions, ages, and distributions. Also, stone tools are "morphologically dynamic," changing form and function throughout their use-lives as they are sharpened and recycled; most do not fit neatly into type descriptions (Andrefsky 2008). Nonetheless, points are usually the only diagnostic artifacts for preceramic time periods.

Ground Stone and Other Rock

Ground-stone artifacts in the region were made by chipping rock into rough shapes then abrading it. Gravel deposits include quartzite cobbles in the river beds, especially the lower Chattahoochee, that were fashioned into artifacts or used as natural round or oblong stones to batter or grind, which leaves use-wear marks. Some larger grinding stones are flat rocks with abrasions, and pitted stones have rounded depressions from cracking nuts or drilling. The large grinding stone from the Trestle Bridge site (8Ja186), in the upper Apalachicola (Figure 2.2), probably from the Early Woodland component, has a 20-cm-wide depression. A tiny Late Archaic jasper bead (Plate XI) is of Mississippi valley material. Pendants and celts were of quartzite and other stone (Plate XII, Figure 2.3). Quartzite bola stones are pear-shaped, of unknown function, and probably Early Archaic in age. The bannerstone or atlatl weight

52   Chapter 2

Figure 2.2. (left) Large, probably Early Woodland, limestone (?) metate or grinding stone from Trestle Bridge site (#8Ja186-3), top and side views. (Nancy Marie White)

Figure 2.3. (below) Groundstone celts (Middle Woodland?) from Richardson's Hammock mound (8Gu10; private collections): (a, b) greenstone; (c, d) quartzite. (Nancy Marie White)

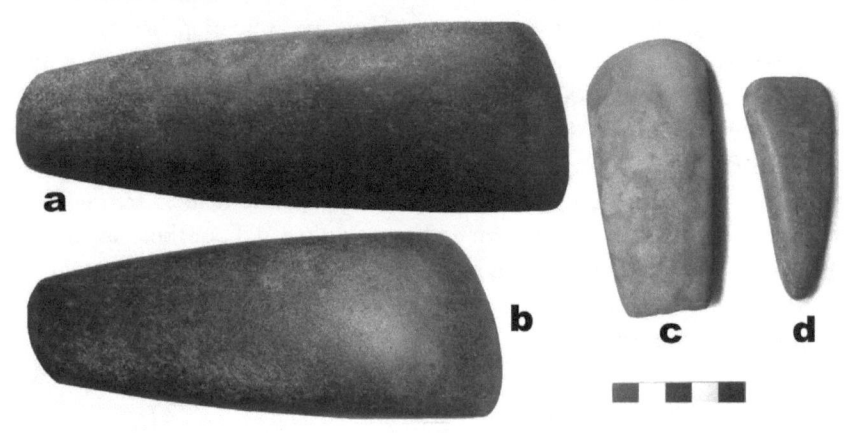

is a flat or rounded, perforated, bilaterally symmetrical Middle Archaic object made of various raw materials (see Chapter 4 on both of these). Many excavated sites have produced small unmodified pebbles that may be natural inclusions or perhaps had utilitarian functions, for stone boiling, polishing, slinging, use in rattles, or even as playthings. Pebbles also occur in apparent ritual contexts, such as the Archaic pits at the McKinnie site (see Plate X) and the Middle Woodland burial mound at Richardson's Hammock. Crystal quartz, an occasional raw material for projectile points, was also used for or made into pendants and other items. Two clear translucent crystal pendants (Figure 2.4), probably Middle Woodland, came from sites on St. Vincent Island.

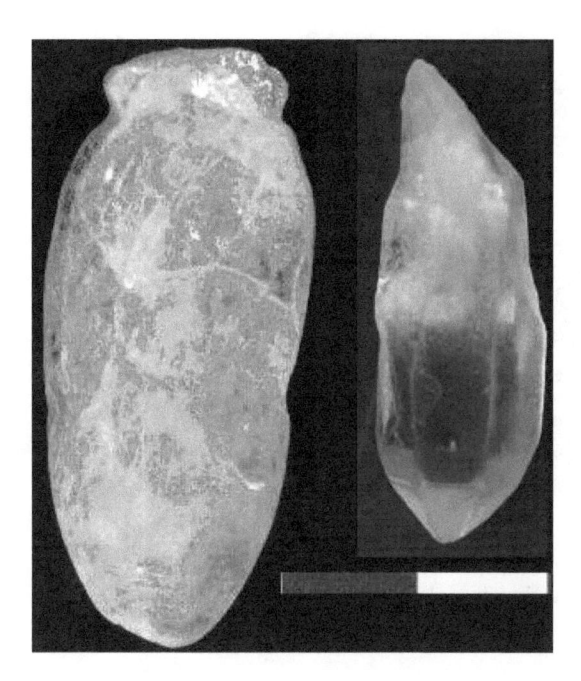

Figure 2.4. Quartz crystal pendants, probably Middle Woodland, from shell middens on St. Vincent Island: *left*, rounded, with groove for suspension around one end, from St. Vincent 5 site (USF#JC8Fr364-15.119); *right*, natural crystal with one end ground to a point, from Little Redfish Creek site (USF#JC-8Fr1367-14-1.13). (Nancy Marie White)

Greenstone, a metamorphosed igneous rock imported from perhaps 1,000 km upriver in the mountains, occurs from at least Woodland times onward; the celt (ax or adze) is the most common form and can be a burial offering. Sometimes these are nicely polished and unused (see Figure 2.3a, b). Others show striations from chopping or rubbing, are broken or heavily worn, or occur only as chips. At the St. Vincent 5 site (8Fr364) on Apalachicola Bay, which has Middle Woodland through Fort Walton components, a collector recovered 44 greenstone celt fragments, both bit and butt ends, most with use wear (White and Kimble 2017). I saw a polished greenstone ring about 5 cm in diameter in a private collection from Jackson County. A greenstone pendant or plummet recovered from mixed Early Woodland and Late Archaic deposits at Clark Creek shell midden (8Gu60) may have been an ornamental item or an everyday object such as a net weight (White 1994b). Pendants of greenstone and other, often exotic raw material are associated with Early to Middle Woodland burial mounds (see Plate XII). Greenstone may have had special meaning, perhaps because of its exotic origins, its greenish-gray color, or the labor needed to make the artifacts, but celts also clearly had utilitarian functions.

Ground-stone gorgets (Figure 2.5) are of greenstone, sandstone, exotic slate, or other rock. They are flat, rectangular or ovoid, and have one or two holes drilled from both sides, presumably for hanging, as the name suggests, around the neck, or anywhere. Though they are attributed to the Late Archaic

Figure 2.5. Gorgets in Hub Chason collection, all from middle Chipola River bottom, of greenstone (*upper left*) and other hard rock (and covered in lacquer so raw material is hard to determine). White square indicates the collector restored it from pieces. (Nancy Marie White)

elsewhere, their cultural affiliation in the Apalachicola–lower Chattahoochee valley region is unknown, and none is associated with a particular site except a rectangular white limestone fragment found by a collector at the Early Woodland Huckleberry Landing Mounds (8Fr12; in DHR collections). Some gorgets are large; I saw one from the Chipola River that was 26 cm wide with an expanded center and two holes.

Steatite was another stone (Figure 2.6) brought downriver from the Appalachian mountains and used all over the eastern United States from Late Archaic times onward. Also called soapstone, it is a metamorphic rock composed of talc and other minerals. It is greenish gray, sometimes with gleaming surfaces, very soft (1 to 2.5 on the Mohs hardness scale), and easy to carve. It was chiseled out of outcrops that extended in a band from Newfoundland to central Alabama (Elliott 2017; Truncer 2004:3–21; Yates 2000:17). Shaped into bowls at quarries, it was then moved over long distances during the Late Archaic. After that it may have fallen out of use, but in Early to Middle Woodland times it reappeared in the research region as ornaments and pipes. Existing studies of prehistoric steatite distribution indicate little or none from around the region (Truncer 2004; Yates 2000). Thus the record is expanded here with evidence from 28 sites, some of which are described in Chapters 5 and 7.

Mica was a significant material, cut into shapes. This shiny silvery-white flat stone that flakes off in thin sheets like French pastry or Greek phyllo was also obtained from mountains far upriver and circulated widely in the

Figure 2.6. Steatite artifacts: exterior and interior views of *left*, Middle Woodland pipe bowl fragment; *right*, Late Archaic flanged bowl sherd from Underwater Indian Mound (9Se27, private [DDM] collection); *below right*, ornament fragment (Middle Woodland?) depicting a rattlesnake or beaver tail from Blue Hole Spring site (8Ja112; Simpson collection, FLMNH#102498). (Nancy Marie White)

East from Early Woodland times onward. Sheet-mica artifacts occur in Apalachicola–lower Chattahoochee region burial mounds and habitation sites. Figure 2.7 shows the arrowhead-shaped cutouts from two riverbank freshwater shell-midden campsites, Sealy Plantation (9Se11) in the river forks, and Otis Hare (8Li172) on the middle Apalachicola. Mica bits naturally occur in the sands of this valley, sometimes a couple cm wide but usually as tiny flecks. Troweling releases these minute particles, which glitter in the sunlight and land on the skin to appear like disco dust. The micaceous clays of prehistoric pottery are distinctive to the region (Bullen 1958).

Sandstone, in flat slabs or concretions, found on the riverbanks and bottoms, was used for pendants, gorgets, and hones, which are tabular shapes with grooves worn by sharpening wood or bone tools. This sedimentary rock can have a high iron content that makes it yellow or red. Iron oxide as crumbly, easily powdered yellow or red ocher was common, probably as a source of pigment or paint. Hematite and limonite rocks, harder iron oxides with red or shiny black surfaces, are available in river gravels and may also have been used for pigment or other purpose (see Plate X). Limestone, the region's bedrock, is fossiliferous, soft, and crumbly, not too useful, yet sometimes shaped into

Figure 2.7. Sheet mica arrowhead-shaped cutouts from freshwater shell middens: *left*, from Sealy Plantation (9Se11; Georgia state collections, Athens); *right*, Otis Hare (#8Li172-355). (Nancy Marie White)

artifacts, including ear spools (Plate XIII). Indigenous peoples obtained salt by boiling seawater or extracting it from saline formations and salt springs, as indicated by distinctive shallow ceramic pans (Brown 1980). But no prehistoric evidence of salt production is yet known in the Apalachicola–lower Chattahoochee region.

Metals

Prehistoric metals in the research region were for special use. Copper appeared in Woodland times (see Plate XIII). Raw native copper came from north Alabama, Tennessee, or around Lake Superior (Goad 1979). Pieces were heated and pounded ("cold-hammered") into desired forms. Copper artifacts from the region include discs and tubes that were probably made elsewhere and imported. A small amount of silver appears as plating on two copper discs from Pierce Mound A (8Fr14). Silver was also cold-hammered and probably came from the same areas that produced copper, sources in northern Michigan and Ontario (Spence and Fryer 2005). Galena cubes or masses, either shiny and silvery or lumpy and white (Figure 2.8), are found in the eastern United States mostly in Middle Woodland burial contexts. Galena is lead

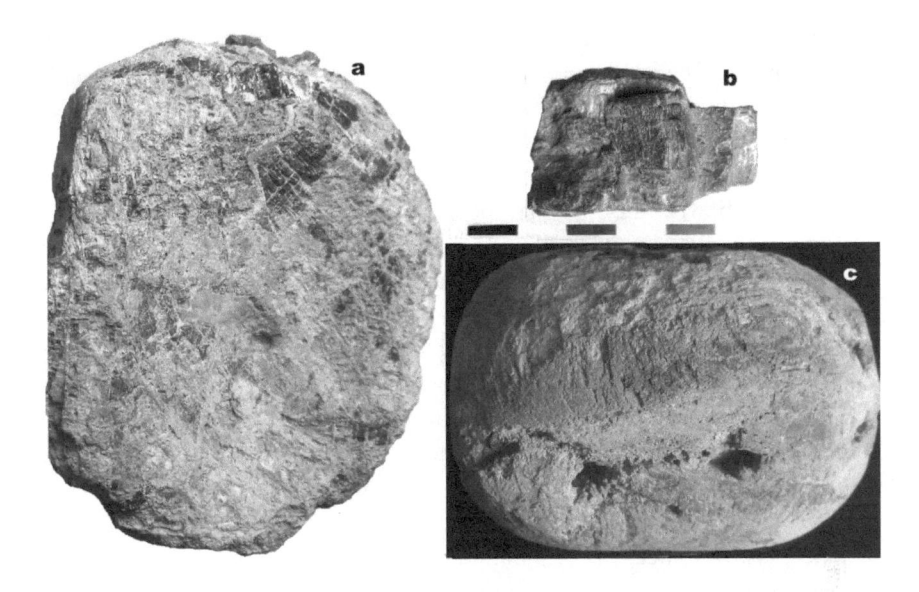

Figure 2.8. Middle Woodland galena: (a) flat chunk with use wear, some shiny surfaces, from OK Landing Mound (8Ca2; NMAI#75149); (b) shiny cubic form from St. Vincent 5 shell midden site (USF#JC8Fr364-15.182); (c) rounded, dull piece with peck marks, from Jackson Mound (8Fr15; NMAI#172052). (Nancy Marie White)

sulfide, a soft, heavy, lead ore that can naturally form in cubic shapes. Gleaming galena pieces might have been used simply as they were or to rub on the body or other things for blackish-silvery or white metallic pigment. However, if ingested or inhaled as a powder, it would have been toxic. Elemental analyses have traced galena from Florida sites to sources in central or southeastern Missouri or the three-state area of southwestern Missouri, northwestern Arkansas, and northeastern Oklahoma (Austin and Matusik 2014; Ghosh 2008), well over 1,600 km (1000 mi.) away from the research region.

Clay and Ceramics
Clay is plentiful in the Apalachicola–lower Chattahoochee region. Its natural mica particles are visible even in pieces of prehistoric daub that were plastered onto house walls or in Late Archaic Poverty Point-style objects. Mica-flecked clay may have been a sign of identity for potters here. Some pXRF studies of potsherds have now identified trace elements indicating variable clays, but limited work has been accomplished on raw clay sources. Objects at many sites labeled "clay lumps" are pieces too small or rounded to be daub. Archaeologist Calvin Jones called them "squeezings," leftovers from pottery-making.

In this same category are burned clay chunks, possibly broken pieces of prepared hearths or encased, cooked animals. At least one probably Woodland-period clay figurine is known from the region.

Pottery appeared in the South over 4,000 years ago, constituting additional containers beyond animal guts, waterproof baskets, gourds, and stone and wooden bowls. The first clay pots may not necessarily have been that revolutionary for their users, though they are exciting for archaeologists, for whom they provide more objects to study. The earliest pottery was tempered with fibers of Spanish moss mixed into the clay. With intact fiber remaining in a sherd I even got a rare case of actually radiocarbon-dating pottery itself (White 2003b). By definition, Woodland times begin when sand, grit, and grog tempers replaced the fiber. Shell and limestone tempers are rare and come much later, as described in Volume 2. Standard ceramic typologies are used for the research region (Willey 1949), refined to be nonoverlapping in our USF sorting guide. Surface treatments, probably not all purely decorative, include incising, punctating or punching a small dent, stamping, and sculpting the wet clay before firing. The southeastern United States is not famous for painted Indian pottery as is the Southwest, but some Woodland pots had red or black paint.

Ceramic variability of course helps illuminate culture change. But we are finally moving away from the days when a new pottery type or series was interpreted to mean that somebody moved in from elsewhere. Even sourcing studies showing foreign manufacture do not necessarily mean movements of people or takeover of cultures by invaders (American homes today are full of electronics made in east Asia). We need more study of ceramic use and recycling. Laborious to produce, pottery was not thrown out when it broke. A study of ceramic function among Central and South American Indians showed large sherds being reused in countless ways, even a punctured jar serving as a chicken house (Deal and Hagstrum 1995). A museum exhibit I saw at the Neolithic site of Banpo, China, featured recycled sherds with use wear from scraping, notches for various uses, and holes drilled to make pendants. This wide range of ceramic reuse has not been recognized in the Apalachicola–lower Chattahoochee region, but we do have abundant sherds with drilled holes for repairs made by tying sides of a crack together. Other sherds were made into discs with beveled edges, for some purpose, perhaps gaming pieces.

Plants

Human use of plants in the research region is explored through study of environments and archaeobotanical remains. Inventories of plant communities (Anderson 1988; Edmiston 2008; Wharton 1978) document vegetation systems, including endangered species. Plants were for food, medicine, fuel, pigment, and fiber to make artifacts including houses, weapons, lines, traps, cloth, containers, zillions of other tools, ceremonial items, decorations, and art. In the dense, diverse forests of the region, most prehistoric artifacts would have been made of plants, especially wood, easy to get and work. Anthropologists know that plant-based diets are typical of most cultures worldwide. Several plant species were domesticated independently by Native Americans in the Midwest and mid-South by Late Archaic times, about 4,000 years ago, but none of these indigenous crops made it to the Deep South very early, if at all, while maize from Mexico caught on in late prehistoric times. The chapters in this volume describe cultures so far known only to have used wild plants, though they may have cultivated bottle gourd, tobacco, and other species. As discussed in Volume 2, even after food production emerges during Late Woodland times, the foundations of the native economy were really mixed farming and foraging. In the Apalachicola–lower Chattahoochee region, no prehistoric evidence of domesticated plants native to the United States is known so far. However, management of forests and plant communities was probably done from the earliest prehistoric times onward. Plant life includes more than food, medicine, and raw materials for artifact production. Unusual species and blooming colorful flowers may have been revered for spiritual or aesthetic reasons.

The meager archaeobotanical evidence in the region provides valuable insights, but much remains to be done in plant retrieval, identification, and analysis, as well as pollen, residue, and DNA study and investigation of past land management methods and how these changed through time and affected today's landscapes. Nonetheless, good data have been obtained on floral remains, as identified by archaeoethnobotanists and in our lab with standard manuals. Fragments are classified to the smallest taxon possible, with some only reducible to larger categories, such as "hardwood." The list includes nearly 100 taxa but is limited, since only small samples from about a dozen sites in the region have been professionally analyzed. Nearly all were preserved because they were charred. Exceptions are the actual Spanish moss fibers baked and sealed into the thick clay of Late Archaic ceramics.

Most of the specimens are wood, nutshell, seeds, fern spores, and occasional burned resin fragments. The only pollen was in the Middle Woodland dog coprolites and soil from the Otis Hare site (see Chapter 7). It is hard to compare these materials across the region because they represent different plant parts from different kinds of sites of many time periods. The data are also biased because the materials come from more recent investigations in which fine-screening and flotation have been done. Furthermore, the specimens identified are the ones from the richest proveniences, with the most diagnostic artifacts or dates, since those samples would have been the ones sent for analysis, and from the middle and lower Apalachicola valley, where more recent research has taken place. Finally, identifications were done by several specialists with different standards. Ethnobotanical evidence is discussed by time period in the appropriate chapters, but the compiled data allow some interesting observations. The most ubiquitous prehistoric remains are of oak, hickory, other hardwoods, and pine, probably from both fuel and food (nuts). Also common are bedstraw, grasses, and other weedy plants that grow in areas where people cleared trees to make living spaces.

Forests and Habitats

The bulk of the archaeological plant materials by weight is wood charcoal. Continually needing fuel from nearby forests might have been a prime motivator for campsite/village relocation after a generation or less. Besides raw material, the huge bottomland forests, pine flatwoods, and uplands of the Apalachicola–lower Chattahoochee valley provided fruits, nuts, and space for vines to hang around. Small seeds of chenopods and amaranths must have been collected and processed by boiling, popping, or grinding, and good amounts of acorn, hickory, other nutshell and occasionally charred nut meats have been recovered. Some of these remains can be deceiving. For example, since acorn shell is more fragile, it preserves poorly compared with the robust hickory shell, which can dominate archaeological plant assemblages but perhaps was less important in diets (Elisabeth Sheldon, personal communication 1987). Also, though nuts are available in the fall, suggesting seasonality, they are also easily stored and consumed at other times, and shells can be saved for fuel. Nuts could have been eaten raw, boiled to extract oil, or ground for gruel. They may have been pounded and sieved to remove shell fragments or crushed with water, then decanted and strained to remove the meat and oil (Gremillion 2011; VanDerwarker et al. 2007). Most acorns would have needed poisonous tannins leached from them to be edible. Then the crushed meats could be used for pottage, bread, or oil extraction. Many species of hickory nuts were important: pignut, water hickory, bitternut, and shagbark. Another, the pecan, might have been introduced prehistorically from west of the Mississippi, where wild groves are still common (Hall 2000).

Wild fruit remains recovered include persimmon, cherries, plums, and various berries. Fruit and nut trees could be transplanted or managed in place for convenience or higher yields. Bushy fruit plants include dewberries, blackberries, blueberries, and huckleberries. Wild grape, maypop or passionfruit, and others grow on vines. Many of these species are easy to encourage in cleared, open areas around settlements (Smith 2011). Fruits could be dried and pounded into cakes (Gremillion 2011). Wild grapevines drape through the forest canopy; grape seeds that have been excavated may reflect foods and also use of vines to weave or twine into artifacts. Flora for which we as yet have no remains but which must have been used include pawpaw (*Asimina triloba*), the largest edible wild fruit on the continent, which is baked or boiled; prickly pear (*Opuntia*), with both fruit and cactus pads edible once spines are removed; and sunflower, for seeds to make gruel. A species not recovered archaeologically (yet) that triggers never-ending horror is *Rhus radicans* (or *toxicodendron*), poison ivy, and its relatives. It grows in vast carpets and canopies in the river swamps. How Native Americans coped with it, or whether it bothered them at all, are intriguing mysteries.

Today much of the region's natural forest has been replaced by commercial planted pine. The varied woodlands of the past would have sustained 90 to 95% more species than do pine plantations, which are larger since mechanization began in the 1960s (Williams 2000). Longleaf pine is the most fire-resistant tree in the East and the first to appear on disturbed land (Outland 2004:15). It needs fire to reproduce, like its companion grasses and forbs, especially wiregrass. Currently control burning is a hotly debated issue in terms of the net yield of resources available to both hunters and ecosystems in general, and also because of risk in populated areas. The longleaf understory is one of the most diverse habitats in North America. The lack of shade they provide and short growing time between natural lightning-season fires mean that grasses, wildflowers, and shrubs can thrive. Longleafs also resist hurricane damage more than other pines. Of the original 60 to 90 million acres of longleaf across the South, an estimated 98% is now gone (Finch et al. 2012). The depletion possibly started with the first human inhabitants. Though we know little of the range of past uses of pine in the research region, as a softer wood it may have been preferred for construction, crafts, resin for waterproofing, and fat-lighter, resin-soaked heartwood, for kindling.

In the lower valley, the sabal or cabbage palm (*Sabal palmetto*), today Florida's state tree (see Plate IV), provided a tender, edible heart (inner pulp), though the tree must be killed to get it, and this species is protected today. This palm did not originally live much farther west along the Gulf Coast than the Apalachicola valley. Palm leaves are great for thatching, fanning, and fibers for plaited fabrics. The saw palmetto (*Serenoa repens*; also in Plate IV), a shrub abundant throughout the region, has similar useful leaves and large edible fruits that even today are of medicinal value. Palmetto leaf stems, lined with sharp thorns, could have been used for cutting; they certainly pierce human skin. Cypresses (*Taxodium distichum*, bald cypress, and others) are in ponds and backswamps. Along wetland edges are cypress "knees," woody upright projections above the water surface that bash people's shins. Orange in winter and blue-green in spring, cypresses are seasonal indicators, water-resistant, and now prized for construction. Shell middens are often marked by cedar trees, which prefer the higher ground and calcium in the soil. When freshly cut, cedar exposes reddish, aromatic inner fiber that could have had ancient significance.

Another important wetland tree is the tupelo, for more than usable wood. The ogeechee tupelo or ogeechee gum (*Nyssa ogeche*) produces an edible, sour fruit. This species and also the water tupelo (*Nyssa aquatica*), swamp tupelo (*Nyssa biflora*), and black tupelo or black gum (*Nyssa sylvatica*) have historically been important for the production of honey. Red maples in dry areas, swamp maples in wetlands, scrubby sandpines on barrier islands, sycamores on riverbanks, and many other trees were undoubtedly chosen in the ancient past for specific uses. The sweetgum, with the lovely biological name *Liquidambar styraciflua*, has an aromatic resin that was probably highly valued. The magnolia (*Magnolia grandiflora*) could have been appreciated for its large fragrant flowers. Though no archaeological evidence of most of these plants exists in the region so far, they might have been collected for multiple uses. Roots and tubers are hard to see because they quickly rot, but they were probably important prehistorically. The prickly smilax (greenbriar) vines, for example, have edible/medicinal shoots and starchy tubers.

Indigenous peoples actively managed plant communities (Barker 2010; Bush et al. 2022; Ellis et al. 2021; Smith 2011). Archaeologists have demonstrated that forests worldwide were altered by humans at least as far back as 45,000 years ago. Details of these human impacts are useful for both heritage study and ecosystem conservation and policy making today (Roberts et al. 2017). Ecologists now realize that disturbance such as fire or flood is constant and generates biodiversity (Dean 2010:6–8; Kelly and Brotons 2017), which native cultures understood. Indigenous Australian groups even know how raptorial birds pick up burning sticks and spread fire themselves to flush out prey (Bonta et al. 2017). Evidence of relationships with plant communities among hunter-gatherers challenges the notion that land clearing and food production began as one sudden shift toward farming. Though evidence is so far lacking for ancient landscape manipulation in the Apalachicola–lower Chattahoochee valley region, people surely knew how to do weeding, watering, pruning, selective harvesting, burning, and planting trees where desired.

Drugs

Hundreds of plants had medicinal uses for Native Americans in the Southeast. Herbs for pain and other ailments were common, but there is little evidence of narcotics or mind-altering substances (Rafferty 2021). There was no alcohol, for unknown reasons (White and Weinstein 2008). The hallucinogen datura or jimson weed (*Datura stramonium*) has been tentatively identified at the Midwestern prehistoric center of Cahokia (Emerson 2003). If it was present, it may have been a ritual item imported from the Southwest. Though several plants may have been smoked and others were remedies for illness, the only two pharmaceuticals used widely in the South were nicotine, in tobacco, and caffeine, in yaupon holly.

Tobacco facilitated connection with the supernatural. At least six species were used, but *Nicotiana rustica* was domesticated possibly in South America and may have moved in through Mexico and the Southwest to the eastern United States. Charred seeds of wild tobacco have been recovered from a 12,300-year-old hearth in the desert Southwest (Duke et al. 2021). Tobacco was chewed, eaten, and smoked, inhaled from fires, cigar-like rolls, or pipes (Dunavan and Jones 2011; Fox 2015). Tubular, elbow-shaped, and other forms of pipes (see Figure 2.6), appearing as early as the Archaic period, probably had cane tubes inserted through which to inhale. Tobacco is addictive; the many varieties cultivated by Native Americans caused different reactions, including unconsciousness and death. Brown (2006) thinks that Middle Woodland shamanism was enhanced by strong tobaccos that produced trances and visions. Use of tobacco was and still is important for American Indian healing, purification, and spirituality.

Yaupon holly (*Ilex vomitoria*) was used to make the Native American tea called black drink, consumed for ritual purification in the Southeast. The dried, parched leaves have the highest caffeine content of any North American plant. Yaupon grows along the Gulf from Florida to central Texas (Hudson 1979) but was exchanged throughout the East. Yaupon bushes grow in great numbers in sandy soils of coastal and estuarine settings of the Apalachicola delta, including at archaeological sites. Easy to collect in the wild, it may also have been planted farther inland prehistorically. Avocational archaeologist John McKinnie had thriving planted yaupon bushes some 120 river miles inland and served my field crew tea made from their leaves. Shell cups from Early/Middle Woodland mounds in the research region may have been for drinking this tea. People go to great lengths for and conduct great ceremony with drugs. Caffeine is in many plants around the globe and is the world's most popular drug (Weinberg and Bealer 2001). If yaupon and tobacco were the only important substances of this kind, they were surely discovered early, distributed widely, highly desired, and important in structuring socioeconomic and ritual interaction.

Industrial and Other Nonfood Plants

Artifacts made of plants are seldom preserved, though they surely constituted the majority of prehistoric material culture. Despite the abundance of water in the research region, wet sites with intact perishable artifacts are not yet known. Anaerobic peat deposits at the Early Archaic Windover site near

Florida's east coast preserved bone, wood, and fiber/fabric artifacts and abundant floral remains up to 8,000 years old including wooden stakes, pestles, atlatl handles and shafts, basketry and mats, and fragments of domesticated bottle gourd (Doran 2002).

Ethnographic and archaeological evidence indicates wood-pole houses were of many styles across the Southeast. Thin saplings could be set into the ground then bent and joined at the top (flexed-pole construction), or straight logs could form vertical walls capped by a separate roof (rigid-pole). Structural evidence is rare in the Apalachicola–lower Chattahoochee region, probably because horizontally extensive excavations are lacking. Walls of buildings could have been of wattle and daub with thin branches woven horizontally between poles to create a framework, and then clay daubed onto the sides. Woven split-cane mats or bark could cover walls and roofs, which could also be thatched with grasses or palm/palmetto leaves. Studies of aboriginal architecture in the Southeast (Lacquement 2007) show that daub washes off walls more easily with curved-roof structures lacking eaves. Experimental archaeology gives some insights: a replica of a flexed-pole wall-trench structure measuring 6.8 × 4.9 m (22 × 16 feet), 2.5 m (8 feet) high, made by inexperienced workers with modern tools, required 568 worker hours, with nearly a quarter of the time needed for obtaining materials and 29% of the time for daubing the walls. Rain and sun-drying hastened daub failure, and chunks fell off interior walls more than exterior (Blanton and Gresham 2007). Such structures would also burn easily, better preserving the evidence. Thatched or woven surfaces offer great places to stash things, say, sticking a sharp knife into the roof on the way into the house so kids will not get hurt. When dwellings decay or burn, these artifacts fall onto the floor.

Though prehistoric fiber arts and crafts of the Southeast seldom escaped decay, we can glimpse them in impressions they left in fired clay (Figure 2.9). Textiles were made of grasses, weedy plants, palm, and other pliable fibers (Whitford 1941), including hair, feathers, skin, bark, and fur. Cotton, so important to the South, was not present until historic times, for unknown reasons. Vines, stems, inner bark, leaves, and other plant parts could be soaked, rotted, boiled, beaten, and otherwise treated to obtain pliable materials for weaving or twining (Weiner and Schneider 1989). In the research region, fabric-impressed and cord-marked ceramics and other fired clay such as daub have preserved impressions of the diverse woven, twined, and twisted fibers in individual strands, multiple-strand cords and yarns, and various weaves. Images on pots, figurines, and other media indicate how cloth might have been used. Though European invaders noted that sixteenth-century Native Americans wore minimal body covering, much clothing may have had social and ideological

Figure 2.9. Woodland ceramic sherds with impressions of perishables from Otis Hare site (8Li172): (a–e) net-marked, from Test Unit 2: (a) Level 5 (#90-86); (b) L9 (#90-163); (c) L10 (#90-177); (d) L11 (#90-189.1); (e) L13 (#90-227); on left of each sherd is its positive impression in modeling clay, to show the variety in mesh sizes, knots, twists of cords; (f) fabric-marked sherd (#90-6) from TU1, L4, with positive impression on left showing at least two different woven patterns. (Nancy Marie White)

significance, as did jewelry, tattoos, and body/face paint. Other wearable objects were of human and animal hair, sinew, seeds, shells, bone, and stones.

Nets were crucial; net bags are the backpacks of forest peoples worldwide. Net-marked ceramics show diverse knot types and mesh sizes. Before modern plastics, fisherfolk spent endless hours repairing nets. Hunting terrestrial game is safer and easier with nets. Scrutiny of fiber-artifact manufacturing processes can identify motor skills and even handedness of the craftworkers (Minar 2000). Plant fibers were twisted and twined into baskets, mats, wall coverings, and probably thousands of other artifacts ranging from utensils to clothing to fish weirs and animal traps, boats, furniture, and houses. The huge range of plant-based artifacts made by wetlands peoples was emphasized for me during a visit to the Brunei Technological Museum, which displays old-fashioned Malay water-village houses and crafts. Just woven bamboo and rattan-vine implements for fishing revealed stunning variability and ingenuity. One fish trap was a large sphere inside of which was a cone with only a tiny opening at the pointed end; fish swam into the wide end then were confined in the sphere. Nested heart-shaped traps, V-shaped weirs, and complex house wall construction were characteristic of just that one cultural tradition. Basketry is an extremely ancient traditional craft, for both utilitarian and artistic or ritual items of near-infinite diversity. A 1926 survey listed over 200 varieties of wicker baskets still being produced in England and Wales, and basket weaving has been called "the original 3-D printing" (Langlands 2018:316–317).

An essential raw material for many of these products was river cane (*Arundinaria* spp.). Thinner and softer than Asian bamboo, this large American grass reaches 12 m tall. It grows in thick, impenetrable canebrakes with other plants, such as greenbriar vine (*Smilax* spp.) with its ornery thorns. Cane is still abundant along stream banks in the research region. It is easy to plant or manage and rapidly grows back when cut. Besides fishing poles, cane was used for projectile shafts, baskets, woven mats, wattle for house walls, fences and drying racks, small artifacts from points and knives to jewelry and musical flutes, easy fuel, and even seeds and shoots for food and medicines. Cane was the plastic of Native Americans (Cook and Cook 2000:194).

Animals

Within the already biologically rich Southeast, the Apalachicola–lower Chattahoochee valley ecosystems sheltered thousands of animal species. Several are now gone, such as the ivory-billed woodpecker and Florida panther (extinct in the region), but high species richness and diversity continue. Besides food, animals were for ritual and spiritual purposes and sources of raw materials for making artifacts. Bird heads, beaks, claws, feathers, fur, hooves, antlers, and other body parts besides bone and shell were used. Pearls from shellfish were decorative, possibly religious objects since they were grave goods (Figure 2.10), as at Pierce Mound A (8Fr14; Moore 1902); elsewhere in this mound were offerings of wolf and panther teeth. Colorful insects may have been special; Amazonians wore strings of iridescent beetles. Obviously, many of these are not preserved, but additional clues to faunal use are images in art and craft. Animals depicted in pottery and other media suggest their importance to humans, such as the many birds and other creatures represented in ceramic effigies. Some beasts are dangerous; panthers, bears, snakes, or alligators can kill a human. Other fauna are just annoying; clouds of mosquitoes, hornets, or gnats require constant vigilance. I sympathize with a passage in an 1836 letter from a Florida woman describing her body covered with mosquito bites and her face looking like a currant pudding (Denham and Huneycutt 2004:41).

Faunal remains recovered archaeologically from the region include over 250 taxa represented by both ecofacts/presumably food remains and artifacts. As with plants, the lists given in the chapters are biased since zooarchaeo-

Figure 2.10. Pearl beads from Pierce mounds (8Fr14; NMAI#171348), probably Mound A Burial 66 (Early to Middle Woodland), shown in tagged specimen bag. (Nancy Marie White)

logical research has been rare and done with samples from only a few proveniences at the few tested sites. Most remains have come from flotation of soil samples from shell middens where the less acidic soil retards bone decay. Therefore shellfish and fish are greatest in represented numbers, volume, and species. Preservation aspects vary: the toughness of garfish scales may account for their abundance in middens, or the fragility of hollow bird bones may make them rarer. Also, before flotation and fine-mesh screening became standard in the 1980s, recovery was biased in favor of larger, more visible bone bits. Some animals recovered are commensals, not collected by past peoples but wandering in later, such as terrestrial snails, or coming attached with some desired resource, such as barnacles or mussels clinging to the oysters people gathered. Species names and common names differ by zooarchaeologists' preferences and changing biological conventions, though I have to love small mollusks called southern fatmucket, slim snaggletooth, or rosy wolf snail. Specialists have differed in emphases. Rochelle Marrinan, analyzing our St. Vincent Island faunal assemblage (Marrinan and Parsons 2010), took bird bones to the FLMNH comparative collections to confirm species. Karen Walker (1988) compared oyster and marsh clam shell by component to show possible environmental changes through time. Arlene Fradkin (1994) identified multiple small terrestrial snails. Brian Parker (1994), with a shell guidebook, discovered in the USF lab that zooarchaeologists had mislabeled some *Polymesoda* shells as *Rangia* (both marsh clams).

My compilations of faunal data in the research region (White 2023) expand on Percy's (1974) summary of Native American animal use in northwest Florida (excluding his sites outside the region). I do not include identifications at the level of class or other more general category (such as vertebrate or mammal), which are less useful for comparative work, but otherwise note the smallest taxon possible. Zooarchaeologists need at least 200 individual animals or about 1,400 bone fragments to show subsistence activity realistically at a single site (Wing and Brown 1979:18–21). So high-level generalizations about sites or subsistence systems in the region are not yet possible, as they are in more intensively investigated areas. Nonetheless, the faunal data do show interesting trends, summarized further on and in the relevant chapters, and also help in understanding modern changing ecosystems.

Hunting, Terrestrial Species, and Manipulating Landscapes
Pleistocene fauna—mammoth, mastodon, horse, camel forms, and giant versions of armadillo, sloth, and bison—were obtained by early hunters/scavengers across North America. Fossil remains of these creatures are plentiful in the Apalachicola–lower Chattahoochee valley region. Though none so far is specifically associated with an archaeological site, collectors did show us a mastodon bone with cut marks (Kelley 2013). Tusks with cuts and other evidence that people harvested these beasts are now well known from Paleoindian sites elsewhere in northwest Florida. Bison/buffalo in the South included two species: *Bison latifrons*, twice as large as modern bison, with a 2-meter horn span, and *Bison antiquus*, with horns spanning up to a meter. After these became extinct, the modern bison (*Bison bison*), the largest animal in North America today, was confined mostly to the Great Plains, though, curiously, it migrated east of the Mississippi River in the 1500s–1600s, as described in Volume 2. A prehistoric possible bison bone ornament came from Pierce Mounds (see Chapter 7).

By the Holocene, when modern fauna were established, there is better evidence for hunting a wide range of animals, though so far we have no zooarchaeological remains older than the Late Archaic, about 4,000 years ago. For all time periods, white-tailed deer are abundant. Typically in the Southeast, deer predominate at inland sites, where they are the largest individual package of meat available, averaging about 45 kg per animal. Deer may have been brought home whole or already split or quartered for roasting. Any animal meats were also probably stewed, leaving more intact, unburned bone fragments. Several sites have produced remains of bear, which provides more meat than deer, as adult males reach 115 kg (250 lbs.). However, as carnivores and more difficult prey than deer, bear might not have been eaten as much as taken for other purposes, from rendering fat to using parts in rituals. The same might be true of alligator and bobcat, and must be the case for panther and wolf, where the teeth are burial offerings. Abundant small mammals such as raccoon, opossum, beaver, rabbit, squirrel, and rodents could have been trapped or shot.

Easier to obtain were the many types of tortoise and turtle (except for snappers, which can take off fingers or dent a shovel handle). Turtle meat and eggs are nutritious, with beneficial fat. The shells are ready-made containers, also useful for making rattles to set music and dance rhythm. Turtles provide a lot of food for relatively little effort, whether netted, speared, or simply picked up; a loggerhead can weigh 136 kg (300 lbs.). Turtle eggs, especially of sea turtles, are still (illegally) harvested today because they are considered a tasty delicacy, and are easily obtained by simply digging them up after watching the turtle lay them. Softshell turtle is a swift creature on land or in the water that must have been taken frequently, as fragments of its distinctively patterned carapace are common in middens. Other abundant turtle remains are of cooters, sliders, and gopher tortoises. The endangered Barbour's map turtle was recognized at the Otis Hare site; only 10–20 cm long, it may have been an easy catch since it floats with its head above water.

Remains of freshwater turtles characterize sites from the interior to the coast, while sea turtle is rare at inland sites. On the coast, sea turtles are well represented in shell middens on St. Joseph Bay. They move into this salty bay until the temperature drops, when they head south seeking warmer waters. Since the south end of the bay is closed off by the peninsula, people probably just had to wait there for supper to arrive. In addition, cold-stunning of turtles when water temperatures drop to 50 degrees F causes immobility (Foley et al. 2007). We might assume the same was true in the ancient past, when these creatures would simply float helplessly and be even easier to get. The cold 2000–2001 winter stranded over 1,700 green, Kemp's ridley, loggerhead, and hawksbill turtles on the bayshore in the largest sea-turtle cold-stunning event ever recorded in the United States. During the 2018 cold winter, rescuers picked up 1,100 cold-stunned turtles in a week.

Alligator remains, especially the easily recognizable dermal scutes, are numerous at sites in the region. The few frog bones probably indicate a food source. Fewer archaeological remains of birds than would be expected have been recovered so far. Many specimens can only be identified to the level of class, Aves. Possibly birds were more difficult to obtain (they do tend to fly away) or less preferred. A similar relative lack of bird bones from Gulf peninsular Florida sites has been interpreted as a resource selection issue (Quitmyer 2013:350). Ivory-bills, thought to be reclusive, were probably widespread and easy to get prehistorically. Woodpecker feathers and other parts were used in Native American rituals and depicted on engraved shell and ceramics throughout the South. Other species extinct today, such as passenger pigeon and Carolina parakeet, were surely valued for their behavior and colorful feathers. Tiny hummingbirds, which pollinate tobacco plants, might have been harvested whole for food, decor, or ritual. Abundant ducks, geese, and turkey are represented in prehistoric middens. Dove, quail, and other small birds for which we do not yet have any bones were probably also taken often, as they are now. Wild turkey was a mainstay in the prehistoric diet. Other large birds—sandhill and whooping cranes, osprey, eagle, woodstork, egret, turkey vulture, and seabirds such as brown pelican, which can gather in flocks of 800–900 on the bayshores (Cerulean 2015:127)—are not yet known in archaeological assemblages. Birds are depicted so often on artifacts that they surely had major significance, based on their appearance, flight patterns, other behavior, and sounds. The "caw" of a regular crow might have been less noteworthy than that of the fish crow, a "ha-ha" that sounds like mocking laughter.

Most snake bones from sites in the region are not identifiable as to species, but hundreds of herpetological species occur here, including all six of the poisonous snakes of the eastern United States: diamondback, canebrake (timber), and pygmy rattlesnakes; cottonmouth/water moccasin; copperhead; and coral snake. Rattlesnake rattles are depicted in native imagery (see Figure 2.6). While sometimes lethal for humans, snakes may have been eaten but also used in ritual or magic. The endangered indigo snake was identified at Clark Creek (8Gu60) in the Early Woodland shell midden. Though no insects have been recovered in archaeological contexts, prehistoric natives could have eaten or otherwise used them. We did excavate the preserved clay chambers of a mud-dauber wasp nest deep in an estuarine shell midden in the lower valley, which suggested it had been on the side of a structure wall. Human coprolites from sites in the West have contained termites, grasshoppers, cicadas, and other bugs that were probably eaten deliberately, perhaps dried and salted or fried, as well as fleas, lice, mites, and other external parasites, weevils and flies that were probably unintentionally consumed, and internal parasites such as stomach worms (Elias 2010:115–117).

Though prehistoric Native Americans mostly subsisted on wild resources, there was probably always one domesticated species: the dog, domesticated from gray wolves in Eurasia and maybe independently in Europe during the Upper Paleolithic (Grimm 2016; Snyder and Leonard 2011), possibly due to their own behavior, scavenging at the edge of human camps. More than just work animals to carry or drag packs or sleds, aid in hunting, and protect people, dogs were companions too, but also food. Genetic and other data show that dogs probably came to the Americas with the first humans (Perri et al. 2021). The oldest archaeological evidence is from coastal British Columbia, dated to 13,100 BP (Fedje et al. 2021). A dog skull fragment from Texas dated to about 9400 BP was in a human coprolite, meaning that the dog was eaten (Stewart 2011).

A study of physical variability of dogs from archaeological sites all over the South, mostly from deliberate burials and ranging in time from the Archaic through protohistoric, showed the more ancient examples were mostly small- to medium-sized, with little morphological variation, while later dogs had greater size and shape ranges (Worthington 2008). While no dog bones have been recovered in the research region, Middle Woodland dog coprolites came from the Otis Hare site (8Li172; see Chapter 7). The only other animals domesticated in North America were turkeys, in the Southwest, but not the Southeast, probably because wild turkey is so abundant there (still). Suggestions that Native Americans practiced aquaculture are based on reasonable evidence of constructed canals and ponds in south Florida. Fish and shellfish populations raised or manipulated by humans would not be hard to imagine in the Apalachicola–lower Chattahoochee region.

Our understanding of the impacts of prehistoric peoples on their environments has evolved. By the 1970s, the traditional view that human effects on forests did not extend more than a few paces outside the settlement gave way to the realization that foragers have altered landscapes and often enhanced biodiversity (Ellis et al. 2021). Indigenous societies in the Apalachicola–lower Chattahoochee region probably engineered their surroundings both deliberately and inadvertently. No prehistoric anthropogenic environments have yet been recognized, but forests had to be cleared when mounds and settlements were built. Burning to drive game or enhance vegetation attracting animals was likely done by the earliest people. Before recent times, the region is estimated to have had natural fires often, every one to three years in fire-prone areas, except for the very uppermost portions of the valley, where the frequency was between four and six years (Noss 2013:205). People may have set fires or managed natural ones. Florida has the most lightning strikes (and deaths) per year, with Georgia ranking second and Alabama fifth, according to insurance companies. Lightning causes natural fires in the summer, while winter fires are set by people. Fire ecologist Huffman (2006) found that natural fires occurred at least every three years around St. Joseph Bay during the late spring–early summer season (the driest, with the most lightning). Fires during other seasons, probably set by humans, were rarer but by the early 1800s comprised 14% of those on St. George Island and 20% on the mainland. This change in fire ecology is attributable to the Euro-American presence (but Huffman's data do not extend earlier than the 1600s).

Fishing and Aquatic Species
Other prehistoric land management strategies may have included fish weirs, traps of poles or stones laid across a stream, or stream rechanneling to drive or cultivate aquatic species. Prehistoric V-shaped and zigzag weirs are

documented in North Carolina rivers (Price 2019). Southeastern archaeology is biased toward overestimating human use of terrestrial animals relative to aquatic species, especially at inland sites (Walker 2000), and Native Americans probably ate more fish than we realize. In warm, forested, watery areas such as the Amazon, fish is the primary source of protein (Oliver 2008). In the Apalachicola–lower Chattahoochee valley, species represented in zooarchaeological assemblages must give only a limited idea of what was caught. The Apalachicola River has more fish species (91 known) than any other in Florida, many restricted to this region (Light et al. 1998:2). Sturgeon, shad, and striped bass were found well up the Chattahoochee and Flint before the dams were built (Yerger 1977). A large number of Florida record-sized fish have come from here (Barnes 1987:7). Netting or spearing fish or other creatures was easier than running after, spearing, or even trapping land animals, and was easily done by kids. Even today, fishing, arguably more than hunting, is crucial to most longtime inhabitants of the region, not a "recreation or a hobby . . . [but] a way of life" (McClellan 2014:28).

The line of prehistoric sites on the east side of St. Vincent Island must have been created as people came to net the mullet that regularly run past that shore. Mullet live in both salt and fresh water, and often, startlingly, jump out of the water. They occur as zooarchaeological remains at both coastal and inland prehistoric sites. Mullet run in the bay in huge schools, especially with the first autumn full-moon cold snap. They are so noisy that fishers probably did not even have to see them to know it was time. Watts (1975:91) describes one man with a boat and gill net circling a school and quickly pulling out over 70 fish. Striped (black) mullet migrations draw other fish, such as jack crevalle, also well represented among the archaeofauna, as well as tarpon and diving birds "into a grand biological phenomenon," as these hand-sized fish "periodically burst into the air like exploding fireworks" (Witherington and Witherington 2007:146). They also draw predatory dolphins into the bays (Cerulean 2015:142–143). Our test excavation at the St. Vincent 5 site (8Fr364) examined Woodland deposits in which nearly 15% of the identifiable biomass of fish was mullet (61% of the fish MNI and 56% of the total vertebrate sample), 12% was drums, and nearly 11% was saltwater catfishes; also represented were ladyfish, herring, jacks, flounder, and the ubiquitous garfish (Marrinan and Parsons 2010). Another anadromous jumper, Apalachicola sturgeon, which still vaults up to bash into boaters, was a genetically distinct variety. Fishing for both its meat and roe/caviar was once commercially important (US Fish and Wildlife Service 2018), though few remain today, and none have been recovered archaeologically. Bream, shellcracker, and channel catfish are represented at some sites; pied bream occurs nowhere else except this valley (McClellan 2014:33).

Commercial catfisheries existed along the rivers until very recently. Now the most numerous fish in the estuary and bay system is anchovy, with Atlantic croaker and seatrout also dominant (Livingston 1983, 1984). Atlantic croaker and seatrout are well represented at prehistoric sites. Zooarchaeological remains of saltwater fish include many marine catfish such as hardhead and gafftopsail cats. Hardhead is often considered inedible today, and both have wicked, poisonous, slime-covered spines that can inflict pain on humans, so I wonder what technology native fishers used to get them. Such species are dominant at Atlantic-coast prehistoric sites, where they were "large-bodied, mass captured" taxa (Reitz et al. 2010:61). Apalachicola estuarine shell middens have also produced remains of sunfish, sheepshead, bowfin, and jack crevalle. Jack can get up to 18 kg and might have been more available in winter when they venture en masse into freshwater springs seeking warmth.

Interesting bones attributed to jack, drum, and other fish are "pneumatized" or hyperostotic or "tilly" bones, named after Tilly Edinger, the paleontologist who first described them. They are swollen and can resemble sea-turtle phalanges, though it is unknown how they got that way (Tiffany et al. 1980). Zooarchaeologists have told me that the swelling might come from air or oil, and these bones might help fish flotation; however, dropped into a glass of water, they sink just like any bone. Human use of some kind is recorded for tilly bones even at South American shell midden sites (Bird 1985:243). In the research region, pneumatized bones must have been used by humans, as several have cuts or cut ends or notches (Figure 2.11).

Many fish found at prehistoric sites are still harvested, such as jack crevalle, famous as fighting gamefish; but some species are not taken today. Garfish (*Lepisosteus*), including the Florida, longnose, alligator, and spotted gar, are abundant in prehistoric middens, though not desirable today. Alligator gar can reach over 45 kg and 3 m long, and huge gar that create havoc for boaters are still sighted in the river (Cook and Cook 2000:152). Gar is recognizable by its distinctive diamond-shaped scales that preserve well and were used for points or other tools throughout the South (Patterson 2004). An Early Woodland child burial in Tennessee had rows of them evidently as beads attached to clothing (Faulkner 1992). While the utility of gar and durability of its remains may account for its archaeological abundance, another reason might be its ease of capture, since it lies still just below the surface. However, few today bother catching a big ornery fish with nasty teeth that is too bony to clean easily.

The hook and line was possibly the least common method of native fishing. It is less dependable if one is after dinner, not thrills. Of course, the goals of prehistoric fishers are pure speculation. They may have made sport out of the process as so many do today, especially bass fishers; however, bass remains

Figure 2.11. Pneumatized fish bones with cuts: *top*, 10 cut on both ends, from St. Vincent 5 site (Woodland, #USFJC-8Fr364-15-1.312); *bottom left*, notched, from Van Horn Creek shell midden TU5 L5, Late Archaic–Early Woodland (#8Fr744-93-230); *bottom right*, two with flat-cut ends, from Mound Near Apalachicola, Stratum II (43–66 cm) Shovel Test 94-1 (Middle–Late Woodland; #8Fr14[Fr20]-94-57.16). (Nancy Marie White)

are recorded from only a few sites. Finely fashioned bone hooks, rare in this region, include barbed versions that were burial goods in the Chipola Cutoff Mound (8Gu5; Moore 1903:366) and a few from other sites, inland and coastal (Figure 2.12). While such artifacts may be called fishhooks, they could have had many functions: hanging things up, holding things down. Often fish bones in archaeological assemblages are tiny, suggesting large quantities of fish were netted, boiled whole, perhaps picking out the meat or straining the broth. Surprisingly, crustaceans are rare in the zooarchaeological assemblages, represented mostly by crab and the occasional barnacle that probably grew on other harvested shellfish or on wooden structures. Shrimp and crayfish were probably commonly eaten but their parts are apparently too fragile to survive.

Other aquatic species are represented in the data. Playful fat otters still cavort in the river, though so far no otter remains are known archaeologically. Turtles are noted above. One cetacean bone fragment from Middle to Late Woodland context at the St. Vincent Island 5 site could have been whale or dolphin; the latter frequently glide close to shore. An interesting faunal item found by the dozens on St. Vincent Island is a fossilized dolphin bulla (inner ear bone). Though these are petrified and pre-date humans, they might have been collected by people. Manatees rarely range as far north as Apalachicola Bay in the summer, occasionally a ways into the river. All these larger species could have been hunted but may also have been obtained when they became stranded; over an eight-year period 132 strandings were recorded in the 1990s, mostly of dolphins and some whales (Edmiston 2008:109). Caribbean monk seals, now extinct, also lived in the Gulf of Mexico, though they are not known in the region's archaeofaunal remains. A tiny fragment of sea urchin, an echinoderm known to inhabit St. Joseph Bay, was recovered on Black's Island there, indicating possible harvest.

The intensively investigated prehistoric record of the Atlantic coast indicates that native fishers mostly used tidal creeks and estuaries, and only rarely the open ocean. Mass capture of small, schooling fish was the typical strategy, which persisted for thousands of years from Archaic times onward, despite environmental and social change. Species diversity increased through time, but mean trophic level of fishes declined, meaning higher-level predator species decreased while species lower in the food web increased (Reitz et al. 2010). A reason for these changes might be landscape alteration inland when people began clearing forests and farming, increasing erosion and flushing of sediments downriver into estuaries, affecting fish populations. Another reason could be overfishing, which can cause decline in mean trophic levels or depletion of selected species over time, or reduction of fish size and/or geographic range, as seen today and in some archaeological cases (e.g., Erlandson and Rick 2008). Yet other historic and ethnographic data show that native systems across the world had complex management strategies that promoted sustainability, including strictly enforced rules about who could fish, how/where fishing was done, and who could eat fish (McClenachan and Kittinger 2013). Knowledge of past fishing regimes can be valuable for modern policy making. Data are still too few in the Apalachicola–lower Chattahoochee region to examine these possibilities, but more intensive study of excavated collections has great potential. Faunal remains at coastal shell midden sites do

Figure 2.12. Broken Early Woodland deer bone hook (#8Gu56-87-33.8) from Depot Creek shell midden TUA L9. (Nancy Marie White)

suggest little change in types of species harvested from the Archaic onward, for at least 4,000 years, as in south Florida and on the Atlantic coast (e.g., Reitz et al. 2010).

Shellfishing and Shell Middens
Prehistoric shellfish collection left copious remains and is thus studied intensively by archaeologists. Shellfish are nutrient-dense and easy to get, but we have now overturned the idea that they were the main dietary staple. Fine screens recover tiny fish bones showing other aquatic species were the primary targets. Salt-marsh fishing ranks higher in return rate of food obtained for the time and effort than does terrestrial hunting, while shellfishing ranks low, though the shellfish provide high-quality protein (Thomas 2014). Mollusks may have been a secondary food, for convenient snacks or lean times. The picture has been skewed because shells comprise such a huge volume of the recovered remains though they represent a relatively small amount of actual food. One good-sized fish has as much meat as hundreds of clams or oysters.

Models of how middens are created explore ethnographies of shellfish collectors worldwide (e.g., Meehan 1982; Waselkov 1987). Shellfish are picked up by hand in shallow water or mud, found with feet or sticks, sometimes rakes, dredges, scoops, or traps for mass harvesting. A prehistoric Louisiana shell mound produced an amazingly preserved burned net bag full of unopened marsh clams (Gagliano et al. 1982:60). Shellfish processing can involve simple shucking, but easier methods to open them are roasting, boiling, or steaming, and they can be dried or smoked for storage. Many models also assume that shellfish must have been collected by women and children, but gender-based division of labor cannot be assumed. However, even young kids can collect mollusks without help. Research in Australia and New Guinea found that adult foragers process larger, higher-quality shellfish right where they are collected and then bring more meat back to camp, while children pick up smaller, lower-quality shellfish to bring back whole. Thus, species in shell middens may reflect kids' choices and obscure what was really being gathered and eaten (Codding et al. 2014).

Within the eastern Gulf region, the Apalachicola Basin supports the highest number of freshwater mollusk species and of endemics: 33 species of mussels (bivalves), 10 of which are endemic (Williams and Fradkin 1999). Bivalves and snails live in shallow-water beds easy to access in low-water times of late spring and early fall. Those from archaeological sites in the region include a new species of Unionid mussel, Apalachicola ebonyshell, *Fusconaia (Reginaia) apalachicola*. It was discovered during analysis of a faunal assemblage from St. Stephen's Church site (8Li76) and then identified in collections from three other sites: Sycamore (8Gd13), Scholz Steam Plant (8Ja104), and Omussee

Creek Park (1Ho26) at the northern end of the region in Alabama (Williams and Fradkin 1999; Williams et al. 2014). Visiting the USF archaeology lab, malacologist Jim Williams also identified it in our materials from the Sunstroke site (8Li217) in the middle Apalachicola, making the range of this species a 70 river-mile stretch. All these sites are Woodland or later in cultural affiliation. Apalachicola ebonyshell is recognized by its circular shape and other characteristics. Evidently it disappeared due to historic large-scale soil runoff. It is the only species of Unionid known to have become extinct before being described. Its discovery shows the value of archaeological data to other sciences and to ecosystem management, even if the news is not good.

Other freshwater mollusks in the region are now rare or endangered (Williams et al. 2008, 2014); most Unionid species in North America are imperiled. Numbers of riverine shell middens in the Georgia and Alabama portions of the research region are underrepresented because less study has been done of them. Deposits probably constitute accumulated refuse from multiple foraging trips or by many and/or different aboriginal groups through time. Percy (1976:118–119) thought snails would be less preferred over mussels as they had less meat and occur in smaller numbers in middens. If all these mostly small food resources were simply scooped up and stuck in pots to boil or steam, it might be easier to extract meat. However, at the Torreya Ranger site (8Li8) some 80% of the Georgia/banded mystery snail shells had the apex (spire) broken off, possibly to suck out the raw meat, and eating shellfish raw may have provided the maximum food value. Freshwater shell middens occur on present-day riverbanks and also on old meanders far from current channels. Though archaeological data may be unreliable to use for dating meander bands, a comparison of old channel locations with prehistoric occupation times might be useful. Freshwater shell middens occur as far downriver as the lower-middle Apalachicola.

Coastal and estuarine shellfish, from brackish and salty waters, supposedly first became available after post-Pleistocene sea-level rise backed up rivers into estuaries and bays for them to inhabit by around 4000 BP, corresponding roughly with the Late Archaic period. The earliest coastal shell middens in the research region are indeed Late Archaic, but they may just be the earliest site components that have not been submerged by still-rising seas. Geological borings into Apalachicola Bay to investigate delta formation have recovered marsh clam at 22 meters below present sea level, dated at 9,950 ± 180 years BP. Since this species lives in shallow brackish water, the conclusion is that sea level began rising, backing up the river water in its entrenched valley at this time (Schnable and Goodell 1968:42–47). Clams were gathered in huge quantities by natives who left estuarine shell middens that are today farther inland. Similarly, buried oyster beds on the barrier islands indicate that sea level stood about 3–5 m lower between 4,000–4,500 years ago (Schnable and Goodell 1968:50) and suggest that oyster too was available farther south than the current evidence indicates. However, prehistoric shell middens in the research region may not be as big as those on the Atlantic coast or south Florida because other resources were so abundant that fewer shellfish were needed.

The following are the region's shell midden site types, based on species, environment, and distributions (White 2014b):

1. riverine, with shells of bivalves and snails, from small features to thick strata;

2. estuarine, with shells of brackish-water marsh clams (*Rangia* and *Polymesoda*) in thick strata, often mounded, usually including some oyster, on or near stream banks in the river swamps;

3. coastal, with mostly oyster but usually some marsh clam too, typically strata along mainland and barrier island bayshores;

4. large-gastropod, dominated by lightning whelk and up to 20% horse conch, around salty St. Joseph Bay, with other saltwater shellfish and fish but just a few oysters.

Estuarine shell middens dominated by marsh clams occur between about 3 and 10 river miles (5–15 km) inland. Interestingly, the *Rangia* marsh clam, called helmet clam on the Mexican Gulf Coast, where it is commercially harvested, inhabits subtidal zones, always submerged. The *Polymesoda* marsh clam (called black clam in Mexico), occurs in intertidal areas (Wakida-Kusunoki and MacKenzie 2004), so their relative proportions in middens may reflect habitat differences. Proportions of different shellfish species at different sites probably depended on fluctuating conditions from tides, storms, and seasons at the time of collection, though cultural preferences surely played a role. Oysters grow more rapidly in Apalachicola Bay than anywhere else in the country (Barnes 1987:68; Ingle and Dawson 1953:24). More and larger oyster shell middens seem to occur where freshwater streams empty into the bay, probably because fresher water enhances oysters' growth and resistance to predators. Interestingly, as described in the previous chapter, invertebrate faunal assemblages at archaeological sites on the east side of the lower delta may demonstrate the eastward movement of the river channel and mouth during post-Pleistocene sea-level rise. Earlier, deeper deposits at the Van Horn Creek and Thank-You-Ma'am Creek sites (8Fr744 and 755), on the west side of the delta, dated to Late Archaic times, about 4,000–3,000 years ago, are characterized more by oyster and other more saltwater species, while later prehistoric strata are predominantly of marsh clams. The single-component oyster shell midden at Sam's Cutoff (8Fr754), on the east side, is all Late Archaic. As the river moved eastward, forming new delta lobes, it brought more fresh water. My "lobes and fishes" hypothesis is supported by the rest of the species composition in faunal assemblages from these sites, suggesting hydrological change around 3,000 years ago, after the Late Archaic.

Other marine bivalves, such as cockle and sunray venus clam, were obtained in smaller numbers prehistorically and occur in St. Joseph Bay middens. Scallop, today a prized delicacy from that bay, is present only in small numbers. Quahogs or Venus clams (*Mercenaria*) are rare in the region, despite their abundance at south-Florida and Atlantic-coast shell middens and just to the west around Choctawhatchee Bay. Their hard, thick shell is useful for artifact manufacture, and so far all specimens recovered are implements or debitage pieces, not food debris. An unusual form is a triangular fragment cut from a quahog shell, for unknown purposes. Both the triangles and the shells with triangles cut out of them were present at the St. Vincent 5 site (8Fr364; White and Kimble 2016). Marine shell at inland sites is rare and always in artifact form, not food refuse.

Shell middens can be more than just domestic garbage piles. Mexican Pacific coast shell mounds were built up over long periods as stations for repeated processing of seafood to export inland (Voorhies 2000). Research on the massive *sambaquis* on the Brazilian coast examined biological species, human skeletons, artifacts, and site formation processes to interpret issues of labor, monument-building, and burial ritual, as well as subsistence, from cumulative trash deposits dominated by shell (Roksandic et al. 2014). Some south Florida and Atlantic coast shell sites are now demonstrated to have been left by combinations of ceremonial and mundane activities (e.g., Thompson et al. 2016). Huge riverine shell middens in the Midwest with burials and offerings have been attributed to repeated feasting and renewal rituals since the Early Archaic (Claassen 2010).

In the Apalachicola–lower Chattahoochee valley, however, the coastal, estuarine, and riverine shell middens left from the Late Archaic period onward appear to be refuse built up in mounded shapes or as strata. Seldom do they even contain perceptible features. Two have isolated individual human burials that seem to have been stuck into the trash. Feasting was not necessarily the mechanism for deposition of a large pile of food garbage. Daily buildup or consolidation of waste could also account for these sites. However, the shell midden matrix was sometimes used for construction. At Pierce Mound complex (8Fr14) and other coastal mounds such as Porter's Bar (8Fr1), Green Point (8Fr11), and Richardson's Hammock (8Gu10), midden shells were used for strata or lenses within sand burial mounds, over or under Woodland graves. We cannot know what function these midden materials had. With the high lime content, shells

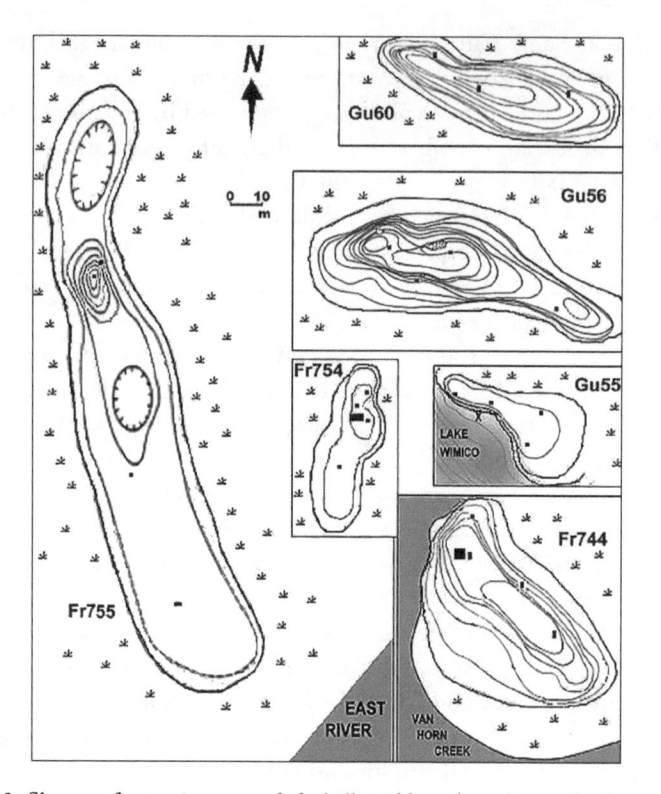

Figure 2.13. Shapes of estuarine mounded shell middens (mostly marsh clam with some oyster) in the lower Apalachicola delta: Thank-You-Ma'am Creek (8Fr755, "8" for "Florida"), mined at north end for road fill, leaving depressions and high elevation; Clark Creek (8Gu60); Depot Creek (8Gu56); Sam's Cutoff (8Fr754), all oyster, mostly submerged; Yellow Houseboat (8Gu55) with X marking human burial location; and Van Horn Creek (8Fr744). Small black squares and rectangles are test excavations. Contour interval is 20 cm except at Fr744, 50 cm. Components are mostly Late Archaic and Woodland. (Nancy Marie White)

might simply have helped mask the smell of death and decay, but they could have had ritual importance as symbols of the ancestors who left them.

Shell midden shapes in the research region are linear, running along banks or shores. None are ring-shaped like some farther east and south along the Florida Gulf and Atlantic coasts. I have visited the shell ring at Bird/Byrd Hammock site (8Wa30) near Apalachee Bay, 90 km northeast of the research region. Nothing like it is known in the Apalachicola delta, and this absence of rings may be another marker of a distinct identity for the region's prehistoric peoples. Some Apalachicola middens owe their current forms to modern removal of shells for construction fill, which can leave an oval or horseshoe shape and deep depressions. Most are curved, even banana-shaped, along small

Figure 2.14. Stilt house standing on shell midden, with woman holding child, Murik Lakes, Papua New Guinea, 1986. (Photo courtesy of Paul Gorecki)

streams or old stream channels (Figure 2.13). Much of the margin around the town of Apalachicola and the western and southern bayshore of Eastpoint (see Figure 1.4) was once continuous shell midden ridges. They may have been just part of garbage disposal or deliberate accumulation to elevate settlements. This could have been accomplished by throwing trash out the house door. Australian archaeologist Paul Gorecki (personal communication 2013) documented an example from a New Guinea estuarine habitation (Figure 2.14) where people have done just that, living in stilt houses and piling shell refuse underneath. However, little structural evidence has been found at Apalachicola middens. If posts for houses were pulled up or rotted in place, shell would fill the holes, leaving little trace of buildings.

Bone and Shell Artifacts

Prehistoric objects made of perishable organic materials are rare in the research region but include a few engraved bone pins, longbone points or picks, hooks (as noted previously), and other items. Many bone fragments have cut marks (see Figure 2.11) but may simply be leftover bits after butchering. No artifacts made of freshwater shell are known. Marine shell artifacts occur from Late Archaic times onward, but even on the coast they are not as numerous as in south peninsular Florida, where there is far less stone raw material

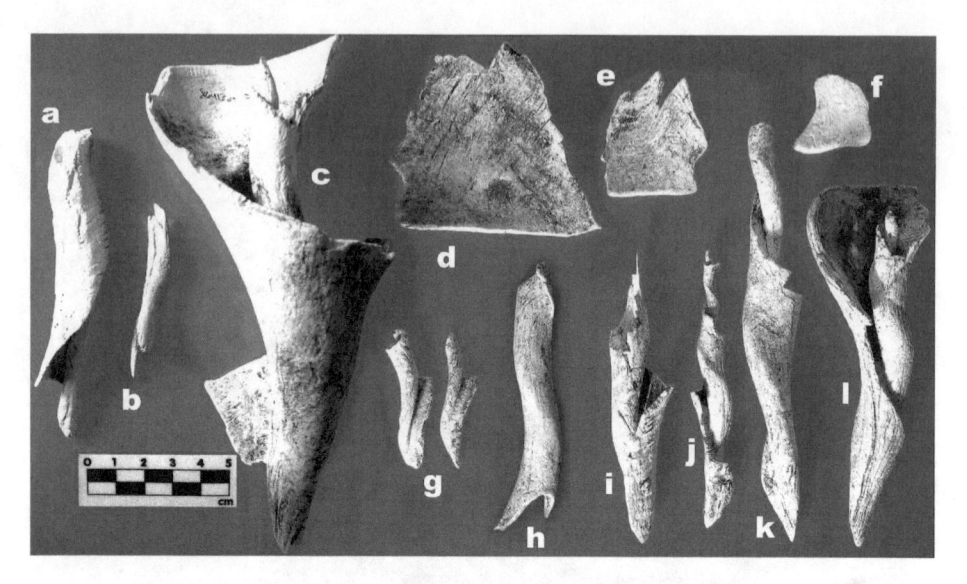

Figure 2.15. Large gastropod-shell artifacts from sites around St. Joseph Bay (all surface-collected): (a–c) right-angle pointed tools (a, from Baby Oak site, 8Gu126; b, from Lost Crew site, 8Gu130; c, from Yellow Flower site, 8Gu132); (d–l) from Gotier Hammock mound (8Gu2-01-1, 2; 03-2): d–f, whelk whorl scrapers, two with notches; g, 2 awls; h, columella tool with notched, bipointed end; i, conch columella awl; j, whelk columella awl; k, whelk columella tool with small chisel end (*at top*); l, right-angle pointed tool with scraper edge at top. (Nancy Marie White)

for tools. Tools of whelk and conch shell (Figure 2.15) are most common at middens on St. Joseph Bay, which is a habitat for these species. Lightning or left-handed whelk has had many name changes—*Busycon sinistrum*, formerly *contrarium*, and now *Busycon* or *Sinistrofulgur perversum* (poor thing went from contrary to sinister to perverse). Horse conch, now *Triplofusus giganteus*, formerly *Pleuroploca gigantea*, is the state shell of Florida. Artifacts made from all these shells (Eyles 2004) include utilitarian hammers, awls (pointed or bipointed columellae), scrapers, chisels, and spatulas, as well as ritual cups, beads, gorgets, and other decorative items. An unusual, undated tool at many sites is a shell with the apex/spire removed to access the sharpened end of the columella, sometimes with a right-angle cut or other shaping on the whorl, presumably to serve as a handle (Figure 2.15c, l). These might be perforators with "governors" preventing them from punching too deep; I call them right-angle pointed tools (White 2005). Some burial goods may be utilitarian. The elegant shell objects (Figure 2.16) from Green Point Mound (8Fr11; Early or Middle Woodland) may be just for cutting, scooping, or pounding, but the two knobbed ones may be pendants.

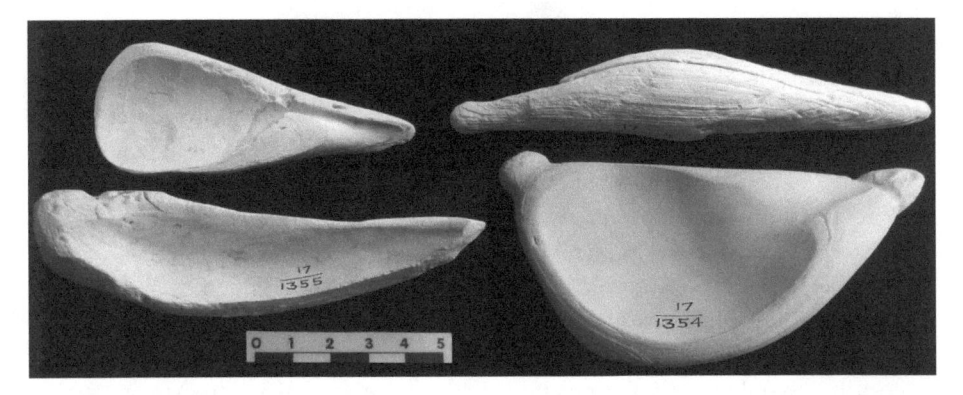

Figure 2.16. Shell artifacts from Green Point mound (8Fr11; NMAI#1354-57). (Nancy Marie White)

Large gastropod shells were prized by Native Americans and became more valuable as they were moved inland and used for ritual and decoration. Gulf shells appear in prehistoric ceremonial deposits, especially graves, well into the Midwest, either unmodified or engraved with designs or cut into fancy shapes such as gorgets. Symbolism of these large shells to Indigenous peoples was probably complex (Claassen 2008), but they were obviously also valued as thick, sturdy raw material. Lightning whelk was revered for its characteristic spiraling with the opening to the left (counterclockwise), unlike other whelks and conchs (Marquardt and Kozuch 2016). So far, sourcing studies for lightning whelk artifacts across the eastern United States only show that they came from both the Gulf of Mexico and the Atlantic. Should more precise determination become possible, many would surely be traced to St. Joseph Bay, since it is so easy to harvest them there and send them north along the river network. A huge lightning whelk that C. B. Moore recovered from the Chipola Cutoff mound (8Gu5) measured 39 cm long and was even kept by the Academy of Natural Sciences of Philadelphia when it got rid of all its archaeological collections (see Chapter 7). The world record for this species is 40 cm, from a specimen from Carrabelle, just east of the Apalachicola valley.

Tulip snail shells (*Fasciolaria*), smaller and thinner than the larger gastropods, are also in coastal middens, but, unlike elsewhere in Florida, they seem to be merely food debris. Olive shells occur at coastal sites as food refuse. Marginella shells, which are seen as beads at many southeastern sites, may be confused with or the same thing as olive shells, depending on the terminology and time of the researcher. So far nothing resembling a shell-working activity zone is known from the research region, though the St. Joseph Bay middens have so much fractured shell that they may be production areas.

Seasonality and Climate

As spoiled moderns, we mostly ignore seasons except for adjusting inside air and wardrobes, and most foods are available year-round. But past peoples had to get resources in cycles, know when species were accessible and how different natural conditions affected them. Calendars and other time measurements were probably based on seasons, menstrual cycles, lunar cycles, and the behavior of other celestial bodies, but they were also based on when things were available (like today's autumn "pumpkin-spice" months). Midden composition also represents elements of food choice, not necessarily everything that was ready at a particular time, and season of capture of a certain species is not necessarily the only time a site was inhabited (Quitmyer 2013:350). Much work remains to be done in the research region to recognize seasonality as well as past climates.

In investigations of climates, the concept of the Anthropocene is now significant. Earth scientists use this term for the time period in which we currently live, when human action has driven climate change, extinctions, and other phenomena. While debate continues on a beginning date for the Anthropocene (Smith and Zeder 2013), archaeologists contribute to the picture greatly with their abundant long-term data and knowledge of indigenous, often sustainable systems (Boivin and Crowther 2021). Though cold and dry during the Pleistocene, for the last several thousand years the Apalachicola–lower Chattahoochee region has had a warm, wet beneficial climate. Spring and fall are warm, summer is hot, with temperatures of 90 degrees F on the coast and warmer inland away from the moderating effects of the sea. During the summer of 1985, south Georgia heat-wave temperatures reached a near-record 108 degrees. The average annual rainfall at the north end of the region is slightly less than on the coast, with Houston and Seminole Counties at 135 cm, Jackson County at 147 cm, and Gulf County up to 175 cm.

The cold, rainy season begins in late fall, and rain and upriver snow swell the rivers. Annual floods inundate riverbanks by March, then water levels slowly fall, and late spring is dry. Typical yearly floods raise the river 15 to 20 m at the forks and 5 m in the middle valley, with record levels in 1929 and 1994 at 23 m and 8.5 m, respectively (US Army Corps of Engineers n.d.). With huge rises in water level, people on the banks would have scheduled activities and habitation accordingly. In summer and fall, hurricanes batter the region more than anywhere else in the eastern United States. Tropical storms Alberto and Beryl on July 4, 1994, caused the "500-year-record" flooding of northwest Florida, south Georgia, and Alabama, killed a few people, and exposed and damaged archaeological sites (White 1996). Recovery from the 2018 catastrophe of Hurricane Michael, which ravaged the entire region, will take many decades. Such natural events and their consequences were undoubtedly significant in past native lives, legends, and cosmology. Other cultures of the world worshipped mountains, volcanoes, amazing natural features. In the Apalachicola–lower Chattahoochee valley region, storms that smashed huge trees and human settlements, or extremely rare cold snaps that froze water or sent a few white flakes falling from the sky might have been so awe-inspiring that they took on magical significance, or at least would have been remembered frequently around campfires.

People

The entire Native American population of North America before 1492 has been estimated at almost four million (Denevan 1992), though calculation methods are controversial, and even this number is less than half the population of New York City today. However, the total prehistoric population in Florida has been estimated at nearly one million (Dobyns 1983), and the southeastern United States was the most densely populated area north of Mexico. With abundant resources and water networks, it is no surprise that the Apalachicola–lower Chattahoochee region contains so many archaeological sites. I agree with archaeologist Frank Schnell that this valley must have held the largest concentration of southeastern native groups outside the Mississippi Valley (quoted in Cook and Cook 2000:193–194).

Populations

Most reconstructions of the numbers and densities of Indigenous peoples in the Southeast are too low. They are based on data gathered often centuries after contact in the part of the country where the earliest European invasion and heaviest loss of Native American lives took place. One estimate suggests a population density in the Southeast at the time of contact between 2.2 and 3.1 people per km^2 (Ubelaker 1988:291). This must be inadequate for a region with intensive agriculture and a warm climate with a double growing season. The same source lists the estimate for California at 7.5 to 9.7 people per km^2. Aboriginal California had no agriculture or large rivers. Late prehistoric population density in the Apalachicola–lower Chattahoochee region must have been at least as high as California's.

Today the number of inhabitants in the region ranges from around 4 per km^2 in rural Liberty and Franklin Counties to double digits in counties with larger cities. The 1930 census of Decatur County showed about 23,600 people, 75% rural, with a higher rural population density than today (Hasty et al. 1939), reflecting a different American South at that time. Gadsden County's population in the 1950s (Thomas et al. 1961) was not much lower than in 2010. (Significantly, Gadsden is the only Black-majority county in Florida; its population includes many descendants of the enslaved people who labored on the vast plantations there.) It is important to note that the research region incorporates only portions of all these counties. Site numbers and sizes must be proxies for estimating prehistoric populations until wide excavations provide real demographic information on house patterns, community layout, cemeteries, and multiple occupation episodes. Nonetheless, it seems that by Early Woodland times, some 2,000 years ago, population densities rivaled those of recent history; prehistoric folks would not have considered the region remote.

Individual People

Elements of individual human biology and appearance in the prehistoric past can be gleaned from human representations on artifacts. The drawing at the opening of this chapter, showing the face of a Middle Woodland human effigy jar from Aspalaga Landing Mound (8Gd1; see Chapter 7), features a hairdo/headdress, pierced earlobes, puffy cheeks, and a not-too-happy expression on a long face with the nose broken off. However, it may not even depict a living person but an ancestor or spirit. Potentially better for understanding people and individuals are their bones, not usually well preserved in the typically acidic soils. Skeletal remains can provide specific details about a person's life as well as demographic data, but research on them may be restricted.

Scientific study of prehistoric human remains has been considered anathema by some Native Americans. Others welcome respectful investigations of ancient forebears in order to learn of daily life, health, diet, genetics, and additional information that can illuminate the poorly known past and be useful today. They may encourage investigation of skeletons and thank ancestors for providing the learning opportunities. However, such research can be forbidden or curtailed by law, especially the Native American Graves Protection and Repatriation Act (NAGPRA), which covers federal lands, as well as state laws against disturbance of unmarked graves on public or private lands. This important civil rights legislation has corrected wrongs committed by archaeologists and looters. Disrespectful excavators casually bagged bones sacred to modern Indigenous peoples who may be descendants or at least more closely related to them, culturally and/or genetically, than is the average archaeologist. After all, marked cemeteries are protected by law, though sometimes they may be excavated to be moved, and study of the skeletons may be allowed. The best approach today is of course "balance between spirit and matter," between science and Native American beliefs, while ensuring the validity of both (White Deer 1997:42). Bone chemistry and DNA studies can be significant methods of connecting modern American Indians to their roots and to each other. Further, they provide evidence that is better than or independent from what the artifacts suggest for hypothesized migrations or other population movements (Reich 2018).

Prehistoric human remains known archaeologically from the Apalachicola–lower Chattahoochee region were numerous but today are mostly nonexistent. Nearly all were dug up a century ago by C. B. Moore from Woodland burial mounds, with a few excavated by looters, collectors, or archaeologists. For most of the over 700 individuals estimated to have been unearthed, the locations of their bones are unknown. Moore must have discarded those he dug up, rudely left them out to rot as many early diggers did, though he occasionally sent some elsewhere for study, and two of his specimens from the region remain curated (see Chapter 7). He also frequently mentioned masses of fragments or decayed bones, for which the number and nature of individual persons represented was unknown. In addition, he constantly noted how burial mounds he investigated were often already severely looted, so it is impossible to calculate how many skeletons were removed and destroyed. The relatively small number of people in burial mounds, assumed to be elites, also raises the question of where the rest of the prehistoric dead were placed.

The few known details of graves and human remains from archaeological sites are given by time period in the following chapters, and general knowledge is summarized here. Prehistoric Native American life was, by today's standards, somewhat rough. Life expectancy probably averaged about 40 years. Accidents and injuries were common among people who did heavier labor and moved around all day far more than we moderns do. Bone chemistry shows that, as expected, coastal populations ate more marine resources and inland groups more terrestrial and freshwater fauna (Hutchinson 2004). Within the research region, human remains from St. Vincent Island, possibly from Woodland-period components of two shell midden sites, included teeth, jaws, and a cranial fragment representing three young adults with worn but healthy teeth, with one having two healed blows to the head, and two middle-aged men with worn teeth and dental problems, one with temporomandibular joint disorder (Bongiovanni 2017). The Early Woodland burial in the marsh-clamshell midden at Yellow Houseboat site (8Gu55) was a man about 158 cm tall (5'2") with a healed fracture on the left ulna (White 1994b). Bones of a young woman buried in the Late Archaic shell midden at Sam's Cutoff (8Fr754) indicated she had done relatively heavy labor involving upper body strength and also had stress on the legs and lower back (White 2003a). These cases are typical for Florida Native American populations, among whom the most common wounds were blows to the cranium and lower arms (Hutchinson 2004:155). They also had heavy tooth wear, from more sand and other dirt in the diet than we have today. People from Paleoindian through at least Early Woodland times, who hunted, fished, and gathered for a living, probably had more arthritis than agriculturalists (Bridges 1991) but fewer or no caries in the teeth since they did not yet have a diet of starchy maize.

A Middle Woodland man from Richardson's Hammock mound, some of whose looted remains were later recovered and studied, had poor dental health, gum disease, and porotic hyperostosis, an anemia resulting from poor nutrition, including lack of phosphate, calcium, iron, or other minerals. He showed fronto-occipital cranial modification, meaning the skull was flattened on the forehead and on the lower back. Other individuals from this site also had such cranial modification (Tullos 2018). This common practice was probably done by binding infants with soft, malleable skulls to cradleboards, producing a desirable appearance, perhaps signifying elite status. Besides modifying head shapes, cultural alteration of human bone seen for the prehistoric eastern United States includes filing teeth, trophy-taking, and fashioning artifacts from body parts, done for reasons of ritual, beauty, reverence for/connection with ancestors, or other purposes. In the Apalachicola–lower Chattahoochee region, not much of this is known beyond possible trophy skulls in Middle Woodland and later contexts. If not trophies, these could be the body elements left for secondary burial after processing, exposure, and decay, not intentionally severed heads. Or they could be all that was left of revered family members. Though most human remains in the region were tragically disturbed, destroyed, and lost, archaeology and other sciences can tell the stories of the people they represented and help something of their lives become known and respected.

3

Paleoindian Period, ca. 15,000 to 10,000 BP (13,000 to 8000 BC), the First People

The first humans probably arrived in the Apalachicola–lower Chattahoochee valley by 15,000 years ago. The Pleistocene climate was colder and drier, sea levels were much lower, the coastline was far out under today's Gulf of Mexico, and the river system was bigger. No clear evidence exists for "preprojectile point" material culture. But plentiful Paleoindian lanceolate points show widespread habitation near springs and chert sources. Archaeologists in northwest Florida are contributing fascinating information to the expanding Paleoindian picture, though in the research region no controlled excavation has been done. But compiled data, especially from helpful collectors, show interesting patterns. Sites cluster along the Chipola River, which may then have been the main river channel. Sites along the big river became covered in fluvial deposits as its channel shifted eastward. Points washing out of coastal shores also suggest that most of the Paleoindian record is deeply buried or submerged. Reconstruction of native lifeways is difficult. Pleistocene fossils are abundant, but big-game hunting was probably not the major subsistence strategy. Small groups may have moved around harvesting diverse animals and plants, probably managing landscapes, and possibly raising dogs and bottle gourds.

Coming to the Americas

Understanding the very first peoples in the Apalachicola–lower Chattahoochee valley research region, given the limited archaeological record, requires ethnographic and biological knowledge. Interpretations presented here of how hunter/gatherer/fisher groups have lived are useful for succeeding chapters as well. Needed first is some background on the earliest Americans. Emerging on the African continent, human ancestors spread over a million years ago throughout Asia and Europe, and people made it to Australia at least 50,000 years ago, then into North and South America by at least 16,000–20,000 years BP or possibly earlier. Evidence for the peopling of the Americas—archaeology, bones, blood, and DNA of persons, animals, plants, even microbes—points to migrations from northeast Asia, both by water along the coast and overland/inland along waterways. Beringia, a land bridge between Siberia and Alaska now under the Bering Strait, was exposed by lower sea levels during the Pleistocene, when ocean waters were taken up into continental glaciers. The great genetic diversity of both prehistoric and modern Native Americans makes it hard to argue for a single population migration. The best current hypothesis is that ancestral groups split into at least two branches, one moving into North America and one into South America (Waters 2019).

Anthropological linguists, using computer simulations of rates at which languages branch off from one another, suggest that it took up to 40,000 years to evolve the 130 to 150 Native American language families, each of which contains hundreds of individual languages. Investigating hypothesized ancient coastal travel is difficult because coasts are drowned by rising seas of the last 10,000 years, submerging shoreline sites. But the coastal route makes more sense and is now the preferred model (Lepper 2019). Water travel is easier: less effort to sit and paddle; food is easily caught; and it is slightly warmer, as the ocean moderates extreme temperatures. Though coastlines were once thought to be marginal places for humans, the archaeology shows that the earliest colonists must have occupied maritime habitats early and often (Braje et al. 2017).

Biological commonalities meant that the earliest Indigenous Americans probably all had type-O blood and many other distinctive genetic characteristics. The lack of Native American resistance to European and African illnesses during the sixteenth-century Spanish invasions suggests that the Arctic cold may have killed off disease organisms among the first humans traveling into the Americas. Moving in small groups perhaps prevented infectious illnesses that require large populations to spread. East coast American Indians met by European intruders many millennia later were taller and healthier than the Europeans. Their supposed "red" skin is a racist myth that began with British accounts of groups who colored their skin with red pigment. Traditionally, archaeologists have called the first peoples in the Americas "Paleoindians." We cannot know the names that American Indian cultures called themselves until there are written records in historic centuries, by which time their societies, and probably names, had radically changed over countless generations. Also, the foreigners who first described them were ethnocentric and made mistakes with ethnic or tribal terms. We might imagine, however, that many populations took names of nearby geographic features, as do cultures worldwide (e.g., "people who live on the tiny crooked stream," or "upriver" versus "downriver" people).

The earliest North American societies were once thought to be specifically associated with a distinctive artifact: the Clovis point, a thin, pressure-flaked, lance-shaped, chipped-stone projectile point with a large flute (channel flake) up the middle. The Clovis horizon is now dated to a short time span, from about cal 13,125 to 12,925 (or 13,050 to 12,750) years ago or about 11,000–10,800 BC, perhaps lasting as little as two centuries (Neely 2020; Waters and Stafford 2007). Clovis is found in the western United States with bones of mammoths and other Pleistocene megafauna, and later fluted and unfluted point types in the West are associated with bison kill sites; all these have strongly influenced Paleoindian interpretations. However, far more fluted and other lanceolate points are known in the East, where Clovis technology may have originated. Furthermore, we now know that Clovis does not represent the very first Americans. It is only one phenomenon within the material record from both North and South America, where stemmed and other kinds of stone spear points were made by cultures contemporaneous with or earlier than Clovis (Becerra-Valdivia and Higham 2020; Wade 2017). Indeed, new research has uncovered potential human evidence from Coxcatlan Cave in south central Mexico dated to over 30,000 years ago (Somerville et al. 2021), human footprints in New Mexico between 23,000 and 21,000 years old (Wade 2021), and remains of a domestic dog that can only have been brought by humans dating to 13,100 BP from a coastal cave in British Columbia (Fedje et al. 2021). Under the Clovis zone at the Gault site in central Texas, small points and other stone artifacts were recovered from a cultural stratum dating 16,000 to 20,000 BP (Williams et al. 2018).

Earlier work on Paleoindian site distributions in the East (e.g., Anderson 1996) suggested that most of the Gulf and Atlantic coastal plains were unoccupied, as few sites were recorded there. But coasts are not undesirable habitats; they just have a visibility problem. Rivers coursing across flat coastal plains dump alluvium that thoroughly buries earlier settlements, both on land and offshore, especially where deltas form. It is no surprise that few sites are recorded in the lowest portions of big valleys in the South, since evidence would be too deep and/or underwater. Site distribution maps show the most ancient settlements to be where the archaeological record is the most visible and where there has been the most research. Now statewide surveys of Paleoindian sites and isolated points, as well as the compiled information on Paleoindian site distributions in the Paleoindian Database of the Americas (PIDBA online; Anderson et al. 2010) show more sites near modern coastlines, and some underwater, nearer to ancient Pleistocene shores. The first peoples in the Apalachicola–lower Chattahoochee region inhabited the interior, what is now the coast, and surely what was the coast in their time too.

Coming to the Deep South and Gulf Coast

Northwest Florida has some of the earliest pre-Clovis Paleoindian evidence as well as classic Clovis points and other more regional point types such as Suwannee and Simpson. A hypothesis of interest for the research region suggests that the earliest peoples traveled down from North to South America and then migrated north again when climates warmed. Because interior eastern North American Indian languages are reduced sets of the languages found in Central and South America, and therefore possibly descended from them, some linguists think they could indicate that Clovis people were the first to reenter North America from the south, an idea possibly supported by resemblances of some South American and Florida point types, as will be dscussed. Whenever people first reached the Apalachicola–lower Chattahoochee valley, they were undoubtedly already superbly adapted to diverse ecosystems.

However, moving into the Gulf Coastal Plain did not mean giving up fur coats right away—it was the Ice Age. Though no ice covered the South, the climate was colder and drier, and the Florida and coastal Alabama landmass was over twice the size it is today. Glacial conditions meant that ice sheets (a mile thick, the textbooks love to say) covered much of the northern hemisphere as far south as central Ohio. Figure 3.1 shows coastlines during the last glacial maximum, 18,000 BP, when sea level was 100 m lower than at present, and also where the shoreline was during the times of the Clovis horizon and near the end of the Pleistocene. By 14,700 BP temperatures were warming, with cold reversal periods over the next 2,000 years. The last cold reversal was the Younger Dryas, about cal 12,850 to 11,650 BP, after which came the rapid warming of the Holocene or Recent era. The melting ice released cold fresh water into the oceans at differing rates over the millennia; sea level rose and fell several times before reaching the current level by around 5,000 years ago (Donoghue 1993), though smaller fluctuations continued. Variable flow of water down major river valleys altered conditions, from wet to dry, cold to warm, when the first people were settling into the South (Dunbar 2016).

Florida has abundant Late Pleistocene fossils and Paleoindian artifacts, usually from springs. Decades of research, including recording of collectors' materials and underwater investigations (e.g., Dunbar 1991) have brought a bounty of archaeological knowledge from the Aucilla, Silver, Santa Fe, and other rivers. Anaerobic underwater conditions even preserve organic remains. Flooded sinkholes are famous for Paleoindian tools, including some of wood, bone, and antler, and human and extinct-animal bones. Some of these have been dated very early, for instance, at Little Salt Spring, between cal 14,700 and 13,400 BP (Clausen et al. 1979). People were living on spring edges when

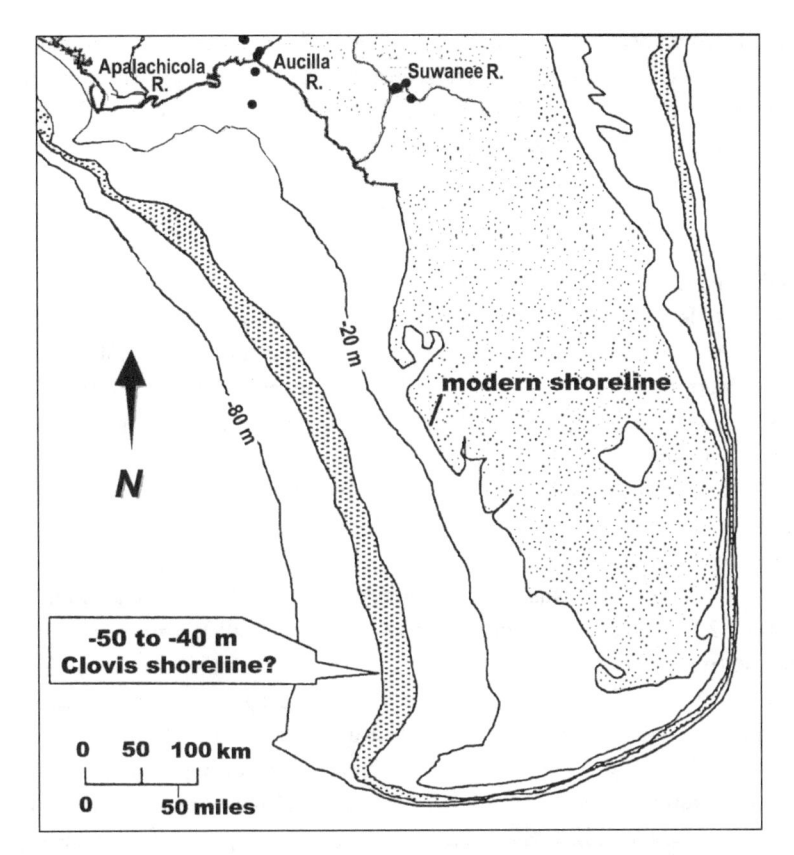

Figure 3.1. Florida landmass during the Pleistocene, showing shorelines at different times, with widest extent at about 18,000 years ago, the Clovis period at about 11,000 BP, and the 20-m-depth shoreline at about 8000 BP (Early Archaic period). The modern Apalachicola delta was far inland. Dots show Paleoindian sites on the Suwanee and Aucilla Rivers, including those now out in the Gulf on the ancient river channel. (Adapted from Dunbar et al. 1992:Figure 2; Nancy Marie White.)

the water was 10 m or more below present levels (Dunbar 2006a). Then, rising seas inundated and therefore preserved the evidence.

Exciting research comes from 115 km east of the research region in the Aucilla River Prehistory Project, where a coalition of scientists, avocationals, and students investigated underwater sites (Webb 2006). The Page-Ladson site, a 9-m-deep sinkhole, produced stone points; bone and ivory tools; mastodon, bison, camelid, and dog remains; and plant fragments including mastodon digesta (dung and stomach contents). A tusk had circular cutmarks where it had been detached from the animal's head. Humans coexisted with and hunted/scavenged the big game animals there for about 2,000 years before these creatures became extinct by 12,600 BP (Dunbar 2006b; Halligan et al. 2016). Page-Ladson is the oldest securely radiocarbon-dated site in North America with unquestionable artifacts of the first Americans. It had two pre-Clovis components with lithic debitage and human-altered animal bone, as well as a Clovis component, a Middle Paleoindian component perhaps associated with Suwannee points, and a Late Paleoindian component, all with good stratigraphic integrity. Over 70 radiocarbon dates from the site range from cal 15,405 to 11,342 BP. Though none of the dated proveniences had a diagnostic artifact in clear association, six stone objects, including a flake knife and a biface, were solidly within the pre-Clovis component (Dunbar 2006b:413–415). The site's strata indicated differing ancient water table levels, suggesting riverine, slower stream, and pond environments at various times during its use.

Also on the Aucilla, the Sloth Hole site, dated between cal 14,650 and 14,050 BP, has mastodon bones (one with butchering marks), flaked mastodon-bone tools, carved ivory shafts, a possible ivory workshop area, Clovis points, and waisted Clovis points (Dunbar 2006b; Hemmings et al. 2004). An ivory point was directly dated to within the Clovis period, at cal 13,000–12,860 BP. Such underwater archaeology is all the more notable for being extremely difficult logistically and more expensive than digging on land. The Aucilla River area has one of the densest known concentrations of Paleoindian sites in North America. On a tributary, the Wacissa River, the Alexon Bison site yielded bones of an extinct bison dating to cal 12,800 BP with a broken chert artifact stuck in its skull (Dunbar et al. 2022; Dunbar 2012:60; Webb et al. 1984). Other rivers, including the Suwannee, have yielded similar Paleoindian bone and stone artifacts, including carved ivory spear foreshafts. Aucilla River sites contained both fluted Clovis and unfluted lanceolate points, the latter more numerous and possibly earlier. A perennial problem is getting stratification clear enough to establish sequences of diagnostic artifacts.

The now-extinct forms of large animals were attracted to the string of waterholes, probable sinkholes or dolines (Halligan 2012:38) that later connected to become rivers. These beasts stayed longer than they planned, getting bogged down in the mud or at least pausing long enough for people to pick them off. Bison are attracted to bogs and swamps, which provide lush grasses for grazing and relief from insects (Frison 2004:117). Fossils found in these rivers can be a million years old, but others are unmistakably associated with humans, since they have signs of human manipulation or occur with artifacts or are artifacts, such as ivory foreshafts. Tallahassee biologist Bruce Means once showed me an ancient bison longbone from the Aucilla with a bone point stuck down its hollow center, maybe from somebody picking out the marrow.

Far offshore in the Gulf of Mexico are drowned quarry sites and springs that were also loci for early human occupation. Paleochannels of the Aucilla and other rivers have been identified running far out under the Gulf (see Figure 3.1). Along the ancient Aucilla, sites 6 to 9 km offshore and 4 to 6 m underwater have yielded Paleoindian (and Archaic) points and habitation evidence (Faught 2004). These sites are at drowned freshwater springs and would not have been coastal settlements, but they shed light on the earliest human activity and sea level fluctuations.

Paleoindian in the Research Region

The Paleoindian record in the Apalachicola–lower Chattahoochee region is probably extremely similar to that of the Aucilla River sites, but it has not had the professional investigation required to demonstrate this. Furthermore, while Apalachee Bay, into which the Aucilla empties, is well known for underwater archaeology, similar study is unfeasible in Apalachicola Bay, where the huge delta means that the river has dumped tens of meters of alluvial sands on top of any ancient cultural deposits. However, professional research on Paleoindian terrestrial sites and drowned sites in river bottoms and sinkholes in the region would have great potential. Meanwhile, lacking controlled information, we can still evaluate the existing database compiled with knowledge shared by reliable collectors, whose locational and other data have allowed finds to be registered in state site files.

Verified Paleoindian sites and isolated artifact finds (IFs) within the research region number over 100 (Figure 3.2). All are classified based on the presence of one or more diagnostic points or the Waller knife. Though the Florida BAR ran an isolated finds program for several years, it was discontinued. However, the information reported here has been accumulated over decades and evaluated for reliability. Student theses (Kelley 2013; Kreiser 2018; Tyler 2008) describe private Florida collections, and I assembled data in new or updated reports (White 2018). For underwater finds, a site was defined by materials from within a 100-m area. Much Alabama information came from Moon's (1999) work, while the Georgia data are far too few, though I know the sites are there. Over half of these Paleoindian finds are on the Chipola River, and 39 of these are underwater. Combining those on the tributary creeks that form the Chipola gives 67% of all known Paleoindian evidence in the region from the Chipola basin. Several points have come from dredging underwater on the lower Chattahoochee, as shown by a 17-river-mile line of dots on Figure 3.2. A huge number of sites that are just recorded as scatters of lithic debitage may also of course be Paleoindian in age, but diagnostic points were picked up long ago. (However, recording such lithic scatters as "possible Paleoindian" sites when only undiagnostic tools and flakes were found is a hindrance to research; such sites could be from any other prehistoric time period.)

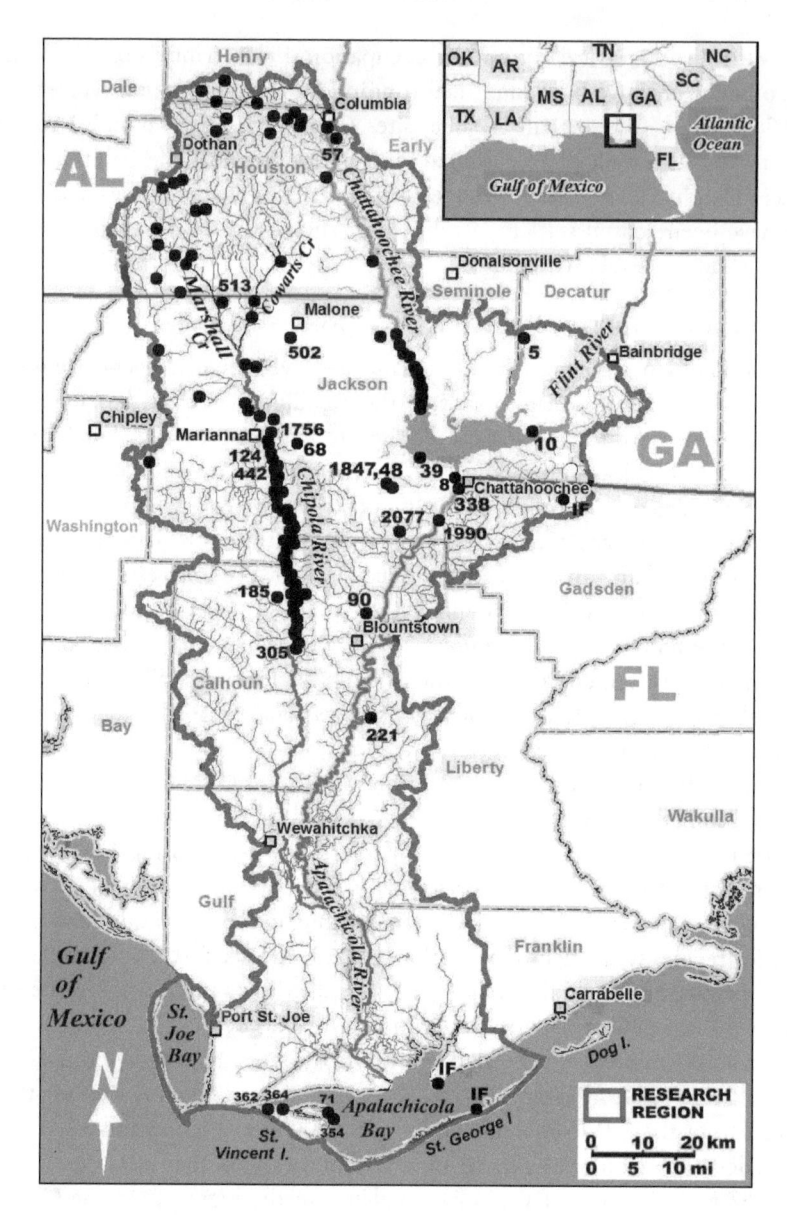

Figure 3.2. Paleoindian sites and isolated finds (IF). Numbered sites are discussed in the text. (Nancy Marie White)

The Paleoindian record is discussed here by subdrainage (see Figure 1.2). The modern main river is underfit for its valley. Its ancient channel was larger, flowed farther to the west, and extended well out into what is today's Gulf, as shown by paleochannels farther west of the current river (Donoghue 1993).

The modern tributary Jackson River and Lake Wimico (see Figure 1.4) were probably the main channel at some point during the Pleistocene, bending sharply eastward to meet with a paleochannel that may have flowed seaward toward today's west side of Little St. George Island. The landscape was very different when the places on the map were occupied. Macrobotanical and pollen deposits in cores from the bottom of Camel Lake, on the middle Apalachicola, show that between 15,000 and 12,000 BP, as people presumably were first arriving, the forest had changed from being dominated by pine to include more hickory, beech, and spruce. These indicate a cold, foggy, wet climate like that of modern southern Quebec (Watts et al. 1992). The map shows obvious gaps in survey coverage and site visibility but presents a new settlement model, with Paleoindian materials now known also from the main Apalachicola valley and the modern coast.

Paleoindian on the Lower Chattahoochee and Flint
Farther to the north, beyond the research region, recorded Paleoindian evidence increases as one moves upriver on the lower and middle Chattahoochee (DeJarnette 1975). But this pattern is less likely the result of ancient human choices than it is of preservation, depositional processes, and the amount of archaeology done. For example, the Alabama coastal plain has relatively few Paleoindian sites reported, while the Tennessee Valley has had much more investigation over the decades (Meredith 2009). The same is true for southwest Georgia, which has many Paleoindian sites (Anderson et al. 1990) but few known within the research region. On the lower Chattahoochee 50 river miles north of the region addressed in this book, the Paleoindian presence is sparse (Jenkins 1978; Schnell 1975). Bullen (1975b) illustrated three thick, slightly fluted Suwannee points from a collection in Blakely, Georgia, some 60 river miles up from the Chattahoochee-Flint forks.

Within the research region, at the north end, Huscher (1959a:18) excavated from site 9Er57 a fluted point base from a zone 60 cm deep but mixed with Early Woodland pottery. Moon (1999) recorded collectors' Alabama finds on Omussee, Marshall, and Cowart's Creeks, noting how little attention was paid to this area. Bullen (1950:105) observed that early sites did not occur on the Lower Chattahoochee because they "were located on old banks now abandoned by the river and buried by subsequent floods." In his later work at the Chattahoochee River1 site (8Ja8 [J-5]), on the west bank at the forks, he dug through many components down to a stratum with ambiguous lithic materials that could have been Paleo or Archaic, over 4 m deep (Bullen 1958:335–336). Along the upper reaches of Spring Creek, tributary to the Flint and probably former river channel, Kelly (1950a, b) documented a probable Suwannee point from the Lane Springs site (9Dr5). Farther down this creek avocational archaeologist Ron Hunt recovered over 15,000 points, a couple of which were Paleoindian, though locations were not officially noted. The key factor for these sites is depth. As the river flows toward the sea, the decreasing steepness of banks and increasing sedimentation mean more deeply buried remains; many sites surely lie below the water table. During boat survey here (Belovich et al. 1982) we occasionally saw, when waters had been artificially lowered by closing dam floodgates, artifacts embedded in the high vertical bank face, sometimes large, chunky cherts as deep as 7 or 8 meters below the ground surface. With the next rising water level, these materials were submerged or washed out into the river bottom. They might well have been deeply buried Paleoindian tools.

Above the forks, the Harrell site (8Ja39), on a hillside overlooking the Chattahoochee, had materials from all prehistoric time periods (White 1981). Now it is in the state park on an island in the reservoir. Materials collected there when the reservoir level dropped include a small, sharpened-down Suwannee point (Figure 3.3a) that must have eroded out of this former terrace; it has a light reddish-brown patina from decades of inundation. Salvage excavations at the multicomponent Montgomery Fields site (9Dr10) on the lower Flint, before reservoir flooding, produced at least four probable Paleo points (White 2019). Other evidence on the lower Chattahoochee remains poorly known. A Panama City avocational reported a Clovis point on a hilltop 2–3 km west of the river at about Mile 15, though neither the artifact nor the site was observed (White 1981:606). Dredged river bottom gravels between Miles 8 and 25 produced many Paleo points and Waller knives (Tyler 2008).

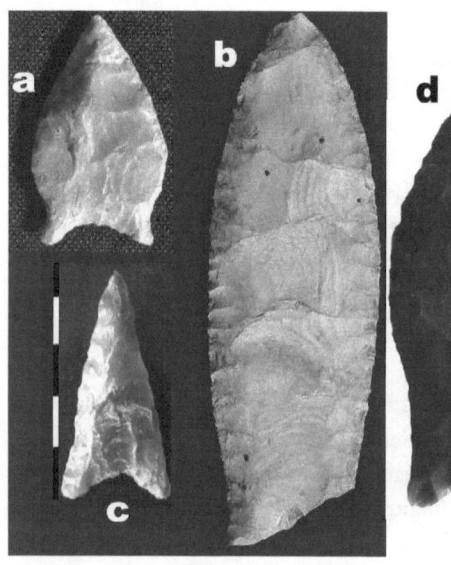

Figure 3.3. Paleoindian points: (a) Suwannee from the lower Chattahoochee, Harrell/3 Rivers State Park site (8Ja39; park collection); (b) Clovis or Simpson from the upper Apalachicola, Tyler CF1 site (8Ja2077; private [CF] collection); (c) Clovis? from the middle Apalachicola, Parish Lake Road site (8Ca90; private [JW] collection); (d) Suwannee isolated find from Gulf shore of St. George Island (private [KJ] collection). (Nancy Marie White)

Since the damming of the rivers at the forks and drowning of many small creek valleys, both the original banks and the more distant uplands have washed away, exposing the deep sides of hills where these points may have originated. Collectors often see Paleo finds at the bottom of washes 1 to 2 m deep. A reported Clovis point came from a sandbar at the dam and was said to be near exposed mastodon remains. Another collector told me he found in a 20-acre field two Paleo points that had washed out of a high blufftop within the ravine formations on the south side of the Flint River, near the Florida-Georgia line. Georgia avocational Jack Wingate showed me an unfluted Clovis point that came from his duck pond on the southeastern side of Lake Seminole. Knowledge of most of these reported but unverified finds is insufficient to warrant inclusion in the database or map. But distribution of confirmed Paleoindian materials in the northernmost section of the research region does reflect the shifting of the river system eastward over time. People would want to settle on the river, wherever it was. Also attractive would have been the abundant springs and chert outcrops along the lower Chattahoochee (see Plate I).

Absence of Paleoindian in the Main Apalachicola Valley?

Few Paleoindian materials have come from the main Apalachicola valley by comparison with its main tributary valley, the Chipola. Over decades of viewing hundreds of thousands of points in collections, I had seen no Paleo types from there and until recently assumed a settlement model suggesting that the earliest people preferred the Chipola's environments. However, the main Apalachicola also has abundant chert sources and springs, even if they are now drowned or buried. Collectors thought the Apalachicola had produced no Paleoindian because the water is too muddy, with swift currents and many boaters, unsuitable for diving (Calvin Jones, personal communication 1994), or the water too dirty so see much (Hub Chason, personal communication 1986). Sites would be hard to find on land if the Pleistocene Apalachicola flowed in the channel now occupied by the Chipola before shifting eastward and burying landscapes in up to 14 m of alluvium along the way in the middle valley (Vernon 1942). The rural nature of the region has also meant less deep soil disturbance. But small clues are now coming to light and merit individual description.

Two unfluted Clovis points were reported from the Mount Pleasant area (unnumbered IF in north-central Gadsden County on Figure 3.2), far up on the drainage of a small tributary of Mosquito Creek, which joins the Apalachicola just below the forks. Gravel "bars" along the east bank near the town of Chattahoochee are famous for artifacts and Pleistocene fossils. These bars appear to be old dredging spoils piles or limestone bedrock areas more exposed during low water, not real sites. Panama City avocational Tom Watson picked up materials there that he logged into the state site file as 8Gd338, including two points labeled O'Leno and Greenbriar, showing fluted bases in the photos. Downriver, submerged on the bottom, was a Chipola point at the Tyler TM2 site (8Gd1990). Near the Jackson-Calhoun County line, a large Clovis (or Simpson; Figure 3.3b) was found by a forester clearing timber near two springs and a cave, 1,400 m west of the river on an old meander (Tyler CF1 site, 8Ja2077). This point is fluted on both sides, slightly waisted, and weathered to opaque white, with tiny burgundy-colored pinpoint-sized fossils. Its light color shows it was buried on land, not weathered underwater. It was at the base of a 20-m-high bluff, and probably eroded out of, or was unearthed from, deep deposits.

Also in the upper Apalachicola, 8 km west of the river on backed-up old channels named Ocheesee Pond, the Keene sites (8Ja1847, 1848) produced at least two unfluted Clovis points, two Daltons, two Mariannas, and a Waller knife. When we recorded them, these points were in family collections that totaled 1,461 artifacts, 862 of which were points. Our test excavations on this high land 10 m above the surrounding waters determined that all cultural components were compressed and mixed from a long history of plowing (Kelley 2013). In the middle valley, avocational Jeff Whitfield found a possibly sharpened-down Clovis point (Figure 3.3c) at the Parrish Lake Road site (8Ca90) after heavy machinery had dug a deep borrow pit. My survey crew recorded the Stuck Truck site (8Li221), with a point that could be of either the Dalton or Tallahassee type, from a dirt road surface (Figure 3.4d). The site

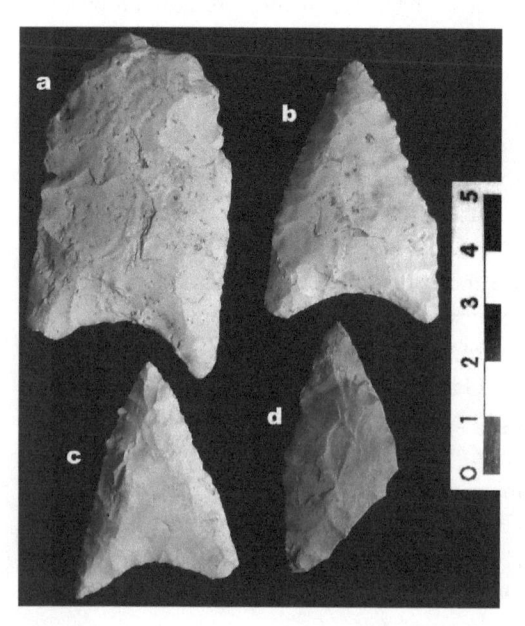

Figure 3.4. Paleoindian points (USF collections) from terrestrial sites: (a) unfluted (?) Clovis from the Baggett site (8Ja442) on the middle Chipola; (b) Dalton from the Bevis site (8Ja502), on an upper Chipola tributary; (c) Clovis from the For Sale site (8Ja513), on a tributary of Marshall Creek above the Chipola; (d) resharpened Dalton (?) from the Stuck Truck site (8Li22) on the middle Apalachicola. (Nancy Marie White)

is on a small stream near its mouth into a larger stream, Outside Lake, an old river meander. This location is similarly at the base of a 12 m hill, so the find may also result from erosion out of deep deposits.

Paleoindian Site Concentration in the Chipola Valley
Marshall and Cowart's Creeks drain a large area veined with myriad smaller tributaries in southeast Alabama. They flow southward 10 km (6 water miles) to meet and form the Chipola River below the Florida line. The Chipola runs parallel to the bigger river for most of its 92.5 waterway miles until it turns eastward toward its mouth at Apalachicola Mile 28, below Wewahitchka. Its upper and middle reaches have more first- to third-magnitude springs than any other Florida river except the Suwannee, and countless smaller springs. The basins of their creeks and the upper and middle Chipola valley sides and stream bottoms have the highest known concentration of Paleoindian materials in the research region (see Figure 3.4) (Figure 3.5). One first-magnitude spring, Jackson Blue Springs, issues 130 million gallons of water per day from its main vent (Rosenau et al. 1977), that flows as Merrit's Mill Creek/Spring Creek (now dammed) over six miles to empty into the upper Chipola near Marianna. At sites around this spring (8Ja68 and others) great numbers of Paleoindian points have been recovered (e.g., Archaeological Consultants Inc. 2006). The many caves along the upper and middle Chipola, including one 2 km long under Jackson Blue Springs, were probably shelters during the Pleistocene when water levels were far lower.

Either the Chipola was a line of sinks/springs that held water year-round and only later became connected as a river, or it was a channel holding the main river, later diminished when stream capture upriver triggered by sea-level rise moved the big river eastward; both scenarios are possible. A diver estimated there are 90 small sinkholes in the Chipola and 5 to 10 large ones, over 3 m deep with straight rock walls (Jeff Whitfield, personal communication 2018). The bare limestone river bottom has little accumulated sediment except near tributaries (Jessi Halligan, personal communication 2020). The surrounding karst topography features abundant lithic resources and quarry sites, also predictive of Paleoindian habitation (Dunbar 2016).

The Chipola's white limestone bed, startlingly clear-blue water, and scenic beauty (see Plate III) make it a favored recreation spot for the three-state area. Thus the numbers of finds are tied to the numbers of people who dive and hunt relics. But this basin may have had the greatest human population density in the region during the late Pleistocene if it was the lowest portion of the river system that reached far into the continental interior. From its waters come abundant fossils of bison, mammoth, mastodon, giant sloth, giant armadillo, elk, camel, and horse, though most may predate the arrival of people.

Figure 3.5. Paleoindian points (Simpson, Suwannee, Clovis, and unfluted Clovis) from the Hub Chason collection, all from around mile 82 on the Chipola River bottom except three large "fish-tailed" Simpsons at top from the terrestrial Four Hole Pond site (8Ca185; left two are glued and patched). Darker patina and shine are from being underwater. Some are varnished; some are reconstructed (indicated by white squares). (Nancy Marie White)

Skulls of such beasts were reportedly found in the 1960s and earlier, and a mastodon skeleton came from a tributary stream (Dunbar 2016:54). A giant sloth skeleton from Spring Creek just below the highway 90 bridge, with possible butchering marks, was reported to a park ranger. Chason (1987:24) believed that the profusion of fossil horse teeth in this river should make it the ancient "Valley of the Horse."

My 1986 survey along the Chipola located only three sites (out of 184) with Paleoindian points (White and Trauner 1987). But we were not divers, and most materials are from underwater. H. L. ("Hub") Chason, a retired teacher from the town of Altha, was a well-known collector. When I met him in the 1980s, he had been diving for decades and sharing his knowledge, including many Paleo artifacts (see Figure 3.5; one is also in the drawing at the opening of this chapter). He told me their stories in person and in letters, emphasizing the beauty of the land, and (at age 72) published a book about them (Chason 1987). He pictured 430 of his points, of which at least 40 to 50 are Paleoindian: 4 Beaver Lake, 3 Gilchrist, 3 Wheeler, 1 Dalton/Hardaway, 3 Dalton, 1 Redstone, 3 Greenbriar, 1 Marianna, 1 Quad, 9 Suwannee, 1 Clovis, 6 Clovis/Suwannee, 12 Clovis/Suwannee/Beaver Lake. He also included 68 points from other collectors, of which perhaps 10 are Paleoindian. His type names vary widely since he admitted in the book foreword his personal goal of identifying 200 types and used published point guides from all over North America; totals noted here include my relabeling of some of his with more local type names. He said most of his points came from within a few miles of Johnny Boy Landing, at about Chipola Mile 82. Only the exceptional specimens from the terrestrial Four-Hole Pond site (8Ca185) had a tighter provenience.

However ambiguous these data are, just the concentration of some 50 Paleo points from one stretch of river bottom extending only a few miles is impressive. Most other collectors have also gotten their Paleo points from the Chipola basin in southeast Alabama and Florida. Artifact hunters here are sophisticated, aware of the great antiquity of these specimens; commercial establishments in Marianna have displayed points. Chason kept in a bank vault his rarest artifacts, three huge waisted "fishtail" Simpsons (Figure 3.5 top) from the Four-Hole Pond site. Serious avocationals organized the Chipola Archaeology Society to document finds ethically and record them with the Master Site File during Florida's Isolated Finds program.

Within the upper and middle Chipola basin, diagnostic materials come mostly from underwater but also from fields and eroding banks. Avocational Jeff Whitfield found a Paleo point in a field on the shore of Cowart's Creek, a meter from the water and a couple meters south of the Alabama line. Farmers here push soil to the edges of fields and expose artifacts. He knows a collector who claimed to have gotten 100 points from this field in the 1970s. Higher elevations were also important, up on river terraces, such as the Malloy site (8Ja124), over 25 m above sea level, and the Baggett site (8Ja442), 21 to 28 m high. At the Baggett site, the landowner had several Suwannee points from a plowed field and donated a reworked Clovis specimen (Figure 3.4a). At the Bevis site (8Ja502), which also had later ceramic components, a

Dalton point (Figure 3.4b) came from a plowed field 40 m in elevation, near a sinkhole pond. The large collection from here included several Early and later Archaic points, 25 bifaces, 32 unifaces, two "turtle-back" scrapers, other chert tool fragments, abundant debitage, and ground stone tool fragments. The For Sale site (8Ja513) is one of the few with no later prehistoric components. It lies on a hilltop 50 m high, 600 m east of Cowart's Creek and 600 m south of a sinkhole pond/marsh area. Its point (Figure 3.4c) was on the highest ground in the burrow backdirt from a gopher tortoise, an animal that can dig 3 m deep. The surrounding dirt road and fallow field yielded lithic debitage and a unifacial tool.

This site distribution is informative: all those in the Chipola basin are from its upper two-thirds, a total distance of 70 miles (115 km) by water. One 16 mile (26 km) stretch between Chipola Miles 48 and 64 (76 to 92 miles inland), in south Jackson and north Calhoun Counties, contains the greatest cluster of Paleoindian occurrences: 27 recorded, most underwater. This is nearly two sites per mile (one per km)—not as dense as the 37 sites within 10 km (6 mi.) of the Aucilla River (Halligan 2012:313), but professional work on the Aucilla has gone on for many years. Chipola sites are distributed in clusters no more than 5 or 6 water miles apart, and even continue around the "Look-and-Tremble" rapids. But no evidence is known below the mouth of Davis Mill Creek at Chipola Mile 41.5. When added to the Apalachicola's 28 river miles up to the Chipola mouth, this means no Paleoindian finds up to about 70 waterway miles (113 km) inland. The terrain does not immediately change here, and large creeks and springs still occur below this point. Possibly there is some geological shift from here moving downstream, with lower valley sedimentation covering sites as the elevation lowers and the water widens into Dead Lakes, with its standing flooded forest and no exposed banks or agricultural fields.

Interpreting site density on the Chipola has problems of ambiguous data and more finds from around bridges, boat landings, and other popular access spots. However, as Tyler (2008:88–92) and local experts point out, this 16-mile segment of valley thickest with sites is narrower, with steeper banks. A possible "bottleneck" phenomenon might be explained as a place where more sinkholes were once present, important in the Pleistocene for trapping game and now for trapping artifacts. Also along this segment are more springs and 20 creek mouths. Perhaps it was the best-watered stretch along an already attractive waterway and was reused for generations. Or it might have been a place where the Chipola disappeared underground into a solution hole before reappearing (as it still does upstream), making it a useful natural crossing for both people and animals, even a sacred spot. The fact that so many Paleo points have been found so close might also mean that they were stored in caches at base camps, or placed in ceremonial deposits, or were at workshops where they were made in bulk. The favored locales on the Chipola were inhabited by later Native American groups, especially during the succeeding Archaic period. People apparently stayed around even through massive climate change, appreciating the water, chert, and other resources. The Chipola has great scientific potential; for example, recently a preserved deer track (of unknown age) was observed in its bed at about Mile 72 (Jeff Whitfield, personal communication 2018).

Paleoindian on the Coast

For a long time, only two Paleoindian artifacts were known from the present coast. A Dalton point came from the surface of the Paradise Point site (8Fr71) on the St. Vincent Island bayshore, on the west side of Apalachicola Bay, during archaeological salvage (Braley 1982), and a visitor to our 1985 USF field camp showed us a Clovis point he picked up at Cat Point, the narrow tip of land protruding into the bay on the east side of the river mouth (unnumbered IF on Figure 3.2). Lack of controlled context haunts archaeological interpretation, so it was easy to explain these two points if they were perhaps left by later peoples and washed out on the surface or up from the bay bottom. They were not enough to adjust the model of Paleoindian clustering far inland on the Chipola—until the discovery of 20 more points from St. Vincent Island.

Only accessible by boat, St. Vincent is a federal wildlife refuge where collecting artifacts is illegal. Because people hunt them anyhow, our survey documented collections (White and Kimble 2017). Since my job is not law enforcement but research and education, and since collectors eagerly shared locational and other detailed information, the project could gain much more beyond our own fieldwork by such consultation. In fact, it would have been unethical not to do so. Knowledge from collectors has been the major way that Paleoindian research in North America has advanced (Pitblado 2014). One avocational picked up the 20 Paleo points from four eroding shoreline sites on St. Vincent Island over the course of two decades, beginning 40 years ago. He had thousands of artifacts, most with locational documentation in a computer database and typed field notes, and he donated his collection for further research (Keffer 2015). These data alter the Paleoindian model for the region. The points themselves confirm his reliability, since he would have had to go far to get so many of such different types and cherts. Eighteen of the 20 (Plate VIII; Figure 3.6) came from the St. Vincent 3 and St. Vincent 5 sites (8Fr362 and Fr364), a few hundred meters apart along a nearly continuous oyster-shell midden ridge on the north shore. Two other specimens came from the northeastern corner, at the Paradise Point site (which had already

Figure 3.6. Paleoindian points from St. Vincent 5 site (8Fr364; USF JC collection): (a, c–f) unfluted Clovis (?) and (b) Clovis; e is dark-gray foreign material. (Nancy Marie White)

produced the first point) and the St. Vincent Point site (8Fr354). A problem on this island, as with stream banks, is that often most of the shoreline has washed away before the site is even recorded. Photos from the 1960s show that St. Vincent 5 site then had double the thickness of shell midden from what is there today (White 2021b).

These bayshore Paleoindian points were deposited when the location was on the mainland far from the sea (see Figure 3.1), probably along an ancient Apalachicola channel now on the west side of the modern bay. At 15,000 years ago, sea level was about 40 m lower than at present and the coastline around 50 km (30 mi.) away (Donoghue 2011). Today these sites are near rich oyster bars in the bay, which may be another environmental indicator. No, Paleoindians were not collecting oysters since they were far inland, but the oyster bars may have arisen near springs that are now drowned in the bay. At St. Vincent 5 site, also called Pickalene Bar, there is a small area of very deep water in St. Vincent Sound (the western arm of Apalachicola Bay) that may have been a spring. Perhaps water still flowing westward from this drowned spring makes the current so strong in Indian Pass, at the west end of the island. Cat Point is another place with a rich oyster reef, called Dry Bar (Edmiston 2008:11) that may have developed near an ancient stream bank or spring that attracted human habitation. In late 2021 another local resident reported a Suwannee point found on the Gulf shore of St. George Island (another unnumbered IF on Figure 3.2). Again, this has to be an item washing out of what were once terrestrial cultural deposits.

Geologists (Joe Donoghue and Frank Stapor, personal communication 2010) caution me that the barrier formations are only about 4,000 years old (or younger; Ahmad 2011). Pleistocene sediments that must have contained these artifacts would be over 5 m below mean sea level today (Schnable and Goodell 1968) and not exposed to processes that could have eroded them out of modern visible shorelines. So my interpretation that these coastal points were originally deposited on now-exposed ancient riverbanks that were the cores of island formation is open to serious question. However, other explanations are even less satisfactory. For example, the points do not appear to have been washed up from deeper deposits and weathered and thrown back onto the shore by waves and storms, since they are mostly of unpatinated or lightly patinated chert. They are so diverse that it is improbable that they were accumulated later and left at sites as far as 10 to 20 km apart. Until a better geoarchaeological understanding of site formation processes is possible, I assume that this Paleoindian evidence was found close to where it was first left. Another crucial issue is, if these artifacts and so many island shoreline sites have sat for over 10 millennia, what recent processes caused them suddenly to be exposed in recent decades?

The 23 points from these shoreline sites are very diverse in type and raw material. The second Paradise Point specimen (White and Kimble 2017:Figure 73), 8 cm long, only 1.5 cm wide, and of dark gray chert, appears to fit the Tallahassee type (which can be much younger) on one face, but is fluted on the other face. The dozen points from St. Vincent 3 site (see Plate VIII) are mostly Clovis or unfluted Clovis; one is reworked into a graver or chisel, another is a large Simpson of a style locally called the "Chipola" point, and another fits the type definition of Beaver Lake. The few dark ones may be of foreign stone, but most are of the local chert, either unweathered, honey-colored, and translucent or weathered opaque white, as they would be in exposed terrestrial contexts.

Only the one St. George Island Paleoindian point is known from the Gulf-side shore. A prehistoric bison horn core was reported by Alabama shrimpers who netted it in the Gulf over 20 miles out from the Apalachicola delta. Its outer curve length was 72 cm and basal diameter, 14 cm (Brooms 1995), giving a good idea of the size of these Pleistocene beasts. On St. Andrews Bay, 70 km northwest of St. Vincent Island, one site near a spring/submerged basin produced a Dalton point (Brown 2015). Woodward (2012) documented other Paleoindian sites on Choctawhatchee Bay, one with a Dalton point and three with Waller knives. The McFaddin Beach site in southeast Texas is a 32 km stretch along the Gulf with a huge array of Pleistocene fossils and artifacts from all prehistoric time periods, but predominantly Paleoindian and Early Archaic points, including over 100 Clovis points. These materials are believed to have come from submerged offshore sources, possibly not far away or deep. They were deposited by storm surges that churned them up onto the beach. The Paleo points, apparently in two clusters, are made of chert from 59 different sources, including some hundreds of km away and one of Mexican obsidian. Both the present beach and the offshore locations were high, dry, mainland until relatively recently. They were between two river valleys and up to 200 km inland when sea level was over 100 m lower (Brown 2009). Since McFaddin, on a Gulf beach, is really a redeposition location, not an intact archaeological site, it is mostly different from the Apalachicola bay shores that have Paleoindian materials seemingly washing out of original deposits. However, the similarities are important. First, they show places where people lived from Paleoindian times onward, for thousands of years. Second, they were interior locales attractive for human settlement, and now their artifacts are exposed by coastal processes. With the diversity of cherts, McFaddin also demonstrates, as the St. Vincent Island data confirm, widespread interaction networks already existing among the earliest peoples.

Summary of Site Distribution Patterns

Modeling Paleoindian habitation in the Apalachicola–lower Chattahoochee valley region is hampered by sampling biases. Immense landscape change since the Pleistocene has buried and otherwise obscured so much. Collectors prefer points, leaving lithic-scatter sites of unknown age. Collecting points has gone on since later prehistoric peoples picked up and reused older things, and historic collection has been intensive. For example, researcher Dan Elliott noted a Georgia collector who accumulated by 1905 over 78,000 artifacts (now in the Smithsonian), of which 96 were Paleoindian points from a site where recent survey found none (Moon 1999:28–29). Jim Dunbar (personal communication 2010) notes that, given over a million motorboats in Florida, tens of thousands of divers, 11,000 miles of rivers and streams, and the fact that sport divers find most of the Paleoindian evidence, we are lucky to have the information we have. Figure 3.2 must represent the tiny, visible fraction of the total Paleoindian presence in the research region. Reconstructing settlement pattern has been a long-standing, slowly unfolding mystery, and analyses of site types such as base stations versus hunting/fishing/gathering camps and other anthropological questions await controlled excavation. But the data are more than we have ever had before, and they now suggest that habitation was quite widespread.

Similar to that on the contemporaneous Aucilla River, the pattern of sites in the research region is structured by Pleistocene water and chert sources. People probably first arrived by waterways. Fresh cold water surging up from the ground may also have had spiritual power, perhaps more so if a cave or rockshelter was included and could provide lodging perhaps with indoor running water. Or, scavenging and hunting brought Paleoindians to water holes, but these might have been dangerous places where carnivores also came to drink and grab prey, and thus not good areas to live (Halligan 2012:357). In the entire Apalachicola–lower Chattahoochee region, delta sediments and heavily vegetated wetlands may mask evidence, but chert and water are the best predictors of Paleoindian site location (the spring's the thing!).

Material Culture

Pre-Projectile Point/Pre-Clovis Artifacts?

Materials dated earlier than Clovis have come from five sites in Florida, including Page-Ladson, as noted previously, though which artifact types are diagnostic of this time remains unclear (Dunbar 2016; Halligan et al. 2016). Humans were undoubtedly present before Clovis in the Apalachicola–lower Chattahoochee valley region too. Hypothetical preClovis artifacts need not have been inelegant implements. It is appealing to think of pioneers in a new continent, first exploiting, with their rough tool kits, the unfearing big game herds, then rapidly developing refined artifacts to improve their expertise —but several things are wrong with this picture. Comparing an exquisitely pressure-flaked Florida Suwannee point and a later Florida Archaic Stemmed point demonstrates that earlier is not necessarily cruder; in fact, this is itself an interesting question: why are Archaic points so much more coarse? A better way to consider the preClovis issue may be in the framework of "nonprojectile-point" assemblages. Though still controversial, very early dates are associated with lithic assemblages devoid of points at some sites in the eastern United States and elsewhere (Bonnichsen and Schneider 2001).

In the Apalachicola–lower Chattahoochee valley region, nothing so far is known of pre-Clovis age. But nearby, rough chert artifacts were suggested for this very old time period. In western Alabama over a half-century ago researchers hypothesized a pre-projectile point complex of pebble tools (Lively 1965). Most of the materials in this "Lively Complex" seem human-made. However, the original reports had limited circulation, and neither the grouping of these artifacts as a distinctive complex nor the supposed great age have been validated (Futato 2004). Sites in the research region have produced similar thick, rough-looking core tools, many with some cortex remaining, associated with diagnostic artifacts of different time periods or no diagnostics at all. These items may have undergone only the initial step in a technological process, rather than the conceptual limitations of some early human fabricator. Rugged bifacial chopping-pounding tools probably were never out of fashion.

During survey on the Georgia side of the proposed Jim Woodruff reservoir, Kelly (1950a, 1950b) described an "early flint industry" at the Lane Springs site (9Dr5). A flash flood had washed out a sand ridge along the small stream connecting a large spring with the creek and had deposited "hundreds of worked flints" on the clay hardpan that had underlain the ridge. These tools and debitage were remarkable for their "crude, primitive technique in manufacture" and the "marked chemical alteration or decomposition of their cortex," unlike most chert in the region. Types were heavy choppers, large unifacial plano-convex blades, large plano-convex "turtleback" end scrapers, and "bun-shaped" quartzitic or sandstone "rubbing stones." Associated points included one Early Archaic Bolen Beveled and one with the "characteristic 'fish-tailed,' elongated, longitudinally expanded thin blade aspect of the so-called 'southeastern folsomoid' type but lack[ing] the fluting," which sounds like a Suwannee. A chert quarry was 100 m north of this site, overlooking the spring.

Kelly related this assemblage to the decomposed "rotten flints" he had recovered on the Macon Plateau, from deep weathered soil zones, which included "cutting tools and projectiles hav[ing] a 'Folsomoid' aspect" (Kelly 1938:7). He saw (Kelly 2010:55–66) that the thousands of pieces of chert in such "old flint" assemblages were more weathered or "decomposed" the deeper they were deposited. McMichael and Kellar (1960) formally described an assemblage similar to this Macon Plateau Flint Industry, which they observed on the Middle Chattahoochee and named the "Standing Boy Flint Industry," after Standing Boy Creek, above the Fall Line. They thought that the light-colored, heavily weathered Gulf Coastal Plain chert was the "definitive backbone of this industry," but considered it to be Early Archaic and included within it the "spinner" or beveled point known as Ecusta or Big Sandy (Cambron and Hulse 1964) or Bolen Beveled (Bullen 1975a).

Huscher (1964:4–6) described three sites on the lower Chattahoochee within the research region in the Columbia Reservoir (Andrews Lake) where the Standing Boy Flint Industry occurred, significantly, on remnants of former levees along old channels west of the river. He stressed the inclusion of beveled points, especially at the most westerly (assumed to be the oldest) of the sites. He thought the heavily weathered "leached" chert came from southwestern Georgia along the Flint River and argued that the correlation of extreme age and extreme leaching of these stone tools was evidence for abrupt post-Pleistocene climatic change in the Southeast (Huscher 1967:7).

The Florida contribution to the discussion of rough, thick, possibly very old tools is the "horse's-hoof core-plane," first described by Warren (1963) for central peninsular Florida and Mexico. Similar tools have come from

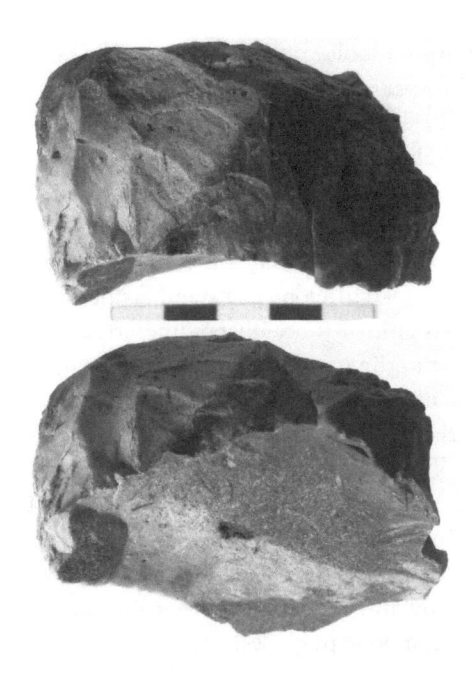

Figure 3.7. Horse-hoof core/plane tool from St. Vincent 3 site, side and underside views (#USF JC-8Fr362-13-1.70). (Nancy Marie White)

the Flint-Chattahoochee forks area and from the other end of the research region, on St. Vincent Island (Figure 3.7). They are large, unifacial, planoconvex implements with steep retouch, shaped like a horse's hoof, probably heavy scrapers or planes similar to Kelly's "turtle-back" scraper. They seem ideal for working wood or hides but might also be specialized cores. Warren notes their occurrence in a wide range of contexts and time periods. Chason (1987:167) obtained dozens of "crudely flaked stone clubs" from the Chipola River that he thought were for clubbing animals—a reasonable conjecture if large game were captured in nets. These thick, coarse, ancient-looking tools in the three-state area all have similarities. They include bifacial and unifacial forms, steeply retouched and directly hammered, retaining a lot of cortex, and often of heavily weathered chert. They could all have multiple functions, and also occur in assemblages of later time periods. Reports of them were neither widely known nor followed by further research. Leaching or heavy weathering of chert is a relative, unquantifiable attribute possibly resulting less from age than from environmental factors such as water and sunlight. However, these artifacts could be candidates for some pre-Clovis culture.

Fine Points of Chronology

For Paleoindian in the Apalachicola–lower Chattahoochee region, the diagnostic artifacts are points. The term "projectile point" is traditional, though use wear and residue studies could give a better idea of true functions; most were probably also knives, gigs, and multipurpose tools. Since hunting can be done equally well with fire-hardened wooden spears, as shown by 300,000-year-old examples from the European Middle Paleolithic, the stone points could also have been made for "costly signaling" (showing off) or some other social or ceremonial reason (Speth et al. 2013). If they were projectiles, flying through the air, they were on spears or darts, as the bow and arrow were not in North America this early. Most likely the points were used with atlatls (spear-throwers), for both stealth and safety reasons, since one can stand farther back from the targeted, sometimes dangerous animal (notwithstanding artists' depictions of hunters positioned right next to the mammoth they are spearing).

Paleoindian points are thin, finely made by pressure-flaking, and sometimes fluted. Some are tiny, like a Marianna, often less than 4 cm long. Some are large, like the broken Clovis that Tesar and Whitfield (2002) estimated at 16 cm long or the Simpsons in the Chason collection that approach 16 cm, and certainly his "fishtail" Simpsons, the largest of which is over 17 cm (see Figure 3.5). The large ones may be less used, unworn or sharpened-down. Since so many might have been unwieldy and expensive as spear tips, maybe they were special objects for solemn or symbolic purposes, say, awarded at puberty or a teen's first kill.

Bullen (1975a) defined the three major Paleoindian point types: Clovis, Suwannee, and Simpson, in both fluted and unfluted forms. Unfortunately, they are among the most questionable of his whole typology (Dunbar 2006b:410). Definitions overlap, especially with the slightly waisted variety of the Suwannee and very waisted or recurvate Simpson points. Relationships among these types is unclear. Dunbar (2006b:408–409) thinks narrow-necked or strongly waisted, wide-bladed Simpsons show a flaking technique slightly different from that of Clovis points. They have large flakes removed by percussion to thin the point, as opposed to the Clovis outrepassé or overshot flaking that produced long, pressed-off flakes that run across the whole width of the point. Therefore, he thinks that Simpsons were actually knives, not projectiles. Other classifications (Farr 2006; Thulman 2007) still have overlapping type definitions and seldom include examples from the Apalachicola–lower Chattahoochee region. Another classic problem is that some types of smaller points may just be sharpened-down versions of other types. Most Paleo points have ground bases, presumably for better hafting, but bases can be reworked after heavy use, and resharpening can change shapes radically. Archaeologists are sometimes slow to recognize this dynamic character of lithic artifacts (Andrefsky 2005:34–40). My grandmother's best kitchen knife was so sharpened-down over decades that it became a thin metal arc.

The classic Clovis has either parallel or excurvate (convex) sides and is not waisted like the Suwannee and Simpson. Other similar types such as Redstone,

Cumberland, Greenbriar, Santa Fe, and Beaver Lake, are found throughout the Southeast. Beaver Lake points are similar to Suwannees but with more of an angle instead of a curve marking the waist. Bullen (1975a:48) recognized that Marianna points were fluted but then put them in a grouping of much later triangular points and said they did not occur north of Gainesville, even though the town of Marianna is far northwest of Gainesville. Most collectors consider Marianna points to be Paleoindian and heavily used. The Dalton point (see Figure 3.4b, d), with a distinct obtuse angle marking the end of the blade and beginning of the base and no waisting, is late in the Paleoindian chronology (Dunbar 2006b:408), but again, could be a sharpened-down something-else. Other types called "Clovis-like" or "unfluted Clovis" defy meticulous classification. Collectors in the Apalachicola–lower Chattahoochee region recognize a "Chipola" point (see Plate VIIIg), a variety of Simpson, Santa Fe, or Greenbriar. It is waisted, almost notched, with basal ears slightly turned upward or expanded and rounded. It is not defined in any professional publication and may simply be another worked-down version of some other type, such as a Gilchrist. For all these types there is little idea of ages, and many appear to be contemporaneous. Simpson and "unfluted Clovis" might be pre-Clovis, even ancestral to Clovis in northwest Florida. Clovis is a continent-wide artifact type that indicates a broad, if relatively short, adaptation, while Suwannee and Simpson points are more confined to the Southeast. As a "lumper" in artifact classification, I remain bewildered by the plethora of type names that different researchers assign to the same artifact. I hope that at least illustrating some from the research region, whether or not my classifications are correct, will advance the discussion.

In the Southeast the Paleoindian period is of course divided into Early, Middle, and Late subperiods, though how to recognize these is debated (Dunbar 2016). Early Paleoindian now means pre-Clovis, with an uncertain beginning date before 14,000–13,500 cal BP (Anderson 2005:33). Middle Paleoindian is the short Clovis horizon, noted above, 13,125 to 12,925 cal BP, though some push dates beyond this range at both ends (Halligan 2012:19, 26). Middle Paleoindian diagnostics are the classic Clovis points, but may also include unfluted Clovis, Cumberland, Suwannee, and Simpson types. The end of Clovis roughly coincides with the Younger Dryas event, a sudden cold climatic episode that happened just as the Ice Age was warming up a bit. This radical climate swing may have lasted 1,000 years, but might well have been observable by the people living through it. It would have meant a sharp average temperature drop of 7 to 15 degrees F. Though geological evidence for it is controversial (Stewart 2020; Voosen 2018), and recently seriously challenged (Voosen 2022), it may have been triggered by volcanic eruptions or by a comet or asteroid exploding over Canada around 12,800 BP, which would have spewed gasses that blocked the sun, bringing extinctions and requiring culture change for survivors. In any case, late Pleistocene environments were unlike anywhere today, with rapid flooding and far more variable climates. The only constants in the landscape might have been chert and water, and successful human adaptations would have been flexible. If a darkened sky or a burning white space-rock did appear (Hand 2018; Stewart 2022), those witnessing it may have incorporated the shocking experience into their storytelling or religion.

Late Paleoindian, from possibly about 12,800 to 10,000 cal BP (10,800 to 8000 BC), is marked by Dalton points, unifacial blades, thumbnail scrapers, and gravers (Anderson 2005). It was apparently a time of fast sea level rise during which coastal adaptations may have shifted constantly. Dalton was a transition presumably seamlessly into the Early Archaic period. Indeed, the Archaic may have begun earlier or the Paleoindian lasted longer, depending on one's definitions. In the Apalachicola–lower Chattahoochee region, so far the only Dalton evidence is the point distribution. Dalton is considered Paleoindian here because the points are still lanceolate and they occur with other Paleoindian materials. Given the numbers of Dalton locations (39% of known Paleoindian sites), this time period may represent a population expansion coupled with the warming climate.

Finer temporal divisions among point types are unclear, given their overlapping definitions and great diversity. Suwannee points, considered Middle Paleoindian, have been found with megafaunal remains of species that supposedly died out by 11,000 BP, so either the points are earlier or the animals survived longer (Dunbar 2016:36, 155). Clovis points have concave bases and basal thinning, but no basal "ears" (bilateral rounded projections), and are not always fluted. In the research region, by my classification, the unfluted Clovis is the most common Paleoindian type. Simpsons are known for their waisted shape and lack of developed "ears," but Suwannees can also be waisted and have bigger ears, while Santa Fe points are narrower, with no ears. Simpson points can have the highly recurvate "fishtail" shapes with very contracted bases and flaring ears. The huge ones from the Four-Hole Pond site are delicate. This site is one of the few terrestrial Paleoindian locales known. It was found in the 1970s during the first clearing of a field bordered by four connected sinkholes aligned in a U shape, 2 km west of the present Chipola River. The points came from the low hilltop overlooking this pond, which was undoubtedly the remnants of a cut-off meander. When I visited there with Paleoindian expert Jim Dunbar in June 1994, no artifacts were visible. The elegant points might have been in a cache or ceremonial set.

This type is also somewhat similar in shape to fishtailed points found throughout South America (Gnecco and Aceituno 2006). Though many South American fishtails are actually stemmed, some specimens from Fell's Cave in southern Chile (Jackson 2006:Figure 6.2) and from Brazil (Loponte et al. 2015) resemble the Chason fishtail Simpsons. Because the South American versions are contemporaneous with Clovis, are made on thicker flakes, and usually have less-prominent ears and other manufacturing differences, they may not be related to the Florida varieties (Dunbar 2016; Faught 2006). However, fishtailed points from Fell's Cave and El Inga sites in southern Chile date between 10,200 and 10,800 BP, Middle Paleoindian, while Clovis-like points there may be earlier than 11,000 BP, overlapping in time with North American Clovis (Jackson 2006:119). More comparative study should investigate possible relationships among these points on the different continents.

Only one northwest Florida site, Sloth Hole, in the Aucilla River, has a chronometric placement for a Paleoindian component with diagnostic artifacts. Both classic and slightly waisted Clovis points, as well as carved ivory foreshafts, overlay a level with nondiagnostic lithic debitage dated to cal 12,300 ± 50 BP (Dunbar 2006b:407). It is only a relative date, seems too late for Clovis, and emphasizes our handicap with the lack of dates for diagnostics. Another problem is that the Dalton point is often confused with the Tallahassee type (Bullen 1975a). Dalton is small, trianguloid or pentagonal, with an incurvate, ground base and a distinct angle where the base joins the blade. It could conceivably be a worn version of other Paleo types. The Tallahassee point is nearly identical to the Dalton except for being possibly longer and thinner, with no flute and sometimes serrated edges; it may be Late Paleoindian but is also found at Woodland sites. Of course both types could be already-ancient tools picked up by later natives and altered. In sum, Paleoindian point types are still chronologically shaky. Probably we should avoid a linear interpretation that sees one type give way to the next and instead recognize the great variability within types.

Other Stone Artifacts

The Waller knife is a distinctive tool named after Ben Waller, a Florida avocational archaeologist and diver who was a stunt double for the old television show *Sea Hunt* and even taught its star, Lloyd Bridges (father of actor Jeff Bridges), how to dive (Dunbar 2006b). Waller collected artifacts and fossils from Florida waters, including the Chipola. The Waller knife is a simple asymmetrical flat secondary flake with two notches, presumably to make a tiny base for hafting (Figure 3.8) and edge retouch approaching serration (Waller 1971). It looks like an expedient tool knocked out quickly to do a job. The notches could be for tying a cord around to keep the tool handy, or for attaching a small handle.

The Waller knife may overlap in attributes with another possible Paleoindian artifact, the Edgefield scraper, which is more triangular, with larger,

116　Chapter 3

Figure 3.8. Waller knives, shown with unifacial side down: all from Chipola and lower Chattahoochee River bottoms, except far right (lighter color), from the terrestrial Tyler TM1 site (8Ja2081); from private collection (numbers are the collector's). (Photographs by William Dan Tyler)

ground notches, and occurs throughout the South (e.g., Lauro 1982). Waller knives are mostly from Florida river-bottom Paleoindian sites, but it is unclear whether they are Paleoindian or Early Archaic in age. Though the notched point is a hallmark of the Early Archaic period, after the end of the Pleistocene, Archaic points are fully shaped, bifacial, finished tools, while Waller knives are simple notched flakes. They probably were indeed knives, and many are sharpened down to be very long and thin. They are so simple as to appear within a different cognitive category from projectile points, and they apparently do not last very far into a time of notched bifacial tools; hence, I include them

Figure 3.9. Large, unifacial, possible Aucilla-type adzes from the Chason collection, middle Chipola River. (Nancy Marie White)

here with Paleoindian. Waller knives are well known in the Apalachicola–lower Chattahoochee region, from sites with both Paleo and Archaic points.

Other diagnostic Paleoindian chert artifacts in the research region remain to be recognized. Butchering/processing tools, used with different forces, angles, and substances, required constant maintenance and different haftings from those of spear points. Continually sharpened large thin percussion flakes work better than points for skinning something with thick hides like bison (Frison 2004). Heavy, clunky tools may have been for woodworking. Some implements resemble the adze defined at Aucilla River Paleoindian and Early Archaic sites, which is large and unifacial but waisted or tapered for hafting. Possible Aucilla adzes (Figure 3.9) were recovered in the Chipola by Chason (1987) and others. Chason also retrieved a few lunate-shaped unifacial scrapers that resemble the crescent or limace form at Paleoindian sites in the Amazon and elsewhere. Besides chipped stone, Paleoindians would have had ground-stone cobbles and other rocks to hammer and grind.

Perishable and Other Organic Artifacts
No osseous artifacts—bone, antler, ivory points, pins, knives, and carved shafts—attributable to Paleoindian times have so far been found in the Apalachicola–lower Chattahoochee region. Swift river movement may break bone to pieces. Collectors brought to our field camp in 2010 a large probable mastodon bone with possible cut marks made when it was fresh (Kelley 2013). Bone or ivory foreshafts, barbed tools or needles, items made of tooth, claw, hoof, thorn, quill, cane, and wood were likely common for everything from tattooing or making decorative objects to daily work. Most of Paleoindian material culture would have been of the fiber arts and crafts: hides,

nets, cord, woven textiles, baskets, artifacts of bark, vine, skin, gut, and leather (Adovasio et al. 2007). Cordage, basketry, bags, mats, and woven sandals/shoes preserved at dry caves and rockshelters in the West were made of various animal and plant materials, with sophisticated craftwork, well over 10,000 years ago. Especially in the rich forests of the Southeast, there were many softer, easier materials with which to fashion everyday items.

Aucilla River underwater sites have yielded such interesting objects: two seed beads, a barbed ivory harpoon, and the greatest number of carved bone and ivory points or foreshafts known from one locale (Dunbar 2016). These shafts sometimes have incised linear designs. Most were splinters of mastodon or mammoth tusks sharpened on one end and obliquely cut or roughened on the other, apparently for hafting (Dunbar 2006b). The Sloth Hole site produced over 900 bone pins, 33 beveled ivory points, bead preforms, a needle tip, and a socketed handle (Hemmings et al. 2004; Largent 2004). Bone or ivory foreshafts probably minimized breakage when hafted to the stone point; if the spear broke, the foreshaft gave way and resulted in less-expensive damage, since the point required more labor to make.

Cultural Adaptations

The first people in the Americas, the oldest artifacts, the strange landscapes full of huge animals and premodern climates are exciting. But much evidence is misrepresented or interpreted with faulty assumptions. Modeling Paleoindian societies through ethnographic analogy can be misleading since no written records exist for any human groups moving into enormous, completely unpopulated lands (except the Antarctic and the moon—and nobody lived off the land in those places). But accounts of foraging cultures worldwide, especially those in bountiful, forested environments, can help illuminate this deep past.

Models of Movement

One reconstruction of Paleoindian settlement patterns in the Southeast suggests that a few areas in the midcontinent had the earliest colonization and more settled, denser populations. From these "staging areas" people proceeded to fill up the rest of the land, with the Gulf Coastal Plain reached later (Anderson 2013). At staging or marshalling areas, groups would aggregate to plan strategies for dispersing into smaller bands, and thus staging sites would have more diverse artifacts, the earliest point styles, and wider spacing (Dincauze 1996). But the proposed staging areas may just be the places where more research has uncovered more and larger sites. Another idea is that the earliest Gulf Coastal Plain communities were separate from those in the heavily populated Highland Rim and Valley-Ridge areas above the fall line in north

Alabama, Georgia, and Tennessee, since chert from those northerly locales seldom occurs at coastal plain sites and vice versa (Meredith 2009). But maps of fluted point concentrations in the eastern United States may not reflect ancient habitation as much as areas of published work and old Clovis biases. The admirable Paleoindian Database of the Americas website (Anderson et al. 2010) has still relatively incomplete data. However, using this model, we might see the Chipola basin, the lower reaches of a major riverine network originating in the Appalachian mountains, as a staging area.

More appropriate here are Paleoindian settlement models developed in northwest Florida. The "oasis" hypothesis suggests that occupation clustered near dependable water at a time when surface water was scarce due to lowered sea levels, attracting both animals and humans (Thulman 2007; Webb 2006). The "river-crossing hypothesis" imagines that shallow places where animals could ford streams and browse or graze, in mud that could trap them, were good hunting stations (Dunbar 2016:184). Both models work in the Apalachicola–lower Chattahoochee region as well as my suggestion that Paleoindians sought shelter in rock enclosures that were then above water. Beyond settlement, however, we can only speculate what the first people in the region were doing, how and why they came, and how they learned new lifeways and persisted (Rockman and Steele 2003). Ecological explanations for migration include population pressure and resource depletion, "push" and "pull" factors that trigger movements of people, but social and ideological reasons are also significant. Plus, the earliest adaptations probably changed regularly. The first people harvested animals that had not experienced predation pressure and were easier to capture—like having a free grocery store—until the different species learned to avoid humans.

Early human groups were probably small, around 50 persons, with aggregations into larger communities at intervals for seasonal/ceremonial/social events or sharing during lean times. People could have set up base camps from which to make day trips in a pattern of central-place foraging, or moved as a group from resource station to station over the yearly cycle. We can only imagine how it felt to step into uninhabited land. Perhaps only fearless trailblazers went first, to scout out locations. Or maybe people just moved so gradually that it was like relocating down the same street. We cannot yet know how quickly the earliest settlers learned the environments and began manipulating them, perhaps with fire-clearing or location markers. Foragers' cognitive maps of the landscape may include cardinal directions, which were sacred to historic Native Americans, routes to geographic features, and distances expressed in time required to go somewhere. In forested regions, streams are the major features to which all else is related (Kelly 2003:50).

Big-Game Hunting

Popular reconstructions of Paleoindian hunting often feature unrealistic imagery ignorant of both animal behavior and basic hunting skills (Frison 2004:xiii–xv, 32). Pleistocene environments had arrays of plants and animals with few modern analogs. Experimental studies using stone and bone tools to throw at and butcher elephants give some insights, but few archaeologists themselves are hunters. I am not, but I have tried to work with hunters and absorb some knowledge. Tactics and technologies vary as animal behavior changes by season and as they learn they are being pursued. On these topics, I respect discussions by George Frison, a rancher, hunter, and guide who became an archaeologist; as a student I volunteered for a week on his project at the Paleoindian Agate Basin site in Wyoming. He describes how hunters use snares, traps, nets, blinds, and other aids (Frison 2004). They require the skills of manufacturing the devices, understanding the behavior of different species, reading tracks and other signs, using scents and baits and sounds, training dogs to help, and understanding the associated social, ethical, and ritual issues. Tracking is crucial; South African hunters are still so good at it that they learn the comings and goings of each person in their community as well as animal behaviors (Suzman 2017:166–168). Frison (2004:13–14) notes the importance of baiting, for example, how a piece of dried hide suspended from a tree attracts bobcats, forcing them to stand on hind feet to investigate and thus step into a trap. I saw such bait in a Gulf County forest, a hanging piece of hog hide to snare invasive coyotes. These examples also show the need to take animals for reasons other than food, whether for obtaining fur or other materials or getting rid of a nuisance.

Large animals may provide the greatest return for the effort but also bring the most difficulties. Abundant remains of smaller animals and plants are also found in good Paleoindian contexts. Regular, organized, deliberate hunting of Pleistocene megafauna was probably rare. Stalking and killing large creatures is far more dangerous than scavenging them after they are killed by other predators, or harvesting them when they are trapped in a bog or net. Paleoindian sites in the North American West, Plains, and Midwest sometimes have rocks or postholes, suggesting paths for game drives or corrals to hold the animals. Having worked at bison-kill sites in Colorado, Nebraska, and Wyoming, I have seen what mass kills looked like. They would have been impossible in thick forest and are indeed absent in the South. The Aucilla River sites appear to be the results of killing and butchering one or a few animals, not herds. Even these sites would have attracted other animals, bears and other scavengers, which could also be seized. Less effort may have been required if the animals came to the hunters waiting at the water's edge. Trapping or netting game is even easier, and teamwork is more effective than the single hunter.

Plus, fewer huge animals would be needed if smaller game, fish, and plant foods were abundant.

Information about targeted resources is important. At the Page-Ladson site, chemical components in annual growth rings of the tusk of a mastodon showed it had migrated in from north Georgia. Mastodon digesta formed a straw-like layer at the site, probably because the animals used the sinkhole for drinking and wallowing, as African elephants do, and thus left a healthy amount of preserved remnants of what they ate. The material was twigs, branches, bark, and woody debris of cypresses and other trees as well as nuts, acorns, fruits, and berries that showed the animals were there in autumn. Some plants in the digesta, such as wild gourds and Osage orange, do not grow in the region today and may have evolved along with the now-extinct megafauna, which were their agents of dispersal (Newsom and Mihlbachler 2006).

The Pleistocene South would have been as rich as the African Serengeti in big game (Russell et al. 2009). The two Pleistocene elephants were mammoths that grazed in open areas and mastodons that browsed in the woods. A single modern bison can produce 160 to 200 kg (350 to 400 lbs.) of meat minus the head and neck, enough to feed a family of five for a month (Frison 2004:115, 224), as well as marrow, grease, bone, gut, horn, hoof, fur, and hide. The extinct *Bison antiquus* was twice as large as modern bison, while horses and camels were smaller than today's varieties. Horses became extinct and absent from the Americas until the Spanish brought them back, while camel forms such as llama remain in South America. Frison (2004:49) was puzzled over why bison could survive in North America but horses could not, especially since feral horses, mustangs, descended from those brought by Europeans, still flourish in the West. The giant sloth was a furry creature several meters tall (a reconstructed one greets visitors in the Daytona Museum of Arts and Sciences) and the giant glyptodont armadillo could reach 2 m long. The tapir had a long snout and resembled a pig.

We must imagine a landscape where these creatures walked, along with saber-toothed cats, dire wolves, and other ferocious beasts. After the 1999 World Archaeological Congress conference in South Africa, I was fortunate to go on a game drive and a game walk in Zimbabwe, which provided terrific insights for interpreting Paleoindian archaeology. In the present US Southeast there is little more than the occasional poisonous snake, hungry panther, or ornery alligator or bear to endanger a person in the forest. But, on foot in southern Africa among so many beasts that, as the armed guide said, want to stomp us, gore us, or eat us, I appreciated the phrase "safety in numbers" and also the need for powerful weapons for defense, if not for getting dinner. Even recent news reports detail animal attacks: an incautious hiker in the western US parks barely alive after being gored and thrown by bison; people seriously injured after bear attacks in northwest Florida. In the Pleistocene landscape, unlike modern hunters, what Paleoindians had to watch out for was animals hunting them.

People surely got excited about the hunt; it was dangerous and tricky but offered high returns. Social and ceremonial behavior intertwined with hunting might have included offerings to the animal's spirit to thank it for allowing itself to be killed, or sharing meat with others based on family or other social rules. South African native big-game hunters consider the owner of the animal to be the one who made the arrow that killed it, not necessarily the one who shot it; the owner then has rights and obligations to allocate meat in specific ways. But bagging a big animal was probably a good time for everyone, not only to share food, brag, and celebrate but also to cook, preserve leftovers, and clean up. All this is purely imaginative, however, and researchers now agree that the emphasis on Paleoindian big game hunting is overdone. Mastodon steaks may have been the original "power lunch," but probably were rare. Archaeology has suffered from biases in reconstructing Pleistocene humans "acting out versions of 'Rambo meets the megafauna'" (Trinkaus 1987:107), and the old model of "Man the Big Game Hunter" is having a hard time dying. Even recognition that fancy projectile points may have been more for social display than utilitarian function is still derived from imagining male prestige systems (Speth et al. 2013).

Archaeologists speculate on gender roles in prehistory, but with scant evidence. Anthropological research documents how women in many cultures hunt, including mothers and grandmothers (e.g., Estioko-Griffin 1986). A South American woman from 9,000 years ago was found buried with hunting and animal-processing artifacts (Haas et al. 2020), as have many other Pleistocene and early Holocene female burials throughout the Americas (Dycus 2022:3). To a multiton mammoth, neither a 200-lb. man nor a 100-lb. woman is threatening. More important is having the right tools and tactics, as men, women, and kids who hunt today realize. With less speed and strength but more stamina than men, women may have been more suited to run down some animals. Calendrical systems, which may have originally developed based on women's menstrual cycles, may have included scheduling optimum times to get animals in connection with blood and hunting taboos. Yurok hunter-gatherers in California apparently scheduled subsistence behavior and mobility around the synchronous monthly cycles of women living together (Buckley 1988). Furthermore, hunting behavior should not be seen as manifesting some innate aggressive "killer" instinct in human nature. Even if only one person makes the shot that gets the beast, the process is usually a group effort, with cooperative tasks from tracking to carrying meat home, and trapping, netting, and clubbing large creatures is easier than spearing them. In

Paleoindian studies, some researchers introduce sexist and other biases that are not inherent in the material they dig up (Chilton 2004). Most foraging communities have highly flexible divisions of labor based on gender and age (e.g., Gould 1980:74–75), with small game harvested more often than large, even little kids swinging sharp tools around, and parents freed to conduct risky activities by the simple concept of the babysitter.

Overkill?
The idea that "overkill" by human hunters led to or aided Pleistocene extinctions is continually debated (Becerra-Valdivia and Highham 2020; Grayson and Meltzer 2015). Some believe that climate change alone was not responsible for the loss of so many megafaunal species. Human pressure could have aided the process, because of naive animal populations not used to human predation, and later, if remaining large game were more clustered in refugia areas and easier to find (e.g., Russell et al. 2009:194). Humans not only killed by hunting but also were doubtless responsible for additional stresses to animals brought on by deliberately set fires and other habitat changes. The best assessment seems to be that both global warming and human action played roles, depending on local conditions (Broughton and Weitzel 2018). We cannot assume that ancient peoples were always careful about or aware of damage they might be doing to their environments (Krech 1999). Pleistocene megafauna evidently survived slightly longer in the Southeast, where there was greater biodiversity than in the West. However, by the early Holocene, even though warming was not as radical as farther north, extinction was more severe, taking out nearly half of the known species (Russell et al. 2009).

Other Resources
Ethnographies of hunting cultures show that up to 80% of the diet is plants and small animals (Lee and DeVore 1968), yet megafaunal remains still tend to overshadow studies of Paleoindian foodways (Peres 2017). Rather than specialize, Paleoindians must have had variable diets including vegetables and small protein sources such as birds, eggs, small mammals, fish, reptiles, and amphibians. Wild seeds and grains were certainly harvested, probably ground, dried, and mixed into gruels. Though modern hunter-gatherers ingest more cholesterol from meat than is recommended today, they have far lower levels of cholesterol and heart disease, get much more daily exercise, and eat much less fat, since wild animals are less fatty than domesticated ones (Kiple 2000). Recent research on 339 forager societies demonstrates that variation in their lifeways, as with birds and mammals, is explained by characteristics of their natural environments nearly as much as by cultural factors (Barsbai et al. 2021; Hill and Boyd 2021).

Specialist studies at Paleoindian sites do detail evidence of fish, birds, nuts, small game, and plants (Walker and Driscoll 2007). Botanical remains from north Alabama rockshelter sites dating from Late Paleoindian through Early Archaic include hickory nut, acorn, and fruits such as persimmon, grape, and sumac (Hollenbach 2009). From the Florida Aucilla Paleoindian sites come remains of medium-sized and small animals such as turtles, snakes, and fish (Dunbar 2016:41). Domesticated species might have been used by Paleoindians. In east peninsular Florida, Early Archaic bottle gourd fragments from the Windover site dated to 8100 BP are of an already-domesticated variety either brought from Asia (Erickson et al. 2005) or domesticated in the American tropics and spread northward (Kistler et al. 2014). Domesticated dogs probably also arrived with the first Americans (Perri et al. 2021). Dogs helped with hunting, safety, and carrying loads, and provided fur, companionship, and other benefits, including food. Dogs and bottle gourds, "utility species" controlled by people, were also the first "invasive" or nonnative species in the Americas—besides humans.

Beyond Subsistence

Ideology, Art, and Craft

Besides material objects, Paleoindian possessions doubtless included songs, dances, stories, and other performances. Nonutilitarian artifacts were decorative or objects of art, magic, games, religion, or social significance that we can only imagine. Red ocher, ground hematite, was used possibly for a preservative, abrasive, or pigment (Frison 2004:219). It occurs at the Anzick site in central Montana, which produced the only Clovis burial known so far, dated between about 12,600 and 13,000 BP. A small boy was buried with a cache of artifacts that is the largest Clovis assemblage ever discovered. In the cache were at least 100 stone tools including Clovis points, preforms, cores, unifaces, and chert debitage from at least six different sources in Montana and Wyoming, as well as eight antler rods, probably spear foreshafts, with incised cross-hatching on their beveled ends; the artifacts and the child were ritually covered with red ocher (Knudson 2015). The Sloan site in Arkansas, at about 10,500 BP, is the only Paleoindian cemetery known. Its 30 burials of adults and children were accompanied by piles of Dalton points, other tools, and red ocher (Morse 1997). Closer to the research area, Paleoindian beads have been found in Florida. At the Wakulla Springs Lodge site east of the research region, a tiny quartz disc 4.3 mm in diameter was in Paleoindian deposits. The Ryan-Harley site, on the Wacissa River, had an even tinier chert disc bead 2.3 mm in diameter, associated with Suwannee points, and two larger ivory bead preforms were at the nearby Sloth Hole site (Glowacki 2012:49).

People and Society
Models of early prehistoric foraging societies have undergone significant change throughout the history of science but are important to consider because such adaptations have characterized most of human existence. We no longer assume that society was only kin-based or patrilineal, supposedly to facilitate hunting by related men. Ethnographic data show that hunter-gatherer groups are made up of mostly unrelated persons and can have patrilineal, matrilineal, or other kinship systems (Chapais 2011; Hill et al. 2011). The few known Paleoindian burials suggest egalitarian societies, with men and women treated the same in death (Lepper 2016). Life expectancy was shorter than it is today, but for the perhaps 60% who made it past childhood, a long life was possible (Holden 2006).

Paleoindian communities were probably more complex than once thought, "transegalitarian" societies with authority based on more than just kinship, though not yet hereditary positions. Historic versions include coastal foragers such as the wealthy ranked groups on the northwest coast of North America and in south peninsular Florida. Complexity implies that human cultures begin to lose their assumed original egalitarian nature. But known egalitarian societies are well documented to be actively self-maintained through typical leveling mechanisms, community sanctions that keep someone from trying to be more important than everyone else (Lee 1969). Impulses to dominate are not absent but are held in check by group pressure and traditions of sharing resources and decisions. The notion that people constantly aim to better themselves and their families is a relatively recent ideal of western culture. Even today, continued study of South African traditional hunter-gatherers over generations demonstrates that they are fiercely egalitarian, with no chiefs or hierarchies, maintaining order by group agreement; they wonder why people would want more than they need, especially if they have to work harder to get it (Suzman 2017). The same is true for other foragers who do not seek to accumulate abundant possessions (Hoffman 2018). The notion that life was constant struggle amid scarcity for foraging peoples was discarded long ago. Quantitative data show how, even in harsh environments such as deserts, these "original affluent societies" needed only to work about three days per week to make a living (Sahlins 1972). Striving for more, contrary to modern standards, is pointless (Lee and DeVore 1968), even something to be mocked (Suzman 2017).

The big questions come later, about how such equitable systems could have broken down, and why people would work harder to produce food when they could obtain it wild for less effort. Some researchers think that no society is completely egalitarian, with at least socioeconomic distinctions based on age and sex. A division of labor based on age is universal; kids or the elderly cannot do some tasks. However, plenty of foragers have no strict division of labor based on sex or gender (e.g., Endicott and Endicott 2008). Stereotypes should be discarded; to survive, these societies had to be flexible and diverse. Even gender is a variable social role. Native American societies descended from Paleoindians often included additional genders beyond male and female (Callender and Kochems 1982; Hollimon 2001), and such persons frequently had supernatural power, did unusual tasks, and merited great respect.

The popular, romantic story of the first Americans portrays heroes conquering a strange new land, fearlessly seeking humongous beasts, pushing the American frontier ever forward. In reality, these origin myths are dangerously inaccurate, reflecting old stereotypes of the noble savage. Asians moving into North America altered lifestyles in response to new challenges. By the time they got to the Apalachicola–lower Chattahoochee region, they surely had well-established but adaptable traditions and probably great cultural diversity. Five separate historic language families in the native Southeast, as well as several language isolates, included hundreds of individual tongues, most of them mutually unintelligible (Drechsel 1997). The region was probably populated by small groups who gathered periodically for larger celebrations, cooking, dining, praying, joking, making music and dance and theater together, keeping news, innovations, and individuals moving around interconnected landscapes and repeating oral traditions over generations—the original social networking.

Plate I. Lower Chattahoochee River, west side, winter 2017. Rock outcrop extends down into caves now drowned in the Jim Woodruff Reservoir or Lake Seminole. (Nancy Marie White)

Plate II. Blue Spring (one of many in the region with this name), 200 m back from the west riverbank on the upper Apalachicola. (Nancy Marie White)

Plate III. Middle Chipola River, with blue-green spring-fed waters, white limestone bank. (Photograph by William Dan Tyler.)

Plate IV. Van Horn Creek, Lower Apalachicola distributary, with cypress-palm swamp and USF survey team in boats. (Nancy Marie White)

Plate V. White sugar-sand Gulf beach, St. George Island State Park, with sea oats on dunes. (Nancy Marie White)

Plate VI. Clark Creek clamshell midden (8Gu60), TUB L5 Feature 1, June 1988, showing fragment of yellow-sand prepared floor (?) 75 cm deep, associated with Early Woodland ceramics. This is one of very few features in Apalachicola estuarine shell middens. Trowel points north. (Nancy Marie White)

Plate VII. Gotier Hammock Mound (8Gu2), near St. Joseph Bay, north wall, TU2A, 2009, showing contrasting gray topsoil, lighter-gray stratum 4, black (3), and white (2) sand strata overlying yellow natural soil (1), with a deep black pit (Feature 1). This unit was opened adjacent to TU2, just to the right, to get all the pieces of ceramic vessels. (Nancy Marie White)

Plate VIII. Paleo-Indian points from the St. Vincent 3 site (8Fr362): (a–f) unfluted Clovis (?); (g) Chipola (or Santa Fe or Simpson); (h) Beaver Lake (?); (i–l) probable Clovis (i is resharpened into a graver or chisel); USF#s JC-13.1-27, -39, -45, -52. Local chert is honey-colored and translucent, weathering to white or tan; dark chert is foreign. (Nancy Marie White)

Plate IX. Middle Archaic Florida Hamilton (?) point and large biface from Chipola River bottom, showing red-violet patina, in private (JW) collection. (Photograph by William Dan Tyler.)

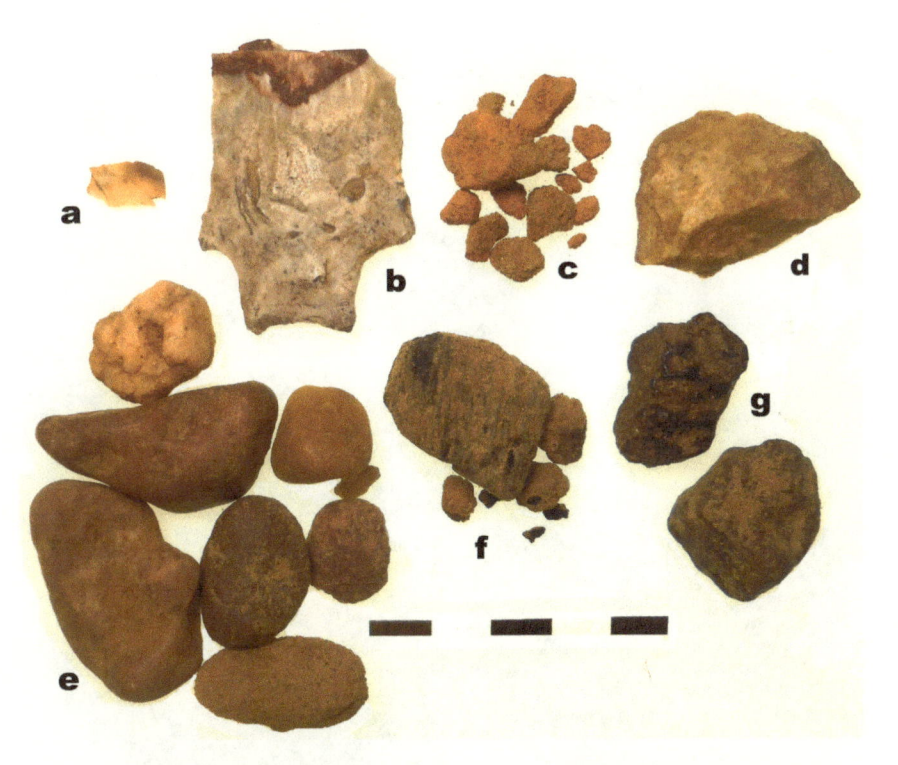

Plate X. McKinnie site (8Ja1869) artifacts in Feature 2, a small pit dated 3630–3375 cal BC: (a) chert flake; (b) Hamilton point; (c) red ocher crumbs; (d) quartzite fragment; (e) 8 smooth quartzite/quartz pebbles; (f) charcoal (some removed for dating); (g) 2 black hematitic stones (#8Ja1869-13-48.1). The site had 22 such features suggesting Middle–Late Archaic ritual. (Nancy Marie White)

Plate XI. Late Archaic red jasper disc bead from St. Vincent 5 site (#USF JC-8Fr364-273). (Nancy Marie White)

Plate XII. Ground-stone pendants or plummets from Middle Woodland Porter's Bar mound (8Fr1) on Apalachicola Bay (NMAI#171797, 1711347): (a) white quartz; (b, c, f, g, h) greenstone; (d) granite?; (e) red sedimentary (?) rock. (Nancy Marie White)

Plate XIII. Discs: (a) copper, from (Early Woodland) Huckleberry Landing Mound (8Fr12; NMAI#172985; upper one has knotted cord fragment in perforation); (b) ceramic backing for them; (c) two sides of copper-covered limestone disc from Middle Woodland Cemetery Mound (8Fr21, Pierce complex; NMAI#170212), with back showing protrusion for secure attachment and bare white stone surface. (Nancy Marie White)

Plate XIV. U-shaped Weeden Island Incised vessel with zones of red paint, from Pierce (8Fr14) Mound A, Burials 2 and 4 group (NMAI#174530). (Photograph courtesy of the National Museum of the American Indian, Smithsonian Institution, by NMAI Photo Services Staff.)

Plate XV. Weeden Island Incised red-painted compound vessel with scalloped neck and cylindrical base from Green Point Mound (8Fr11; NMAI#174534). (Nancy Marie White)

Plate XVI. Weeden Island Plain red-painted cutout bird-effigy jar from Bristol Mound (8Li4; NMAI#173955). (Nancy Marie White)

4

Early and Middle Archaic Periods, 10,000 to ca. 5500 BP (8,000 to 3,500 BC)

We know less in the Apalachicola–lower Chattahoochee region about Early and Middle Archaic than any other time periods, though collectors' data help interpretations. Early Archaic sites are only recognized by diagnostic corner-notched, side-notched, often beveled projectile points—Bolen/Kirk Corner-Notched/Big Sandy types—and a few bola stones. With little evidence from controlled excavation, inferences are based on knowledge of neighboring regions. People filled out the land after the end of the Ice Age, hunting modern fauna, possibly obtaining more plants, fish, and shellfish. Sites are still often obscured or deeply buried by geomorphological processes, or else components are mixed with later cultural deposits. The same is true for the Middle Archaic, for which fewer sites are known, dates are scarce, and generally stemmed point type definitions overlap. Diagnostics include Kirk Serrated, Morrow Mountain, Eva, Sykes, and Benton points, and bannerstones. Reconstructing social and ideological systems remains speculative; probably Native American communities were still small, seasonally mobile, and egalitarian.

Defining the Archaic

With the end of the Pleistocene, Paleoindian material culture disappeared in the Apalachicola–lower Chattahoochee valley region, as in the rest of the Southeast. Megafauna died out, people hunted deer and small animals, and lanceolate projectile points gave way to stemmed and notched types, marking the shift into the Archaic period. This transition included both cultural persistence and change. Many Paleoindian sites also have Early Archaic materials, implying continuity in preferred places. The Archaic was once defined by what it was not, a "stage" in prehistory after Paleoindian and before the emergence of pottery and mound-building, which were supposed to be significant achievements indicating more complex societies. Now we realize how silly such terminology is to describe the huge cultural variability over time, and how ethnocentric ideas that human systems continue to become more elaborate, larger, or settled are outmoded Victorian notions of "progress." We also recognize that the millennia assigned to the Archaic actually saw the first appearance in the South of both mound-building (Middle Archaic) and ceramics (Late Archaic). In the research region, only diagnostic points or chronometric dates permit classification of sites as Early or Middle Archaic. The three-part chronological division of the Archaic is admittedly stereotyped but still useful.

Holocene or Recent-era climate change, extinctions, rising sea levels, and wetter environments accompanied the advent of the Archaic. Developing Archaic lifeways was undoubtedly more complicated than just learning to hunt the smaller beasts that remained, especially since they were already being hunted all along. Big questions concerning social and other systems are now examined across the South. But Archaic research in the Apalachicola–lower Chattahoochee region is still concerned with chronology and settlement. The lack of information from controlled contexts means interpreting this time period in the light of data from more intensively studied regions and ethnographic descriptions of hunter-gatherer-fisher cultures. However, the widespread evidence of Early Archaic in the region comprises far more information than we have ever had before about this period and suggests that humans survived their first global warming quite well.

Archaic research is "some of the most theory-dependent archaeology being practiced in North America" because the hard evidence is so limited, a situation in which theorists prosper (Emerson and McElrath 2009:27). But environmental approaches are useful. The new absence of large creatures would have modified landscapes. If mastodon and mammoth acted like modern elephants, their feeding and ranging would have kept areas free of more closed forest cover. After they were gone, open savannas may have become more forested, also providing more fuel for fires (Dunbar 2016; Frison 2004), as humans continued altering landscapes. Typical descriptions of the Archaic assumed that people decreased mobility and devoted more time to plants, since big game were gone and trees more abundant. Paleoindian groups were said to have been specialized hunters characterized by "logistical mobility," meaning small groups ventured out from base habitations to smaller camps for specific resources. Archaic Native Americans were then seen more as generalists, exploiting a wider range of ecosystems, with settlement patterns of "residential mobility," meaning the whole group seasonally followed the resources (Binford 1980). Some of these stereotypes are now discarded. If Pleistocene cool open woodlands, parklands, and savannas gave way to warmer forests, but deer, racoon, and other small game were still there, little change in subsistence strategies was needed.

Early Archaic in the Region

The Early Archaic period in the research region is estimated to extend from about 10,000 to 8000 BP, or about 8000 to 6000 BC (since this chapter takes us closer to recorded history, I use western calendar conventions, ethnocentric as they are; by 6000 BC, settled farming villages characterized western Asia). Some place the onset of the Archaic earlier, at 11,500 BP, corresponding with the end of the Younger Dryas geological era, but shifts in material

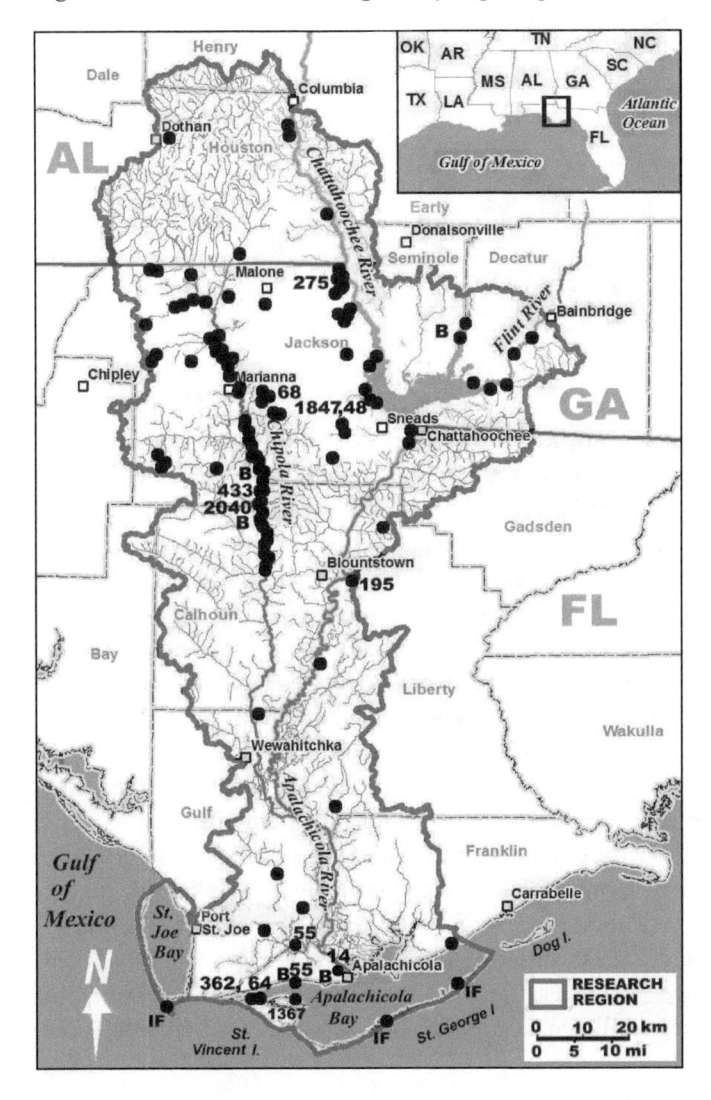

Figure 4.1. Early Archaic sites, isolated finds (IF) and bola stones (B). Numbered sites are discussed in the text. (Nancy Marie White)

Figure 4.2. Early Archaic points: (a) Broward? (b, d) Lafayette; (c) Westo; (e) Leon or Duval? (f) Taylor; (g, h, i, k, n) Bolen Beveled; (j, l) Kirk Corner-Notched; (m) Clay? (o) Kirk Serrated? or Morrow Mountain? (possibly Middle Archaic); (p–r) Hardaway Side-Notched. Sites (all USF#s): (a) J. B. Young (8Ca99); (b) Lightning (8Ca101); (c) Ten Mile Creek Overlook (8Ca108); (d) Spivey Road Borrow Pit (8Ca128); (e–f) St. Vincent 3 (#8Fr362-13-1.24 and .36); (g) St. Vincent 5 (#8Fr364-15-1.86); (h) Saul's Creek Road East (8Gu33); (i) Cypress Ridge (8Gu58); (j) Yellow Houseboat shell midden (8Gu55); (k) Homer Sims 3 (8Ja448); (l) Dudley (8Ja450); (m) Bevis (8Ja502); (n) Lonice (8Ja522); (o) Welch (8Ja537); (p) Keene Dog Pond (#8Ja1868-10-15-DP32-1); (q) Nameless Creek (8Li95); (r) Estiffanulga Dump (#8Li207-2). (Nancy Marie White)

culture seem to have taken a little longer. In fact, the Early Holocene rapid ecological transformation is thought to have no modern analogues (McWeeney and Kellogg 2001). Climate records from a pollen core at Camel Lake in the Apalachicola National Forest suggest that the region was changing from the cold, foggy boreal forest of the Pleistocene to a warmer, dry Early Holocene (Watts et al. 1992), but then rising sea level resulted from postglacial meltwaters. The transition into Early Archaic was happening at a time of declining pine forests and increasing hardwoods, especially hickory and spruce, followed by increases in beech, oak, and prairie species indicating open areas. Then by around 7700 BP more pine and wetlands were evident, developing into modern forests and wetter climates. Waterways were expanding but still not as abundant as today. As sea levels rose, river channels shifted often.

At first glance Early Archaic here looks different from what came before, as site distribution (Figure 4.1) is more widespread (compare Figure 3.2). Whether this means more people or more movement is unknown, though populations were probably growing. Site locations are based on the occurrences of diagnostic points: corner-notched or side-notched, sometimes serrated, sometimes beveled types, usually with ground basal edges (Figures 4.2 to 4.4). Type names are Bolen, Big Sandy, Kirk Corner-Notched, Lost Lake, Lafayette, Eva, and a few others.

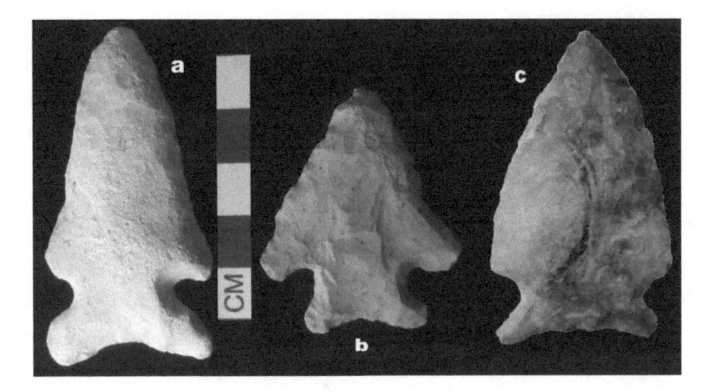

Figure 4.3. Early Archaic points from St. Vincent Island: (a, b) Lost Lake? (weathered) from St. Vincent 5 site (#USF JC-8Fr364-15-85 and -100); (c) Bolen? or Gilchrist? from Little Redfish Creek site (#USF JC-8Fr1367-14-1.13). (Nancy Marie White)

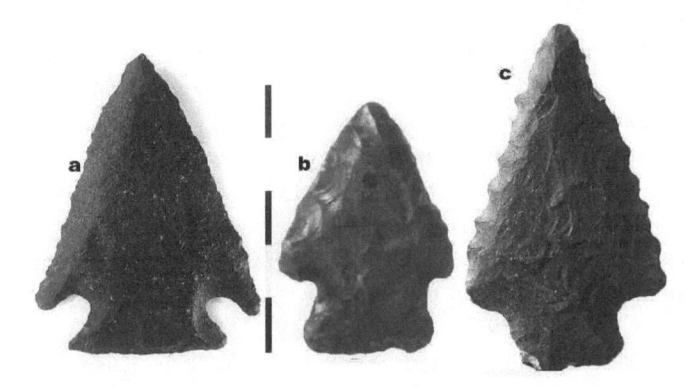

Figure 4.4. Early/Middle Archaic points from Gulf beaches: (a) Bolen Beveled (#IF-MT) from Cape San Blas of dark (foreign?) chert (curated at St. Joseph Bay State Buffer Preserve) (courtesy of Michael Trabue); (b) Wacissa (USF#IF94-1) from northeast side of St. George Island (patinated, water-worn); (c) Hardee Beveled from southwest side of St. George Island (USF#IF2006-1). (Nancy Marie White)

Settlement Pattern

Deep Archaic cultural deposits in the eastern United States now give insights into human lifeways in these earliest times of relatively modern environments. Though Early Archaic in the Apalachicola–lower Chattahoochee valley is known mostly from surface-collected points, this is still far more information than we have ever had before. Some 150 known sites occur along water sources and often have earlier Paleoindian materials and later prehistoric components. Many Early Archaic points have also come from plowed fields and deep borrow pits. A larger number, over 60%, were found underwater in the Chipola River. Though we do not know any other Early Archaic chipped-stone diagnostics, the points are abundant throughout the region (Kreiser 2018; Tyler 2008; White and Kimble 2017). Of Chason's (1987) 430 points from the Chipola valley, 30 to 45 are Early Archaic. The Keene sites' (8Ja1847, 1848) family collection in the upper Apalachicola totals 862 points, with the Early Archaic specimens including 34 Bolen (20 beveled), 6 Kirk Corner-Notched, and 15 Big Sandy (Kelley 2013; I reclassified some in this thesis). From Jackson Blue Springs (8Ja68, other numbers), which flows into the upper Chipola, have come countless points (Archaeological Consultants Inc. 2006). When the Blue Springs water was artificially lowered in the 1990s, people were finding 50 points a day in the underwater cave alone, but decades earlier the park trail was covered with points that people picked up and threw in the water to avoid cutting their feet (Jeff Whitfield, personal communication 2017).

The site map in Figure 4.1 reflects sampling error. In the lower Chattahoochee and upper/middle Chipola basins, more exposed ground in plowed fields and more river divers mean more sites, but the Alabama and Georgia portions of the region have had little survey coverage beyond riverbanks (Figure 3.2 reflects interest only in Paleo points) (Moon 1999). The main Apalachicola valley is heavily alluviated; its continual eastward migration altered or buried sites. Yet even these inadequate data contradict the old viewpoint that Archaic sites were few due to people's difficulties in adjusting to postglacial environments (Caldwell 1958).

Dating this time period in the research region has been elusive, even when diagnostic points are found below the surface. Bullen's (1958) excavations at Chattahoochee River 1 site (8Ja8 [J-5]), on the Chattahoochee west bank just above the forks, reached a preceramic stratum that may have been extremely old. It was from 4 to 4.6 m deep, separated from the stratum containing Late Archaic fiber-tempered pottery by 122 cm of culturally sterile sands. His meter-wide cut produced nearly 150 pieces of lithic debitage, 2 quartz(ite?) hammers, other cobbles, a thumbnail (tiny curved) scraper, and a (bifacial?) flaked knife. Without diagnostics, this stratum could be anything from Paleoindian to preceramic Late Archaic.

Within the west side meander belt of the lower Chattahoochee–upper Apalachicola, a few deep deposits have looked promising. At the Robinson 4 site (8Ja275), on a bluff overlooking a creek one km upstream from its mouth into the river, a Bolen Beveled point was in situ 60 cm deep in a shovel test (White 1981). At the Keene Dog Pond site (8Ja1848), on a large old backed-up channel, a 2-×-2-m test produced a point tip, lithic debitage, a Kirk point base, and a Bolen Beveled point (Figure 4.2p). The Bolen was in situ 60 cm deep in Level 4. But Level 4 charcoal was dated cal AD 400–640, and an additional date on charcoal from Level 6 was cal 40 BC–AD 80 (Kelley 2013). These Middle and Early Woodland dates demonstrate how the Early Archaic components can be mixed in with later materials in compressed stratigraphy from generations of prehistoric disturbance and modern plowing.

On the middle Apalachicola at the Nameless Creek site (8Li195), a Bolen Beveled point (Figure 4.2q) was recovered washing out of a stratum some 4 m below the riverbank face at a time of low water (White 2018). Deep, undisturbed Early Archaic deposits like this are usually unreachable. In the lower valley Late Archaic points have been similarly mixed in with later materials and lack original context. For example, at the Yellow Houseboat site (8Gu55), an estuarine clamshell midden on Lake Wimico (see Figure 2.13), a Kirk Corner-Notched point (see Figure 4.2j) occurred with other surface artifacts from four later components.

Early Archaic evidence is emerging from what is today the coast. On the St. Vincent Island bayshore, a collector obtained several points (see Figure 4.2e, f, g, and Figure 4.3.) at three multicomponent sites, St. Vincent 3 (8Fr362), St. Vincent 5 (8Fr364), and Little Redfish Creek (8Fr1367). Just in the last two decades, surface finds have also come from the Gulf side of barrier formations. An isolated Bolen Beveled from the tip of Cape San Blas peninsula (Figure 4.4a) was brought to the St. Joseph Bay State Buffer Preserve by a helpful visitor. Its dark chert looks foreign to the region, and it is so unweathered as to suggest it just eroded out of the ever-decreasing dunes on the west side of the Cape, which is one of the most rapidly eroding locations along the Gulf. Another collector had found at least four Archaic points from Cape San Blas over the years, especially after storms threw them up, and they were always black, so perhaps the dark chert is not foreign but unusually weathered. A Wacissa point (see Figure 4.4b) eroding out of the Gulf shore on St. George Island was recovered by another visitor. It is heavily weathered, with a dull brown patina from sitting in water for a while, but it retains beveling and serrated edges. Also on St. George Island, a resident found and donated a Hardee Beveled point (see Figure 4.4c) from the southwest shore.

Good coastal evidence also comes from adjacent to the research region: at least one Early Archaic point from the bay side of Dog Island, within the Apalachicola delta (White et al. 1995:Figure 17), and Early and Middle Archaic points from the barrier formation at Tyndall Air Force Base, 50 km northwest of Apalachicola Bay (Brown 2015). This is a small but real body of evidence from today's coast, which would still have been far inland when Early Archaic people lived there, as post-Pleistocene sea level rise did not happen overnight. Offshore about 8 km (5 mi.) in neighboring Apalachee

Bay, 100 km to the northeast (see Figure 3.1), underwater archaeologists have found Early Archaic deposits with Bolen Beveled points along the paleochannel of the Aucilla River (Faught 2004), with possibly associated oyster shells.

Projectile Points, Dates, and Other Chipped Stone
Early Archaic points show what some consider a decline in flintknapping quality. They appear cruder, are often minimally finished and are hard-hammered, contrasting with the earlier elegant, pressure-flaked lanceolate Paleoindian points. However, Archaic points may reflect a change in the nature of the artifact from an object tied with status or ceremonial systems to a mundane tool just needed to get the job done, like so many other things, from the fork to the automobile, have shifted over time in meaning from unusual to mundane. Or perhaps these points were more beautiful to their makers than to our modern eyes, as are styles of new but faded, shredded blue jeans. We can only guess whether Archaic points represented revisions of hunting, butchering, or other tasks, though they were still spear or dart points, since bows and arrows came later. They are often small, perhaps reflecting the frugal nature of users continually sharpening them down for reuse instead of throwing them away.

Bolen points are the most recognizable Early Archaic types. Big Sandy, Kirk Corner-Notched, Lost Lake, and others seem to be alternate names for the same types. Beveled points such as Bolen and Hardee are beveled on the left side of both faces, like the one drawn at the opening of this chapter. This shape may be attributed to human handedness; 90% of us today are right-handed. The beveling could be for aerodynamic properties such as spinning, but experimental work shows that the spear will flex and spin independent of point form, and the point will not cause spin during the throw but might do so within the flesh target (the researchers used melons; Pettigrew et al. 2015). Laudable efforts to refine point typologies have a long history. An early study of beveled Big Sandy/Bolen points in northwest Florida (Lazarus 1965), including nine from the Apalachicola valley, determined that they were of fairly consistent dimensions, though more variable than those in the Alabama point guide (Cambron and Hulse 1964). Most likely a general side-notched beveled point and its un-beveled companion were popular standardized traditions spanning a great temporal and spatial range. The Wacissa point is also a good candidate for Early Archaic; the one in Figure 4.4b is beveled and has serrated edges. Beveling is rare after the Early Archaic.

Some good Early Archaic dates are now available from close to the research region. The Page-Ladson site, underwater in the Aucilla River 115 km to the east, was described in the previous chapter for its astounding Paleoindian evidence. Above that, in good stratigraphic context, Early Archaic deposits with Bolen points were radiocarbon-dated as old as cal 9,959 BP or 7959 BC. The corner-notched and side-notched Bolens, Beveled and Plain, were associated with chert preforms, possible adzes, stone wedges, antler tool handles, a bone pin, worked wood including carved stakes and a chop-marked cypress tree, hearth features, and the first bola stones recovered in controlled provenience. Animal remains included a drilled turtle shell and a worked partial deer skull possibly made into a cup, as well as deer and other bone food debris. A major site function was probably woodworking (Carter and Dunbar 2006). The Sloth Hole site, another one on the Aucilla with a major Paleoindian component, also has Early Archaic deposits, with 17 Bolen points and a possibly associated bobcat jaw carved in geometric patterns (Largent 2004). Other Aucilla Paleoindian sites have Bolen components left by people living around the permanent water sources of the sinkholes, possibly closer than did the Paleoindians because the large mammals that made the sinks dangerous were no longer around (Halligan 2012:309). Two other sites that have produced nearly identical dates and Early Archaic materials similar to those from Page-Ladson are the X-156-1 site (8Le2105) near Tallahassee, with Bolen points, unifacial scrapers, adzes, and apparently fluted preforms, and the Warm Mineral Springs site in southwest Florida, 6 m underwater, that had a human burial (Carter and Dunbar 2006:512).

Several Early and Middle Archaic habitation sites in Florida have cemeteries, with burial of the dead in ponds or wetlands. The most spectacular is Windover (8Br246) near the Atlantic Coast at Cape Canaveral, 485 km southeast of this book's research region. Windover burials in the wet, anaerobic conditions preserved Early Archaic human skeletons, soft tissue including brain matter, and organic artifacts from up to 8,100 years ago (Doran 2002). Interestingly, the abundance of normally perishable remains was accompanied by amazingly few stone tools—only five chert bifaces, a flake, and a limestone abrader. Three bifaces were points with long, straight rectangular stems, which fit into the type Florida Archaic Stemmed, except that one, accompanying a burial of a 47-year-old woman, was beveled. Both this point and another one buried with a middle-aged man had pitch or asphaltum on the stem, used as a glue for hafting. These specimens do complicate our interpretation of how to designate the Early Archaic merely by point types. They also show how many sites might be missed or deemed insignificant because so little of the material culture was of stone and nothing else survived.

Biface caches in the South have been attributed to the Early Archaic. They are clusters of large chert ovoid bifacial artifacts that might be preforms for later tool manufacture, or actual tools, or ceremonial items. At least two such caches are known from the Apalachicola–lower Chattahoochee region. On the west side of the lower Chattahoochee, the Ragland Foundation site (8Ja1846) cache had five bifaces 17 to 19 cm long, 7 to 8 cm wide, and 2.3 to 3 cm thick (Byrd 2009). From St. Vincent Island's Paradise Point site (8Fr71) came 15 bifaces of about equal size (White and Kimble 2016). Hub Chason (1987) recovered at least four such generic bifaces from the Chipola River. These artifact clusters or caches can also occur in Early and Middle Woodland.

Other chipped stone artifacts—scrapers, debitage—are part of the Early Archaic assemblage. The heavy unifacial scraper/core known as the "horse's-hoof core-plane" (Warren 1963), a potentially Paleoindian artifact (see Figure 3.7), and related to Kelly's (1938) concept of the aged, "rotten" flints he saw on the Macon Plateau, could also be Early Archaic, as could the Aucilla adze (see Figure 3.9). Such heavy woodworking tools would have been needed if forests were expanding in the Early Holocene. Kelly's (2010) definition of this whole ancient lithic industry is somewhat loose, but the deeply buried, heavily weathered "Old Flint" material was preceramic and included beveled points. Bullen (1975a:52) thought Bolen points were the most patinated in any collection, but rates of weathering and patina formation are so far not determinable.

Ground-Stone Artifacts

Ground-stone tools, important in definitions of the Archaic, are said to indicate more plant use. Nuts were cracked open and seeds pulverized into gruel, but also meat can be tenderized and fish paste or bird-liver pâté can be mashed with quartzite cobbles. In the Apalachicola–lower Chattahoochee region most ground-stone tools are rounded cobbles with use wear, which occur in all time periods, as do hones or abraders, usually irregular sandstones or limestones with worn grooves from sharpening bone or wood implements. The bola stone is a well-made ground-stone Early Archaic artifact. It is pear- or egg-shaped, with the wider end rounded or gently pointed and the smaller end often concave, leading to its also being called a "dimple-stone." The first in-situ occurrence of a bola in datable context, with a diagnostic artifact assemblage, was on the Aucilla River in the Page-Ladson site's Bolen-age deposits (Carter and Dunbar 2006). Neither the function of the bola nor the reasons for its shape are known. Bolas have been called "sling-stones," objects swung around in leather thongs and hurled at the legs of game animals to bring them down (Milanich and Fairbanks 1980:39). They could also be net sinkers or other weights or plummets, gaming stones, or charms.

While the three Aucilla bola stones and two preforms are of limestone, the five examples in the Apalachicola–lower Chattahoochee region are of quartzite (Figure 4.5). They occur from the lower Flint to the coast ("Bs" on Figure 4.1). One from near Spring Creek in the Flint-Chattahoochee forks was associated with a Dalton and several Early Archaic points, all recovered by an avocational whose collection included over 1,000 points (Hunt 1975).

Another, found by a diver in the upper Chipola at the HJ-AU Rocky Creek site (8Ja2040), is smooth, pale quartzite weathered tan and gently pointed on the wider end, with a concave, truncated narrower end. This site, at Chipola Mile 58 or 86 miles (140 km) upstream from the coast, also produced Clovis, Chipola, and Archaic points. A similar bola stone was reported by a diver who got it underwater farther up the Chipola near the Peacock Bridge site (8Ja433), which also had Paleoindian and Archaic points. On the west side of the Apalachicola River mouth, a bola stone found in the mid-nineteenth century at the Pierce Mounds complex (8Fr14) is now curated in the British Museum. Its accession card reads "Pres[ente]d by A.W. Franks, Esq. Oct. 20. 1869. Waters. [probably the dealer] Florida, N. America Pale coloured egg-shaped Stone (artificially formed) conical at the larger end, & having a small concavity in the smaller. L. 2 ¼ in, D. 1 ½ in. Found in a 'shell bank' (?) at

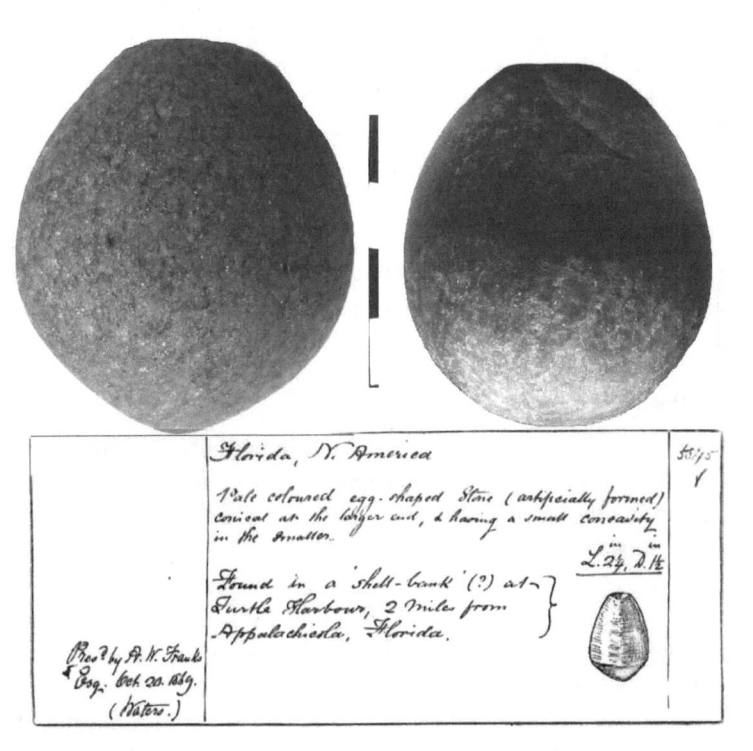

Figure 4.5. Bola stones from the region: *top left*, from upper Chipola River bottom at HJ-AU Rocky Creek site (8Ja2040; private [HJ] collection); *top right*, from Eight Mile site (8Fr55) on Apalachicola bay shore (private [JM] collection); *bottom*, from shell ridge at Pierce Mounds complex (8Fr14) at mouth of Apalachicola River, shown in drawing on 1869 British Museum accession card. (Nancy Marie White)

Turtle Harbour, 2 Miles from Appalachicola [*sic*, meaning the town]." It is similar to the Chipola specimens. Finally, 13 km (8 miles) west-southwest of the river mouth, another, similar bola was recovered on the bayshore at the Eight Mile site (8Fr55). The bola demonstrates proficiency in grinding hard rock into a standardized shape. It may be the oldest ground-stone tool in the South, representing a horizon of a brief but distinctive technology.

Perishables

Most Early Archaic material culture was of softer, now-decayed materials. A glimpse is available at Windover (Doran 2002), where the wet-peat pond deposits contained 119 artifacts of faunal material: bone pins, points, awls, a dagger, needles, and a hooked barb; antler atlatl handles and cupped hooks, points, and a flaker; and cutting or engraving tools made of dog and shark teeth. Many of these had traces of asphaltum adhesive, and several of the atlatl parts had segments of wooden shafts. There were also turtle-shell containers, bird-bone tubes with elaborate carving in geometric patterns, wooden stakes, a wooden pestle, sharpened cane fragments thought to be snare triggers, fabric and matting, and tree branches stacked over the burials. The textiles demonstrated sophisticated tight-weave technology using palm or palmetto fibers; one was a fine-mesh bag enclosing an infant skeleton. Tanned deer hide enmeshed with fabric wrapped some burials. These constitute the largest collection of prehistoric textiles in the Americas and show exceptional diversity. Equally ancient sites in the western United States have produced organic artifacts such as woven cloth, bags, footwear, even fiber figurines or dolls that were preserved in dry contexts.

Middle Archaic in the Region

As with the Early Archaic and Paleoindian time periods, the Middle Archaic is lacking in extensive material evidence, yet we have far more in recent years. Defined as stretching from about 8000 to 5500 BP or 6000 to 3500 BC, the Middle Archaic may correspond with the Hypsithermal or Holocene Climate Optimum, a warmer, dryer time that might have triggered changes in human adaptations. In the South, the earliest shell midden sites are known from this time, attributed to the warmer temperatures and rising sea levels that backed up rivers into estuaries featuring shallow aquatic resources. However, coastal adaptations were probably as old as the earliest people, who could themselves have confined waters into pools to hold fish and enhance shellfish growth, though any signs of this are long drowned by sea-level rise.

The Middle Archaic is recognized from diagnostic points, usually with short or small stems (Figure 4.6 and Figure 4.7). Types include Abbey, Benton, Boggy Branch, Cottonbridge, Elora, Eva, Halifax, (Florida) Hamilton, Hills-

Figure 4.6. Middle Archaic points: *left*, Marion, from Dan Gray site (#8Ja520-2) on the Chipola; *right*, Kirk Serrated (note black tip) from Eight Mile site, on the Apalachicola Bay shore (#USF JC-8Fr55-13-1.26). (Nancy Marie White)

Figure 4.7. Middle Archaic points from coastal sites, USF JC collection: (a–g) from St. Vincent 5 site: (a) Sumter (?) of translucent chert (#8Fr364-15-1.77); (b) Abbey (#8Fr364-15-1.79); (c) Ledbetter? of agatized coral and (d), Ledbetter? (#8Fr364-15-1.84); (e–g) Benton (#8Fr364-15-1.96); (h–i) from Eight Mile Point site: (h) Marion (#8Fr55-13-1.20); (i) Levy (#8Fr55-13-1.29). (Nancy Marie White)

borough, Kirk Serrated/Stemmed, Ledbetter, Morrow Mountain, Pickwick, Savannah River, St. Albans, Sumter, Sykes, Thonotosassa, White Springs, and varieties of Florida Archaic Stemmed (Alachua, Levy, Marion, Putnam). Type definitions overlap, so classifying individual specimens can be difficult. In addition, several of these types hold on into Late Archaic and beyond.

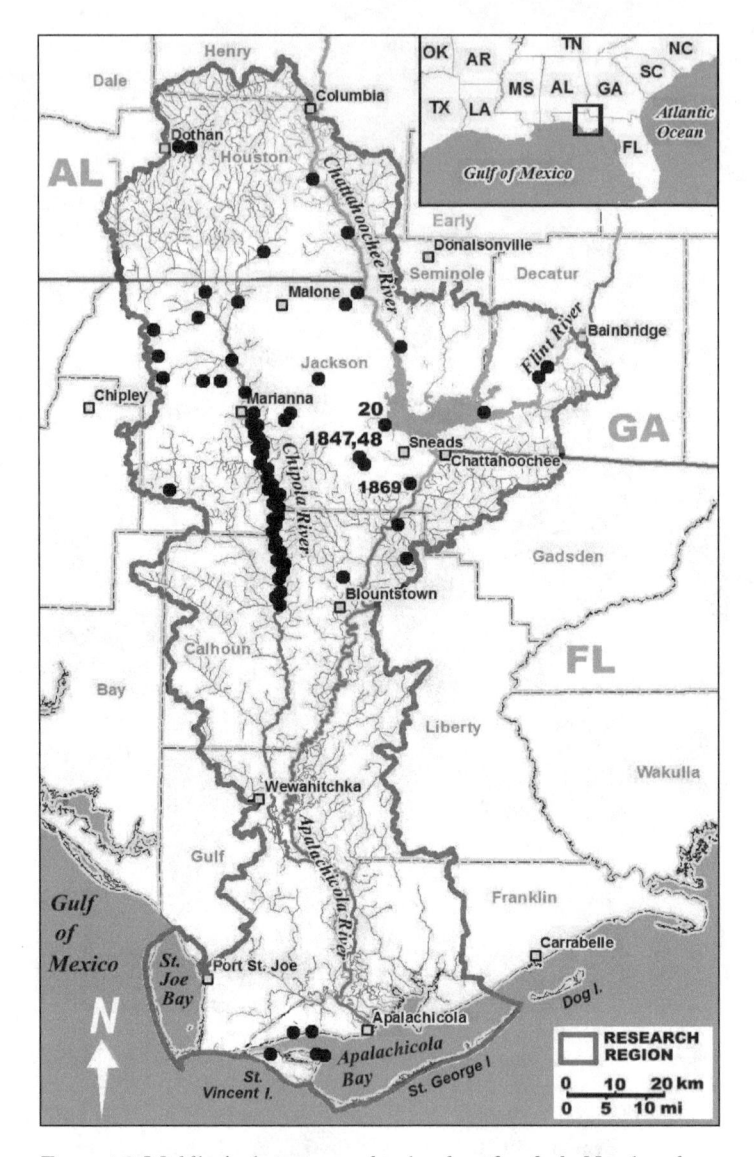

Figure 4.8. Middle Archaic sites and isolated artifact finds. Numbered sites are discussed in the text. (Nancy Marie White)

A possible sea-level stand 1–2 m higher than at present, at around 6200 to 4900 BP (Balsillie and Donoghue 2004) may mean that coastal Middle Archaic sites within the Apalachicola–lower Chattahoochee research region are well inland today. Deep testing could probably show that shell middens were developing by this time, along both rivers and bayshores. The oyster shell in Apalachee Bay noted previously dates to around 7800 BP, and also the

Econfina Channel site, 5 km offshore in Apalachee Bay, produced a Middle Archaic Putnam point and abundant quarry debitage from what would have been a terrestrial site near a spring run, with evidence for subsistence on marine resources too (Cook Hale et al. 2018). West of the research region 170 km, shell middens are dated as early as 7200 cal BP on Choctawhatchee Bay (Saunders and Russo 2011:42–43). Offshore from Louisiana on the continental shelf, a *Rangia* clamshell midden along a buried, submerged river channel is dated to over 8000 BP (Pearson et al. 2014).

Settlement Pattern
Unfortunately, no clearly Middle Archaic dates are known from the research region, with the possible exception of one from an unusual feature. Furthermore, the distribution of known Middle Archaic sites in the region (Figure 4.8) is surely unrepresentative, with fewer (about 90) than for any other time period. The same biases apply as for Early Archaic: more sites in the upper valley's plowed fields; less information from the Alabama and Georgia portions of the region; ambiguity on what diagnostics actually define the Middle Archaic; and the obscuring of sites by river movement and delta formation that left many deeply buried. Shallower sites, on less changed landscapes, were attractive locations disturbed by later peoples whose materials were mixed with the earlier cultural deposits. Finally, again, most Middle Archaic finds are underwater in the Chipola River, where more people collect artifacts. Chason's (1987) 430 points included up to 45 that could be labeled Middle Archaic. Collections from the Keene sites (8Ja1847 and 1848) on old river channels in the upper Apalachicola include among the total 862 points about 145 that are definitely or possibly Middle Archaic (Kelley 2013).

Site locations are on waterways and springs, bayshores, both mainland and St. Vincent Island, and even rarely on the Gulf shores. A point that looks like a Morrow Mountain was reported to me by a resident from the Gulf side of the St. Joseph Peninsula, though the location is not shown on Figure 4.8, and another Morrow Mountain/Putnam point was picked up on the Gulf-facing east side of Dog Island, outside the research area but part of the Apalachicola delta formation (White et al. 1995:Figure 17).

Points and Other Chipped Stone
Middle Archaic points are highly variable and not well dated but are the only indicators so far for this time period beyond chronometric dates. Demarcation of the end of the Early Archaic and beginning of the Middle Archaic is also ambiguous. We do not know whether people made new point styles to hunt or do other tasks differently, or whether the plethora of new types indicates more cultural diversity or more labor specialization, or whether the shift from notched to stemmed bases is significant beyond just style. If both hardwood

and pine were expanding in warming Middle Holocene forests, perhaps subsistence strategies called for newly designed tools. Elsewhere in Florida, greater use of silicified coral is seen during the Middle Archaic, corresponding with an increase in thermal alteration (heat-treating) that flintknappers did to work the stone more easily (Austin et al. 2014). These trends have yet to be confirmed in the Apalachicola–lower Chattahoochee region.

The limitations of existing point typologies render some individual site classifications tentative. One type in great need of refinement is the Florida Archaic Stemmed (Bullen 1975a:32), with its subtypes Putnam (rounded-base stem); Levy (stem with incurving sides, straight or convex base); Marion (stem with excurvate sides, straight base); and Alachua (stem with straight sides, straight base). With so many varieties, named after Florida counties beyond whose boundaries they regularly occur, a lot is fit into this broad type. Middle Archaic points continued to be spear or dart tips, though a minority opinion is that the bow and arrow first appeared sometime during the Archaic (Bradbury 1997). However, physical experimentation and other studies have still not demonstrated how to distinguish between spear and arrow points except perhaps by maximum size or weight that an arrow shaft can hold, and small spear points could be those sharpened down and reused often or could even be for kids. A few other chipped-stone artifacts may be Middle Archaic. Heavy woodworking tools and drills were known since Paleoindian times; some with Middle Archaic–looking drill bases have been recovered from the Chipola River.

The Atlatl and Bannerstone

The atlatl or spear-thrower, which probably came to the Americas with the first Paleoindians, was known in the Paleolithic worldwide. Charles Darwin recorded aboriginal people using throwing sticks in Australia in 1836 (Whittaker 2010). Atlatls come in an amazing variety of shapes. The name is from the Nahuatl language spoken by Aztecs, who used them to propel spears or darts. Usually the atlatl itself was a flat wooden stick that would decay. However, the handle at one end and hook at the other to hold the spear shaft might have been of antler or other materials that preserve better. The spear might also have had a foreshaft affixed behind the point to provide an easier breaking spot and protect the more expensive stone tip. The whole composite kit could be assembled and adjusted for different uses. No artifacts like these have been recovered in the Apalachicola–lower Chattahoochee region.

However, the bannerstone, thought to be an atlatl weight, is well known in the region (Figures 4.9, 4.10). Atlatls probably continued to be used beyond the time that the bow and arrow appeared, which was most likely during the Woodland period. But bannerstones first appeared in the Middle Archaic,

Early and Middle Archaic Periods

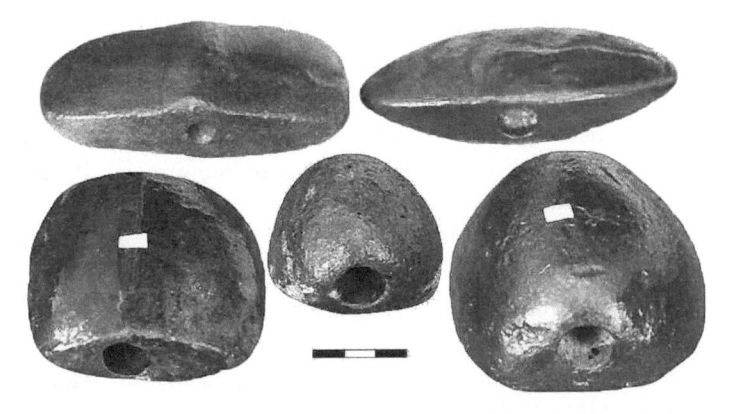

Figure 4.9. Bannerstones from the Chason collection, Chipola River. White squares show repairs. (Nancy Marie White)

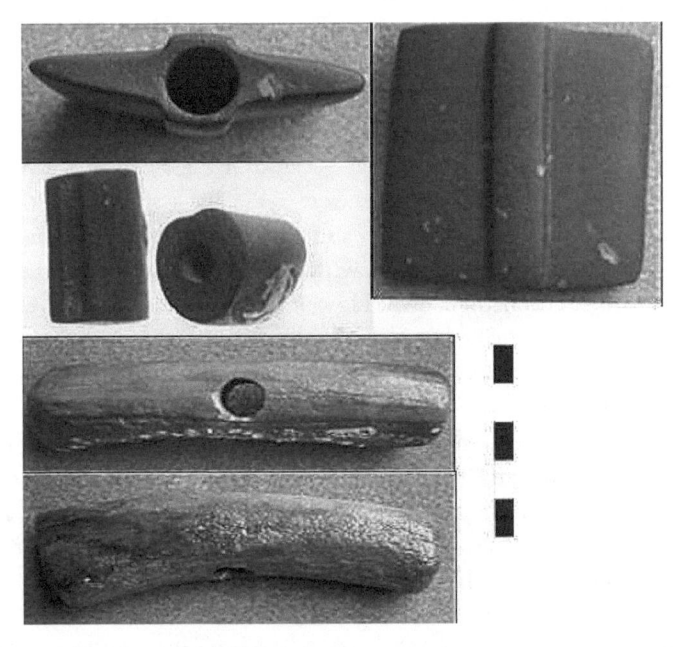

Figure 4.10. Bannerstones, top and side views: *top*, winged shape from Peacock Bridge South 1 site, Chipola River (#8Ja432- HJ2017-277); *middle*, small grooved cylindrical shape, isolated find from St. George Island bayshore (private [AC] collection); *bottom*, cylindrical, of antler, from HJ-A site (#8Ja2069-HJ2017-9), Chipola River. (Nancy Marie White)

possibly lasted through Late Archaic, then disappeared (Kwas 1982). They are fascinating artifacts found throughout the East whose function and age are continually debated. Made by grinding sandstone, limestone, quartz or quartzite, banded slate, or other hard material, bannerstones come in various sizes, and their forms can be winged, cylindrical, L-shaped, flat, round, crescent, or oval. They are usually bilaterally symmetrical, with a hole up the middle 1 to 2 cm in diameter. They show prodigious creativity and skill and probably required immense patience to make, with the tedious jobs of bashing the rock to rough out a form, then pecking and grinding away until the desired configuration was reached, then more grinding maybe with a hollow cane and sand to drill out the hole, then polishing the whole thing. Collector Hub Chason obtained five bannerstones from the Chipola River. Another collection from the Chipola had six more, including one of antler. A specimen from the St. George Island bayshore is very small. Bullen (1958) got a fragment of a possible steatite bannerstone at the Tan Vat site (8Ja20/J-18). Most bannerstones appear to be of foreign rock obtained from far upriver.

The bannerstone was so named because it could be more than just a utilitarian object and once was thought to be maybe the top of a ceremonial staff. Now it is considered to be an atlatl weight since some were found positioned next to atlatl hooks (made of antler) in Shell-Mound-Archaic graves dating as early as 5700 BP along Kentucky and Tennessee rivers (Webb 1957). A bannerstone may have given more power to the throw by its weight but also may have been a status or identity marker. Because of the association with spear-thrower prowess, bannerstones once were typically associated with men as hunters, and when found in women's and children's graves, were said to show status the women got from affiliation with some man (Kwas 1982), as opposed to anything they did on their own. However, if earlier prehistoric cultures in the Southeast were matrilineal, as were historic Indians, then family association would be through women, and these artifacts could have marked clan membership. Also, given the composite nature of the spear and atlatl package, the whole kit, whose purpose is to give more power and accuracy to the throw, would have been adjusted for people of different sizes, strengths, and skills, including women, as would be possible for any weapon set (Doucette 2001).

Some think that proficiency with a bow and arrow is easier to attain than with a spear and atlatl (Whittaker 2010:213). Others suggest that the spear-atlatl combination was easier to learn, could be used well at an earlier age, and could have been wielded effectively by a wider segment of the population than bows and arrows; so atlatl use might have been associated with more egalitarian society (Grund 2017). The laborious grinding to make bannerstones might have been a safer task for those doing childcare than is flintknapping, when sharp, dangerous chips fly around. Throwing a projectile using an atlatl does require upper body strength, precision, and practice. I have seen experts propel a spear into the heart of a hay bale as if pitching a fastball strike, and throw distances average 10 to 30 m (Whittaker 2010:213). Atlatlists have developed the practice as a sport, with organized competitions, which may help us understand ancient use of these devices. One champion thinks bannerstones do give a decided mechanical advantage but would not have increased distance or accuracy. He fashioned his own bannerstone using only materials available to Archaic craftworkers, needing over 10 hours just to drill the hole 2.8 cm long and 1.4 cm wide. He thinks they would have served best as a counterbalance on the atlatl shaft, taking weight off stressed muscles and allowing the user to remain motionless longer in "pre-launch" position while waiting for the best shot (Kinsella 2013). A heavy weight might help balance, but other avocational archaeologists who make and use atlatls think that the weights are clumsy and hinder the throw (Jeff Whitfield, personal communication 2016). Online videos show good performances using spears and atlatls without any weights. One features a seven-year-old with equipment tailored to his size easily bagging a doe at 20 yards (complete with music from the movie *Rocky*) (Wide Open Spaces 2017).

The best explanation for bannerstones may be that they had both technological and social or magical/spiritual importance (Hall 1997). Maybe they designated hunting honors, but in Kentucky and Alabama they were in graves of men, women, and children, even infants, and were conspicuously not associated with points that might be part of the spear-atlatl combination, unless they were wood or bone points that did not preserve. Further, most bannerstones at these sites were from nonburial contexts (Kwas 1982). Northeast Florida Archaic bannerstones and miniature bannerstones found on the chests of burials or as isolated finds are also not associated with points and could be parts of necklaces (Brookes 2001). The lack of associated points, occurrence exclusively in the eastern United States and not in the rest of the world where spear-throwers are used, uneven distribution throughout the South, and frequent association of a specific shape with a specific raw material might mean that bannerstones were products of craft specialists and were used to express power or status (Brookes 2004).

Other Ground Stone and Unusual Features
Quartzite cobbles and pebbles, sometimes with use wear, from Middle Archaic sites indicate hammering, grinding, and drilling. Hematite for coloring things red, grainy or as unmodified pebbles, is also known. Unusual features are a so-far localized but interesting phenomenon dating to near the end of the Middle Archaic, unearthed at the McKinnie site (8Ja1869) on the upper Apalachicola. The site is 150 m in from the riverbank up a spring-fed creek, at the base of the first terrace. It is a multicomponent camp with a little Early Archaic and considerable Middle Archaic evidence, as well as ceramic Late Archaic, Woodland, and Fort Walton components. The collector's points include seven Early Archaic Bolens and Kirks and 15 Middle Archaic: Sumter,

Morrow Mountain, Hamilton, and Thonotosassa. During his digging, the collector recognized 22 small features that looked like hand-scooped pits extending into the hard clayey-sand subsoil. Each feature contained similar materials: chert flakes and/or a broken tool or point, shiny black hematite stones, quartzite shatter fragments, smooth river pebbles (some battered), soft red or yellow ocher, and charcoal. He had bagged materials from each feature separately. During our testing at the site, another such feature was exposed eroding out of the creek bank, extending 7 cm below the midden stratum. It had vague outlines but contained similar objects, including a Hamilton point (see Plate X; note dark-red, glassy inclusion at the break). Charcoal from this feature dated to cal 3630–3375 BC, at about the Middle/Late Archaic boundary (Prendergast 2015). This is the earliest radiocarbon date from the Apalachicola–lower Chattahoochee valley research region.

Ethnographic and archaeological literature was explored to try to interpret these features, which are so far unknown anywhere else in the region. Prendergast (2015:124–125) noted that they were probably not medicine bundles, bags of sacred objects, but may relate to processing or use of the ocher pigment, which was not found elsewhere at the site. They could be from a ritual, though the contents are really mundane items. Perhaps they denoted rites of passage in which the pebbles smoothed something, skin was colored red, the sharp flake or point cut something, and the charcoal came from burning something specific. Possibilities are a birth or coming of age ceremony, commemoration, or seasonal offering of items used in the previous year. The site's late Middle Archaic to Late Archaic use could be tied to its increasing attractiveness as the creek and adjacent wetlands developed during the Holocene.

Early and Middle Archaic Lifeways

Subsistence and Resource Use

Without plant or animal remains or excavated data on site layouts, we can only imagine how Early and Middle Archaic people lived in the research region by using related information from elsewhere. Reconstructions of hunter-gatherer-fisher lifeways based on archaeological and ethnographic data are discussed in the previous chapter. The traditional interpretation of the Archaic has been that people were no longer ranging great distances to follow herds, but settled into local environments, moving less often, accumulating substantial midden deposits. If populations were becoming denser and more territorially restricted, the Archaic may have seen increased use of traditional foods and first use of new ones (Milanich and Fairbanks 1980:50). Coasts were still distant from modern shorelines and still unstable until sea level rise slowed at about 8000 BP to something near its current rate (Halligan 2012:45). Local environments were becoming warmer and wetter and presumably more desirable. While canoes had already been used for millennia, some of apparently more complex design occur by the Middle Archaic (Wheeler et al. 2003), possibly resulting from thousands of years of technological innovation and responses to changing aquatic systems.

Across the South, nuts and acorns were important resources during the Archaic, as well as fruits and seeds from weedy plants. North Alabama rockshelters have produced abundant floral remains including mulberry, grape, wild squash, chenopod, hazelnuts, and black walnuts, as well as nonfood plants such as cane, used for torches and other artifacts (Hollenbach 2009). By the end of the Middle Archaic in the midcontinent, people were going beyond just collecting; they were manipulating three native wild annuals, chenopod, squash, and sumpweed, toward domestication. Mobile forager groups in southwest Mexico were already domesticating maize and squash by 8,000 years ago.

Plant remains at the Early Archaic Windover site in northeast Florida included hickory, pine, magnolia, elm, and other tree and shrub species. A wooden bowl was made of live oak. Remains of grape, hackberry, prickly pear cactus pad, maypop, amaranth, and other flora represent foods. Fragments of an unidentified holly may indicate early use of "black drink" made from yaupon holly leaves (Newsom 2002). Pieces of bottle gourd rind and other nonfood species indicate additional uses of plants for utilitarian and medicinal reasons (Doran et al. 1990). Bottle gourd (*Lagenaria siceraria*) is not typically eaten; today it is mostly used for purple martin birdhouses. It was domesticated worldwide some 11,000 years ago to make containers, floats, musical instruments, and other implements. It is native to Africa, so its presence in the Americas at very early dates is intriguing. DNA research demonstrated that it must have been domesticated early, and the variety that spread in Asia was thought to be the one brought to the Americas (Erickson et al. 2005). But newer genetic study of both modern and archaeological gourds (Kistler et al. 2014) indicates that those in the prehistoric Americas are closer to the African varieties, which could have floated across the Atlantic during the late Pleistocene and gotten domesticated in the American tropics. After that they must have quickly spread as far as Florida by the Early Archaic. Human manipulation of many plant species was probably far earlier than once thought—at least 50,000 years old in southeast Asia (Jones et al. 2016). Other gourds and *Curcurbita pepo* pumpkin, squash, and ornamentals were still wild but used by humans as early as Paleoindian times for artifacts but possibly also for food. Domesticated dogs were probably brought by Paleoindians (Perri et al. 2021). Skeletons of Early Archaic dogs show that they carried heavy loads (Lapham 2011:414).

Meanwhile, though Windover was a cemetery, not a habitation site, and might not have materials representative of how the people were actually living, Windover skeletons show the diversity of Early Archaic diets. Bone-chemistry and archaeobotanical analyses confirm that, for a millennium between 7000 and 8000 BP, the community subsisted by opportunistic use of aquatic resources, probably both freshwater and estuarine, as well as harvesting fruits. There was little evidence of terrestrial animals or marine mammals despite the near-coastal location (Tuross et al. 1994). The increasing availability of shellfish, both freshwater and marine, during the Archaic must have opened new avenues for meals, with broad-scale foraging for what was most abundant and easiest to get, not resource specialization. What technological or dietary changes were necessitated by the evolving and often radically different ecosystems of the Early Holocene are so far unknown for the research region, except that there were no more mammoth steaks.

Sociopolitical and Ideological Systems
Mobility and social organization are similarly not yet able to be reconstructed well for Early and Middle Archaic groups. The notion that they were small, wandering family bands gave way long ago to recognition of the great diversity that probably existed (e.g., Price and Brown 1985). In fact, cultural diversity is an important factor in human resilience amid climate change (Burke et al. 2021). How people were organized across the landscape of the Apalachicola–lower Chattahoochee region, whether in larger or smaller communities, more or less sedentary, or in what different types of settlements, is so far unknown. They were probably still egalitarian societies. The skeletons at Windover included roughly equal numbers of men and women, with bone evidence showing similar workloads for both sexes. In many known hunter-gatherer-fisher societies, men and women do most of the same tasks (e.g., Endicott and Endicott 2008). For example, hunting parties among the Agta of the Philippine jungles can be all male, all female, or mixed, and usually with dogs. One study showed men's hunts obtained meat 17% of the time; women's, 31%; and those with both men and women were the most efficient, at 41%. Only women in advanced pregnancy, the elderly, and the lame did not hunt but performed easier collecting jobs (Estioko-Griffin 1986). Traps, snares, nets, and weirs are other ways to obtain meat. If Archaic societies mirrored ethnographically known cultures, they probably ate mostly plants, fish, and occasional game.

During the Early and Middle Archaic, egalitarian societies may have been evolving toward greater social, political, and ideological complexity. Suggested evidence includes the construction of mounds and earthworks in a few places of the South as well as obtaining raw materials from afar and making elegant bannerstones and other artifacts that appear to be more than utilitarian. However, hierarchical society is not needed to accomplish these things

(White 2004). People were likely organized in small bands of 25 to 50 people, as many foraging societies are, which might then aggregate periodically into "macrobands" for social and celebratory reasons. Models of Archaic foragers' settlement/subsistence patterns have a long history (Kelly 1995). They are all usually variations on the same theme of whether societies had long-term or short-term living sites and how to recognize these, since repeated short occupations, especially during different seasons, can also look like year-round use when the evidence is mixed around in the ground. If one year's hunting/nut-collecting camp becomes next year's base camp, signature features are blurred, such as the percentage of special-function tools, leaving a site with squashed, deflated strata instead of clear layers for each individual occupation. Also, many researchers forget that housekeeping includes sweeping away debris to pile it somewhere else.

Economic and ideological systems in the research region, similarly, can be suggested with reference to what is known elsewhere. Throughout the East there is more burial of the dead by Middle Archaic times, sometimes with artifacts. Deliberate burials at a Miami Archaic site were right below a level that produced a Bolen Beveled point (Carr 2012). At the Windover site at least 168 graves were excavated, constituting about half of those buried there; 60% were adults, most in flexed position on the left side, interred beneath the pond. Stakes marked graves or held bodies down. The dead had been clothed or wrapped in woven textiles, and seeds of grape, prickly pear, and other plants as well as ground fish bone within some could be either gut contents or food offerings. A 30- to 40-year-old man had a bone point stuck in his pelvis, though whether by attack or accident is unknown. A woman had 15 artifacts, more than any other adult, including bone tools and an animal tooth. Adults usually had more grave goods, but a burial of an 11-year-old girl and a newborn had one of the highest counts and diversities of objects in the cemetery, including a stone knife, and bone and antler tools, while the grave of a 2-year-old had beads made from drilled shells, palm seeds, and catfish vertebrae. Antler tools and atlatl parts were often buried with men. In general, the graves contained everyday items but also some fancy things (Doran 2002). The picture is one of social distinctions, possibly ranks, respect for elders or relatives, but not real economic inequality, which is unequal access to necessary resources.

Whether Archaic communities experienced conflict as great as warfare is unknown but improbable, though interpersonal violence is documented in some skeletal remains; real warfare is discussed in the next chapter. Mobile foragers traditionally have systematic means of avoiding conflict, as detailed in the previous chapter. These include institutionalized mutual aid toward those in need and customs of caring for the ill and elderly (Cronk and Aktipis 2015; Lee 1992). Such cultures lasted thousands of years. Ranked societies may recognize the best hunters or tool makers or group organizers, achieved statuses. When these do transform into political leadership or become inherited ranks, such as clan mothers, they are ascribed statuses, but are not necessarily tied to greater economic wealth.

The earliest deliberate construction of earthen mounds is a significant characteristic of Middle Archaic in the Southeast that some researchers have tied to inequality. At Watson Brake, in northeast Louisiana, an oval complex of 11 mounds, connecting ridges, and middens dates to as early as 3500 BC. The site had year-round occupation and broad-spectrum collection emphasizing nuts, fish, deer, small mammals, turtle, dog, freshwater clams and snails, and weedy seeds. The enclosed area was kept clean, possibly for ceremonies. Since some building episodes occurred at times of El Niño–Southern Oscillation (ENSO) events, which are Pacific current shifts causing droughts and other erratic climates, researchers suggest that this great construction project was a ritual response to the stresses of unpredictable food resources (Saunders et al. 2005). Other earthen structures dating to Middle Archaic occur in north and east Louisiana, some with diagnostic points, stone beads, and possible mortuary structures. Equally old are some mounds of shell and sand, sometimes with burials, on Florida's Atlantic and southern Gulf coasts. Because they lacked ceramics, exotic objects, and definitive Archaic artifacts and were built up of shell midden debris, they have not until recently been recognized as deliberate constructions (Russo 1994). These examples are far earlier than when archaeologists once traditionally thought mound-building began. They could indeed have been built for sacred purposes, but also for marking territory, elevating spaces above water, or other reasons, and they did not need hierarchical leaders to organize the construction labor. The Archaic in the research region so far has no such earthworks, mounds, or indications of social difference.

The People
No Early or Middle Archaic human skeletal remains from which we might glean specific health or life-course data are known in the region. Studies from elsewhere in the South give a general picture. Bones of Archaic individuals of both sexes show degenerative joint disease, with arthritis in the shoulder, elbow, and knee (Bridges 1991). Vertebral arthritis in the lower back was common, probably from carrying heavy loads, with asymmetrical patterns probably resulting from being right-handed. Relatively high levels of arthritic neck vertebrae may be due to use of a tumpline or forehead strap to carry burdens. One study showed that men had more broken ankles and women more broken forearms than in later times, perhaps from accidents during foraging (Smith 1996). Archaic peoples' teeth had far fewer cavities than those

of farmers, since they were not yet eating a diet heavy in starches, but they were very worn from grit in the diet. At Windover, among the 168 individuals recovered, some men and women had upper arm fractures, facial wounds, or blunt trauma to the head. About 41% of the skeletal sample showed anemias, and there were also enamel hypoplasia and other indicators of physiological or nutritional stress. Some neural tube defects and dental anomalies possibly reflected unintentional inbreeding in a small population group. The pathologies on some skeletons indicate that persons who were disabled enough to be unable to hunt, gather, or fish were still cared for by the rest of the group.

Comparing chemical study of human teeth from 50 burials and faunal analysis of midden remains from the Tick Island site in interior east Florida, dating to cal 3650 to 4889 BC, researchers found that the Middle Archaic people buried there had mostly eaten local terrestrial and freshwater foods. However, there were six animal species from the coast, which is at least 50 km away, and two people who had migrated from the coast, as well as two others who came from the central Atlantic seaboard area, perhaps as far north as Virginia (Quinn et al. 2008). Demographic, genetic, fertility, and other biological studies of prehistoric and ethnographic foraging cultures indicate that life expectancy was lower than today. However, diets of primarily plants and fresh foods are healthy, and high blood pressure, high cholesterol, and heart problems were absent. Seasonality of resources may have been important to health. Microbiomes of the Hadza, East African hunter-gatherers, showed a cyclical pattern that reflected the seasonal availability of foods. Striking differences in gut microbial communities included the disappearance and reappearance of some taxa according to season, possibly providing protective effects that humans might be gradually losing as they modernize (Peddada 2017). Well-known studies of South African foragers show that women travel great distances daily to get resources. They carry children along and breastfeed for three to four years, only weaning kids when they can walk well enough to keep up. Since lactation inhibits conception, women do not get pregnant during this time, making births about four years apart and fertility rates low. In agricultural societies, soft foods allow weaning at an earlier age, reducing birth-spacing intervals. But contradictions to this classic model are now raised by bone chemistry research that produces once unknowable information about past human bodies. For example, a study of 37 Holocene forager skeletal populations found no difference in weaning ages between them and non-hunter-gatherers. These data suggest that the human breastfeeding period was already shortened by Archaic times (Tsutaya and Yoneda 2013), affecting fertility rates and other aspects of life that had consequences for women and everyone—as populations would be growing.

5

Late Archaic Period, ca. 3,500 to 800 BC

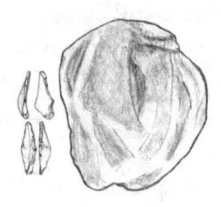

The Late Archaic is recognized by the appearance of various stemmed and notched points, chert microtools, soapstone bowls, and the earliest pottery, thick, fiber-tempered, hand-built vessels. Preceramic Late Archaic is hard to characterize but may be the time of the earliest shell midden accumulations on riverbanks and bayshores. Late Archaic sites occur throughout the Apalachicola–lower Chattahoochee region along waterways; none have mounds or earthworks. At coastal and estuarine shell middens, baked-clay objects show connections with the Poverty Point complex stretching from northeast Louisiana across the Gulf. Radiocarbon dates and biotic studies demonstrate subsistence by collection of local animals and plants in diverse, probably increasingly wetter environments. Seasonal movement must have continued, but reconstructing sociopolitical or belief systems remains speculative. Late Archaic peoples were probably small egalitarian hunter-gatherer-fisher groups.

The Archaic period in the eastern United States was once defined as a time when preceramic, nonfarming cultures continued foraging under modern environmental conditions, with the Woodland period being the time of the earliest pottery and mounds. But Willey (1949:351–352) recognized early that this "preceramic" era "was marked, toward its close, by the appearance of the first pottery . . . a crude fiber-tempered ware." These ceramics are the earliest in North America, appearing some 1,000 years before any in Mexico. Late Archaic projectile point styles, microlithic tools, and clay objects related to the Poverty Point complex stretching from north Louisiana across the Gulf South hint at more subsistence and technological specialization and long-distance interaction. Many Late Archaic sites are shell middens, easier sites to find and with more organic remains since the shell neutralizes the acidic soil and helps preserve bone. Though only a few sites have been tested in the Apalachicola–lower Chattahoochee valley region, we have more data for this time period than for anything earlier.

For Late Archaic in the geographical area encompassing the research region, additional terminology includes "Norwood phase," "Elliott's Point complex," and "Gulf Formational" stage. Each of these names implies something special beyond the generalized adaptation seen across the wider Gulf Coast, and so they are not used here. Regional variation is poorly understood, and giving something a different name means it should be distinct. The first two terms are discussed herein. Gulf Formational is cumbersome for comparison across the South, and "formational" or "formative" imply value judgments about what were the most "advanced" "stages" of a particular culture, ethnocentric concepts we no longer use. An additional proposed term for the later Late Archaic has been "Transitional Period" (Bullen 1959), to mean the time span including fiber-tempered pottery with added sand ("semi-fiber-tempered"). However, at least in the research region, fiber-tempered pottery with added sand is contemporaneous with and might even be earlier than pottery tempered with fiber alone, and most fiber-tempered sherds also contain sand.

Late Archaic Settlement

As for earlier times, many Late Archaic sites in the research region are undoubtedly still buried by alluvial deposits heaped on as the river has moved eastward and built its delta southward, or they are inundated in the Gulf or bays by rising sea level. However, even with so many potentially invisible, they are better known than those of previous periods. Coastal and estuarine sites are mostly shell middens. Inland sites might be freshwater shell middens but are usually in sandy soils exposed by borrow pits or other deep disturbance, often underlying later prehistoric components. Traditional models once portrayed Late Archaic habitation as concentrated on the coast (Milanich 1994), but that was because more sites were known there as more land was exposed by construction.

Also Late Archaic coastal sites appear to have been long-established, not necessarily new groups adapting to changing environments. At least one site, Sam's Cutoff (8Fr754), was abandoned after the Late Archaic because of radically altered conditions. It is an oyster-shell midden rising barely 50 cm above the surrounding estuary, with its dry portion only 56 m north-south by 16 m wide (see Figure 2.13). It is on the east side of the Apalachicola River mouth and has only Late Archaic cultural deposits. Located 700 m from the nearest stream today, it has been nearly submerged by continual sea-level rise combined with the river's movement eastward since the end of the Pleistocene (White 2003a). On the west side of the river, other sites confirm the picture of continually changing hydrology and salinity. Two *Rangia* marsh clam middens are dominated by Woodland deposits that overlie earlier Late Archaic materials having only oyster shells, indicating saltier waters at that earlier time: Depot Creek (8Gu56) shell midden rises 2.5 m from the surrounding swamp and is today over 150 m from the creek (Figure 5.1). Clark Creek midden (8Gu60) rises 2 m (Figure 5.2) and sits 300 m from the nearest tiny creek. Both sites (also in Figure 2.13) became elevated enough for later peoples to return; trails in the figures were made by apiarists who kept bees there to make tupelo honey in the 1930s.

The distribution of known Late Archaic sites/components throughout the research region (Figure 5.3) shows the same biases of uneven survey coverage, site burial, and ambiguous projectile point typologies as for earlier Archaic sites. However, the presence of more diagnostics, mostly fiber-tempered pottery but also chert microtools and steatite bowl sherds, makes recognizing the Late Archaic easier. Of over 110 sites, only 17 are defined by points alone, and most of those are underwater in the Chipola River. Knowledge varies for each site; a few have been tested while others are known from a single surface sherd. The least amount of research has taken place above the Georgia-Alabama border, where survey has usually covered only riverbanks (Belovich et al. 1982). Similarly, the lower valley is so low and wet that most sites known are the more visible shell middens.

Despite these shortcomings, the data are interesting. Late Archaic sites are spread along waterways, many on old meanders that probably were flowing streams at the time of occupation. Interestingly, none are known so far from around St. Joseph Bay, where they may be too deeply buried. But the

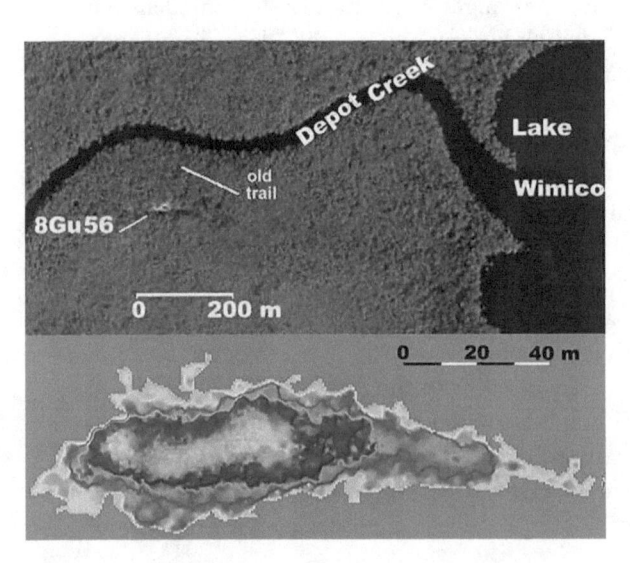

Figure 5.1. Depot Creek site (8Gu56), a mounded estuarine clamshell midden: *top*, Google Earth image with still-visible watery, straight trail running 150 m from the creek to the site (white streak); *bottom*, lidar image by Kaitlyn Kingsland from 2007 NOAA data, with contour interval of 2 feet (0.61 m; the darker the shade, the higher, except for white summit), shows site elevation reaches 2.43 m above surrounding wetlands (compare with Figure 2.13). (Nancy Marie White)

Apalachicola Bay shores on both the mainland and St. Vincent Island have good evidence. Also fascinating, by comparison with site distributions of earlier periods is the higher number of sites along the east side of the valley, especially on the bluffs of the upper and middle Apalachicola. Perhaps this is due to the greater amount of survey there, where surface collection of deflated sites with mixed components often meant a few fiber-tempered sherds lay among later prehistoric artifacts. Or there could be a real reason for increased habitation on these higher elevations, whether for gathering specific resources or avoiding annual flooding.

Sites from the later part of the Late Archaic, during which ceramics were present, have produced good information. At the multicomponent McKinnie site (8Ja1869), 1.3 km up a creek in the upper Apalachicola, a collector dug up a dozen large fiber-tempered sherds, most being vessel bases with partial

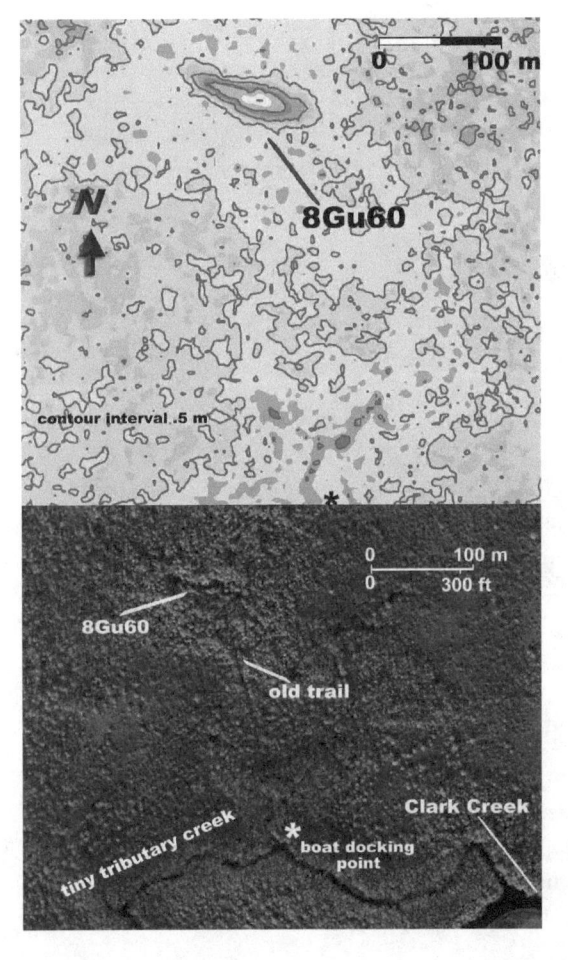

Figure 5.2. Clark Creek site (8Gu60), a mounded estuarine clamshell midden: *top*, lidar image courtesy of Christopher N. Hunt from 2007 Florida DEP aerial data shows site elevation reaches > 2 m above surrounding wetlands; *bottom*, 2007 Google Earth image with still-visible watery, straight-line trail to the site from the tiny tributary creek (compare with Figure 2.13). (Nancy Marie White)

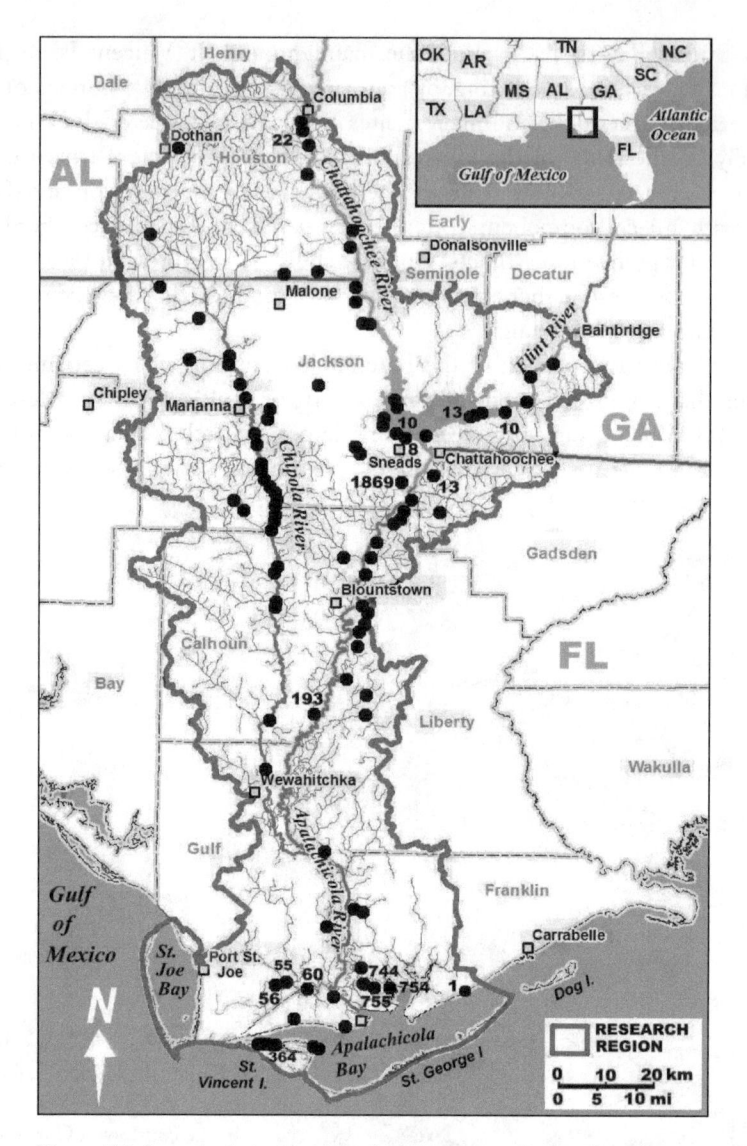

Figure 5.3. Late Archaic sites. Numbered sites are discussed in the text. (Nancy Marie White)

sides; he loaned these for the analysis discussed here. Five sites on St. Vincent Island spread along much of the north shore shell midden ridges produced 551 fiber-tempered sherds weighing 5.28 kg (White and Kimble 2016); three were recovered by our survey and the rest were obtained by collectors over 20 years. These numbers show how intensively some sites were occupied as well as the difference between professional and avocational data.

No evidence for structures or within-site settlement patterns has yet been found. But at the Bayou Park site on Choctawhatchee Bay, 175 km to the west around the Gulf, two possible Late Archaic structure patterns were delimited by postmolds as a 2 m oval and an open rectangle 7 × 2 m. These houses seemed to be arranged in an arc with the open side facing upslope, and midden materials accumulated around them (Austin et al. 2014). They were probably stream-bank dwellings, and the household trash of the middens suggests long or repeated habitation. Similar shelters could have been used in the Apalachicola–lower Chattahoochee region. Comparison of marine foragers' houses in Norway and Tierra del Fuego showed that distinctions between permanent and nonpermanent dwellings were unclear, but house remains were visible for years and attracted later peoples to sites (Fretheim et al. 2016).

As with earlier Native American peoples, those in Late Archaic communities may have seen great environmental change within their lifetimes, maybe adjusting often to moving shorelines. As sea level rose in the Early Holocene, the ancient Apalachicola channel, which today extends south under the bay, filled in and the delta prograded and receded several times between ca. 6400 to 2500 BP. An eastern deltaic lobe existed between ca. 5800 and 5100 BP. Barrier formation began in today's western bay as early as 6400 BP (Osterman et al. 2009). These conditions provided dry, forested land to inhabit, and oysters appeared as early as 5100 BP (Twichell et al. 2010). Interestingly, fiber-tempered pottery washes out of bayshores but is also buried in peat layers on the barrier islands, under dune sands, exposed after storm-scouring. The barriers are only 4,000–5,000 years old, formed as rising seas inundated the former mainland, then winds and waves thrust up sands to make dry land again. As soon as there was some solid surface, humans were there to camp while getting bay and marsh resources.

Dating the Late Archaic

A dozen Late Archaic radiocarbon dates have been obtained for the region, the oldest two possibly indicating preceramic Late Archaic. At the McKinnie site (8Ja1869), as noted in the previous chapter, the small unusual pit feature (see Plate X) was dated to cal 3630–3375 BC with an intercept of 3520 BC, at the Middle-Late Archaic boundary. Another date from this site, cal 1735–1565 BC, came from charcoal 30 cm deep on Floor 3 of TUB, 33 cm horizontally away from a generic, unfinished projectile point. This second date may be preceramic but is within the time frame for ceramic Late Archaic. Though our small tests at the site did not recover any fiber-tempered sherds, the collector had plenty of them, as noted. At Clark Creek shell midden (8Gu60) in the lower valley, described above, the date of cal 2900–1980 BC, with an intercept at 2470 BC, was on charcoal from Level 11, at the water table 165 to 180 cm deep, 15 cm below both plain and Simple-Stamped fiber-tempered ceramics. This date might also be for preceramic Late Archaic, or may reflect an area where people did not leave pottery.

Five other Late Archaic dates are associated with fiber-tempered pottery. Two were run on the actual fiber in the sherds (Prendergast 2015; White 2003a): one from the upper valley McKinnie site (8Ja1869) at cal 1220–1020 BC and one from the lower valley Sam's Cutoff shell midden (8Fr754), at cal 2290–1930 BC. Bullen's (1958) date on the Chattahoochee River 1 site (8Ja8 or J-5) Zone 9, given as 1200 BC ± 250, has a calibrated range spanning over 600 years. Whatever their problems, the dates show that fiber-tempered pottery was manufactured for over a millennium. Burned residue on a steatite bowl sherd from Thank-You-Ma'am Creek site (8Fr755), another estuarine oyster and *Rangia* clamshell midden, provided the latest Late Archaic date at cal 980–830 BC. The sherd was on the disturbed ground surface, but the deposit on its exterior should be contemporaneous with its use (see steatite discussion further on and in Chapter 2). This date suggests that steatite bowls were there at the same time as fiber-tempered pottery, with the disappearance of both marking the end of the Late Archaic.

Lithic Materials and the Possible Preceramic Late Archaic

Projectile Points

Point types diagnostic of the Late Archaic are variable stemmed and notched forms (Figure 5.4 and Figure 5.5). To compile data for Figure 5.3, types used were Clay, Cotaco Creek, Gary, Ledbetter, Wade, Westo, and a few others (Bullen 1975a; Cambron and Hulse 1964; Ford and Webb 1956), but many of these overlap with earlier or later types. In the Apalachicola–lower Chattahoochee region, types specific to the Late Archaic, whether preceramic or ceramic segments, are poorly known. The Chattahoochee River 1 site (8Ja8 [J-5]) was the first Late Archaic occupation excavated in Florida. Bullen (1958:352) said it had more stone tools than any contemporaneous site in the state that he knew of then. It is also the only inland Late Archaic site so far subjected to extensive excavation—4.6 m deep by 15.2 m wide. Zone 9, which was 2 to 2.5 meters deep, contained the Late Archaic deposits, with 23 points and others reworked into large or medium-sized scrapers. They seem (Bullen 1958:Plate 67) to fit within the general Florida Archaic Stemmed type, with small to medium, mostly straight to incurvate-base stems; in the Alabama typology they are Cotaco Creek, Ledbetter, or Pickwick points. Zone 9 also had fiber-tempered pottery. About 1.2 m below it, separated by mostly culturally sterile strata, Zone 14 was preceramic but produced only a scraper, knife, hammerstones, and flakes, and so could have been from any early time

Late Archaic Period

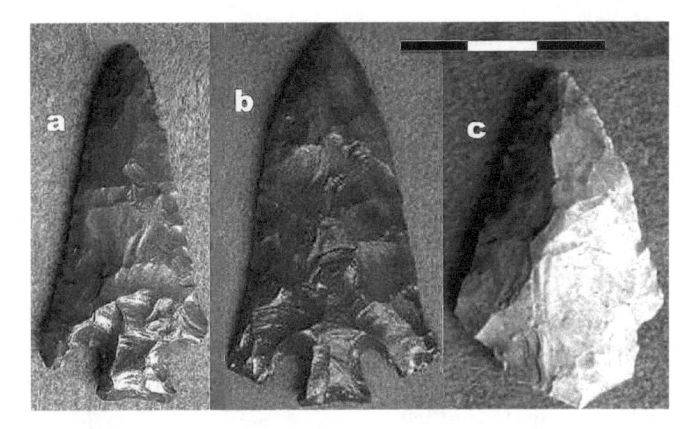

Figure 5.4. Late Archaic points from the Chipola River bottom (private collections): (a) Clay, from HJ-BJ site (8Ca293; photo by Kelsey Kreiser); (b) Clay from Ring Jaw Island site (8Ca92) (photograph courtesy of William Dan Tyler); (c) Westo from Magnolia Bridge site (8Ja437) (photograph courtesy of Kelsey Kreiser).

Figure 5.5. Late (or late Middle) Archaic points: from the McKinnie site, (a, b) two sides of a Levy or Pickwick, from TUB Floor 3 (#8Ja1869-13-69.1), dated 1640 BC; (c, d) two sides of an Ottare? from TUA L5 (#8Ja1869-13-32.4) (photographs courtesy of Eric Prendergast); (e) Ledbetter? from Duncan McMillan site (#8Ca193-98-2). (Nancy Marie White)

period, including preceramic Late Archaic. Bullen said the riverbank stratification suggested that the river channel might have been on the other side of the site during the time of these early occupations, which fits with the picture of continually eastward fluvial migration.

At the McKinnie site (8Ja1869; noted above) in the upper Apalachicola the Hamilton point (see Plate X) could be late Middle or early Late Archaic. Besides abundant points in the private collection, two more uncovered by our work (Prendergast 2015) might be diagnostic (see Figure 5.5). The crudely made or unfinished Levy or Pickwick is associated with the 1650 BC date. The short-wide-stemmed possible Ottare or Paris Island point from TUA L5 was relatively deep and not with any ceramics, and could even be Middle Archaic. At the Duncan McMillan site (8Ca193), in the middle Apalachicola on an old meander 2 km west of the river (White 1999), a shovel test produced a small possible Ledbetter point (see Figure 5.5e). One side of its base is rounded, indicating a stem, and the other is notched; this shape may be the result of damage repair. This point must be Late Archaic since no later materials came from this or another test, which also produced fiber-tempered sherds, lithic debitage, and fired clay bits. Even when found with other Late Archaic diagnostics, the points are ambiguous, but they all seem to have moderate stems with mostly straight bases.

Chert Microtools
One distinctive lithic artifact, the microtool, is specific to the Late Archaic (Figures 5.6, 5.7, and drawn at the opening of this chapter), and appears at coastal and estuarine shell middens. While my work has recovered a couple

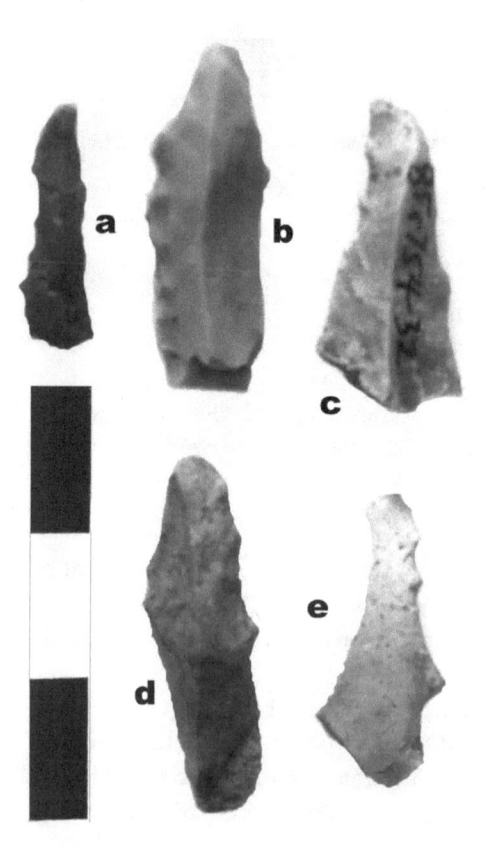

Figure 5.6. Late Archaic microtools from excavated contexts in estuarine shell middens: (a, b) Sam's Cutoff TU1 L3 (#8Fr754-32); (c) Clark Creek TUA L2 (#8Gu60-111); (d, e) Sam's Cutoff TU3 L2 (#8Fr754-41). (Nancy Marie White)

dozen of these from good contexts, one collector has picked up hundreds over the years, including at least 75 from St. Vincent 5 site (8Fr364) and over 200 from the Yellow Houseboat site (8Gu55). An analysis of 23 microtools from controlled proveniences (White and Estabrook 1994) showed that they were consistent with the types established in the Poverty Point and Jaketown complexes of Louisiana and Mississippi. Jaketown perforators and their expended-form variant, blunt perforators, with wide bases and narrow tips, comprised 15 of the 23 tools. Most of the rest were side-scrapers, with a few double-ended perforators and needles. Ford and Webb (1956:79) considered the side-scraper to be a tool-use stage antecedent to the Jaketown perforator.

These incredibly tiny tools, some only 1 to 2 cm long, are usually of local chert, occasionally of other chert or clear quartz. They all have use wear, step and hinge fractures on the edges of the tips or sides, similar to that of Jaketown perforators, suggesting they were for scraping or engraving but not drilling or perforating, despite the type name. They probably were hafted into a handle and might have served to work bone and wood, or scrape or grate roots or tubers. In-depth study of microlithic industries worldwide has

Figure 5.7. Late Archaic microtools from St. Vincent 5 site (#USF JC-8Fr364-15-1-120); collector's numbers on some. (Nancy Marie White)

shown that these little artifacts could satisfy a great range of needs and help adjustment to new resource regimes (Torrence 2002). I think the Late Archaic microtools in the Apalachicola estuarine region were for making wood and fiber fishing equipment and other things needed in these watery environments. Most artifacts would have been of wood, not only because it was cheap but also for convenience: if you drop something out of the boat, it floats and can be recovered. Microcores for microtool manufacture are also at estuarine shell middens. Since microtools and cores occur at Late Archaic sites near the coast, sometimes where no fiber-tempered ceramics are known, they may represent a specific kind of localized activity and/or a shorter horizon within the longer Late Archaic period. Meanwhile, the rest of the lithic assemblage at Late Archaic sites is undistinguished, consisting of (so far) undiagnostic items and debitage, though the chipped-stone waisted adze Bullen (1958:Plate 68l) recovered from Zone 9 at J-5 might be characteristic.

Steatite Bowls

The steatite bowl first appeared in the region, as in the whole eastern United States, during the Late Archaic. Steatite or soapstone is greenish- or brownish-gray, sometimes glittery, and so soft that it is easily cut with a fingernail or wooden tools. It had to be obtained far to the north in the Appalachian Mountains; 67 quarries are known in north Georgia alone (Elliott 2017). Steatite vessels (see Figure 2.6 *right*) were ovoid or circular bowls, often with a flange or lug on each side, presumably for carrying, and ticked lips (tiny notches). Rough vertical striations on exterior surfaces may be from hacking and chiseling them out of the rock and were left unchanged after the interior was smoothed, for aesthetic and/or functional reasons, perhaps more surface area for heating/cooling. Bowl sherds occur at Apalachicola–lower Chattahoochee valley sites from well inland to the coast, though never many. They are from large heavy vessels that would have weighed 9–14 kg (Yates 2000:88). As noted, a good Late Archaic date of cal 980–830 BC came from burned residue on a steatite vessel sherd from Thank-You-Ma'am Creek shell midden. This sherd has a ticked rim and external striations (Figure 5.8) and weighs 78 g; a similar-sized ceramic sherd weighs about 30 g.

Steatite demonstrates Late Archaic long-distance exchange. The bowls represent a new technology and probably arrived already manufactured. No workshop with steatite debitage is known in the research region. Elsewhere in the South the bowls have sometimes occurred in Middle Archaic contexts. West of the region on Choctawhatchee Bay, soot on a steatite sherd was dated to cal 7270–7150 BP (Mikell and Saunders 2007). If that date, some 4,000 years earlier than the one from the Apalachicola region, is correct, it shows really long-term use of this artifact type.

Figure 5.8. Interior and exterior views of Late Archaic steatite bowl rim sherd with ticked lip, from surface of Thank-You-Ma'am Creek site (#8Fr755-7), with black residue dated cal 980–830 BC. (Nancy Marie White)

Steatite vessels are heat-resistant and allow direct cooking over a fire. They might have been for boiling acorn and nut mast, as suggested by residue analysis, and are better thermal conductors than ceramics, though thicker and heavier (Truncer 2004). Traditionally, steatite vessels implied that Late Archaic people were becoming more sedentary, since such heavy objects would have been harder to transport. But archaeological and ethnographic research shows that mobile foraging societies do indeed carry weighty objects as they move around, or else they store them until their return. In the comedy skit *The 2000-Year-Old-Man*, entertainer Mel Brooks remarks that "thousands of years ago, there was no heavy industry" (Brooksfilms Limited 1994); however, hauling around these stone vessels seems like it would have been heavy labor. Steatite bowls disappear after the Late Archaic, perhaps falling out of use when ceramics—lighter, easier, made locally—appeared. However, the two are contemporaneous during the Late Archaic, possibly for different functions, and it is unclear which came first. Though vessels of other rock are known elsewhere in the South, so far only one sandstone bowl sherd has come from the research region, also from the Thank-You-Ma'am Creek shell midden site (8Fr755).

Other Ground Stone
Quartzite cobbles with use wear, smoothed limestones, and sandstone hones for sharpening softer tools appear during the Late Archaic, but also in other prehistoric periods. Stone pipes occur in the South, though none in the research region are known to be this early. Gorgets of flat, oval, and other shapes, usually with two biconically drilled holes, may have originated in the Late Archaic (e.g., Ford and Webb 1956:98–99). Those known in the Apalachicola–lower Chattahoochee region have mostly come from the river

bottoms. Specimens from the Chipola (see Figure 2.5) are of greenstone and other rock, ground into flat, oval, or squared-off forms up to 10 cm long, most with holes at each end. An oval gorget pointed at both ends and measuring 18 cm long was reported from the upper Apalachicola river bottom (H. Means, personal communication, December 2000). Another from the Chipola is oval with rounded ends, nearly 5 cm wide at the center tapering to less than 2 cm at the ends, and a whopping 26 cm long (Louis Tesar and Jeff Whitfield, personal communication 2017). A greenstone pendant/plummet from the Late Archaic component at Clark Creek shell midden (8Gu60) is pear-shaped with a groove around the narrow end for suspension. Pendants and gorgets may have been ornaments or tools.

A significant Late Archaic stone artifact from the research region is a jasper disc bead (see Plate XI) similar to those of the Poverty Point lapidary industry in Louisiana as early as Middle Archaic (Sam Brookes, personal communication 2003). This tiny red decorative object came from the barrier island St. Vincent 5 site (8Fr364). It is one of the proofs of relationships with the Poverty Point interaction network, not only in type but also in raw material, as the distinctive red stone is from Mississippi-valley gravels. Other less fancy ground-stone items must be mentioned again. The previous chapter details the materials in features at the McKinnie site, noted previously, dated to the Middle-Late Archaic boundary. These features were small pits that contained unmodified black shiny hematitic stones, quartzite pebbles, chipped-chert objects, and crumbly chunks of reddish sandstone or red ocher that were probably ground for pigment (see Plate X). The best guess is that they were some kind of ceremonial offerings.

Ceramic Artifacts

Fiber-Tempered Pottery

Willey's comment (quoted above) that fiber-tempered pottery was crude is accurate. It is so ugly that only an archaeologist could love it (Figure 5.9). But it was useful and emerged around 5,000 years ago across the South. Some think it was earlier along the Atlantic and later in the interior (Saunders and Hays 2004), but we have fewer data from the interior. Whatever its origins, it spread rapidly. Vessels were of clay mixed with plant fiber, reported as Spanish moss, palmetto, palm, or grasses, used maybe to prevent pots from exploding during firing (Simpkins and Allard 1986). My work was the first in the region to get ethnobotanical identification and radiocarbon dates on individual plant fibers still amazingly preserved, undecayed, and unburned, in the sherds (White and Estabrook 1994:69). That plant is indeed Spanish moss (*Tillandsia usneoides*), an epiphyte commonly hanging from trees, and the date, as noted, is cal 2290–1930 BC. Bulk sherd organics from the McKinnie site

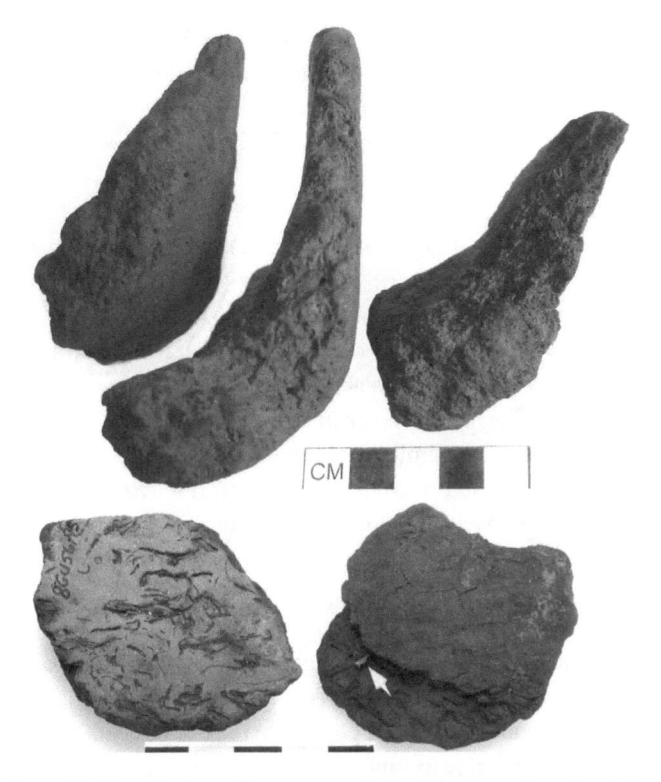

Figure 5.9. Late Archaic fiber-tempered pottery: *above*, three bowl fragments from St. Vincent Island sites (private [JC] collection); side view, showing flat, thick bases and nearly right-angle side walls; *below*, interior and exterior surfaces of sherd from Depot Creek shell midden (#8Gu56-95) with unburned, undecayed Spanish moss fibers (arrow indicates largest) preserved in recently broken edge. (Nancy Marie White)

dated to cal 1205–1055 BC, showing the technology lasted over 1,000 years.

Plain and simple-stamped fiber-tempered pottery are hallmarks of the later Late Archaic in the Apalachicola–lower Chattahoochee region, as well as adjacent areas along the Gulf and well into interior Alabama and Georgia. The pots were hand-molded from slabs, with thick walls (1 to 3 cm or more), even thicker bases, and sides at right or obtuse angles, up to 125 degrees, to the base. This is very different from the coiled pottery made during the rest of prehistoric time in the East. Bullen (1958:338, Plate 68e) recovered one vessel base impressed with woven-splint basketry, suggesting potters might have shaped the wet clay in baskets. The fibers usually burned away during firing, leaving squiggly voids or casts running through the clay, but sometimes surfaces were smoothed to obscure these voids. Exteriors are usually plain, but occasionally were simple-stamped, impressed with a dowel leaving parallel grooves. Fiber-tempered Simple-Stamped sherds in the region have come from only three estuarine shell middens.

Twelve large, chunky sherds from the McKinnie site were studied in detail. They were predominantly from the vessel "heel," where the base and wall meet, with walls between 9.9 and 11 mm thick and bases from 17.2 to 24 mm thick. Prendergast (2015) suggested that the slab construction method made the base-wall joint the sturdiest, most preservable portion. He used pXRF to compare the chemical composition of these sherds with those of 53 other samples, including sherds of later time periods, from McKinnie and nearby sites, and clay samples from 12 locations about every 15 to 20 km along the whole Apalachicola valley. The pXRF instrument measures trace elements in the clays to see if samples have similar or different origins. The McKinnie fiber-tempered sherds constituted a group themselves, not resembling clay in the creek bank or later sherds at the site, nor from any other location or time period in the valley. Their chemically distinct clay was from an unknown source not tested in the study. Such results suggest that all the sherds were from similar vessels brought to the site by mobile peoples. These were large, heavy bowls that weighed about 10 pounds (Kimbrough 1999). But the same consideration applies here as with steatite bowls: foragers lugged them around.

How people used fiber-tempered pottery here is unknown. So far no sherds from the region have exterior residues from sitting right on the fire, though this was supposedly the advantage of ceramics over containers of skin, gut, wood, or basketry. Combined with the technology of fired clay chunks and shaped clay objects possibly also for cooking, which were probably earlier, fiber-tempered pottery probably did usher in changes in food preparation methods.

Food is a conservative part of culture; cooks might resist new methods, but if advantages become clear, technologies can spread rapidly. Heating water for soup or tea or cleaning may have been less important than boiling it to make it cleaner to drink or cooking/soaking foods to detoxify them (Arnold 1993:117). Cooking in a pot allows soaking, stewing, and intermingling of ingredients and juices that are otherwise lost in flames and makes it harder to burn food. Pots might have been valued by shellfish-eaters since the clay caught the tasty clam or oyster liquor (Wilson 2012). Ceramics also withstand rapid temperature change better and can save cooking time and effort. They may allow improved long-term storage for fruits, seeds, and other solid and liquid foods, protecting them from insects, rodents, and dirt. Possibly technological, social, and even ideological factors were significant in the introduction of pottery. But ceramics with fiber or other organic tempering occur often among mobile peoples, as they are easily made and weigh less than stone bowls (Skibo et al. 1989).

Ceramic Nomenclature and Production
Confusion abounds with type names for these earliest ceramics in the region. St. Simons Plain or Orange ware (Willey 1949; Bullen 1958) were the original terms for the plain or simple-stamped vessel. Then it was named Stallings (Fairbanks 1971:38) or "Norwood" (Phelps 1965), and Norwood somehow became a phase name. Norwood is the most poorly defined of several taxa of southeastern fiber-tempered ceramics, yet the name continues to be used without question except when experts notice that Norwood and Orange are essentially the same (Milanich 1994:97). One analysis (Shannon 1987) showed that all fiber-tempered ceramic types were products of local archaeological interpretation, not consideration of a whole tradition, and what is called Norwood is not distinctive, since all the fiber-tempered ceramic series in the Southeast have overlapping attributes or are indistinguishable from one another (like so many other pottery types of all time periods). Distribution maps for the various types show more about where and when research was published than about prehistoric cultures and often have blank spaces for the Apalachicola–lower Chattahoochee region, the entire Gulf Coast, and other areas of the South (e.g., Saunders and Hays 2004). We cannot yet say that fiber-tempered wares in the research region were a tradition diffusing in after developing elsewhere as they appear similar to and as early as those anywhere else in the South.

Exceptions are the Stallings Island/Wheeler types, which are decorated with incisions and punctations or dentate stamping and are found on the Atlantic coast and from Tennessee to north Alabama. Stallings Punctate sherds are known in the Apalachicola–lower Chattahoochee valley region from only three places. Huscher (1959a) recorded an unknown number from the Bullpen site (1Ho22) at the north end of the region; Milanich (1974:37) excavated six from the Sycamore site (8Gd13) in the upper Apalachicola; and two sherds are in a donated collection from the middle valley. Some punctated fiber-tempered sherds came from farther up the Flint River beyond the region (Frank Schnell, personal communication 1981). Meanwhile, as discussed in Chapter 2, the proliferation of "phases" in archaeological description does more to obscure than to inform. The term "Norwood" should be abandoned in favor of "ceramic Late Archaic," and generic type names are best: plain or Simple-Stamped fiber-tempered. While Orange wares on the east coast may have more palmetto-fiber temper, and Wheeler ceramics of Tennessee and north Alabama may have grass fibers (Shannon 1987:49–53), quantitative investigations of temper characteristics could isolate regional differences.

I studied attributes of fiber-tempered sherds from 23 sites in the research region (White 2003b) to investigate this lack of distinctiveness and other characteristics, such as whether adding sand to the clay with the fiber prefigured the emergence of sand-tempered Woodland pottery, as assumed by some researchers and contradicted by others (e.g., Saunders and Hays 2004:11–12). Nearly all of my sample of 200 sherds had some sand in the paste, like most fiber-tempered types (Shannon 1987), which were often originally defined that way (e.g., Wheeler Plain in Alabama: Heimlich 1952:8). A few sherds also had grog, and most had the mica flecks natural to the region's clays. Differing amounts of fiber meant that the sherds ranged from smooth on both surfaces to completely riddled with voids from burned-out Spanish moss strands. Simple-stamping, similar to that on other fiber-tempered wares such as Wheeler in Tennessee and north Alabama, is rare, as noted, and confined to the lower valley. The plain and less sandy-paste sherds were not stratigraphically earlier, logical as it may seem to have both increased sand and simple stamping as transitions into Early Woodland, where those two attributes are widespread. In fact, the simple-stamped fiber-tempered sherds may be earlier. At Thank-You-Ma'am Creek (8Fr755) and Clark Creek (8Gu60) they were deeper in undisturbed strata than sherds with plain surfaces.

Occasionally sherds tempered with something other than fiber are associated with Late Archaic fiber-tempered ceramics in the region. At Bullen's (1958) Chattahoochee River 1 site the Late Archaic Zone 9 had a handful of chalky-paste, sponge-spicule-tempered St. John's sherds that he thought were from peninsular Florida and were contemporaneous with the latest fiber-tempered wares. His date from the site is late, as noted above, and these sherds could be later artifacts mixed in with earlier materials, though Bullen noted that all of Zone 9 was about a meter below the stratum with Early Woodland Deptford ceramics. Early non-fiber-tempered pottery from elsewhere or from local experimentation could have ended up in Late Archaic contexts. At Van Horn Creek shell midden (8Fr744; White 2003a) I recovered two tiny sand-tempered sherds (totaling 1 g in weight) deep in Level 8 (-120 cm), in what appeared otherwise to be undisturbed, submerged Late Archaic deposits containing six fiber-tempered sherds (17 g). The sand-tempered sherds could have come in from disturbance by later people or downward movement of tiny things through the spaces between the packed shells, or crumbs of fiber-tempered pottery that just did not have much fiber. Or, they are indeed evidence of early ceramic production of a different sort, as they are indistinguishable from sand-tempered sherds in later deposits at the site. Until there is better evidence, we cannot date the transition to Woodland sand-tempered ceramics earlier than about 500 BC. Sporadic examples exist of pottery tempered with sand and some tempered with sponge spicules that is roughly contemporaneous with fiber-tempered pottery in south Florida and elsewhere in the South (Saunders and Hays 2004).

Clay Figurines
Figurines in the Late Archaic South are interpreted within Poverty Point–related cultural manifestations as important in symbolic and/or social realms, though they could be toys or just artwork. At Poverty Point they are solid, fired-clay human effigies, often of women, sometimes pregnant, but other times of indeterminate sex, with modeled faces and torsos, clefts across the forehead, but little shaping of the rest of the body. They can have slit eyes or round punctations for eyes, and some have heads broken off. In the Apalachicola–lower Chattahoochee region, so far the only fragment of a clay figurine could be Late Archaic, from the surface of the Clark Creek shell midden (8Gu60). It is more likely Early Woodland.

Poverty-Point-Type Clay Objects
Fired clay balls or Poverty Point objects (PPOs) are other Late Archaic artifacts found in the research region. They are hand-molded chunks of baked clay in forms including biconical, spheroid, cylindrical, grooved-cylindrical, crisscross-incised, squeezed handfuls, and amorphous shapes (Ford and Webb 1956). They occur in the Poverty Point area of northeast Louisiana and along the Gulf Coast, where they are often associated with shell middens, hearths, and earth ovens and found clustered in pits (e.g., Broyles and Webb 1970). Those in the Apalachicola coastal/estuarine area, from a dozen sites, are usually roughly ovoid or melon-shaped, often with finger grooves, like the one from Clark Creek shell midden (8Gu60) drawn at the opening of this chapter, and those from the Porter's Bar site (8Fr1) in Figure 5.10. This variety is one of the most common within Poverty Point assemblages in Louisiana and elsewhere (Gibson 2000), including along the northwest Florida coast (Lazarus 1971). Usually these objects are recovered in pieces and in small numbers. But the 20 from Porter's Bar, on the bay shoreline, were found under nineteenth-century burials eroding out of the multicomponent prehistoric shell midden. They appeared to be a cache (Calvin Jones, personal communication 1993; Knigge 2018) and were evidence of a previously unknown Late Archaic component at this site; collectors found even more clay ball objects there (Tim Nelson, personal communication 2019).

Experts who have long studied these objects speculate that they were for cooking—boiling in baskets or wooden bowls or dry-roasting or steaming meats or shellfish—as well as gaming devices, fishnet weights, or even identity tokens marking pilgrimages to Poverty Point itself (Hays et al. 2016). The wide variety of shapes is sometimes taken as an indication that they are just too elaborate for utilitarian use. However, dry-roasting, keeping meat off the ashes of the fire while heating to high temperatures, is a good explanation of their function and is confirmed by experimental archaeology (Hunter 1975),

Figure 5.10. Some Poverty Point–type clay objects from Porter's Bar (8Fr1), in DHR collections, Tallahassee. (Photograph courtesy of Kerri Knigge Klein)

though steaming, boiling, and slow cooking are equally plausible (Wheeler and McGee 1994). They also could have been toys. We seldom note how much of the material culture that litters human living spaces is children's playthings. Native American communities would have been full of giggling, wiggling, meddling children. These artifacts often have small finger grooves. They are also associated with things like miniature bowls and irregular clay rings (Jahn and Bullen 1978:Figures 21–24). Wet clay is a fun and safe medium for keeping children occupied. When it was time to use these objects to cook they could be heated, then later reused. The different shapes do have different thermal properties and might have been for different kinds of cooking. If they were also ethnic identity markers, all these functions could have combined into a single activity set; today's "Easy-Bake oven" toy actually cooks foods and also is associated with western middle-class culture.

Elaborate varieties of Poverty Point objects are rarer in northwest Florida, though unusual shapes do exist (Woodward 2012) beyond the ovoid, finger-grooved globs of clay in the Apalachicola region. These artifacts were part of a general Gulf Coast Late Archaic adaptation. Austin and colleagues (2014) suggest that the origin of the technology was earlier, in the Middle Archaic, and the thousands of baked clay objects from the Bayou Park site and others around Choctawhatchee Bay, 200 km northwest of the lower Apalachicola, date as early as cal 7270–7150 BP and as late as cal 3637–2997 BP. Mineral and trace element analyses of the objects show that they moved around within the Poverty Point exchange sphere and between the Gulf and northeast Louisiana. At the Poverty Point site itself they are made of local loess, those from coastal Louisiana sites are more sandy, and most in northwest Florida that have been tested were of the local clayey silt (Hays et al. 2016; Tykot et al. 2013). These artifacts may have been in traveling cooking kits brought by people moving around the Gulf, or mementos of a trip to the Poverty Point site itself. At Bayou Park, Austin and colleagues (2014) found no fiber-tempered ceramics but thousands of these clay objects and microliths. This evidence also implies that the notable elements of the region's Late Archaic—fiber-tempered pottery, clay objects, stone beads, microtools—may all have been adopted individually at different times in different places.

Fired-Clay Lumps/Irregular Chunks
Irregular chunks of fired clay are common at Late Archaic sites in the Apalachicola–lower Chattahoochee region, especially in coastal/estuarine settings, but also inland, in features or loose in middens. They may be pieces of Poverty Point–type objects or daub or fragments left over from pottery-making; most have no definable shapes. But some are large chunky pieces with signs of intense heating that might have been for the same kind of dry-roast cooking. Another possibility is that they were remnants of "clay cooking," encasing large hunks of meat or whole animals in wet clay to bake or roast. This method yields tender, juicy meat and is found in many cuisines worldwide (O'Donnell 1969:236), including among historic Native Americans in the Southeast. Mann (2016) calls these chunks "nodules" and has recovered many in Late Archaic contexts in southeast Alabama that he thinks, based on experimental study, resulted from this cooking method. At Van Horn Creek shell midden (8Fr744) a concentration of 0.5 kg of such pieces in the lower levels of Test Unit 4 might represent such cooking techniques or might be fragments of a clay-lined fire pit or cooking surface. Many of the thousands of baked-clay chunks at the Bayou Park site were irregular shapes, some concentrated in features (Austin et al. 2014). At Thank-You-Ma'am Creek site (8Fr755), Parker (1994:164–166) recovered one Poverty-Point-type object as well as many smaller clay chunks, some of which looked to him like they were formed by pressing wet clay into a clamshell.

Other Material Culture

Bone points, long and thin with one or both ends tapered, and at least one engraved bone pin (Figure 5.11) have been recovered from Late Archaic contexts at Apalachicola estuarine sites (White 1994b). Two points came from deep levels at Depot Creek (8Gu56), among the *Rangia* clamshells. A 12-cm-long broken point fashioned from a deer metapodial was in Test Unit A, Level 15 (225 cm depth, 30 cm below ceramic levels), just at the water table. It is grooved down the middle and 1 centimeter thick. The other point, from TU B Level 11, 150 cm deep and 15 cm below ceramic levels, possibly with the proximal end tapered into a chisel, is otherwise similar, 6.4 cm long and 0.9 cm thick. Both points have small cut marks left during manufacture. A similar point came from far inland at Chattahoochee River 1 site (8Ja8 [J-5]), which also produced a worked deer-antler tine (Bullen 1958). These points could be for projectiles, composite tools, fish throat gouges or other functions. The tiny engraved bone pin fragment (see Figure 5.11c) from Van Horn Creek shell midden (8Fr744) is subconical, with six engraved lines encircling it. This pin came from the flotation sample taken below the water table in the nonceramic zone, Level 11. Since a single fiber-tempered sherd was recovered from Level 10, some 15 cm above it, the pin could be from either the ceramic or preceramic Late Archaic. It resembles Archaic engraved pins with symmetrical geometric designs from south and east Florida shell middens (Wheeler 1994:Figure 13C).

Shell artifacts are more numerous than those of bone in Late Archaic estuarine shell middens. They include scoops/spatulas, picks, awls or other pointed columella tools, and debitage. Raw materials are usually lightning whelk, sometimes horse conch. As for other kinds of artifacts, we can imagine the remaining majority of Late Archaic perishable material culture made of skins, gut, fur, feathers, wood, cane, reeds, and other plants. This includes canoes,

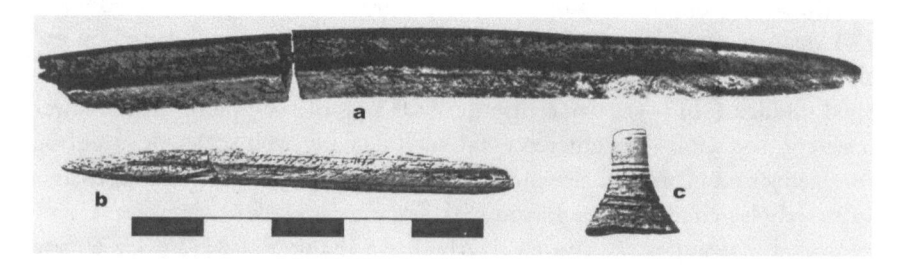

Figure 5.11. Late Archaic bone artifacts from estuarine shell midden sites: from Depot Creek (#8Gu56-87): (a) broken point from TUA L15; (b) point from TUB L11; (c) from Van Horn Creek: broken engraved pin from TU3 L11, below water table (#8Fr744-87-67). (Nancy Marie White)

floats, spears, harpoons, clubs, gigs, cordage, nets, baskets, mats, traps, drying racks, shelters, clothing, bark for paintings or walls, even toys.

Subsistence, Seasonality, Environments

Late Archaic subsistence is well studied all over the Southeast with sizable collections of biotic remains. They show great variability and use of mostly local resources. Hickory nuts, acorns, deer, and other terrestrial mammals and turtles were important, and dog bones within midden garbage (Jahn and Bullen 1978) show that puppy stew was still on the menu. The Late Archaic is the earliest time period in the Apalachicola–lower Chattahoochee research region for which we have identified animal and plant materials. Though only a few sites were tested and only tiny samples were sent for analysis, they give a glimpse into food and environments.

Faunal Remains

Animal remains at inland sites are few due to poor preservation and are all from shell middens. An example is the Chattahoochee River 1 site (Bullen 1958), where the Late Archaic Zone 9 contained diverse species of mussel and snail shells, abundant deer and turtle remains, and a few bones of beaver, lynx or bobcat, muskrat, and opossum. Similar freshwater shell middens were Whaley's Mill site (9Se10), also on the lower Chattahoochee, and Bird Field site (9Se13) and Montgomery Fields (9Dr10; White 2019) on the Flint, all of which were around the river forks. Dug right before dam construction, they received only hurried attention, but they indicate resources easy to get, whether as a dietary mainstay or supplement.

Faunal remains from estuarine and coastal sites are better preserved. Late Archaic components were tested at six shell middens: Van Horn Creek (8Fr744), Sam's Cutoff (8Fr754), Thank-You-Ma'am Creek (8Fr755), Yellow Houseboat (8Gu55), Depot Creek (8Gu56), and Clark Creek (8Gu60). Recovered remains were of deer, opossum, rabbit, raccoon, rodents, alligator, various turtles, a few snakes, birds, and amphibians, and abundant fishes such as croaker, drum, bowfin, jack, various marine catfish, and mullet, as well as the ubiquitous gar fish, and a little seatrout, sawfish, and sunfish. Associated shellfish were marsh clam, both *Rangia* and *Polymesoda*, with a few oysters and crabs. Raw shellfish require sharp, specialized knives and a great force to shuck. If people forced them open, mechanical damage would be prevalent, but it is not, so they were probably steamed, boiled, or roasted open. They may have been dried, smoked, or salted for future use or trade, which would also have reduced their volume and made packaging easier. Also listed among the fauna are sea snails, which prey on oyster and probably came in with the catch, and land snails that may have crawled into middens.

When these six shell middens were occupied, the landscape configuration was very different. The faunal assemblages support the idea, noted above and described in Chapter 1, that the river was farther west during the Middle Holocene and continually pushed eastward by sea-level rise (Donoghue and White 1996; White 2003a). Van Horn Creek and Sam's Cutoff are the two northeasternmost of these sites. At Van Horn, the deep Late Archaic oyster-shell deposits contrasted with the upper, later Woodland and Fort Walton levels dominated by *Rangia* clams. At Sam's Cutoff, farther east, with only a Late Archaic component, the species were all oyster and saltwater fish. Saltier water before 4,000 years ago on the northeast side of the lower valley changed when the river brought more fresh water as it moved eastward. Similar conditions prevailed elsewhere along the Gulf, such as at the mouth of the Guadalupe River in Texas, where a shift in midden composition at site 41CL9 just before 770 BC from oyster to clam shows an influx of fresh water into the estuary attributed to sea-level fluctuation (Gadus et al. 1999:71). The archaeological sites help elucidate the history of delta development.

Floral Remains

From the same estuarine shell middens, plant remains are less illuminating, consisting mostly of oak and pine charcoal and fragments of bedstraw, fern, smartweed, possible wild grape, possible sedge, and the Spanish moss in the sherds. These are more than are preserved at inland sites but can only suggest harvesting a wide variety of plants. Probably acorns, nuts, and fruits were key resources. Some of the weeds may simply be opportunistic species that grew up in cleared areas, but their tiny seeds are edible. Abundant materials from the Late Archaic Bayou Park midden west of the research region (Austin et al. 2014) included hickory nuts. One researcher there had worked in the Caribbean and recognized fragments of possible ceramic griddles. Though no fiber-tempered ceramics were recovered at this extensively excavated site, the possible griddle fragments appeared flatter and thinner among the thousands of baked-clay Poverty Point–type objects and had starch grain residues identified as bottle gourd, hackberry, and possible coontie or zamia, a cycad that does not grow there today.

Indigenous environmental knowledge in the Late Archaic Southeast included manipulation of many species. Domesticated bottle gourds and dogs were already present. Domestication means genetic engineering, cultural selection for desired characteristics. In the Midwest, some crop plants were domesticated between 5000 and 3800 BP: squash, sunflower, marsh elder, and chenopods, weedy plants with edible seeds. However, these local cultivars were not in the South, including in the Apalachicola–lower Chattahoochee region, where no cultivated crop dominated subsistence pursuits until maize, around

AD 1000. People may not have needed or wanted to produce their own food if it took more effort and resources were already plentiful.

Seasonality and Diet
It is difficult to evaluate mobility, sedentism, or seasonality for Late Archaic groups in the research region. Ethnographic data on shellfish-collectors show that they often move seasonally because of winds, precipitation, insects, weather and temperatures, and species availability. Midden deposits piling up over time can be from different activities, seasons, and time periods (Meehan 1982), and degrees of permanence or mobility can fluctuate (Fretheim et al. 2016). Determining season of capture has yet to be done for Late Archaic shellfish. However, the bones of duck (unknown species) at Yellow Houseboat site and snow goose (*Chen caerulescens*) at Van Horn Creek site suggest fall occupation, when those birds were migrating and available.

Though the sample sizes so far studied are small, they do imply broad collection strategies beyond the few dietary staples of deer and turtle. Late Archaic adaptation probably continued earlier Archaic lifeways, with people perhaps altering subsistence labors as ecosystems shifted, but often remaining at or returning to the same sites their ancestors used. The traditional view is that Late Archaic people were experimenting with new ideas and resources with increasing efficiency (Caldwell 1958). Comparison with other regions may be instructive, as new scientific methods expand the picture. At Dry Hinds Cave, southwest Texas (Reinhard et al. 2008), zooarchaeological, palynological, and DNA analyses of human coprolites showed that Late Archaic people ate deer and also a wide range of small animals, including a lot of rats. These small animals were entirely consumed; the dried human feces contained fur, teeth, fish scales, head bones, and even plant remains already processed in rat guts. However, plants made up the largest portion of the diet. The 47 taxa identified included nuts, berries, abundant cactuses, and medicinals. The richer environments of the Apalachicola–lower Chattahoochee region surely allowed far greater dietary diversity.

Archaeologists' emphasis on hunting terrestrial mammals may prevent our appreciation of early fishing adaptations (Walker 2000), especially since nets and lines are not preserved. Fine-screen techniques now show the importance of fish and turtle, in comparison with the less-nutritious shellfish that are, on the other hand, easier to get. The research region's inland Late Archaic sites, interestingly, have no reported fish remains, though they lie in riverine settings, but fish bones are fragile and soils were seldom screened when those sites were dug.

The size of the useful subsistence landscape, and possibly even the social landscape, was probably greater than we imagine in this water-veined wilderness. The standard measure of a catchment area as a 12-km radius or 2-hour walk from home was developed in such places as the open Kalahari desert (e.g., Lee 1969). If travel was faster by water and in forested landscapes, then different standards apply. Though the assumption that current environments and climate are not much different from those of 4,000 years ago might be inaccurate, Apalachicola shell midden faunal assemblages differ little so far from Archaic through late prehistoric strata, suggesting relatively similar environments over millennia. Similarity of subsistence systems across very broad space is also implied by the Late Archaic record in the region. Chert microtools and Poverty Point–type clay objects suggest a continuity in wetland adaptations and interaction across a wide swath of the lowlands of the northern Gulf and well up the Mississippi River. The distribution of these artifacts strikingly parallels the extent of modern hurricane evacuation maps. Indeed, Hurricane Katrina in 2005 sent debris floating out of flooded New Orleans to wash ashore in the Florida Panhandle. Wind and water might have aided travel within a Poverty Point interaction zone.

Social and Ideological Systems

The data on Late Archaic sites in the research region do not allow extensive reconstruction of social organization or beliefs. Undoubtedly ceremonial or magical activities were represented by some of the artifacts discussed. Claassen (2015) lists possible evidence for Archaic spiritual customs in the eastern United States, including rock art, burial practices, unusual stone and bone objects, caches, shrine features, offerings in sinkholes and springs, and mound construction. Concerning social systems, we can hypothesize that ecological dynamism required small, mobile communities and precluded the complexity found later when people settled down to farm. But more complex society is often linked to coordinated, directed group activity, whether food production, long-distance trade, or mound building.

The previous chapter mentions Middle Archaic earthworks in Louisiana; Late Archaic earthwork construction is equally enigmatic. The Poverty Point culture, the height of Archaic elaboration, emerged in northeast Louisiana after 4000 BP, with earthwork building greater than anything previously seen and large-scale long-distance exchange (Broyles and Webb 1970; Gibson 2000). The Poverty Point site itself extends 3 km and includes huge and small mounds, six concentric arcs of raised earth, and evidence of filling in wetlands for construction foundations (Sherwood and Kidder 2011). The meaning of the whole phenomenon and what labor and politics it required are constantly debated, though usually no great social inequality this early is proposed. There is no evidence of houses, and the population was supported by fishing, with no real dependence on gardening. A remarkable aspect of the site is the amount and variety of imported stone and other raw materials, and the huge numbers and varieties of baked-clay Poverty Point objects (PPOs). Poverty Point–related sites extend over nearly 2,000 km, spreading into northwest Florida.

In southwest Florida, a 5,000-year-old mounded shell midden includes human burials and evidence of year-round coastal habitation by nonhierarchical, egalitarian societies (Russo 1991). Ring-shaped shell middens on the Florida, Georgia, and South Carolina coasts are interpreted as ceremonial places with plazas in the middle, though they may just have been circular villages arranged for better interaction. Dwellings are speculated to have been just inside the rings but could have been sitting on them, as stilt houses (see Figure 2.17), which occur worldwide in wetlands. Debate continues over whether these sites are planned social and ritual spaces, expressions of corporate social bodies or political power, nodes in economic systems, or just elevations for better drainage (Gibson and Carr 2004), or whether mounded shell middens are just garbage piles whose contents are sometimes used for other purposes (Marquardt 2010; Voorhies 2000). A director is not necessary to build a mound, nor must there be a great labor cost for just dumping garbage daily to build it (Russo 1994:106–107). If foragers only had to work a few days a week to make a living (Sahlins 1972), they had plenty of time and flexibility. Coerced labor should not be assumed either. People can willingly work cooperatively, with nobody in charge, but all contributing. Whatever leaders existed need not have been individual men—maybe the clan mothers asked everyone to pitch in for mound building.

No Late Archaic mound or earthwork construction is known in the Apalachicola–lower Chattahoochee research region, nor any other social indicators so far. Generalized hunter-gatherers who were mostly egalitarian, mobile, and allied by kinship ties may have been transforming during this time. Perhaps they became more complex "intermediate" or "transegalitarian" societies, more sedentary and territorial, with more stored surplus, "prestige technologies" such as the stone bowls or beads, that might indicate socioeconomic power (e.g., Hayden 1995). Some models propose that people did not really start developing artifacts with more than just everyday functions until they had a stable food supply and more elite leaders. However, we have finely made nonutilitarian projectile points and beads as early as Paleoindian times. Change toward greater social complexity is no more natural or logical than change toward simpler organization. Social ranking may have been developing during the Late Archaic, but not real economic stratification. Some also think that there was no reason to invent or use pottery if other containers were available, unless it was for novelty or social display contexts (e.g., Hoopes and Barnett 1995), but Late Archaic fiber-tempered bowls may just reflect more efficient ways of cooking that became mainstream.

In the Apalachicola–lower Chattahoochee region, we have Late Archaic site distributions, but no data on populations, sedentism, or territoriality, or any cemeteries, mounds, or earthworks. There are only midden sites and mounded shell middens made of domestic refuse and attractive for repeated visits probably over generations. None of them is ring-shaped, though many are ridges curved around stream banks. In fact, Late Archaic shell midden contours are mostly hidden under those of later components and by modern mining for road fill. The matrix is usually solid shell with very little black sand. Even if they were deliberately constructed out of already deposited midden, it would be hard to recognize basketloads of white shells piled on top of other white shells.

In sum, the meager evidence prohibits a good understanding of Late Archaic social organization in the region. The lithic microtools or clay objects might indicate part-time craft specialization, or just be things that everyone made. In these lush watery environments resource abundance and lack of sedentism due to ever-changing surroundings may have fostered complex scheduling but continuation of egalitarian society. As for ideology, we have few clues. Stone beads may have been merely for decoration. The small features at the McKinnie site suggest ritual and are the only evidence so far from this early time period of a repeated observance of the intangible or magical. In reality, Late Archaic Native American religious or ceremonial life, like that of hunter-gatherer-fisher peoples worldwide, was probably quite elaborate.

Long-Distance Interaction and Economics

Some Late Archaic artifacts in the research region were obtained from afar, through wide-ranging interaction networks across the South. The steatite vessels came from the mountains, perhaps 700 to 1,000 km upriver. Specimens from the Chattahoochee River 1 site were traced to Virginia, and the Chattahoochee-Apalachicola system was probably one of the main waterways for steatite distribution in the eastern United States (Smith 1991; Yates 2000). Finished steatite bowls could have moved directly from quarries or workshops or by down-the-line interaction. Only one Poverty Point–type clay object from the Apalachicola–lower Chattahoochee region, from Clark Creek, was subjected to trace element analysis, which showed it was made of local clays. However, in a group from around Choctawhatchee Bay to the west, most were local but a few matched results from the Poverty Point site itself (Tykot et al. 2013), suggesting movement down the Mississippi and along the Gulf. The jasper bead from St. Vincent Island was made in the Poverty Point region, where diverse types of stone characterized the lapidary industry (Ford and Webb 1956:125); it is one of several recorded along the coast and well into Florida.

Lazarus (1958) first recorded the extension into northwest Florida of sites producing Poverty Point–type artifacts and named it the Elliott's Point complex. Calvin Jones (1993) listed 90 sites in the Florida panhandle with Poverty-Point-type clay objects. The Apalachicola delta area seems to be the easternmost contiguous extent of the distribution of these artifacts. But their spread across the South makes it inappropriate to single out those in Florida with different terminology. Though clay objects have been collected elsewhere in Florida and on the Georgia coast, no new names have been proposed for those occurrences. Coupled with the microliths and the single jasper bead, the connections between the Apalachicola region and Poverty Point could fit Jackson's (1991) trade fair model, with selected rarer things and accompanying ideas filtering down the rivers and along coasts. We cannot say whether people themselves from Poverty Point and other mound centers were part of spreading ideologies or religious notions, but socioeconomic interchange is obvious. However tenuous or profound the interaction, it took place across incredible distances both east–west along the Gulf and north–south into the interior. Late Archaic interaction systems of the East and Midwest were even more extensive than just the Poverty Point network. Gulf Coast shell, including beads, made it to places as far north as Michigan, and steatite circulated everywhere. Given all these connections, northwest Florida should not be singled out for exceptional nomenclature such as Elliott's Point; this name should be discontinued.

Late Archaic People

Indigenous populations may have been growing during the Late Archaic, but so far we have no demographic information for the Apalachicola–lower Chattahoochee region. As for individuals, only one definite Late Archaic burial and some isolated teeth are known from the region, from three lower valley shell middens (White 1994b, 2003a). These remains suggest that people's lives included a lot of physical labor, natural grit in the diet, frequent accidents, and using teeth as tools.

At Sam's Cutoff shell midden, a young woman was buried at a very shallow depth. She was laid out flexed on the right side, with face turned left, left arm thrown outward, and right hand behind her back. She had shovel-shaping on both labial and lingual surfaces of her incisor teeth, molars with some wear, possible gum infection, but no caries. Her lower back and upper body bones showed stresses of an active life typical of foragers. Her upper leg bones had clean breaks, but whether from human action or postdepositional processes such as soil weight is unknown. There were no grave goods. A stable isotope study on a tiny sample of bone and a third molar tooth provided data on diet (Rob Tykot, personal communication 2003). The bone had no collagen preserved, and apatite delta 13C was -8.2 per mil. Bone apatite reflects average diet over the last several years of life. This result suggests that about half her diet was seafood, and even more than that if it was only saltwater seafood, especially because at this early date she would have consumed no maize that could have affected the results. The tooth enamel delta 13C was 10.7 per mil. Enamel reflects diet only during the time the tooth was formed, which for this molar would have been age 10 to 12. The results suggest less seafood consumption, perhaps 30% of her diet, at this earlier time in her life. This bigger picture is of shifting patterns of acquiring animals over the years by this individual and her family, or perhaps changing dietary customs or preferences over a lifetime, or even migration from an area with different food habits. Tykot's small study corroborates well with the faunal assemblage at Sam's Cutoff.

At Clark Creek shell midden (8Gu60), four isolated adult teeth came from Test Unit C Level 2: a canine, lower first molar, lower left incisor, and possible right second incisor. This level is within a Late Archaic context, or mixed Late Archaic–Early Woodland within the compressed stratigraphy of the midden slope. All the teeth were worn, and the possible right incisor had heavy wear resulting in its occlusal surface slanting upward mesially, which might happen if the front teeth were used as tools for cutting. The teeth could have been deposited after being knocked or pulled out, or falling out of the mouth of a living person with dental disease, or falling out of a skull. A single deciduous human molar attributed to the Late Archaic was recovered at Depot Creek shell midden (8Gu56), from Test Unit C, Level 6, a level with no pottery 20 cm below the deepest level with Early Woodland sherds and 10 cm above the level with fiber-tempered sherds. Since the tooth has an attached root, it cannot have fallen out naturally. It was either deliberately or accidentally separated from a living child or fell out of a skeleton. No marks suggest extraction, and the tooth has moderate wear. It came from a child between about 4 and 9 years old.

Data from Late Archaic cemeteries in the mid-South are useful to reconstruct life and health. Hundreds of graves show that Late Archaic burials were usually in the flesh and without grave goods except beads or other items of marine shell and bone. Life expectancy was 20 to 30 years, and infant deaths were common. Men's skeletons displayed more cutmarks, including intentional trauma and other stresses, than did women's, possibly relating to more risky behavior or heavier work, though strenuous daily activity was done by both sexes. These active, mostly healthy Native Americans were continually engaged in behavior we would consider unsafe in today's world of life jackets, seatbelts, bike helmets, and modern medicine. In the Kentucky shell-mound Archaic, many young women had parry fractures in the forearms, suggesting warding off blows by holding the arms over the face. This might indicate violence against women or relate to subsistence or other practices (Belovich 1994). Western Tennessee burials from the Kentucky Lake Reservoir area have evidence for Archaic scalping, and middle Tennessee Archaic burials have indications of decapitation and removal of the forearms for trophies; however, only 10 of 439 skeletons, all male, had uncontestable indication of lethal violence (Milner 1999; Smith 1997). Trophy heads and evidence of dismemberment and defleshing of the dead, seen more in late prehistoric burials in the Southeast, evidently did occur as early as the Late Archaic. Accident or death ritual can be hard to distinguish from war casualties, but parry fractures, body part trophy-taking, and scalping cutmarks and blunt force trauma to the skull do demonstrate violence.

Warfare?

The trick is differentiating individual or small-group violence, vengeance-taking, blood feuds, or murder, from something bigger. Real warfare is organized, wider-scale armed physical attack by the whole society, sanctioned by leaders, and often claiming victims who are noncombatants or uninvolved in the causes. Countless theoretical explorations of the origins, timing, and locations of prehistoric warfare seldom include hard data proving its existence. Archaeology has limitations, but it is all we have, and it does not have the bias of historic time, during which most information was written by the victors. It has other biases, however: the only real archaeological indications of warfare are skeletons of multiple contemporaneous victims and defensive structures (Milner 1999), and even those can be ambiguous.

Archaeologists and other anthropologists examine warfare in different frameworks, ranging from whether it glorifies the male warrior to whether battlefield debris confirms or expands historic accounts. Conclusions may reflect less of what actually happened and more about the intellectual and political atmosphere of the times when they are published. An oft-cited study (Wilk 1985) showed that interpretations of Maya archaeology invoked warfare as a cause for culture change more often during the late 1960s, when the United States was fighting in Vietnam. By the early 1970s, when that war had grown unpopular and environmental concerns became paramount, explanations turned to ecosystem degradation as the major cause, only to shift again to religious motivations by the late 1970s. Linking past human events and processes to modern issues is a benefit of archaeology, but we must suspect stories that are trendy but unsupported by the evidence. War leaves death and destruction that should be visible in the material record, but clues can be questionable. For example, an abundance of Australian microliths interpreted as spear tips or barbs for weapons of war was thought to demonstrate a time of intense conflict among foragers over a 1,500-year period. Then a detailed functional analysis showed they were not used against humans but for very different tasks (Robertson et al. 2009).

Ideas about ancient warfare have come from philosophers envisioning what humanity once was. Since the days of imagining prehistoric life as "a time of war . . . [of] no arts; no letters; no society; . . . continual fear, and danger of violent death; . . . nasty, brutish, and short" (Hobbes 1996 [1651]:84), popular opinion has held sway while scientists collect real data. But war is not biologically programmed into human nature. No universal, innate instinct includes inherent violence or aggression in everyone's behavior or in men's more than women's. In fact, studies of testosterone levels show they increase after violence or aggression, not before. Physical brutality and animosity are learned. Anthropologists describe myriad methods of nonviolent conflict resolution, with lessons for modern society about achieving security by peaceful means (e.g., Fry and Söderberg 2014). Indeed, cooperation is increasingly seen as more natural and critical for human survival, stability, and creativity since human ancestors emerged in Africa millions of years ago up through the time of the first true state civilizations (Ferguson 2018). The ethnographic record holds descriptions of some 70 cultures worldwide that are nonwarring, not including religious groups (such as Quakers) within larger societies (Fry 2006:91–96).

Though some see prehistoric Native Americans societies in the South as endemically violent (e.g., Jennings 2011), these interpretations are often based on historic Indigenous groups who were invaded, devastated, and trained by foreigners; on prehistoric depictions of what might be sacrifice or other smaller-scale activity; or on conceptions of "violence" that actually connote oppression, slavery, or other behavior not involving much physical assault. Ritual confrontation as spectacle, without casualties, or capture of individuals to be servants/slaves, are examples that do not fit the definition of real warfare. Though present-day hunter-gatherer-fishers are not necessarily the best models for ancient cultures, a study of 32 such societies worldwide found amazing cooperation and egalitarian systems. Men or women may leave or stay with their family groups, adult siblings often live together, and most people in the group are genetically unrelated, while interaction networks of many unrelated adults result in cumulative cultural patterns (Hill et al. 2011). Similar kinds of social networks in the Late Archaic might be represented by the widespread connections with Poverty-Point-type material culture, the importing of steatite, or even the spread of fiber-tempered ceramics.

Homicide and violent feuding are not warfare. Late Archaic societies did not have standing armies but probably smaller-scale violence. Most archaeologists agree that no solid evidence exists for true warfare until about the time of early farming villages. War was probably absent from the largest part of the human past, especially among hunter-gatherer-fishers in rich environments such as the Southeast. In the research region, no good evidence of warfare or wide-scale conflict is known until the Contact period, when foreign invaders brought unimaginable large-scale violence (discussed in Volume 2). Unless and until some obvious marker of group violence is discovered, we can characterize Late Archaic Native American life in the research region as short, according to modern standards, but not necessarily nasty or brutish, and probably more peaceful and with more leisure time than that of twenty-first-century humans.

6

Early Woodland Period, 800 BC to AD 300

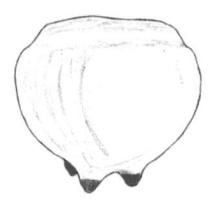

The Woodland period in the Southeast is indicated by the earliest burial mounds and new kinds of pottery. In the Apalachicola–lower Chattahoochee valley region, Early Woodland ceramics increased in numbers and types, were made by the coil method, and were tempered with sand and some grit and grog. They include plain, check-stamped, linear check-stamped, simple-stamped, and fabric-marked types of the Deptford series, sometimes with tetrapodal supports on vessel bases. During later Early Woodland times, Swift Creek Complicated-Stamped pottery and the earliest exotic grave goods appeared. Despite radical change hypothesized for the Archaic-to-Woodland transition elsewhere, little alteration of settlement or subsistence patterns is evident in the research region. Sites are along waterways; many are shell middens. People continued hunting-gathering-fishing lifeways, although greater social complexity may have been developing.

Archaeologists once marked the beginning of the Woodland period in the eastern United States by the appearance of pottery. Now this is understood to mean pottery tempered with sand or other mineral substances, with the recognition that fiber-tempered wares were earlier. The new ceramics may indicate shifting adaptations in the face of cooler, wetter climates, periods of increased storms, flooding, and great sea-level fluctuations. Wide-scale culture change, even abandonment of some areas, has been attributed to risk-reduction strategies in the face of radically changing, unpredictable weather (e.g., Kidder 2006), and new pottery is sometimes thought to mean migrations or repopulation by groups with various regional traditions. But such traditions may be more recognizable because Early Woodland material culture is more visible, with ceramics, a medium expressing great variability, far more numerous than during the Late Archaic. In the Apalachicola–lower Chattahoochee valley region, despite a different artifact record in Early Woodland times, continuity is also evident. Early Woodland occupations overlie Late Archaic middens, and faunal assemblages are similar, so there is considerable persistence of lifeways. The biggest changes are the disappearance of hand-built fiber-tempered ceramics and the emergence of coil-made pottery tempered with sand, grit, and/or grog by around 500 BC. Perhaps a few centuries earlier, chert microtools and clay balls disappeared. Later in the Early Woodland, burial mound construction began and complicated-stamped pottery appeared. These innovations may have emerged slowly and individually. So far no evidence for population migrations or large-scale abandonment of areas is known.

Sea-level fluctuation curves for the Gulf (Balsillie and Donoghue 2004; McNabb 2012; Sankar 2015) indicate a drop by about 950 BC that could be associated with the emergence of Early Woodland. One study of storm rates west of the Apalachicola–lower Chattahoochee region suggests that between 850 and 350 BC hurricanes were more prevalent (Lane et al. 2011). Another study (Coor 2012) determined that higher storm rates, averaging 7.6 great hurricanes per century, occurred between 550 BC and AD 150. Data from coastal Alabama suggest periods of intense fires following the major hurricanes as well (Liu et al. 2007). All these altered local ecosystems certainly affected human communities. But whether diversification of ceramic production meant just technological elaboration or social transformation as well is so far unknown. New tempers, thinner vessel walls, and impressing patterns on pot surfaces could be mostly functional improvements. Fiber-tempered pots were apparently easier to make, but Early Woodland vessels had better heating effectiveness and longer use-life (Skibo et al. 1989). Only when elaborate stamped designs develop later in Early Woodland times do decorative arts and potentially social meanings apparently come to the fore with ceramic production.

Early Woodland Settlement in the Region

Early Woodland sites in the Apalachicola–lower Chattahoochee research region are hard to identify, as diagnostic artifacts and chronometric dates are few. Ceramics become numerous, but types distinctive only to Early Woodland are minorities. Plain-surfaced pottery with mineral tempers was made from this time onward for 2,500 years. Similarly, check-stamped pots appeared at the beginning of Early Woodland and lasted into historic times, with little distinguishing variation except some rim treatments or tetrapodal bases. The rarer Early Woodland diagnostics are the Linear Check-Stamped, Simple-Stamped, and Fabric-Marked, of the Deptford series, and later Complicated-Stamped types of the Swift Creek series. Projectile points or other clearly Early Woodland artifacts are also difficult to isolate. Another problem is that Early Woodland was once seen as primarily a coastal adaptation, with interior sites considered to be smaller, short occupations by coastal peoples making limited inland forays for specific resources (Milanich 1994; Willey 1949). Now we know that Early Woodland sites, large and small, occur far inland. Further, they were obviously valued locations, reinhabited for centuries/millennia afterward, covered or mixed with the debris of many later peoples who also left check-stamped and plain sherds. Once, the abundant sites in the region producing only check-stamped and plain pottery were typically thought to be Late Woodland, with little search for other clues of age. I

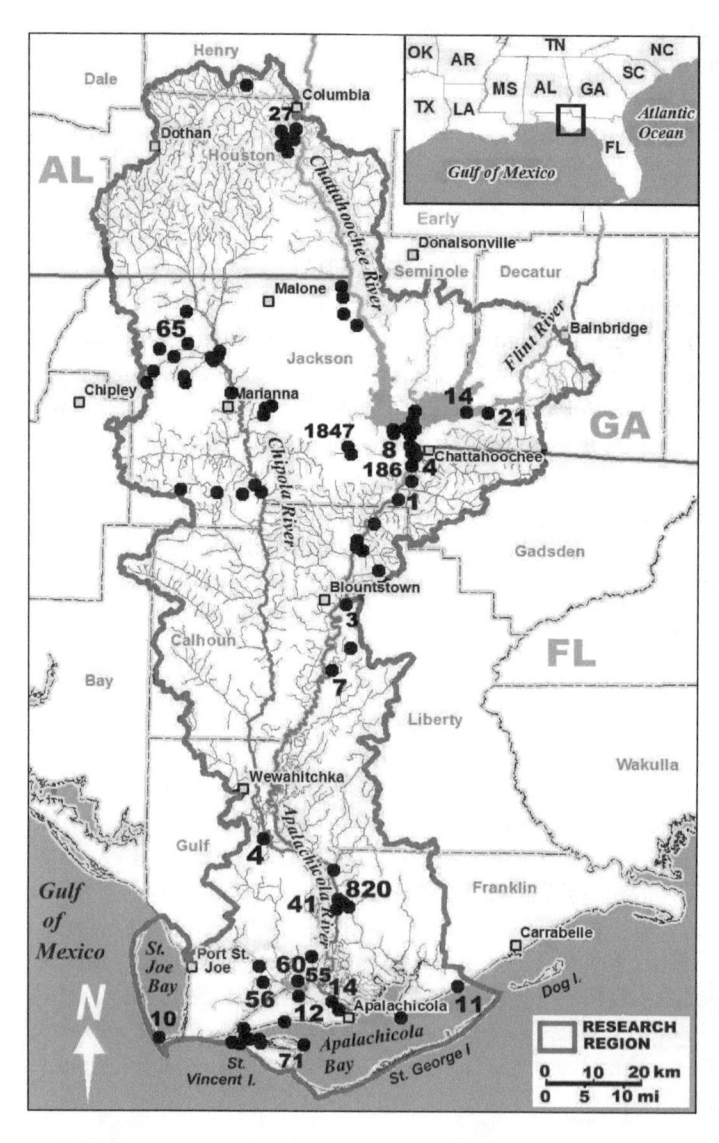

Figure 6.1. Early Woodland sites. Numbered sites are discussed in the text. (Nancy Marie White)

was one of many making that mistake, saying that these sites showed a population increase during the Late Woodland (White 1981), until I got some radiocarbon dates and understood the ubiquity of check-stamped pottery through space and time. By the 1990s, we were listing these sites as "indeterminate ceramic," dating to any time within the last 3,000 years (Schieffer 2013; Simpson 1996).

Thus, the distribution of known Early Woodland sites/components in the Apalachicola–lower Chattahoochee region (Figure 6.1) is biased. Attribution to this time period was made using only diagnostic pottery, radiocarbon dates, or the few reliable projectile point types. Using such limited temporal markers for Early Woodland thus leads to a picture of an apparent decline in site numbers (barely over 90) from those of the Late Archaic. Another source of error is the continued potential for burial of Early Woodland deposits by fluvial shifts. Though elsewhere in the Southeast the Early Woodland has been portrayed as a time of fewer and smaller sites (Kidder 2006), this decline in the research region may not represent population shrinkage, only the failure to see what actually belongs in Early Woodland but might be unrecognized, too deep to reach, or mixed with later materials.

Habitation Sites

Early Woodland sites are along waterways. Inland they are on stream banks, old meanders or ponds, and higher river terraces. Bullen's (1958) Chattahoochee River 1 site (8Ja8 [J-5]) was on the riverbank, with the stratum containing Early Woodland Deptford ceramics about 1.4 m deep, 30 cm below the Fort Walton zone, separated from the even deeper Late Archaic component by nearly a meter of culturally sterile soil. On the coast, some bayshore oyster shell middens have Early Woodland components. Estuarine sites are usually mounded *Rangia* clamshell middens occurring only up to the equivalent of 10 river miles (16 km) inland. Unlike many shell middens elsewhere in Gulf estuaries, no Apalachicola sites have clear separation of strata but only solid deposits merging with those of earlier and later times. Hardly any Early Woodland sites are single-component; most have Middle Woodland and later cultural deposits above and/or Late Archaic components below. No shell rings are known, but mounded shell middens are often shaped to curve around a stream channel or former channel (see Figure 2.13).

Early Woodland settlement sizes are not well known, nor are there structure patterns or other domestic data that would allow distinguishing among camps, villages, or households. Even mapping the mounded shell middens is not conclusive, since coring off their edges into the surrounding wetlands shows a continuation of cultural deposits under the water table. A possible structure floor or other prepared surface was an intriguing feature encountered at Clark Creek (8Gu60). It was a lens of packed, light-yellow clayey silt

(10YR5/4), 2 to 5 cm thick, containing no cultural materials but obviously fashioned by human action (see Plate VI). The portion in the corner of Test Unit B was 38 cm by 16 cm and seemed to be a corner of a deliberately laid floor or foundation for some activity. It was not flat but convoluted, maybe because of the weight of the shell deposited on top of it. After removing the part of this feature within the unit, we noted its appearance in the wall as a thin, slanted yellow lens. This feature was completely unlike the extremely rare dark stains of possible postmolds or other activity at estuarine shell middens.

Mounds

Burial mounds first appeared during the Early Woodland period all across the eastern United States. Along the Ohio and Tennessee River valleys, Early Woodland Adena mounds had graves with elaborate artifacts; similar phenomena emerged throughout the South. Some mound-building developed in the Apalachicola–lower Chattahoochee region, apparently in the latest two or three Early Woodland centuries. So far, at least 13 mounds with Early Woodland materials are known, from the upper valley to the coast. These materials comprise earlier components in Middle Woodland mounds.

At Lake Douglas Mound (9Dr21) near Flint River Mile 25, A. R. Kelly (1953) uncovered some 22 burials on the east side, beyond the disturbed areas. Several had few or no grave goods, mainly shell disc beads, and mostly check-stamped and plain pots, some of the former with conoidal bases. This pottery may have been with the earliest interments, before later Middle Woodland use involved graves with more elaborate objects. More Swift Creek sherds were in mound fill than in the east-side cache, suggesting Early Woodland village debris being swept up to construct this burial mound. At Kerr's Landing Mound (9Dr14) on the east bank at about Flint River Mile 20, check-stamped pottery predominated and was considered "inferior ware"; with it were a few complicated-stamped pieces, some cord-marked, and sherds that "had belonged to vessels bearing feet" (tetrapodal pots) as well as ceramics decorated by the impressions of a "roulette" (Moore 1907:453), now understood to be linear check-stamped, impressed by a paddle or a rolling stamp. All this also accompanied a large Middle Woodland burial component.

Once thought to exist only in late prehistoric Mississippian times, platform mounds or flat-topped pyramids are now recognized as early as the Early Woodland (e.g., Kassabaum 2018). At least one was recorded at the Block-Sterns site in Tallahassee (Jones et al. 1998). A potential Woodland platform mound within the research region is at Waddell's Mill Pond site (8Ja65), in the upper Chipola basin (Tesar and Jones 2009). This site had Swift Creek Complicated-Stamped pottery but no definite early Weeden Island types that would indicate Middle Woodland; its 13 red-painted sherds could also have been from the Fort Walton component, which included burials placed into this mound. A pit feature associated with a red clay floor (Floor 10), the earliest structural element of this mound, yielded charcoal dated to cal AD 65–420.

Farther downriver, other conical burial mounds may be Early Woodland or at least have Early Woodland components. The largest of three Aspalaga Mounds (8Gd1), on the east bank of the upper Apalachicola, contained few burial goods. Amid the majority Middle-Woodland ceramics were several Early Woodland tetrapodal vessels. One interesting Swift Creek Complicated-Stamped pot with a tetrapodal base had a constricted then outflaring neck and rough complicated stamping on the entire exterior in a concentric-circle pattern (Moore 1903:487). At the Mound Below Bristol (8Li3), the only pottery Moore (1903:474) obtained was check-stamped and "faint and carelessly-applied complicated stamp on three or four vessels and one sherd." He said of this site that never had it "been our fortune to open a mound where a number of vessels presented so low an average of excellence." This comment supports the notion that complicated-stamped designs started out as only slightly more fanciful ways of doing the utilitarian, until people began executing them more elaborately. The ceramic record suggests this mound was mostly or wholly Early Woodland. It has not been investigated further or even relocated. Similarly, Moore's (1903:466) Mound near Estiffanulga (8Li7), which also has not been relocated, produced only plain and check-stamped ceramics and a single complicated-stamped sherd, making it another candidate for an Early (or Late) Woodland construction.

On a tributary of the lower Apalachicola, the Howard Creek Mound (8Gu41) appears to be Early Woodland. It was known from a private collection containing only plain ceramics and one Swift Creek Complicated-Stamped (early variety) jar, a piece of sheet mica, and two copper discs (White 1992). Farther south, about 7.5 river miles above the mouth of the Apalachicola on the tributary Jackson River, Huckleberry Landing Mounds (8Fr12) had at least 34 burials in a sand mound accompanied by check-stamped, complicated-stamped, and plain ceramics, three of the last with tetrapodal bases. Other grave goods were clay pipes, copper discs with ceramic disc backing (see Plate XIII), turtle shell, chert tools and debitage, a mica sheet, hones, and pebble tools (Moore 1902:234–238). At least one and maybe two *Rangia* shell mounds sit atop the large riverbank shell midden ridge at this site. The burial mound had shell patches, presumably of repurposed midden, at the base and with some burials, and patches of clayey sand with other burials. The absence of early Weeden Island ceramics suggests Huckleberry is single-component Early Woodland.

Near the river mouth, Pierce Mounds complex (8Fr14, etc.) includes at least two conical burial mounds with Early Woodland components. Moore

(1902:217–228) dug Mound A, uncovering 99 graves with exotic goods, and we cleaned up looters' backfill a century later after they trenched through Mound A's remains (White 2013). Nearly all the materials in this sand-and-shell construction were indicative of elaborate Middle Woodland ceremonialism. But two things hint that its accretion began in Early Woodland: abundant check-stamped sherds and a plain miniature tetrapodal vessel. Pierce Mound C, also on the west side, 75 m north-northeast of Mound A, provided additional data. Refilling its huge looter hole that may have intersected Moore's original trench, we recovered from the screened backdirt several Deptford Linear check-stamped sherds and shell disc beads (all these will be discussed). Other unexplored mounds at Pierce may have Early Woodland materials amid the Middle Woodland and Fort Walton components.

At Green Point Mound (8Fr11), on the north shore of Apalachicola Bay east of the river mouth, Moore (1902:252–253) also recorded earthenware that was "distinctly inferior," "the commonest kitchenware" placed with the dead, much of it with tetrapodal supports. The mostly complicated-stamped pottery was of the early Swift Creek style, stamped all over the exterior, as opposed to later Swift Creek, which is stamped in a band around the neck (Willey 1949). Green Point also contained elaborate Middle Woodland objects and was next to the fully Middle Woodland Porter's Bar Mound. This situation is similar to that at Pierce, showing continued use of the same locale for burial rituals from Early through Middle Woodland. Perhaps as one mound became large, or the family using it died out, another mound was begun nearby. Abundant check-stamped (presumably Deptford) sherds were present at Green Point, but hardly any at Porter's Bar, supporting the picture of one mound preceding the other (Knigge 2018).

The Early Woodland materials at these mounds could represent the earliest construction or later stages when earlier occupational debris from local habitation areas was scraped up and piled on top of a later mound. Less clear examples are the many other burial mounds in the region for which Moore mentions retrieving check-stamped ceramics, though those pots could conceivably be of the more rare Middle Woodland Gulf check-stamped type (Willey 1949). The potential error in seeing mounds or any sites with only check-stamped pottery as Early Woodland is illustrated by the case of Singer Mound, part of the Pierce complex, where Moore dug 19 burials and only check-stamped and plain sherds; now radiocarbon dates place it solidly within Fort Walton times (discussed in Volume 2). Controlled data are needed to assess the timing and dates for Early Woodland mounds in the Apalachicola–lower Chattahoochee valley.

Important to describe here is the Mandeville site (9Cy1 or Cla1), up the Chattahoochee 30 river miles (50 km) above the research region in Clay

County, Georgia, and now under the Walter F. George reservoir at Fort Gaines (see Figure I.1). Mandeville had two mounds and a village on a creek bank. It was investigated before dam construction and is crucial for understanding the Early Woodland. Deptford Simple-Stamped, Check-Stamped, Linear Check-Stamped, and Fabric-Marked pottery, including tetrapodal vessels, characterized its earliest significant component. Mound A was a flat-topped platform built over dark habitation deposits. Its initial stage, or primary mound, was 60 cm high, of stiff yellow clay, with lenses and a cap of bright golden-yellow sand and ramp-like extensions leading down from the summit. To this were added layers of dark midden sand, red clay, and more yellow mound caps in several construction stages that expanded multiple smaller mounds into one large one 4.3 m high, with a flat summit 43 × 24 m. The final mound cap was Mississippian in age, but intermediate stages were associated with later Early Woodland complicated-stamped ceramics. There were few artifacts, no burials, little structural evidence, and only areas of ash or charcoal to suggest ceremonial activities. Conical (?) Mound B, with basin features for human cremations, both Deptford- and Swift Creek–series ceramics, and exotics such as copper, galena, and whelk shell, appeared to overlap the later Early Woodland time of Mound A. Radiocarbon dates were AD 1 ± 150 for the sub-Mound-A midden and AD 540 ± 150 for the Mound A Layer III with Swift Creek ceramics (Kellar et al. 1962). Mandeville was dug in an era when archaeologists had trouble accepting that platform mounds could be Early Woodland.

Dating the Early Woodland

Radiocarbon Dates
Dates for Early Woodland in the region are mostly from habitation sites in the lower valley, and they are few. The oldest is from the Lost Dog site (8Fr820) in the Apalachicola National Forest, a creek-side camp with generic check-stamped pottery and a single Deptford Simple-Stamped sherd. A pit feature originating from a layer with a grog-tempered plain and two check-stamped sherds produced charcoal dated to cal 805–415 BC (Parker and White 1992). No other component was discernible at the site, but the lithic artifacts, mostly debitage, all came from under the Early Woodland midden in a paler stratum that could have represented earlier inhabitants or changes in site function.

The Depot Creek shell midden (8Gu56) has a thick Early Woodland component atop the Late Archaic deposits (White 1994b). Charcoal from Test Unit B (1 × 1 m) Level 7, on the mound summit, with Deptford Simple-Stamped and Check-Stamped sherds, dated to cal 755–405 BC. Another date, from TU C, on the south slope, Level 3, estimated to be in the middle of the Early Woodland occupation, with 136 g of Deptford Simple-Stamped and Check-Stamped sherds, was cal 350 BC to AD 230 (Kingsland 2017). These dates imply centuries of continuity. Above the dated deposits are so-far undated levels that contained some Swift Creek Complicated-Stamped and cordmarked sherds, suggesting the easing-in of later Early Woodland pottery types.

The Paradise Point site (8Fr71) on St. Vincent Island produced a date of cal AD 77–259 on shell from the lowest oyster midden stratum. The position of this stratum below the bluish-clay layer that suggests higher-than-present sea level, and the sea-level fluctuation curves indicating a drop before Early Woodland times (Walker et al. 1995), suggest that Native American inhabitants occupied a landscape very different from that of today on this barrier island. They might have stayed back from the bay shore when they came seasonally to collect fish and shellfish, and perhaps they abandoned the site in the wake of rising seas after Early Woodland times, then but returned later.

Beyond these reasonable dates from shell midden sites, a few other potential Early Woodland dates from inland sites have confusing contexts. The premound midden at Omussee Creek (1Ho27/101) produced Fort Walton–period ceramics but a date of cal AD 20–240, though no Early Woodland artifacts were known (Blitz and Lorenz 2006). While the date is probably incorrect, it could also indicate that people settled for centuries at this prime riverbank spot, with their earlier evidence obscured by later cultures. At the Keene Dog Pond site (8Ja1847), charcoal from 20 cm below the sub-plowzone stratum that produced Early Archaic points was dated to cal 40 BC–AD 80, showing that possibly later inhabitants did mix their debris with earlier deposits. The site had only one tetrapodal basal sherd and one complicated-stamped sherd among the thousands of surface-collected artifacts, so Early Woodland folks were apparently there only briefly (Kelley 2013). Finally, the Corbin-Tucker site (8Ca142) Fort Walton cemetery produced a date of cal 50 BC–AD 420 on charcoal from under a copper disc near a burial. The date seems highly erroneous, but it might be from natural wood or a very ancient grave offering (see Volume 2).

Geomorphological Time
Temporal and geomorphological aspects of the landscape encompassing some Early Woodland shell middens need examining to understand fluvial processes. Depot Creek site sits near a creek (see Figure 5.1) that empties into Lake Wimico, itself an old river channel (see Figure 1.4). The main body of the site runs 100 m east–west and 40 m wide, with a smaller projection another 30 m to the southeast, 16 m wide (see Figure 2.13). Midden deposits are wider and deeper than the extent of visible shell, as much is now submerged. The site was used by Early Woodland people inhabiting the already

raised shellfishing station left by Late Archaic foragers. It is parallel to the creek but 200 m distant from it today. Similarly, Clark Creek (8Gu60) (see Figure 5.2), another mounded shell midden in the estuarine wetlands, also has an Early Woodland habitation overlying a Late Archaic component. Off a tiny tributary of another creek running into Lake Wimico, it is 100 m long and 35 m wide, and parallel to but now 300 m away from that tiny stream. We have no dates for its Early Woodland component, which has typical Deptford Check-Stamped, Linear Check-Stamped, and Fabric-Marked ceramics. These two sites have no cultural deposits later than Early Woodland. After long or repeated habitation over centuries, they must then have been abandoned by about AD 300 after their streams moved too far away, possibly obliterating shellfish beds or making them too distant.

Lithic Artifacts

Early Woodland groups in the region still used spears and darts, but they either made few distinctive projectile points or did not leave enough clues for us to recognize them. Abundant generic bifacial and unifacial tools and points at Early Woodland sites range from Archaic through Woodland in cultural affiliation, but few are exclusive to Early Woodland. An example is the Hernando point, with its distinctive notched base, originally defined as Early Woodland (Bullen 1975:24) but later thought to be as early as Late Archaic and as late as Middle Woodland or later (Ste. Claire 1996). Even the large quantity of Hernando points from the St. Vincent 3 site (Figure 6.2), amid dozens of other points and multiple prehistoric components, does not conclusively establish an Early Woodland presence here. Hernando point occurrences were not used to make the map of Early Woodland sites in Figure 6.1.

The guides say that Adena, Florida Adena, Greenville, Swannanoa, and perhaps a few other projectile point types might be temporal markers of Early Woodland (Bullen 1975a; Cambron and Hulse 1964; Whatley 2002). These are usually relatively crude, with short stems, hard to classify (Figure 6.3). One interesting point from a good Early Woodland context defies classification (Figure 6.4). It was found at the Trestle Bridge site (8Ja186), on the upper Apalachicola bank, washing out of the midden with Deptford ceramics. It has an expanding-stem base that is thinned, with flake scars having a tiny tang between them; its notches produce asymmetrical barbs, and its tip might be described as spurred, tapering to what looks like an awl point. There is no shortage of Early Woodland lithic debitage. Plenty of stone tools were made, even if we do not recognize which ones are characteristic.

Early Woodland ground-stone implements include quartzite cobbles and pebbles with use wear from grinding or hammering. The greenstone pendant from Clark Creek noted in the previous chapter may be Early Woodland. A

Figure 6.2. Hernando points from St. Vincent 3 site (#USF JC-8Fr362-13-1.53; collector's numbers on some). (Photograph courtesy of Kaitlyn Keffer)

Figure 6.3. Early Woodland points from the Keene sites (8Ja1847, 1848), in private (BK) collection: (a–d) Florida Adena; (e–g) Swannanoa. (Adapted from Kelley 2013:257, 267; Nancy Marie White.)

probable Early Woodland grinding rock or metate from the eroding riverbank surface of the Trestle Bridge site (see Figure 2.2) is a large, almost flat, wide slab measuring 33 × 27 cm, nearly 8 cm thick, with a 20-cm diameter smooth basin worn into the top. Rating between 4 and 5 on the Mohs hardness scale, this artifact appears to be of calcareous limestone, with fossil inclusions, and is irregularly shaped, not modified other than by the worn depression on top. It weighs 7.3 kg and might have been left at the site for return visits instead of being carried around.

The category of stone includes the two copper discs (see Plate XIIIa, b) from Huckleberry Landing Mound (8Fr12; Moore 1902:238), Burial 26, on either side of the person's head. They have central large convex circular areas with small central perforations. Nearly 7 cm in diameter, each was accompanied by a ceramic disc 4.3 cm in diameter that was the backing for attachment to pierced earlobes. One disc retains a tiny lump of a knot of preserved cord (sinew?) in the central perforation that would have held the discs together. While these decorative and possibly sacred artifacts seem more typical of later Middle Woodland times, no Middle Woodland ceramics are known from the site. Two similar copper discs were unearthed at the Howard Creek Mound (8Gu41; White 1992), which is also devoid of clear Middle Woodland evidence.

Figure 6.4. Unusual Early Woodland point from the Trestle Bridge site (8Ja186; private [RC] collection). (Nancy Marie White)

Ceramics

By definition, Early Woodland means that fiber-tempered pottery is gone. Suggestions that a later type of Late Archaic ceramics included both sand and fiber mixed into the clay were dismissed with a detailed study (White 2003b), noted in the previous chapter. Another change was that Woodland and later potters no longer worked with clay slabs but shaped vessels from coiled lengths of rolled clay, then paddled or pressed to merge the coils into vessel walls. The earliest Early Woodland ceramics in the region were originally assigned to the Deptford series and thought to have originated farther north in Georgia and/or on the Atlantic coast. However, since the few dates we have are as early as Early Woodland anywhere else, while the typological names persist, the geographic origins of these ceramics remain unknown.

Ceramic Forms

Similar unknowns surround our understanding of individual ceramic types and their huge variability after over 1,000+ years of mostly plain fiber-tempered pots. Early Woodland types and styles, from surface treatments to vessel shapes to temper, might indicate different communities or subcultural units, but they may also indicate different functional, social, or aesthetic choices. Except for smoothing, all the surface treatments—stamping with checks, parallel lines, or woven fabrics—may be variations on a theme. They give the vessel greater surface area perhaps for better heating or cooling, and also may have made pots easier to grasp. Plain-surfaced pottery perhaps had totally different uses. Near the end of the Early Woodland when Swift Creek Complicated-Stamped designs first appear, we might hypothesize that they are conveying larger social messages while maintaining those technological advantages. Early Woodland ceramic pastes are most often sand-tempered. Grit or crushed quartzite rock is less prevalent, supposedly distinguishable from larger sand particles by its sharp edges, while sand grains are smoothed. Grog or crushed, hardened or fired clay/recycled sherds can be present, as well as mixtures of the three. Individual potters usually know exactly what they are doing and may have chosen tempers for specific reasons. In addition, as with most aboriginal ceramics in this region, glittery mica flecks were already naturally present in the local clays and possibly even understood as a geographical or ethnic identity marker.

Early Woodland vessel shapes include bowls and jars with straight and squared, rounded, or folded rims and round or slightly conical bottoms. A distinctive form only in this time period is the tetrapodal base. The four conical podal supports are seen on plain, check-stamped, fabric-marked, and occasion-

Figure 6.5. Early Woodland tetrapodal ceramics: *left*, tiny plain pot from Pierce Mound A (8Fr14; NMAI#174531); tips of podal supports painted black); *right*, Deptford Fabric-Marked basal sherd with large podal support, from Trestle Bridge site (#8Ja186-79-11). (Nancy Marie White)

ally complicated-stamped vessels. They range from small nubs to large cones (Figure 6.5). The tiny vessel from Pierce Mound A, also in the drawing at the opening of this chapter, is only 4.5 cm in diameter and could have been for pigment or condiments or even a toy. The large fabric-marked podal support from Trestle Bridge site (8Ja186) may be from a pot with more mundane use.

Ceramic Types

Most Early Woodland ceramics are recognized by their surface treatments involving stamping the wet clay before firing (Figure 6.6). Deptford Simple-Stamped features parallel straight lines impressed with a thin rod and resembles other Simple-Stamped ceramics throughout the South. The few fiber-tempered Simple-Stamped sherds known from coastal Late Archaic in the region have been suggested as transitional forms leading toward this Deptford type but, so far, they appear to be contemporaneous with, even earlier than, fiber-tempered plain (White 2003b). Deptford Simple-Stamped has sometimes been differentiated from "cross-stamped" when the parallel lines cross (leaving raised squares or rectangles, as in Figure 6.6g), but obviously this comes from overstamping. A single vessel displaying both parallel and crossed lines cannot have two type names. Deptford Simple-Stamped can have local attributes. For example, at the Trestle Bridge site (8Ja186) in the upper Apalachicola, sherds of this type were friable, crumbling when immersed in water, and also often broke on coil marks (White 1982). Simple-stamped sherds are less numerous in Early Woodland assemblages than are check-stamped sherds, but permit temporal assignment.

Figure 6.6. Definite and probable Deptford ceramics from Chattahoochee Landing mounds (8Gd4): (a–c) rim, and (d–f) body sherds of generic check-stamped; (g) Deptford Simple-Stamped; (h) Deptford Linear Check-Stamped (all #8Gd4-3-a, Mound 2 area surface, except for *bottom right*, #75-10-1 Mound 2 profile, 60 cm deep). (Nancy Marie White)

Deptford Fabric-Marked pottery (see Figure 6.5) is similar to other Early Woodland fabric-impressed types in the South, though rarer in the research region. It may be early or late in the Early Woodland sequence and often does not occur with other diagnostics, suggesting it might be less completely indigenous there, or used for specific functions. In sherds with smoothed or eroded surfaces, it can be hard to distinguish from cord-marked pottery (impressed with twisted cords), which is mostly later. Fabric marking shows individual cords woven over and under other cords. Some impressions indicate only strips of woven material (sashes?) or complex weaves with raised elements. This pottery illustrates sophisticated textile-production traditions for which we have no preserved examples. It also implies that cloth was used to hold or mold wet clay pots before firing.

Check-stamping, impressing pot surfaces with a crisscross or checkerboard pattern that leaves raised edges (lands) of small squares or rectangles, is ubiquitous in space and time across the South. Again, this must have been a utilitarian surface treatment, with alternate functional capabilities from those of plain-surfaced vessels. But different technologies may be subsumed under this category. Most diagnostic is Deptford Linear Check-Stamped (Figure 6.6h), the first Early Woodland type presented by Willey (1949:354–356), which he thought was the earliest. It has checks with the parallel lands of one direction more pronounced than those of the transverse direction. In reality it may differ from regular check-stamped by being executed not with a carved paddle but with some kind of notched roller. Willey's (1949:357) "Bold" Check-Stamped is now simply known as Deptford Check-Stamped. There is nothing particularly bold about it, and Willey admitted it was difficult to distinguish. His estimated check sizes, 3 to 7 mm, as well as tempers and other attributes, overlapped characteristics of other check-stamped types of all later time periods; Figure 6.6a–f show a range of check sizes. There seem to be no distinguishing attributes for this type beyond the occasional tetrapodal support. Rims are plain or stamped, rounded or squared, sloppily or neatly folded or straight, resembling those of later check-stamped types. Pots range in size from small bowls to larger open vessels. The bowl from Trestle Bridge site (8Ja186) is 22.5 cm in interior rim diameter, grit and grog-tempered, and has some of the rim fold remaining (Figure 6.7).

Swift-Creek-series ceramics first appeared near the end of Early Woodland in the region, as originally noted by primary investigators Willey (1949) along the coast and Caldwell (Smith 1978) on the lower Chattahoochee. Complex designs were impressed with carved paddles of wood, clay, and possibly stone. Swift Creek pottery saw its height of diversity and ubiquity during the following three to five centuries of the Middle Woodland period and lasted into Late Woodland, as discussed in the next chapter and in Volume 2. But its

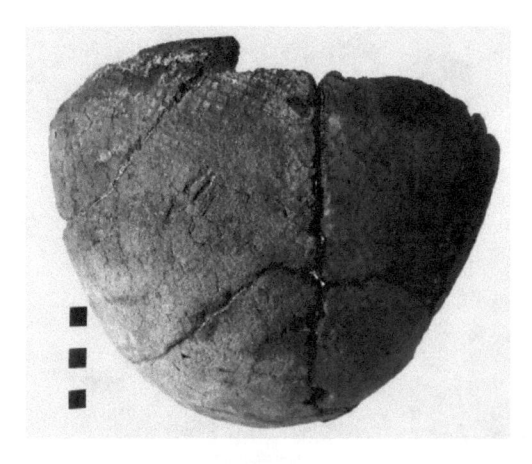

Figure 6.7. Deptford Check-Stamped bowl from Trestle Bridge site; bottom and lower left surface eroded (#8Ja186-1, -2). (Nancy Marie White)

occurrence on some tetrapodal vessels and with other Early Woodland types at sites with no clear Middle Woodland components, indicates it emerged during Early Woodland times. It began the trends toward elaborate craftwork and complicated imagery that blossomed during the Middle Woodland. An interesting artifact found on Choctawhatchee Bay at the Bell site (8Ok19), 125–150 km to the west of the research region, illustrates the difficulties of pigeonholing types and time periods. From this estuarine shell midden, with Early Woodland and later components (Florida Master Site File data), came an actual fired-clay paddle used for pottery manufacture. One side of it is cut in checks and the other in a complicated design; it is displayed at the Fort Walton Beach Temple Mound Museum. The types in this series are Swift Creek Complicated-Stamped, with complex designs, symmetrical or not, in curvilinear patterns (Figure 6.8); St. Andrews Complicated-Stamped (Figure 6.9) and Crooked River Complicated-Stamped, with rectilinear patterns; and New River Complicated-Stamped, with designs combining checks and curvilinear elements. Willey (1949) distinguished between early complicated-stamped, in which the stamping covered most of the pot, and a later variety, with stamping only in a band around the upper vessel.

With large sherds or whole pots, extensive study of the stamped designs has been possible. Frankie Snow (2007) compiled a database of known patterns, showing their incredible range of rhythmic elements, from blunt and simple to complex. Some have names reflecting what they look like (bullseyes, teardrops, snowshoes), but Snow's database numbers the patterns and lists sites where they occur, showing their wide distributions. For example, the sherd in Figure 6.8b somewhat resembles his pattern #7, and Figure 6.8c, with a motif that resembles spoked wheels, is Snow's design #90, found as far away as central Georgia. The Figure 6.8d sherd is suggested as an early variety because the pattern extends over the whole vessel, though the rim projection may be

Figure 6.8. (above) Early Swift Creek Complicated-Stamped ceramics: (a–c) from Green Point Mound (8Fr11) (NMAI#180247; b has notched rim, c has straight rim); (d) from Richardson's Hammock Mound (#8Gu10-HJ18-23), with horizontal triangular rim projection. (Nancy Marie White)

Figure 6.9. (left) St. Andrews Complicated-Stamped vessel with notched rim, from Isabel Landing Mound (8Gu4; NMAI#174012). (Nancy Marie White)

more typical of Middle Woodland. Pottery at Green Point and Howard Creek Mounds and others also included vessels with notched rims, typical of early Swift Creek types. Though interpretation of these two sites depends on secondary data, confirmation of Swift Creek–series pottery in Early Woodland times also comes from controlled excavation. At Depot Creek shell midden, complicated-stamped sherds, including New River Complicated-Stamped, were mixed with the diagnostic Deptford types in only the top four 15-cm levels of the summit test units, which had included up to 13 Early Woodland levels, for a total of 34 out of 1,643 sherds (3% of total sherd weight), and only Level 1 (top 15 cm) of one slope unit that had compressed stratification.

Similarly, at Clark Creek shell midden complicated-stamped sherds occurred with the Deptford types only in the uppermost levels (White 1994b).

At a few Middle Woodland sites there is minimal evidence for a rocker-stamped type that must be labeled Santa Rosa Stamped. In the USF database for the entire region there are only a handful of coastal sites and one inland (Waddell's Mill Pond, 8Ja65) with two or three sherds that can be securely classified within the Santa Rosa series originally defined by Willey, which occurs mostly to the west of the research region, around Pensacola. The Santa Rosa Stamped pattern was done with a curved edge, probably a shell, rocked across the wet clay surface to leave connected curved zigzags. Santa Rosa–series types were so important in Willey's initial definitions of time periods that we are unfortunately left with not only a ceramic series but a whole temporal/cultural unit named "Santa Rosa-Swift Creek," which is inappropriate in general but especially for the Apalachicola–lower Chattahoochee valley region, where Santa Rosa types are so rare. Other Early Woodland ceramics may include cordmarked, described above, and net-marked (see Figure 2.9). These types have no formal names but are surely related to known Woodland types across the South. Their surface treatments may have been analogous to check stamping, for the same utilitarian reasons.

Continuity is indicated in the transition from later Early Woodland, when Swift Creek–series pottery first appears, into Middle Woodland, when it flowers, accompanying the first appearance of fancy early Weeden Island–series types of pottery. Early Woodland has the earliest burial mounds and imported exotic grave goods. At Mandeville mounds, far upriver, ceramics of the later Early Woodland strata were Swift Creek Complicated-Stamped with the notched lip of the early style, New River Complicated-Stamped, rocker- and dentate-stamped Santa Rosa–series types, and cord-marked, while check stamping dwindled; these were associated with Hopewellian-type flake knives, quartz crystals, copper, galena, mica, and other exotics. In the research region, both Huckleberry Landing and Howard Creek Mounds had exotic burial goods such as copper.

Archaeological tradition sometimes explains any new artifact type as something introduced from elsewhere. For pottery we must allow the possibility that it was the contents that were brought in. Pots or foodstuffs could be from economic exchange or gifts from visitors, socially or ideologically significant because of distant origins or because of the giver. Research using pXRF to identify trace elements in a sample of Deptford ceramics from Depot Creek shell midden showed that they mostly clustered as a group apart from pottery from other time periods and from sites farther upriver (Koppe 2010; Tykot et al. 2013), suggesting local clays and local potters. But the Swift Creek Complicated-Stamped sherds from the site have not yet been tested.

Figure 6.10. Clay figurine fragment or ceramic rim effigy of human head from surface of Clark Creek shell midden (#8Gu60-88-28). (Nancy Marie White)

Other Ceramic Materials

In the Apalachicola–lower Chattahoochee region so far only one fragment of a figurine (Figure 6.10) is known, probably associated with Early Woodland deposits. It came from the surface of Clark Creek shell midden and has a lesser chance of being from the site's deep Late Archaic component. This small sand-tempered clay human effigy has a pointed head possibly indicating a topknot, a V-shaped slight cleft at the base of the point, slit eyes, a protruding nose and chin, the suggestion of a right ear, and a turned-down slit mouth. It is broken at the neck and curved flat in the back, as if that surface was the inside of something; so it might be an outward-facing rim effigy on a pot instead of a stand-alone figure. The Mandeville site, noted previously, far up the Chattahoochee, produced several female figurines associated with the latest Early Woodland deposits (Kellar et al. 1962). Clay objects at Early Woodland sites besides ceramic vessels also include the discs for backing copper ear decorations (see Plate XIIIb).

Other Material Culture

Shell tools, usually of sturdy lightning whelk and rarely of quahog clam, have come from Early Woodland sites. These include scoops or spatulas, hammers, and columella (inner whorl) tools, as well as debitage with cut marks from artifact manufacture. Many of these are probably purely utilitarian, but the three lightning whelk "gouges" in the Mound Below Bristol were burial offerings, as were a finely made shell scoop and three pendants of interesting shapes from Green Point mound (see Figure 2.16). Tiny shell beads, perforated discs, are associated with Early Woodland contexts, whether mounds or habitation sites. Kelly (1953) noted their presence at Lake Douglas Mound. They include a wide variety of styles. Some are near-perfect perforated circles, such as the two

Figure 6.11. Shell disc beads from Pierce Mound C (#8Fr14-07-25.1, except *bottom far right*, 07-6.9). (Nancy Marie White)

recovered at Clark Creek shell midden (White 1994b:Figure 23). One of these is not perfectly flat and measures 3 mm thick, 7.8 mm in diameter, with an off-center hole 2.3 mm in diameter. The more regular, smoothed, rounded one is 4.7 mm thick and 7.4 mm in diameter, with a centered hole 3 mm in diameter. From the looters' backdirt at Pierce Mound C we recovered seven disc beads (Figure 6.11) that were probably Early Woodland. All were of lightning whelk shell, with central perforations but only roughed-out shapes that suggest they were unfinished. Most were more square than round; they measured 12 to 28 mm long, 11 to 29 mm wide, and 12 to 74 mm thick (White 2013). With these dimensions they might be in a different artifact class from the Clark Creek beads; however, after finishing they might have been similar.

Bone tools from definite Early Woodland contexts are rare. Notable is a deer-bone hook recovered at Depot Creek shell midden, from TUA L9, 135 cm deep. It is U-shaped, broken at both ends and only 3.5 cm long (see Figure 2.12). This is an unusual find, as prehistoric hooks are most often V-shaped and made as composite tools, separate pieces secured together (Karen Walker, personal communication 1988). However, this implement may not be for fishing but just hooking or hanging anything. Bone points and pins known from Late Archaic contexts at estuarine shell middens undoubtedly continued through Early Woodland times. Not difficult to carve, sharpen, and engrave, bone was undoubtedly used for both practical implements and decorations. Another bone item worthy of note is the pneumatized fish bone (see Figure 2.11). These small, banana-shaped bones show cut marks for some human use. As with all other time periods, most Early Woodland artifacts would have been of perishable materials.

Subsistence, Seasonality, Environments

How Early Woodland groups made a living in the Apalachicola–lower Chattahoochee region is inferred from site locations; from the species identified in faunal and floral assemblages, mostly at estuarine shell middens where they are preserved; from ethnographic analogy; and from the archaeology of related regions.

Animal Remains

Major components of the estuarine shell-midden matrix are *Rangia* and *Polymesoda* marsh clam shells, usually with a few oysters. This combination suggests that people were exploiting different brackish and freshwater environments, or that salinities near their camps fluctuated over time. Whether they got whatever was closest at different times of occupation or went farther from home to get desired resources is unknown. Fewer oyster shell middens on bayshores have Early Woodland deposits. Other species represented in unambiguous Early Woodland proveniences include deer; small mammals such as rat, rabbit, squirrel, opossum, raccoon, and muskrat; a few birds; alligator; a variety of turtles; and a large number of fish including croaker, mullet, herring, seatrout, marine catfish, rays/skates, porgies/drums, shark, and gar. Other shellfish include gastropods such as crown conch, tulip, and terrestrial snails, and a few quahog clams for tools. Many more species come from mixed Early Woodland and later contexts in the shell middens. At Richardson's Hammock on St. Joseph Bay, the tiny amount of Early Woodland ceramics, the earliest evidence of the site's occupation, are mixed with Middle Woodland deposits (White et al. 2002). However, the presence of sea turtle in the faunal assemblage may indicate the reason for and season when people first came. Though turtles do not nest on the bay shores, they swim south in winter, and really cold waters cause them to be cold-stunned and even easier to harvest. Inland sites in the region have few faunal remains preserved, but freshwater shell middens contain both river mussels and snails. In general, Early Woodland sites indicate fishing and hunting of everything available during all seasons, certainly with the assistance of the long-domesticated dog. Coastal and estuarine sites maintain and sometimes expand the list of fauna seen during the Late Archaic, demonstrating persistence yet flexibility in subsistence strategies.

Plant Remains

The only plant remains identified from unmixed Early Woodland contexts in the research region are oak, pine, hickory, and the generic "hardwood." They were preserved by being charred and are probably bits of fuel. Bullen (1958) did get a nut fragment from the Early Woodland Zone 6 at the

Chattahoochee River 1 site. Mixed proveniences that may be from this time period have produced a few additional macrobotanical fragments of grasses and fruit (grape). Indigenous peoples must have used hundreds of plant species, and probably managed some in the region's forests and marshes. Though in parts of the eastern United States, actual food production was going on since the Archaic, right along with gathering wild plants, so far no evidence of managed, cultivated, or domesticated plants has come from Apalachicola–lower Chattahoochee region Early (or Middle) Woodland contexts.

As elsewhere in the South, people probably harvested acorn, hickory, and other nuts; wild fruits, especially persimmons, grapes, huckleberries, sparkleberries, and dewberries; tubers such as groundnut; and leafy greens, maybe in early spring when stored resources were running out (Fritz 2000:233). Domesticated bottle gourds, by Early Woodland times known for thousands of years, must have continued in use as containers or floats. Beyond cultivation, a separate question is whether Early Woodland subsistence behavior included food storage and/or surplus accumulation, which could be linked to the beginnings of social, if not yet economic, inequality. Nuts and dried fruits are easily storable, as was surely known long before the Early Woodland. There is no information so far on whether sites were inhabited long-term or just seasonally.

Early Woodland People, Society, and Ideology

Human Biology

The only extant Early Woodland human skeletal remains from the research region came from the Yellow Houseboat site (8Gu55), a multicomponent estuarine shell midden (White 1994b). A burial of an adult man lying flexed on his right side was exposed in the clamshell along the shore of Lake Wimico at low tide. It was scraped by boats landing there, so removal was necessary. He was 35 to 45 years old and 157 cm (5'2") tall and had a healed fracture or lesion on the right ulna. A rib fragment was dated cal AD 80–320. There were no grave goods or delineated burial pit. While flexing the body would facilitate burial since a smaller grave could be dug in the hard shell, we cannot know why he was put within the food refuse deposits; perhaps the shell midden matrix was sacred because it was left by ancestors. Interestingly, this site also later yielded skeletons and artifacts of historic individuals from the late 1800s (described in Volume 2).

A secondary adult burial from the base of Lake Douglas Mound (9Dr21), with no grave goods, suggesting Early Woodland affiliation, included a skull with marked frontal and slight lambdoidal flattening (Kelly 1953:7). Wrapping an infant's head in a cradleboard produces this kind of cranial modification to the soft young bones, which results in a sloped profile in side view and a wider top of the head in front view. The practice was probably deliberate, done for beautification or other social reasons. Other ideas of what people looked like could come from figurines, such as one from Mandeville showing a woman with a serious face, a torso with small protruding breasts, a short skirt, arms and hands at her side, and long hair falling to the middle of her back (Kellar et al. 1962). The Clark Creek human effigy previously noted indicates a plain face and high head.

The biology of human populations from this time period cannot yet be described. But we can infer general characteristics from other anthropological work. As noted in previous chapters, hunter-gatherer-foragers usually have healthier, if more worn, bones and teeth than do agriculturalists, due to good diets and lots of physical labor. Ethnographies of seasonal foragers in east Africa show that they ingest up to 100 g of fiber per day and have far more diverse sets of gut flora than do people in today's western society, since they absorb bacteria from fresh meats and other environmental sources. The research suggests that their lifestyles and diverse microbiomes may help prevent "modern" diseases such as diabetes, cancer, and cardiovascular illness, though their shorter lifespans are other reasons for such statistics (De Vrieze 2014).

Social and Ceremonial Systems

Reconstructing social organization is often done based on burial ceremonialism. Since we cannot be sure which graves in mounds in the Apalachicola–lower Chattahoochee region are Early Woodland in age, only speculation based on the archaeology of this time period elsewhere in the South is possible. Conical burial mounds and apparently flat-topped platform mounds do exist in the region as early as Early Woodland. They imply ritual practice, social integration, and communal labor, but possibly not hierarchical leadership. Accumulation of shell middens that ended up being mounded and ridged is not the same thing. In this research region shell middens all appear to be piles of domestic garbage from continual or repeated disposal, not ceremonial structures or intentionally designed edifices. However, shell midden materials were used in individual graves in sand burial mounds. We cannot yet know whether many people quickly constructed a mound or a few people built one over a long time, or how this activity was directed. The building up of mounds containing individual graves may have been done in activity bursts whose timing depended on seasons, aggregation of the right people, collection of the remains of all the deceased, the importance of those who had died, and other factors.

Current knowledge suggests that complex Native American social systems involving hereditary elites with greater political and/or economic control over others did not yet exist during the Early Woodland. However, there were doubtless people with more respect and authority, if not real power. As noted in previous chapters, warm, lush forests are often settings for egalitarian hunter-gatherer-fisher peoples who may not even have a division of labor based on gender, let alone recognize different social statuses (e.g., Endicott and Endicott 2008). But anthropologists have been mistaken before in seeing egalitarian foragers in such settings as recorded in the ethnographic present to be representative of past societies that were really much more complex and stratified, as in Papua New Guinea or the Xingu Amazon (e.g., Heckenberger 2005). Yet, ethnographic analogies applied to prehistoric data are always questionable because no recorded cultures have remained unchanged for thousands of years, and even historic forager groups, few as they are, have amazing diversity.

Terms for the Early Woodland include "intermediate societies," "emergent complexity," complex foragers, or early tribal entities. Nothing is known of group interaction, cooperation or competition; no evidence exists for warfare. Networking along connected waterways was doubtless constant. As for symbolic or ceremonial systems, not much can be said without well-dated evidence showing something special beyond everyday life except for the mound graves with elaborate artifacts. But belief systems may have been enormously complex, involving different elements of the natural and spiritual worlds. To quote Mel Brooks again in *The 2000-Year-Old Man* comedy skit, "back then, mainly sitting and looking at the sky was a big job!" (Brooksfilms Limited 1994). Tracking the movements of heavenly bodies, seasons, winds, animal behavior, life cycles, and rites of passage probably involved many teaching moments, celebratory times, and special artifacts. Some culture change during the later part of Early Woodland began the trajectory toward fancier pottery, more exotic burial goods, and far more diverse material culture in general. These suggest innovation, possibly outside influence, expansion of social systems, and probably enormously significant ideological developments. So little is known of the Early Woodland in the region that we can only explore the glory of Middle Woodland and look for ancestral behaviors that were its foundations.

7

Middle Woodland Period, AD 300 to 700

Middle Woodland in the Southeast marks the height of burial mound ceremonialism, with ornate ceramics and exotic artifacts imported via long-distance networks. The uneven distribution of these valued objects signals more complex social differentiation and elaborate ritual behavior, though probably not economic stratification. Within the Apalachicola–lower Chattahoochee valley region, about 200 Middle Woodland sites include some 40 burial mounds, usually with nearby villages. Fancy material culture means people were fascinated with the showy and unusual. Swift Creek Complicated-Stamped pottery continued on from Early Woodland times to accompany early Weeden Island types that first appear before AD 500 in diverse designs and shapes, including animal and human effigies. Chipped-stone tools were often made of foreign cherts; greenstone, steatite, mica, quartz crystal, and other shiny rocks came from afar. Marine shell, copper, galena, and even silver appeared in grave goods. Settlement and subsistence systems of hunting, gathering, and fishing continued as in earlier times, although populations may have been expanding. The transition from Early Woodland was an in-place intensification of cultural processes already underway, with new ostentation but perhaps no great change in fundamental lifeways.

The Middle Woodland period often commands more attention in the southeastern United States because the material culture is extraordinary and the mounds are conspicuous. It is characterized by distinctive artifact styles and raw materials, apparent widespread ritual traditions, and "spheres of interaction" or networks connecting regions (Struever and Houart 1972). A vast literature is devoted to both scientific research and imaginative reconstruction of Middle Woodland society and ideology. Investigation in the

Apalachicola–lower Chattahoochee region began with Moore's 1901–1918 mound explorations, though well before he arrived exquisite artifacts were dug out of graves. Later excavations tied burial mound ritual to that already defined for the archaeological manifestation called Hopewell in the Midwest. Moore and others recognized connections between Midwestern Middle Woodland and mounds in the South, including the Pierce Mounds complex at the mouth of the Apalachicola River (Greenman 1938; Prendergast and White 2014). Today, habitation sites are more investigated, for a fuller picture of Native American life at this time, but emphasis remains on exotic raw materials, unique artifact designs, mortuary programs, and complex earthen architecture over broad regions. Though many associated characteristics, from mound construction to sedentism to food production, were present in the East earlier, Middle Woodland was a time when these combined into something bigger (Williams and Elliott 1998).

In the research region Middle Woodland is recognized by the disappearance of Early Woodland Deptford pottery, the continuation of Swift Creek–series ceramics, and appearance of early Weeden Island–series types, burial mounds, and chronometric dates. Another aspect of this time period is the immense diversity in material culture, greater than at any time before or after. The distinctive pots were the main reason that Moore kept returning to the region over 16 years. But two issues haunt Middle Woodland research here. The first is pottery terminology. Swift Creek and Weeden Island are ceramic series, but unfortunately these terms have come to mean "cultures" and even separate time periods. Though Swift Creek pottery emerges during Early Woodland, both series characterize Middle Woodland, together for several centuries. A goal of this chapter is to underscore this long-recognized overlap and advocate for more appropriate language and categories. A second concern is misunderstandings introduced by work at Kolomoki Mounds, upriver and outside the region, but with interpretations still causing widespread confusion.

Middle Woodland Settlement

At least 200 Middle Woodland sites are recorded in the region (Figure 7.1), of which 20% are burial mounds. Site locations are along waterways. Map biases include those noted in earlier chapters: the gaps in areas not extensively surveyed, away from riverbanks in the lower Chattahoochee and Flint, and the lower Apalachicola alluviated areas, where sites are probably still buried by natural processes. A site concentration on the east side of the upper Apalachicola is the result of FSU surveys in the Torreya Ravines area, not necessarily because bluff tops were preferred for settlement. Criteria for inclusion on this map expose other biases. To be called Middle Woodland, the sites needed to have early Weeden Island ceramics, with or without Swift Creek ceramics,

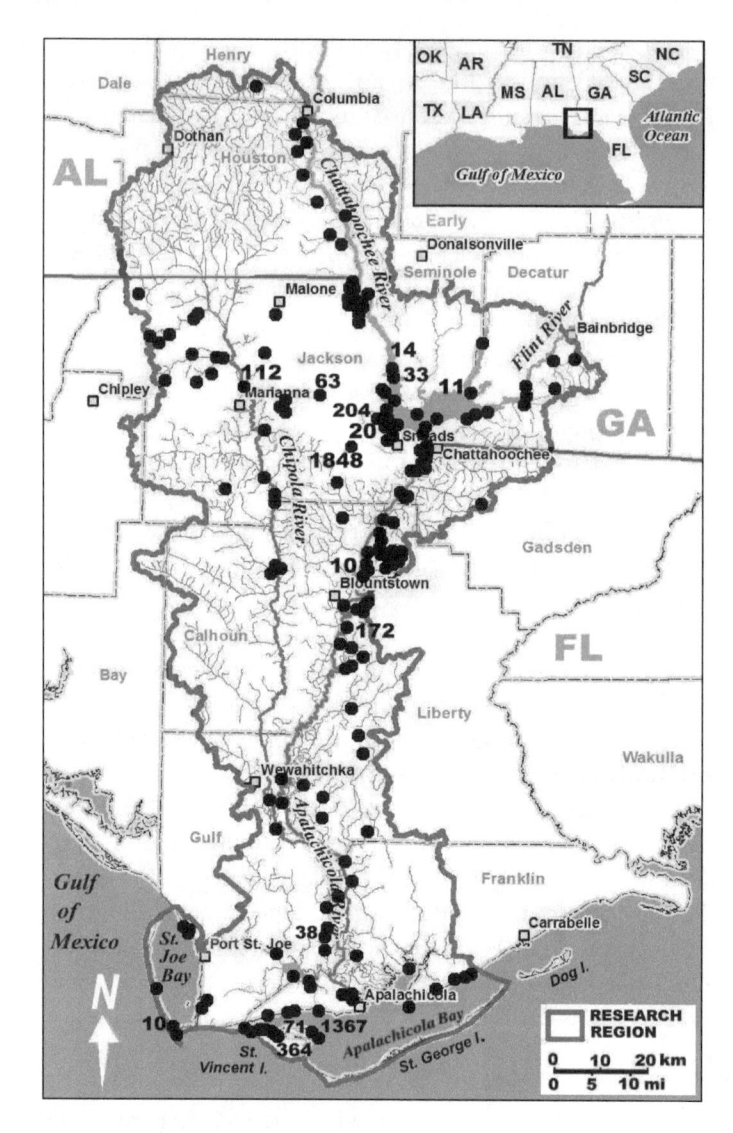

Figure 7.1. Middle Woodland sites. Numbered sites are discussed in the text. (Nancy Marie White)

or typical burial mounds, or appropriate dates. Unfortunately, interpretations are loose, and this site distribution is difficult to compare with maps of sites labeled either "Swift Creek" or "Weeden Island," the two contemporaneous ceramic series; however, gaps and biases can be addressed with strategic sampling and tighter concepts (Smith and Stephenson 2017).

Mounds

Middle Woodland mounds and sensational artifacts have drawn the most archaeological attention in the research region. According to Gordon Willey

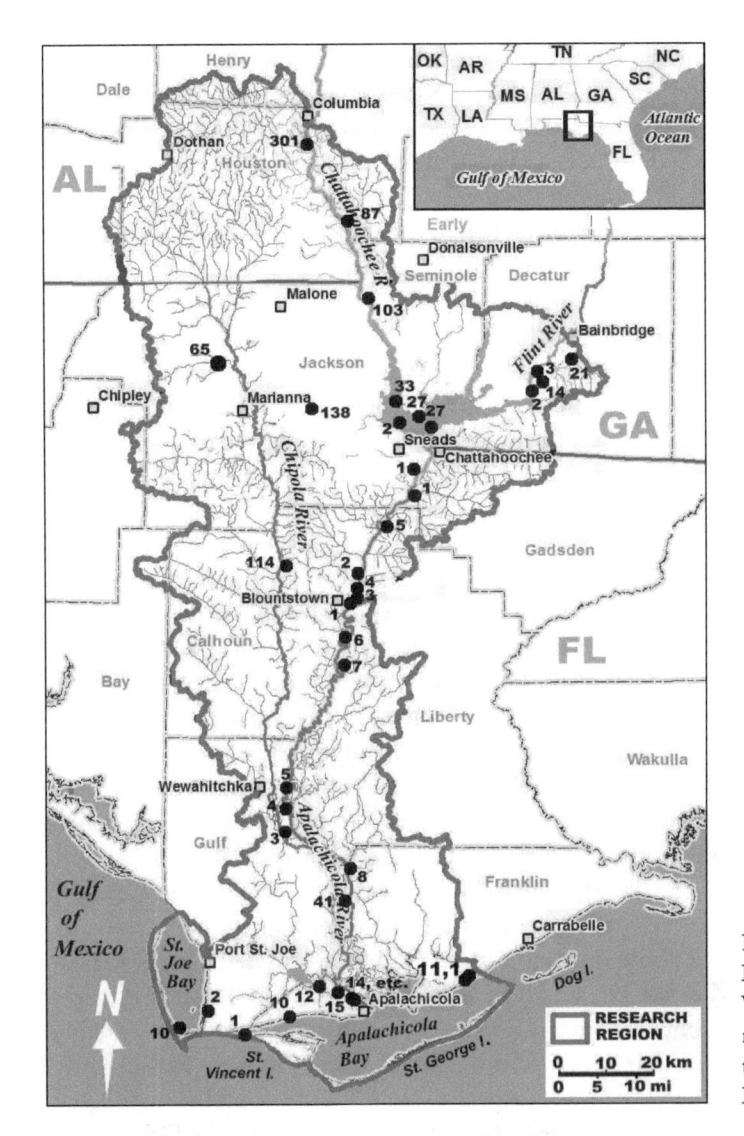

Figure 7.2. Middle Woodland mound locations. (Nancy Marie White)

(personal communication 1999) his fascination with northwest Florida's flamboyant early Weeden Island ceramics led to his landmark *Archeology of the Florida Gulf Coast* (1949). Despite centuries of looting, about 40 Middle Woodland mounds (Figure 7.2) are recorded in the region, though some have minimal information (Lockman 2020). They are all individual mounds except for two groups: Aspalaga (8Gd1), with three, though two may not have been for burial; and the Pierce complex (8Fr14 and other numbers), with 13 mounds, though only five have clear Middle Woodland components. Many more mounds probably once existed. One was reported to me in 2012 by a lifelong resident of the city of Apalachicola who said it was a sand mound on 5th Street, razed long ago and now a baseball field. Most of C. B. Moore's mound locations are known, though at least a dozen still elude rediscovery. His Hare's Landing (9Se33; Caldwell et al. 2014), and Kemp's Landing (8Ja2; Bullen 1958) Mounds, both on the lower Chattahoochee, were relocated only after bulldozing and forest clearing before the reservoir, and both are now underwater. Seven mounds unknown to Moore have been documented thanks to local residents.

In the Midwest and mid-South, Early Woodland Adena mound ceremonialism preceded the more elaborate Middle Woodland expressions of Hopewell, though the relationships and dating of the transitions remain unclear. This is also true in the Deep South. In the research region, over a half dozen of the Middle Woodland mounds have Early Woodland components. A few also have later Fort Walton–period components and possibly unrecognized Late Woodland components, with or without burials, that suggest reuse of sacred places. These burial mounds were conical, though flat-topped mounds built in Early or Middle Woodland times are now recognized across the Southeast (Kassabaum 2018). However, the research region has only one possible Woodland platform, at Waddell's Mill Pond (8Ja65). No mound sites in the region have earthen berms, enclosures, or ditches. Nor do any so far show astronomical alignments, as are seen with Hopewellian earthen enclosures in the Midwest, though all these peoples surely had meticulous knowledge of the sky. The research region's mounds are humble and small compared with many elsewhere in the East, but the material culture is equally noteworthy.

These mounds are all either adjacent to or within a few hundred meters of fresh water. They average 16 m in diameter and over a meter high. These dimensions resemble those of Middle Woodland mounds elsewhere; for example, 14 in the Midwest averaged 14.2 to 17 m wide and 1.7 m high (Charles 1992:182). The 40 mounds in a region extending over 160 river miles could be seen as spaced on average every four waterway miles (6 km), an easy distance. But the numbers are deceptive, since the mounds are not evenly distributed. More evidently cluster along the coast, the middle valley, and the forks. Landscape models might assume that spacing between mound centers reflected the farthest distance able to be traveled by land or water in a day or two (e.g., Dengel 2015 for the St. Andrews Bay area, west of the region).

We do not yet know whether mounds were hidden sacred places or highly visible community markers, isolated ceremonial centers or integrated into daily life, with regular villages or just areas where people stayed periodically for burial activities. At Hare's Landing (9Se33), Jackson (8Fr15), and Porter's Bar (8Fr1), middens were adjacent to the mounds and continued well beyond them along shorelines. At Indian Pass (8Gu1), on a peninsula jutting into St.

Vincent Sound, the associated shell midden is 150 m away from the mound, on more sheltered bayside waters. The closest habitation to Gotier Hammock Mound (8Gu2), which sits over 200 m east of St. Joseph Bay, is a low-density shell midden right on the bayshore that has not produced unquestionable Middle Woodland evidence. We shovel-tested extensively there, looking for any habitation, and found nothing closer. Patterns of mound use seem to have been quite diverse.

Habitation Sites

Middle Woodland residential sites in the research region can be large villages or small occupations such as hamlets or homesteads (Wright 2017:45), but specific households have so far not been recognized. Many habitation sites have produced fancy artifacts once thought to be exclusive to mounds. Either these objects were being made or prepared at home, or else they also had domestic use before being interred with the dead. Only a few domestic sites have been tested, and they often have earlier and later components both vertically stratified and horizontally overlapping. Freshwater shell middens may have individual horizontal shell scatters ranging from a few meters to 30 or 40 m in diameter, separated by nonshell zones that still contain domestic debris. This is the case at Hare's Landing (9Se33) and Fairchild's Landing (9Se14), 5 river miles apart on the lower Chattahoochee (Caldwell et al. 2014) and also, nearly 100 river miles downriver, at the Otis Hare site (8Li172) on the middle Apalachicola.

No structure patterns or discrete activity areas are yet known at habitation sites. Percy and Brose (1974:17–18) reported a "Weeden Island I" house spatially removed from a cluster of Late Woodland houses at the Parish Lake site (8Ca10), but no documentation is available. The 1953 Fairchild's Landing excavations exposed a block of about 140 m^2, with another 85 m^2 opened in trenches, but no postmold or other structure patterns, though two red-clay floor-like areas, one given as 2 × 1.2 m, might have been living surfaces (Caldwell et al. 2014:12–13, Figures 2, 3). The site also had large Early and Late Woodland components, and some 64 features, mostly garbage pits. The features might have marked domestic places sheltered with lean-to buildings that left few traces. The Middle Woodland Block-Sterns site (8Le148) in Tallahassee, 65 km east of the region, did have two structures indicated by postmold patterns, called oval, though one looks rectangular on the map; they were 4 m wide and 10 m long (Jones et al. 1998).

Elsewhere in the East, circular house patterns are common for the Middle Woodland (over 65%); oval, rectangular, and square structures are also found, and all range from 7 to 146 m^2. Building outlines are recognized by postmold alignments or packed earthen floors, sometimes sunken or with differently colored soil. Houses may have been made with poles stuck in the ground, bent to meet in the middle, and tied at the top to support a roof, perhaps of thatch or palmetto branches. Walls may have been of wattle and daub, woven cane mats, or bark. Hearths and pits for refuse or storage might be inside or outside. Use life for such houses is estimated at 10 to 20 years (Steere 2017:18–22, 79) before repair or reconstruction was needed.

Interpretive Constraints

The Kolomoki Mound group and its misinterpretations (discussed below), as well as the McKeithen Mounds, have influenced interpretations of Middle Woodland in the Apalachicola–lower Chattahoochee region, even though these two sites are far away. They are the closest Middle Woodland centers to have had modern extensive excavation, and they are contemporaneous, clearly culturally related, but different from Middle Woodland in the research region. Typical discussions of ceramics or belief systems or other aspects of Middle Woodland culture still reference these well-known sites as if their size and the amount written about them mean they were the places from which all else emanated. But in between them, the Apalachicola–lower Chattahoochee valley looks different.

At McKeithen (Milanich et al. 1984), 250 km to the east, in north-central Florida, Swift Creek pottery is rare and mostly early Weeden Island ceramic types overlie Early Woodland deposits. Kolomoki does have both Swift Creek and early Weeden Island ceramics, with greater connections to the research region. But it is in the upper part of the lower Chattahoochee, nearer to the fall line, 22 waterway miles (35 km) away from the farthest north end of the region, in a contrasting, more hilly environment. Kolomoki's many differences include its huge size (ca. 1 km^2); log-lined graves in mounds; large rocks used in mound building; abundant fire-cracked rock; earthen enclosure; and semisubterranean house pattern, a keyhole-shaped basin floor, which is the southernmost expression of this structure type in the East (Pluckhahn 2003; Steere 2017). These phenomena are unknown in the region of concern in this book. In addition, around Kolomoki, as in much of Georgia farther to the north and east, complicated-stamping of pottery continued in types that persisted through Late Woodland and Mississippian times, while it disappeared after early Late Woodland in the research region. Similarly, quartz as a raw material is relatively abundant at Kolomoki, used for about a quarter of the chipped-stone tools (Pluckhahn 2003:104). It is common for lithic artifacts farther north in Georgia, but rare in the research region. These material traits help establish the distinctiveness of the Apalachicola–lower Chattahoochee region as a cultural entity, though of course Middle Woodland long-distance relationships extended across the whole eastern United States.

Dating Middle Woodland in the Region

Burial mound ceremonialism reached its greatest elaboration early in the Midwest, by the end of Early Woodland times, a few centuries BC. Textbooks often define Woodland burial-mound-building cultures as phenomena that began or had their heartlands in the Midwest with Adena and Hopewell, implying that from there things spread. Many illustrate this in maps with much of the South left out. In reality, native groups all over the eastern United States built Early and especially Middle Woodland mounds. Terminology structures interpretation, and names of "cultures" and "phases" are really parochial constructs, implying timing, place of origin, and dominance. Because Hopewellian burial mounds were once considered the most exciting prehistoric archaeology in the East, everything explored afterward was related to this and subsumed within this nomenclature. Now southeastern archaeologists realize the amount of temporal and material variation in what is both strictly and liberally called Hopewell (Brose and Greber 1979), and how Middle Woodland cultures in the Deep South are related but different, needing description in their own terms (Wright 2017). The Hopewell horizon in the Midwest to mid-South emerged around 200 BC and transitioned into Late Woodland by about AD 400. In the Deep South, including the research region, Middle Woodland similarly emerges from an Early Woodland foundation up to a couple centuries later, then lasts a couple centuries longer.

Radiocarbon Chronology

Over a dozen Middle Woodland radiocarbon dates are known for the Apalachicola–lower Chattahoochee region. As noted, the beginning of this time period is fuzzy, marked by the earliest appearance of Swift Creek Complicated-Stamped ceramics without Deptford pottery but with burial mound ritual, elaborate artifacts, and early Weeden Island–series pottery. Early and Middle Woodland are artificial formulations based on established criteria to give some structure to prehistoric time. The transition from one into the next was probably not something those living through it even noticed. The significant phenomenon came when people began to build burial mounds in the first place; they intensified this practice during the Middle Woodland.

A few sites in the research region figure prominently in this chapter because they have had more investigation. The first is the Otis Hare site (8Li172), a Middle through Late Woodland and early Fort Walton freshwater shell midden on the middle Apalachicola riverbank. It was tested in 5-cm excavation levels to subdivide the heavy midden stratum, which was 1.6 m thick and 1.5 m deep. Its radiocarbon dates document ceramic frequency changes through time, though some mixture is apparent from continual reoccupation. The site has yet to be thoroughly reported but provides good chronological information

(Hutchinson et al. 1991; White 2018, and see Volume 2). Two features from the earliest occupation had Middle Woodland dates: Feature 22 in TU1, at cal AD 420–665, and F15 in TU2 at cal AD 261–640, both pits with plain and Swift Creek Complicated-Stamped ceramics. Charcoal in the stratum from which these features derived, 5–10 cm above them, in TU1 L14, dated to cal AD 415–640, and charcoal in a dog coprolite from TU1 L13 dated to cal AD 620–690. Another site is Richardson's Hammock (8Gu10), a large-gastropod shell midden on the St. Joseph Bay shore with a Middle Woodland component and burial mound (White et al. 2002; White 2018). Some looters' collections from this site were regained and studied. One that C. B. Moore missed, Richardson's Hammock Mound, had both showy and mundane ceramics and other grave goods. A few recovered human remains were examined before reburial. Three individuals were associated with dates of cal AD 230–410, 250–420, and 610–700. Finally, on the lower Chattahoochee at the J-Y Field site (8Ja63); Bullen (1958) recorded a single early Middle Woodland date of AD 350 ± 250; though he gave no provenience, it is associated with both Swift Creek Complicated-Stamped and early Weeden Island sherds.

Three radiocarbon dates fall within the Middle Woodland time span but are from sites/proveniences with ambiguous material culture. At Keene Dog Pond site (8Ja1848), in the upper Apalachicola, charcoal next to a sub-plow-zone Bolen Beveled projectile point, expected to be in undisturbed Late Archaic context, was dated at cal AD 540 (Kelley 2013). Either Middle Woodland people reused the point or the tiny bit of charcoal from later human activities made its way downward in the soil; another, deeper Bolen point was associated with charcoal dated to Early Woodland times. Only one complicated-stamped sherd and no early Weeden Island sherds are known out of thousands from this site. A similar situation holds for Chattahoochee Landing site (8Gd4), at the Flint-Chattahoochee forks, where a feature in Mound 1 returned a date of Middle Woodland age though no artifacts from this time period are known there; an explanation is that the soil organics dated gave an erroneously early age and the date is really later (White 2011a, 2021a). In the shell midden unit at the St. Vincent 5 site (8Fr364), a date of cal AD 560–660 on charcoal from the deepest 10-cm level of the meter-thick midden was not accompanied by any diagnostic artifacts, only one check-stamped and 12 plain sherds. It could be simply missing Middle Woodland diagnostics like those from elsewhere at the site with less-controlled proveniences (White and Kimble 2017).

The terminus of Middle Woodland is clearer, with the latest known burial mound manifestation. Two dates on carbonized residue caked onto vessel exteriors at Gotier Hammock Mound (8Gu2) were both cal AD 640–650 (White 2010). One pot is plain and the other is Basin Bayou Incised. So the "end" of

Middle Woodland is set at about AD 700, recognizing that chronometric determinations for any archaeological time periods are often moving targets.

Research Biases and Errors
The term "Hopewell" can obscure understanding of broader Middle Woodland mound building and lifeways. Willey (1999:203) emphasized that eastern United States archaeology, "in any organized, academic way, had its beginnings in the Middle West . . . and it was mostly 'mound-digging.'" But the concept of a Hopewell "interaction sphere" (Struever and Houart 1972) is usually understood within wider contexts linked to distant locations (e.g., Carr and Case 2005). Middle Woodland in the South can be just as spectacular as in the Midwest. And if the timing of research in both regions had been different, we might today talk about Marksvillian or Swift Creek–early Weeden Island spheres of interaction extending into Ohio and Illinois, instead of using the term "Hopewellian" as the default monolithic phenomenon from which those in the South derive (David Brose, personal communication 1979). As a student I attended the landmark first conference on Hopewell archaeology and saw how artifact sourcing and perspectives beyond classic Ohio sites helped develop an awareness of the hugely diverse repertory encompassed within Middle Woodland (Brose and Greber 1979). Recent work more appropriately considers different scales, from artifacts to site complexes, for comparative regional analyses (Wright 2017).

A more serious problem for Middle Woodland chronology came from work at Kolomoki. This distant mound center merits discussion here. The "Kolomoki problem," a name from at least the early 1970s, has colored interpretations for over a half century. As early as 1942, Charles Fairbanks recognized Swift Creek and early Weeden Island ceramic series at Kolomoki that were "combined . . . as on the N.W. Florida Coast" (Trowell 1998:41). But William Sears (e.g., 1956), conducting years of excavations at Kolomoki beginning in 1948, could not reconcile the presence of a huge platform mound, which then meant late prehistoric Mississippian culture, with all the glorious complicated-stamped and early Weeden Island–series Middle Woodland ceramics. Further, he forgot that people build mounds by scraping up dirt from earlier cultural deposits and piling it on top, giving inverted chronological layering. Thus, he hypothesized a "Kolomoki culture" contemporaneous with later Mississippi period cultures elsewhere in the South, even though such a sequence was unknown anywhere else, and accurate ceramic stratification had already been outlined by other researchers. As a student, I became enmeshed in the professional disagreement with Sears's work. I saw letters in the Smithsonian and the University of Georgia archives in which other archaeologists working in the region in the 1950s (Bullen, Caldwell, Kelly, Miller) realized

Sears's chronology was wrong (Caldwell 1958:56–58). But few colleagues, out of courtesy, disagreed with it in print, incorrect as they agreed in private that it was (Trowel 1998). Sears might be forgiven if he had no dates. But, though none appear in his publications, he did have radiocarbon dates.

The Kolomoki dates were published in *Science* in 1956, described as follows: #M-49, 1920 ± 300 years, on charcoal from "a small fireplace at the eastern edge of a mass pottery deposit in mound D. Sequentially, the deposition of the sample fell about midway in the mound-building program"; and #M-50, 2120 ± 300 years, on "charcoal from [a] burned timber over the central grave of mound E. . . . On the basis of ceramic typology, this sample should be slightly older than the mound D sample" (Crane 1956:665). In the *Ohio Journal of Science*, Prufer (1962) described these dates as "36 ± 300 AD (M-49) and 164 ± 300 BC (M-50)." On a copy of that article that was sent to Caldwell, now on file at UGA, Prufer had scribbled "Hopewell Ho!" With modern calibration, these dates range between 762 BC and AD 686, and 833 BC and AD 557, respectively. The huge standard deviations, typical for early radiocarbon assays done shortly after the technique was invented, make accurate placement difficult. But the hovering of the date midpoints around the end of the first century BC should have suggested Early to Middle Woodland associations for both mounds. Prufer (1962:316) even quoted Bullen's (1958:331) date of AD 350 ± 250 from the J-Y Field site since it had similar ceramics and overlapped the Kolomoki date ranges. Milanich et al. (1984:Table 2.2) did later publish Kolomoki village dates (AD 405 ± 25 and 385 ± 75). Further intensive work at Kolomoki has more accurately dated its occupation range from about AD 350 to 750 (Pluckhahn 2003), covering all of Middle Woodland, with the early Weeden Island–series ceramic types showing up in larger numbers later, and the Swift Creek–series pottery there from the beginning.

Meanwhile, from the early 1950s onward, southeastern archaeologists agreed that Early–Middle Woodland manifestations in the South, including at Kolomoki, were roughly contemporaneous with Hopewell in Ohio. They mostly noted the Kolomoki problem only mildly (Knight and Schnell 2004), though many called for abandonment of the "Kolomoki Culture" term and concept (it is now gone), and Chase (1978) was one of the first to suggest a hyphenated "Weeden Island–Swift Creek." Others, such as Fairbanks (curiously, after his statement already quoted) doggedly supported Sears's chronology (Williams 2003), even as various researchers noted this cultural sequence had long been rejected (Percy and Brose 1974). Finally, over thirty years later, Sears (1992) apologized for being wrong about the Kolomoki sequence even in the face of overwhelming evidence that it was incorrect. Yet he still did not mention the dates.

Thus, generations of archaeologists were stuck with inaccurate chronologies and terminology, and Middle Woodland studies were set back considerably (Knight and Schnell 2004; Pluckhahn 2003:4–6). Significantly, Sears's (1959) NSF study, aimed at learning more about sites on the Gulf Coast related to Kolomoki, barely investigated the Apalachicola–lower Chattahoochee–Flint region at all, confused river names and locations, and mixed up some mound site identities (White 2013). It is surprising that he did not relate Kolomoki to what was downriver from it. Decades of work now clarify ceramic stratification and site relationships. Caldwell's 1950s excavations at the Fairchild's Landing (9Se14) and Hare's Landing (9Se33) sites on the lower Chattahoochee within the research region were hugely significant in this. Had Caldwell finished reporting them, he might have prevented decades of bewilderment. Betty Smith (1978) edited his unfinished report into a limited-circulation version. Mark Williams, Karen Smith, and colleagues later produced an expanded version (Caldwell et al. 2014), with commentary including how Caldwell did say Sears's ceramic sequence was mistaken. Though Fairchild's Landing is a typical Woodland freshwater shell midden in the Apalachicola–lower Chattahoochee valley region, it was unusual at the time for its chronological clarity.

Lithic Artifacts

Chipped Stone

Middle Woodland peoples in the research region used many nonlocal cherts. Waterway access well into the continental interior helped for importing stone. Surface sites are easy to spot, with colorful, often jewel-like flakes. Chert varieties can be bluish, pink, golden, or dark gray, often translucent or transparent, in addition to the local honey-colored or white chert. Quartz also occurs. Much of the chipped stone is thermally altered, making it lustrous and reddish. Diagnostic projectile points for the Middle Woodland can be hard to pin down and are often less emphasized, since earlier types are also common in mounds. The most typical are often straight-based or straight-stemmed generic types that could appear at almost any prehistoric time, but the Baker's Creek (Figure 7.3) and Broward Subtype 1 or Hamilton types are more distinctive.

An example of an exotic lithic tool is a clear quartz small-stemmed point from the Arnold Soybean Field site (8Ja204), a freshwater shell midden on an old meander of the lower Chattahoochee (White 1981). Other specialized lithic items such as Hopewellian prismatic blades do not occur in the region. Chipped-stone celts or axes can appear as grave goods, sometimes with ground-stone versions of the same thing. Large bifacial blade caches are well known from Middle Woodland sites in the East, though when found apart from mounds they can be attributable to other time periods. A cache of 15 large subtriangular and ovate biface blades from Paradise Point site (8Fr71)

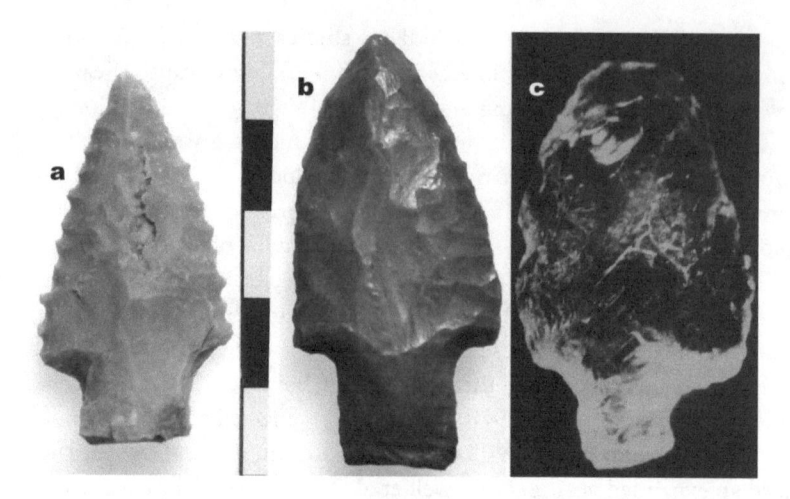

Figure 7.3. Middle Woodland Baker's Creek–type projectile points: (a, b) from St. Vincent 3 site; b has shiny patina from being underwater (#USFJC-8Fr362-13-1.50; photograph courtesy of Kaitlyn Keffer); (c) of clear quartz, from Arnold Soybean site (8Ja204; in private [WB] collection) with tip broken and reworked. (Nancy Marie White)

on St. Vincent Island (White and Kimble 2017), may be Middle Woodland. Block-Sterns Mound 1 in Tallahassee had a cache of 26 such blades covered by sheet mica (Jones et al. 1998; Dan Penton, personal communication 2021).

Ground Stone and Other Rock
The usual quartzite cobbles with use wear, sandstone hones, limestone objects, and other utilitarian implements occur at Middle Woodland sites. Some of these may have been more special than they look. From Aspalaga Mounds Burial 39 (8Gd1; Moore 1903:482), a quartzite discoidal in the National Museum of the American Indian looks like a chunkey or gaming stone used by later Mississippian peoples in the Southeast. Perhaps the origins of this sport go back to Middle Woodland times, but the stone also has a pit ground into one surface, possibly worn from drilling or grinding. The same mound produced another unusual item, which Moore called a "pebble hammer." It is a long cylindrical probable sedimentary rock, thicker around the middle. A finely made rectangular gorget fragment of white limestone, less than 1 cm thick and 3.8 cm wide, came from Huckleberry Landing Mounds (8Fr12); its circular hole was drilled from one side only. Another white-stone object Moore (1902:243) called a "kaolin clay" cylinder came from Porter's Bar (8Fr1). It looks like chalky limestone and is nearly cylindrical with widened ends, shaped like a dumbbell or double pestle. It is 28 cm long and 7 cm in diameter and weighs 787 g. An object like this also came from Warrior

River Mound B, in Taylor County, Florida, 160 km to the east, and Moore (1902:339) thought these might be ceremonial batons because the clay was so soft there would be little practical use. However, they could have been for soft pounding, or perhaps they were sources of white pigment. Irregular incised lines on the smoothed surface might be from deliberate engraving or use wear.

Greenstone and other stone celts were burial goods that may have previously been everyday tools. Several were at Richardson's Hammock Mound (see Figure 2.3), and a cache of them was reported from the Cemetery Mound, part of the Pierce complex. Pendants and other objects of greenstone are common, as are pendants (or plummets) of other rock, such as limestone or quartzite. The great variety recovered by Moore (1902:240) from Porter's Bar Mound (8Fr1), on Apalachicola Bay (see Plate XII) all have grooves for suspension. The raw material ranges from white quartz/quartzite to speckled granite, greenstone, and a bright-red stone that Moore called indurated shale but could be polished sandstone. The elongated greenstone example is similar to one from Pierce Mound A. Functions served by these artifacts are unknown; perhaps they were decorative weights for nets or sides of hide-covered shelters or other things needing to be prevented from blowing/washing away. Other suggestions are that they were "charmstones," magical objects hung around the neck or from the waist, even phallic symbols, to achieve good fishing or other luck (Reiger 1999). They seem too heavy to be body ornaments, but people do endure discomfort to be stylish or devout. An olive-colored slate gorget with a suspension hole and a hematite plummet came from Lake Douglas Mound (9Dr21). Hematite was locally available and significant through the centuries; red sands colored with hematite covered some mound graves.

Quartz crystal pendants are similar to others throughout the Middle Woodland Southeast. The two from St. Vincent Island (see Figure 2.4) were from shell midden sites but certainly served more exalted purposes than simply being weights. The ability to reflect or channel light gave this material its allure. Historic Native Americans used quartz crystals as magical charms (Hudson 1976:167), and Hopewell experts suggest shamanic use to contrast light/shiny with dark (Carr and Case 2005:43–44). The pendant from little Redfish Creek site (8Fr1367) is a natural crystal with one end ground to a point. The one from St. Vincent 5 site (8Fr364) is grooved at one end and rounded at the other. Both could have hung from cords. Other clear quartz items are a ground hemisphere from Otis Hare site in the middle valley and a fragment of another hemisphere from the Overgrown Road site (8Gu38) in the lower valley.

Smoking pipes appear as early as 500 BC in the Southeast, then expand in numbers with burial mound ritual and tobacco as a sacred substance. In the Apalachicola–lower Chattahoochee region, steatite pipes are Middle Woodland in age. They are large and heavy, cut into near-right-angle elbow shapes,

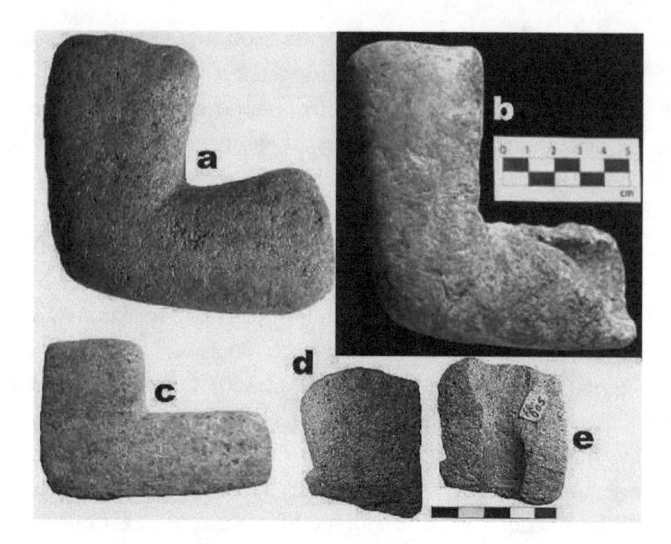

Figure 7.4. Middle Woodland steatite pipes: (a) Jackson Mound (8Fr15; NMAI#171824); (b) Pickalene midden, St. Vincent 5 and 6 sites (8Fr364-365; BAR#91.100.1.1); (c) Log Landing Mound (9Dr27; NMAI #17909); (d, e) exterior and interior views of pipe bowl from Pierce Mounds (#USF JC-8Fr14-12-01.1; collector's catalog number is on interior). (Nancy Marie White)

with squared bowls and stems, into which a hollow cane was likely inserted to inhale the smoke (Figure 7.4; see Figure 2.6). At least six of these are known from the region: at Log Landing Mound (9Dr27) and Underwater Indian Mound (9Se27) on the Flint; Jackson (8Fr15) and Pierce (8Fr14) Mounds on the coast; and a shell midden on St. Vincent Island. Another (not pictured) was recovered from somewhere in the Chipola River (HC collection); it has a bowl 9 cm tall, 5 cm wide, and stem 6 cm long, 4.8 cm wide. Decorative steatite objects may be of Middle Woodland age. Bullen (1958) found at the Tan Vat site (8Ja20 [J-18]), a multicomponent river-terrace habitation, a conical fragment of an ornament or bannerstone; and from the J-Y Field site (8Ja63) he described a diamond-shaped artifact with a plain, convex side, a flat side incised with nested diamonds, the pointed end battered, and the broken end with notches. Another decorative steatite artifact is a carved fragment resembling a rattlesnake rattle or beaver tail from Blue Hole Spring (8Ja112), probably Middle Woodland as it is so fanciful. Steatite can be polished to a high gleam and is another substance good for light reflection.

Cut mica is found often in Middle Woodland contexts. Tiny mica flakes and rarely larger fragments are omnipresent in the alluvial soils of the region, but sheet-mica cutout objects were grave goods all over the East at this time, and they occur in at least a dozen mounds in the region as well as at domestic sites. Mica may have been valued as a mirror or reflector, another shiny material for harnessing light. Some mica objects are cut in seemingly amorphous shapes: one from St. Vincent 5 site (8Fr364; White and Kimble 2017:Figure 80), a coastal oyster-shell midden, is nearly square and 5 cm wide, while another from Howard Creek Mound (8Gu41; White 1992), nearly 25 waterway miles inland, is subtrapezoidal and 10 cm wide. But these shapes may result from the flaking-off of the edges of an original piece made in a more identifiable form in this fragile stone.

Recognizable mica cutouts from Hopewellian mounds include geometric and animal shapes. One distinctive form is an "arrowhead" shape (see Figure 2.7) found at four sites in the research region. Two of these are mounds: Aspalaga (8Gd1), and Bristol (8Li4; Moore (1903:475, 482), and two others are domestic sites, freshwater shell middens. One midden is Sealy Plantation (9Se11), on a creek feeding into the Flint River, that Kelly (1953:35–37) briefly described, never mentioning the mica artifact now in the UGA collections. The second is Otis Hare site (8Li172), in good Middle Woodland stratigraphic context in TU1 L12 (172–183 cm deep). Outside the region, to the north, a mica arrowhead came from Kolomoki (9Er1) Mound D (Sears 1956:29), and a mica piece from Mandeville (9Cy1) appears to be of this shape (Kellar et al. 1962:Figure 3h). Moore also found mica arrowheads in burial mounds at Hare Hammock, on St. Andrews Bay, 50 km west of the region; Yent, 85 km southeast near Alligator Point; Gigger Point, 330 km around the Florida bend to the southeast, near Cedar Key; and Reddie Point, on the St. Johns River in northeast Florida, 365 km away. The two from Sealy Plantation and Otis Hare, the only examples I have studied, look very different in execution, suggesting different artisans. So far no "workshop area" for mica is known in the region. On the Ohio River in southeast Indiana, a Middle Woodland habitation site produced mica arrowhead cutouts and over 600 pieces of mica debitage from making them (Blosser 1996); unworked mica may have been brought southward, as well as finished products.

A wide variety of other stone artifacts and unmodified pieces appear at Middle Woodland sites in the research region. Moore (e.g., 1902:e.g., 240–241, 252) recorded bitumen or natural asphalt, plumbago or mineral graphite, various volcanic rocks, and petrified wood. These were probably imported in finished form. They were for special purposes, possibly only the last of which was interment with the dead. Other stones in human graves include hematite, sandstone hones, other sandstone pieces, and waterworn pebbles. A looter digging fancy grave goods from Richardson's Hammock Mound amassed a pile of 50 smooth quartz/quartzite pebbles that I observed; they averaged 25 g each. These humble objects (also see Plate X and discussion of Middle-Late Archaic features with pebbles in Chapter 4), not natural to the area, may have been smoothers, slingstones, inclusions for rattles, toys, or ritual objects, perhaps curative aids or medicine stones (Koldehoff and Bukowski 2010).

Metals

Middle Woodland people imported metals, surely also as part of the fascination with shining and reflecting light. Copper was available as raw nuggets from sources around Lake Superior, western North Carolina, north Georgia, southeastern Tennessee, and northeastern Alabama (Goad 1979; McKnight 2007). Eight Middle Woodland mounds in the Apalachicola–lower Chattahoochee region had copper artifacts. Copper disc ear ornaments are common all over the East. Those from Huckleberry Landing and Howard Creek Mounds were noted in the previous chapter. On the east side of the Pierce complex, the Cemetery Mound had a limestone disc with a thin copper veneer on the exterior and a lipped underside, probably for holding within a perforated earlobe (see Plate XIII). Pierce Mound A Burial 66 was accompanied by a copper tube (White 2013). A copper flat-strip bracelet was recovered at the Underwater Indian Mound (9Se27; White 1981).

Silver was rarer in the South. The closest silver sources are northern Michigan and northern Ontario (Spence and Fryer 2005). In Pierce Mound A, at the mound base under a deposit of oyster shell (Moore 1902:224), Burial 81 had on each shoulder a copper disc with silver plating on the raised central circular boss (White 2013:Figure 28). These could have been shoulder ornaments or earrings, if earlobes had been stretched down that far. Silver-plated copper discs are known from other Middle Woodland mounds in the Midwest and Southeast, but the Pierce examples are the only silver known in the research region. Silver-plated copper-covered cane panpipes came from the Mandeville site Mound A, 30 miles upriver on the Chattahoochee (Keller et al. 1962:352) and from the Tunnacunhee Mound in north Georgia (Jefferies 1976).

Galena, lead sulfide that naturally occurs in cubic or octahedral forms (see Chapter 2, Figure 2.8), is another significant Middle Woodland metal, found at five burial mounds and one domestic site in the research region. The domestic site is a St. Vincent Island shell midden that had other Middle Woodland exotics, with a 3.7 × 2 cm galena cube weighing 90 g. I saw another galena cube in a collection obtained from river bottom sediments brought up by the dredge boats on the Apalachicola. Soft, silvery galena chunks could have been gleaming charms, or were rubbed onto skin or other surfaces for silvery, black, or white pigment. At Hare's Landing Mound (9Se33) Moore (1907:430) described the faceted mass of galena as being the size of a child's fist. It had use wear, as do other galena chunks from OK Landing (8Ca2), Jackson (8Fr15), and Porter's Bar (8Fr1) Mounds. These pieces are smoothed from grinding, with some pecking, perhaps to get powder to coat something.

Galena powder may have been mixed with oil to rub on the body as silver paint (Walthall 1981). Elemental analyses of galena samples from nine Florida sites showed they originated from sources in the Mississippi valley, central and southern Missouri (Austin and Matusik 2014).

Ceramics

Typologies and Terminology

Middle Woodland pottery is the most ornamented, diverse, and enchanting of any made by Native American peoples in the eastern United States. In the Apalachicola–lower Chattahoochee region, Middle Woodland was defined based on pottery types, but terminology problems abound. Willey (1949) unfortunately established two ceramic series that are now misunderstood to be actual cultural entities: Swift Creek, with complicated-stamping, and early Weeden Island (his "Weeden Island I"), with incised, punctated, modeled, excised, cutout, and red-painted pottery. Interestingly, Swift Creek is named after a type site in Bibb County, central Georgia, and Weeden Island's type site is on Tampa Bay, central peninsular Florida, where those types of pots were first recorded. Thus, the two type sites are far from the research region, where both ceramic series flourished, and where they occur together at nearly all Middle Woodland sites. Of the 40 mounds in the region, only two have early Weeden Island pottery but no Swift Creek, and the few with Swift Creek but no early Weeden Island ceramics may simply be Early Woodland only. However, these few exceptions to the Middle Woodland norm in the region may also result from the amount of work at and materials reported from those particular mounds. Nearly all habitation sites have sherds of both ceramic series.

These Gulf and Appalachian pottery traditions that apparently originated in different areas of the South flourished together in the research region. Complicated stamping does emerge 200 to 300 years earlier, in late Early Woodland times, a prelude to full-blown Middle Woodland, as Willey noted long ago; it lasts a bit into Late Woodland times. The early Weeden Island series, which does not occur north of the Gulf Coastal Plain (Jenkins and Sheldon 2014:104), appears in the Apalachicola–lower Chattahoochee region by about AD 450. One interpretation of the two combined ceramic series in the region is that they reflect craft and design standards of different ethnic groups, possibly demonstrating movements of people into new areas. But ethnicity is notoriously difficult or impossible to see in material culture. The societies who participated in these widespread and diverse pottery-making traditions were part of far-flung exchange networks that brought together multitudes of different objects and ideas. Willey (1949) observed that northwest Florida was the only place where the two cultural sequences known in the 1930s for the Southeast could be related (Milanich 2007:18): the complicated-stamped pottery resembled that of central Georgia, and it was often found in association with incised and punctated ceramics, his Weeden Island I series, which resembled the Lower Mississippi Valley pottery in Louisiana.

However, some later workers took Swift Creek and Weeden Island beyond the realm of ceramics and made them into archaeological culture names, implying separate ethnic groups. This concept is not yet tested, and diverse other possibilities could explain such artifact assemblage diversity—different functions or social factions, not necessarily different peoples. It is crucial to note that, even though complicated-stamped pottery is earlier than the incised and punctated wares, they occur together in the Middle Woodland of the Apalachicola–lower Chattahoochee valley region, in what is best labeled ceramically "Swift Creek–early Weeden Island." The "early" is crucial, since the continuing and later types in Willey's Weeden Island sequence, his "Weeden Island II," unfortunately all named under the same ceramic series, are characteristic of Late Woodland (see Volume 2). The still-common characterization of a site as "Weeden Island" is meaningless here since this category makes no distinction between Middle and Late Woodland assemblages.

Middle Woodland pottery continued to be tempered with sand, grog, and grit, plus the natural mica flecks in the clays. For all types, including humble check-stamped and plain vessels, there was an amazing variability of shapes and embellishments. Rim treatments include folded and/or delimited with a horizontal incision, scalloped, fashioned into four or more points or horizontal protrusions, incised on top of a flat lip, and others, including adornos (rim effigies) in bird, other animal, and human forms. Potters seem to have been compelled to add ornate flourishes. Willey (1999:202) was impressed with the unusual flamboyance and imaginative nature of Middle Woodland pottery on the Florida Gulf Coast, unlike that of the Adena-Hopewell Midwest or Marksville in the Lower Mississippi Valley. He saw its endless variety as demonstrating a fascination with "the outré and the bizarre" and wondered what were the "liberating, energizing factors" at play during this time period. Some of these pots seem made for display. The cutout vessels might have held lights or burning incense, but they have no signs of scorching or smoking. Diagnostic and nondiagnostic types are described here.

Swift-Creek-Series Types
Swift-Creek-series pots were stamped into the wet clay exterior surface with carved paddles. They include Swift Creek Complicated-Stamped (curvilinear patterns), St. Andrews Complicated-Stamped and Crooked River Complicated-Stamped (rectilinear patterns), and New River Complicated-Stamped (checks plus curvilinear elements). Willey (1949) distinguished varieties as early, with stamping on the whole pot, and late, with stamping in a

band around the vessel. Patterns ranging from fine, small, and neatly stamped to large, heavy, "sprawling" designs occur together (Kelly 1953:15). Pots with scalloped or notched rims are earlier, while motifs with wider grooves and lands might be later. Earlier stamping might have been more finely applied, with elements more often left open and decoration more continuous around the pot, while later vessels showed more discrete, less fine paddle impressions, later becoming overstamped, simply malleated to compact the clay, with less concern for the decoration (Caldwell et al. 2014:87). These hypothesized trends over time need more study.

Snow's (2007) design database establishes connections over space. Figure 7.5 shows vessels from the Mound Near Hardnut Landing (9Dr18) on the lower Flint. Two have large "sprawling" designs in a band around the pot, with "b" resembling part of Snow's designs #21 and #70, known from southeast and central Georgia. The large jar, "c," also drawn at the opening of this chapter, has continuous stamping in smaller concentric circles. The sherds from the Otis Hare site (Figure 7.6) include one with a possible bird-head figure, like Snow's design #101. This sherd is from Test Unit 2 Feature 15, dated to cal AD 261–640. It appears similar to the stamped pattern on four sherds from Rock Bluff Mound (8Li5; NMAI#75413), about 20 river miles upstream, and to that on a large sherd from Jackson Mound (8Fr15; Moore 1902:Figure 169), at least 75 river miles downstream.

Figure 7.5. Swift Creek Complicated-Stamped vessels from Hardnut Landing mound (9Dr18): (a) jar with large snowshoe-like pattern (NMAI#75133); (b) bowl with large design unusual in the region (NMAI#75168); (c) large jar with concentric circle design (NMAI#75162). (Nancy Marie White)

Figure 7.6. Swift Creek Complicated-Stamped sherds: (a, b) from the Otis Hare site (#8Li172-90-308), surface of eroding riverbank, and (c) TU 2 F15 (#8Li172-90-299); (d) herringbone design on sherd from Otis Hare site surface (#8Li172-95-5) and (e) sherd from Clark Creek shell midden, TUB L3 (#8Gu60-47). (Nancy Marie White)

A herringbone design on a sherd from the Otis Hare site resembles that on a sherd from Clark Creek estuarine shell midden (8Gu60), which is of Early Woodland age (Figure 7.6d, e). These two sites are 130 km apart by water, but the herringbone pattern is known as far away as north-central Georgia, 500 km distant. Willey (1949:384) did not include a herringbone shape within the rectilinear designs of Crooked River Complicated-Stamped or St. Andrews Complicated-Stamped. A similar herringbone sherd came from Morgan County, Georgia (Wauchope 1966:Fig. 208Z), east-southeast of Atlanta, about 475 km away in a straight-line distance. Finally, this herringbone pattern also appears on sherds from the original type site, Swift Creek (9Bi3), in central Georgia (Frankie Snow, personal communication 2010), which is over 350 km away and in a drainage system connecting with the Atlantic Ocean, not the Gulf. Though the same paddle was not used to stamp all the pots represented by these sherds, the same idea was present, maybe the same craftworker, and the products moved across major river basins. The similarities also show continuity from Early to Middle Woodland. Many other cross-matches can be made. For example, a design of a concave-arm cross with hatching and concentric circles seen on a sherd from St. Vincent 5 site (8Fr364) on the coast

(White and Kimble 2017:Figure 82) is the same as Snow's (2007) #115, which is found in central and southeast Georgia, 480 km distant.

Bettye Broyles (1968), who replicated these paddle designs by hand in an era before electronic scanners, was the first to show spatial distributions not only of designs but also of paddles. She drew some 250 different designs from the Fairchild's Landing site, where 19 vessels with a pattern that combined loops and parallel curved and straight lines were represented by 210 sherds from 10 different proveniences. This design also appeared at other sites, both mounds and villages, and was distributed along the Chattahoochee all the way up to Kolomoki. In one case she identified sherds stamped by the very same paddle, recognizable by measurements and flaws left from visible cracking in the wood, at both Fairchild's Landing and a site 85 miles upriver. Caldwell noted how a couple dozen designs at the Hare's Landing site (9Se33) were also at Fairchild's Landing, including at least one example at each site made by the same paddle, recognizable by a scratch in its surface (Caldwell et al. 2014:86). This is no surprise since these two sites are only 6 river miles apart. Later researchers have approached the study of stamped patterns from a structural perspective, looking at elements that make up the designs, how artisans applied them, and how they vary in space and time (Smith and Knight 2014). More study of paddle designs and relationships for the Apalachicola–lower Chattahoochee region will no doubt demonstrate more geographic and technological connections. We are working with Karen Smith's SnowVision/ World Engraved project that uses 3D scans of complicated-stamped designs and machine learning to seek connections among them. I hope that designs from the research region, from dozens of sites along a large area, will be useful to compare with those from single large sites.

These stamped decorations depended on the potter's skill, tastes, and group norms, which exploded in variability during the Middle Woodland. Paddles, often assumed to have been of carved wood, were also of clay. The hundreds of designs show enormous creativity and imply that potters highly valued imagination and originality, striving for uniqueness (Smith and Knight 2017), as part of the general Middle Woodland obsession with the novel and ornate. Designs could be abstract renderings of animals or other symbols tied to beliefs, geographic areas, family names, craftworkers' identities, or simply pleasing art that was widely appreciated and understood. Perhaps they marked clan affiliation, which allowed people to be welcomed as they moved across social networks. The stamping probably also had technological as well as artistic and/or social functions.

Since they have stamped surfaces, Santa Rosa Stamped and Alligator Bayou Stamped, of the Santa Rosa ceramic series, are noted here. These pots are "rocker-stamped" in zigzag patterns made by rocking a shell's edge. They are extremely rare in the Apalachicola–lower Chattahoochee region, making inappropriate here a "Santa Rosa–Swift Creek" "culture" or time period (Willey 1949) as is recognized farther west around Pensacola. Besides a few individual rocker-stamped sherds from a handful of sites in the region, a nearly complete vessel of Alligator Bayou stamped came from Porter's Bar Mound, though Moore (1902:247) does not mention the stamping, which is barely visible in his illustration.

Early Weeden Island Series Types
It is crucial to differentiate the more ornamented early Weeden Island types (Plates XIV–XVI; Figures 7.7–7.11) from the others in the Weeden Island series. Here is where Willey left confusion, since several of the others hang on through Late Woodland, after the fancy ones are gone. However, the early Weeden Island types (Willey's Weeden Island I) in the series, lasting for a briefer time and constituting a relatively small proportion of ceramic assemblages, disappear with the end of Middle Woodland. These types are Weeden Island Plain, with eccentric vessel shapes such as joined bowls, multiple necks on a bowl, cutout portions or latticework, or animal or human effigy forms; Weeden Island Incised, with complex incised patterns, sometimes recognizable as faces, hands, and other elements, incisions ending in large, round or triangular punctations, and sometimes smaller punctations; Weeden Island Punctated, with similar elements but no incisions, in both large and smaller punctations that are often in "punch-and-drag" technique; and Weeden Island Zoned-Red, with red paint applied inside incised zones or elsewhere on vessel exteriors and sometimes interiors. Since interior surfaces were not incised, and since sometimes whole vessels were painted red, another type name might be Weeden Island Red. This is the earliest time period during which paint was used on pottery. The blood red is easy to distinguish, by brush strokes, from the orangish natural clay color. Occasional sherds have black paint.

In reality, the type attributes overlap, and red paint may be applied to them all. For example, Plate XV shows a compound-shape jar with a scalloped rim and incised design resembling a grinning, bug-eyed face (see drawing in the introduction) from Green Point Mound (8Fr11) on Apalachicola Bay. Plate XIV shows a U-shaped, double-mouthed vessel with heavy red paint inside incised bands, from Pierce (8Fr14) Mound A, Burials 2–4 group. Plate XVI shows a cutout jar with a bird-head adorno, painted red all over, from Bristol Mound (8Li4). Bird shapes are common, but the two other forms are not. The compound jar is similar in shape—but not decoration—to an Alligator stamped vessel from Pharr Mound E in northeast Mississippi and to another from Marksville in east central Louisiana (Mainfort 2013:219–220,

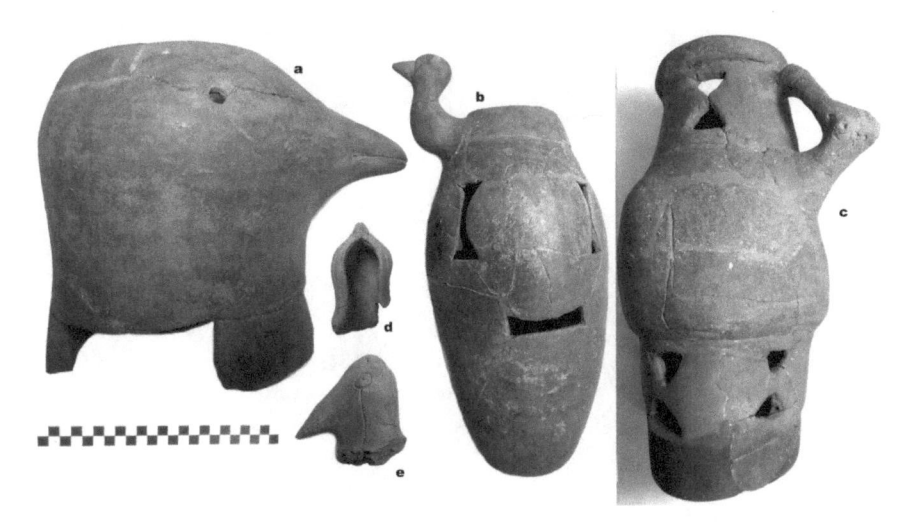

Figure 7.7. Weeden Island Plain ceramics featuring birds, all painted red on exterior: (a) large bird-head jar on cutout base from Hardnut Landing Mound (9Dr18; NMAI#75172); (b, c) cutout jars with bird heads and necks from Hare's Landing (9Se33; NMAI#174452, 174451); (d, e) back and side view of bird head adorno from Bristol Mound (8Li4; NMAI#170276). (Nancy Marie White)

Figure 7.8. Weeden Island Incised turkey or turtle effigy bowl from Underwater Indian Mound (9Se27), side and back views and closeup of head; drilled holes in front and back below rim are presumably for suspension (private [JW] collection). (Nancy Marie White)

Figure 7.9. Weeden Island Plain ceramic human effigies: (a) sherds with two modeled human hands from Porter's Bar Mound (8Fr1; NMAI#174997); (b, c) side and front views of jar representing a man (?) from Aspalaga Landing Mound (8Gd1; NMAI#173410); (d) jar representing a woman from Pierce Mounds (FLMNH #2345-45255); (e, f) straight-on view of face and top view of jar representing a man (?) from Hare's Landing Mound (9Se33; NMAI#180412). (Nancy Marie White)

Figure 8.22). The U shape is known from only two other places, Mound C at Helena Crossing in eastern Arkansas, and a mound in Minnesota (Mainfort 2013:213, Figure 8.11). The similarities might be due to movements of people or ideas over very long distances, but also perhaps more containers of these shapes were made of perishable materials. Figure 7.7 shows bird-form ceramics with exterior surfaces painted red, including the pot from Hare's Landing also shown at the opening of this chapter. Bird pots came from many more mounds, including several not known by Moore: Gaston Spivey (8Ca114), Richardson's Hammock (8Gu10), and Underwater Indian Mound (9Se27). From the last, a collector recovered a lovely small bowl that may represent a turkey with a Mona Lisa smile (Figure 7.8).

Figure 7.9 illustrates human effigy ceramics. The modeled hands from Porter's Bar Mound (8Fr1) are realistic, though not shown necessarily in the position they might have been on the pot. They contrast strongly with the three whole-human vessels, from Aspalaga (8Gd1), Pierce (8Fr14), and Hare's Landing (9Se33) Mounds, where arms are stylized or rudimentary, hands are absent, and legs are represented by nubs. But heads are detailed, with pierced earlobes and headdresses or hairdos with a V shape on the forehead and modeled rising peaks or topknots. The two presumably male figures have noses broken off or pecked away, and eyes each done differently. The Hare's Landing figure has a navel and also a large punctation within the V of the forehead decor. The Aspalaga person (head also drawn at the opening of Chapter 2), has a small mouth but prominent curved line above the chin. The female figure, collected from Pierce in the mid-nineteenth century and displayed at the FLMNH, portrays a folded-arm kneeling woman and resembles Hopewellian figurines. Notable are the protruding but small breasts, one of the few ways of telling the sex of these human images. Why nothing is portrayed below the minimal upper legs is a mystery. The jars are hollow, with the front of the figure higher than the back side. A Middle Woodland human figurine from the research region that was not a pot but a statue of a woman was reported to have come from Richardson's Hammock; it is now lost.

Figure 7.10 shows more of the incredible art of Middle Woodland potters. The bowl from Porter's Bar has incised loopy zones full of punctations and is covered with red paint. The tall, flat jar from the same mound is more like an austere, bare-clay envelope with straight-line incisions ending in those large triangular punctations. The pattern on the small Weeden Island Punctate bird effigy bowl from Richardson's Hammock Mound is made with punch-and-drag lines, which, on the sides, represent wings that look like three-fingered hands. One Weeden Island Punctated tall jar from Rock Bluff Landing Mound has a whimsical, undulating rim margin, while another from the same mound, equally whimsical, has an outflaring squared-off neck with a tiny animal-face adorno with a large bug eyes. The Weeden Island Incised cup from Pierce Mound A, Burial 2–4 group shows two hands reaching toward what looks like an upside-down person, with red paint around the fingers; Moore (1902:223) showed a rollout drawing of this design, and excerpts of it accompany the preface and acknowledgments in this book.

Figure 7.10. Early Weeden Island ceramics: (a) red-painted Weeden Island Incised bowl from Porter's Bar Mound (8Fr1; NMAI#173109); (b) small Weeden Island Punctate bird-effigy bowl from Richardson's Hammock Mound (8Gu10; private [TJ] collection); (c) Weeden Island Punctate jar from Rock Bluff Landing Mound (8Li5; NMAI#75157); (d) Weeden Island Incised tall flat jar from Porter's Bar Mound (8Fr1, NMAI#174061); (e, f) Weeden Island Punctate jar with outflaring neck and small big-eyed adorno and closeup from interior of this adorno, from Porter's Bar Mound (NMAI#75156); (g) Weeden Island Incised cup from Pierce (8Gu14) Mound A Burial 2-4 group (NMAI#174076), with incised human hands surrounded by red paint (see Moore 1902:223, Figure 159). (Nancy Marie White)

Other eccentric ceramic forms of early Weeden Island types include compound pots with merged shapes. One version consists of double small bowls, vertically joined, from Rock Bluff Landing (8Li5; Brose and White 1999:back cover; Moore 1918:Plate XV). A vessel with four individual bottlenecks came from Jackson Mound (8Fr15; Moore 1902:Figure 170) and one with three necks from Pierce Mound A (Moore 1902:Figure 164). A pot from Gotier Hammock Mound (8Gu2) has four small conjoined subcircular bowls surrounding a central rectangular bowl (White 2010). At Chipola Cutoff Mound (8Gu5), a compound vessel had a central square chamber melded to three surrounding circular bowls (Moore 1903:Figure 111). Each early Weeden Island creation seems to be unique to the craftworker's imagination, yet continuities are present. The types are widespread across the South, with other names; for example, French Fork Incised in Louisiana and Arkansas is the same as Weeden Island Incised. Animal effigies are most often birds (owls, woodpeckers, other crested species), but there are also mammals, nonrecognizable forms, and others that are composites with attributes of many beasts. The jar from Shoemake Landing Mound (9Er1/87), on the lower Chattahoochee (Moore 1907:Figures 14–16) is interpreted as a horned owl, with its "ear" tufts or raised feathers that look like horns, incised-scroll wings, tail, and legs, and punctations representing feathers, and the beak broken or hacked off (Moore 1907:438–441). This treatment might be related to the bashing of human noses on pots in Figure 7.9, suggesting some ritual.

Various vessels have pedestals that would have allowed them to stand alone (see Plate XV, Figure 7.7a) while others might have been held up on poles through their basal perforations for display. It is hard to imagine these stunning ceramics being made as just grave goods and not being shown off first. Cutout portions on the sides of pots, made before firing, can be geometric shapes such as triangles or rectangles, or thin lines with wider excised shapes at the ends, mirroring the Weeden Island Incised incisions with larger punctation at the ends. The excised parts on the jars with protruding bird heads from Hare's Landing (Figure 7.7b, c) seem to mirror the dumbbell or club shape of the kaolin object from Porter's Bar previously noted, while the removed portions of the unusual bird-head pot from Hardnut Landing (Figure 7.7a) are actually in the pedestal itself. With such perforations, these cutout vessels could not hold liquids or wet foods. Given hypothesized Middle Woodland fascinations, perhaps they allowed light to shine through.

The type Basin Bayou Incised is rare in the research region. With its swirled or looped incised designs, its attributes overlap those of Weeden Island Incised, and it greatly resembles the Middle Woodland sand- and grog-tempered Marksville ceramics of the lower Mississippi Valley. As noted, residue on a Basin Bayou Incised jar (Figure 7.11) from Gotier Hammock Mound was dated AD 640–650, consistent with dates for similar Middle Woodland ceramics farther west along the Gulf in Alabama (Price 2008).

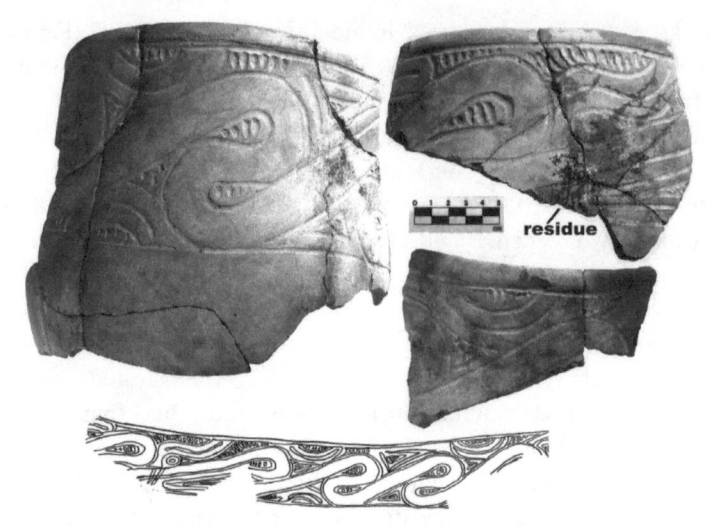

Figure 7.11. Basin Bayou Incised jar from Gotier Hammock Mound (#8Gu2-08-39, etc.) from TU2 N1/2 and TU2A balk; sherds make up upper portion of vessel; rollout of incised design is below. (Nancy Marie White)

Persistent Types of the Weeden Island Series
The ornamented ceramics already described are the early Weeden Island types seen only in Middle Woodland times. Other types first appearing during Middle Woodland are less dazzling, persist longer, and may be more utilitarian. Indian Pass Incised has thin, fine-line parallel curvilinear incisions but no punctations. Tucker Ridge Pinched has parallel ridges made by pinching with fingernails. Keith Incised has crisscross straight-line incisions and rarely single punctations within the small rectangles or diamonds that the incisions create. Carrabelle Incised and Carrabelle Punctated have a neck band of parallel diagonal incisions or punctations. More generic types are net-marked, cordmarked, and some fabric-marked. Extremely significant is that these types, which are also within the Weeden Island series as originally defined, first appear in Middle Woodland but last through Late Woodland, Willey's Weeden Island II. So assemblages composed of these types alone are not enough to distinguish time period and are often confusingly grouped into a "Weeden Island" period.

Check-stamped pottery embodies an even more complex case of this confusion. Stamping with a paddle carved in a checkerboard pattern was introduced with Early Woodland, in the Deptford series and continued for over 2,500 years. For body sherds, specific types and ages are impossible to tell apart, despite decades of attempts and tedious long days of measuring of check sizes (White 1982). Willey defined Gulf Check-Stamped as the Middle Woodland representative of this genre, but it is only recognizable with rim sherds if rims are notched, scalloped, or otherwise unusually shaped. Two

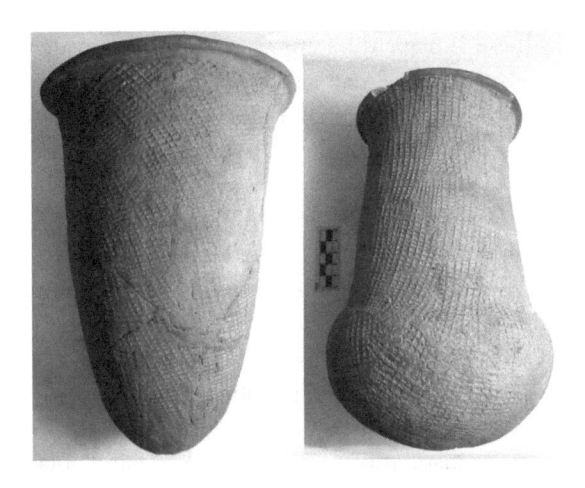

Figure 7.12. Check-stamped unusually shaped vessels from Bristol Mound (8Li4; NMAI#173954, 173415). (Nancy Marie White)

check-stamped jars from Bristol Mound (8Li4) are peculiar enough to be Middle Woodland (Figure 7.12). One is conical and the other is tall-necked, with a globular base; both have outflaring rims. Other examples are a rim sherd with two rows of horizontal punctations, below the lip and at the base of the neck, setting off the check-stamped body, and another rim with triangular horizontal protrusions, both from the St. Vincent 3 site (8Fr362; White and Kimble 2017). From the Lake Douglas Mound (9Dr21) Kelly (1953) got a check-stamped bowl with similar triangular horizontal rim protrusions, and tall, conoidal check-stamped jars, one with an outflaring rim. A sherd I saw from Wakulla County, east of the research region, is Weeden Island Incised on the wavy rim and neck, and check-stamped on the vessel body (Tray Earnest, personal communication 2004).

Ceramic Artistry and Creativity

We cannot say what designs of ceramics or other Middle Woodland objects mean. Archaeologists intensively study iconography to see how symbols or motifs might link to spiritual concepts or power sources (Hall 1997). Analyses of complicated-stamped patterns (Snow 2007; Williams and Elliott 1998) include suggestions of meanings, such as some resembling masks or faces, and others with a four-part division that may indicate world sectors important in Native American ideology. General functional concerns might mean that cooking vessels and those for transporting, storing, or processing liquids would have constricted necks and be better able to withstand heating. Constricted necks are better for carrying as well, with a cord around the neck (no handles yet). More open vessels might have been for display and serving, containing more significant imagery.

Knight's structural analysis of Middle Woodland ceramic symbolism (in Milanich et al. 1984) hypothesized that zoomorphic shapes were cult objects depicting anomalous animals. These inhabit different worlds, such as water birds that are also aerial, and owls that prowl day and night, species that are not usually food, or that do unexpected things that violate taboos. In passing, I wonder why we lack depictions of crabs, shellfish, lizards, butterflies, and especially dragonflies, which magically hover. The curved tubular pot from Pierce Mound A called a grubworm effigy (Moore 1902:Figures 156–157, 163) is a ribbed semispiral tube that does resemble grubworms we saw while excavating there. But it has also been interpreted as a ram's horn portrayed by someone who might have ranged far enough west to see bighorn sheep (DeBoer 2004:90–91; Milanich 1994:139). Animal shapes could also be clan totems that, for Native Americans, often characterized members (e.g., deer people ran fast, bear people were strong), with abstract forms for things such as winds, clouds, or water. Whatever the inspirations for Middle Woodland pots, they do indicate that artisans had great artistic freedom and that idiosyncratic portrayals of familiar things or unusual compositions were celebrated.

Ethnographic studies of American Indian potters show their sophisticated knowledge of the raw materials and manufacturing steps, and individuals' styles are recognizable (Arnold 1993). Their skills might reflect social organization, especially prehistoric matrilineal kinship and matrilocal residence systems. Such possibilities have not yet been explored in the Apalachicola–lower Chattahoochee region, though if women owned the homes and made the pots, paddles, and designs, tracing them in households might isolate different local styles. A celebrated study of matrilineal Pueblo potters in the Southwest (Bunzel 1929:51–57) described how women indeed learned to make their designs from their mothers, aunts, or other family, but also from dreams, and even from sherds picked up at ancient villages (!). Many made up new designs with each production just to be original and said they would never copy those of another, or would copy only with permission. In some villages, symbolism in design was important, but in others it played no role. Different villages were known for different patterns; one craftworker, a third-gender Laguna artisan, visited a Zuni village and liked the designs there enough to introduce them into Laguna craftwork. Some archaeologists have thought that all the fanciest early Weeden Island pottery was made at one center and distributed widely, but trace element analyses of sherds from the research region (Koppe 2010; Tykot et al. 2013) indicate that most ceramic production was local.

Ceramic Chronology
In Willey's original characterizations of Weeden Island I and II series, equivalent to Middle and Late Woodland, he recognized that complicated-stamping began earlier and hung on into Late Woodland. As dating improved, his original ceramic sequences were confirmed and refined. Important in this process

was Fairchild's Landing (9Se14), the lower Chattahoochee shell midden with continuous Woodland deposition, exposed by high floodwaters of 1948–1949 (Caldwell et al. 2014). Kelly (1950a:32) first listed its ceramic sequence from bottom to top: Deptford Simple-Stamped Early Woodland; St. Andrews Complicated-Stamped and Swift Creek Complicated-Stamped with 30 to 35 cm of freshwater shell midden; more Swift Creek accompanied by Weeden Island I incised and punctated wares in three 3 Middle Woodland strata; then Weeden Island II, Late Woodland, with no shell but abundant check-stamped sherds. Relative type frequencies for the strata were not tabulated. Caldwell's report also includes data on the Hare's Landing site, particularly occupation areas around the mound that Moore dug. But ceramic types are given only by horizontal zone. Abundant features could probably also be seriated based on types they contained, and charcoal in them could be dated, should work continue on the stored collections.

At Lake Douglas Mound (9Dr21) on the lower Flint, Kelly (1953) gave ceramic type frequencies in both mound fill and the east-side cache and showed that they all appeared to be contemporaneous. Of a small total of 600 sherds, nearly half were sand-tempered plain in both mound fill and cache; check-stamped was 17% of the cache and 11% of the mound fill; complicated-stamped was 16% of the cache and 29% in mound fill, over two-thirds of which had large heavy stamped patterns and the rest small, neatly executed stamping; and the remainder were Weeden Island Incised, effigy and cutout forms, red-painted, and other types such as Carrabelle Punctated. While the assemblage was quantified, these percentages were by sherd counts, not weights. Furthermore, the basal portion of the mound might be Early Woodland since it had only check-stamped and complicated-stamped ceramics and few other burial goods beyond shell beads. Also, this mound was so disturbed when Kelly got there that the numbers may not be representative. The abundance of check-stamped sherds suggested either an Early Woodland beginning or a Late Woodland continuation of its use, or both, along with the Middle Woodland component. Though Kelly said no occupation area was found nearby, he later said the village was 200 m away. He thought that mound fill soils might have been scraped up from domestic midden, or that reservoir construction might have destroyed village deposits.

The ceramic record and supporting radiocarbon dates at Kolomoki (Pluckhahn 2003:10), though far to the north of the research region, indicate early Weeden Island types first showing up around AD 350, comprising 1–5% by AD 450, and up to 15% by AD 550, declining after AD 650 when Late Woodland assemblages were emerging. Karen Smith's (2009) research tied ceramic decorative modes to social change in the entire lower Chattahoochee valley, from the fall line to the Gulf, and from Middle through Late

Woodland. Though her study covered more time and space than discussed here, her examination of quantified "ceramic distances" between sites and ceramic diversity within sites suggested that both declined if populations became smaller and more mobile, increasing interaction. She assumed that foraging groups were not stationary, and therefore they could be represented by individual ceramic assemblages and certain Swift Creek paddle designs occurring across landscapes, and residential systems might have cycled between greater and lesser sedentism. Pertinent to my discussion here is her determination that times of dispersed settlement may correlate with four periods of drought: AD 388–420, 659–724, 811–891, and 934–1039. The last two are in Late Woodland times, but the earliest drought could correspond with the introduction of early Weeden Island ceramics in the research region, and the second span of years corresponds with the end of Middle Woodland. If native societies broke up into smaller units when environments deteriorated, it could be reflected in artifact assemblages.

Revising Willey's work, George Percy and David Brose (1974) refined Willey's subdivisions of Weeden Island I and II in the research region. Their "Weeden Island period," from Middle through Late Woodland, had five temporal units based on ceramics:

1. earliest were a few Weeden-Island-series incised and punctated types and a dominance of late-variety Swift Creek Complicated-Stamped in middens;

2. then a greater variety of Weeden Island types;

3. next came the first appearance of Wakulla Check Stamped, with a slight decline in the importance of complicated-stamped;

4. then the disappearance of complicated stamping;

5. finally, a dominance of check-stamped, with a limited representation of incising and punctating, and a minor occurrence of corn-cob-marked pottery.

The Percy-Brose model seemed reasonable but was never tested, did not include mound sites, and did not date or quantify ceramic frequencies for the five categories. A half century later, it needs a few refinements. Rather than "Weeden Island" as a time period, Middle and Late Woodland are better chronological terms because of other culture change, such as the cessation of mound building and beginnings of food production in Late Woodland (see Volume 2). Complicated-stamping first appeared during Early Woodland and disappeared sometime early in Late Woodland, as in their category 4. Weeden Island Punctate, Incised, and Red appear slightly later during Middle

Woodland than their subdivision 1. Since Wakulla Check-Stamped usually cannot be differentiated from Deptford, Gulf, or other check-stamped types, we must say that check stamping continues throughout the entire Woodland. Cobmarked pottery, indicating food production, appears only at the very end of Late Woodland.

Data from the Otis Hare site (8Li172) support this chronology. A freshwater shell midden like Fairchild's Landing and 45 river miles downstream from it, Otis Hare extended 50 m along the middle Apalachicola riverbank and was only 20 m wide. Probably 75% of it had washed away by the time I tested it in 1990. Three units produced abundant faunal and artifact assemblages (Hutchinson et al. 1991), including nearly 20,000 sherds, weighing 70 kg. Radiocarbon dates help track ceramic type frequencies. The Middle Woodland levels had abundant complicated-stamped sherds (around 20% of total assemblage, by both number and weight); fancy early Weeden Island types (Punctated, Incised, Red) as only a minority (1%–3%); little check-stamped (5%); and the rest plain (50% to 65%). Late Woodland levels still had some complicated-stamped, Keith Incised, Carrabelle Incised and Punctate, and a few netmarked, cordmarked, or fabric-marked sherds, but nearly half the ceramics were check-stamped and about the same proportion were plain. The early Weeden Island types appeared only between around AD 400 and 700.

Other Clay Artifacts

Middle Woodland clay pipes in the research region include at least two styles (Figure 7.13). The plain right-angle elbow shape is similar to that of the steatite pipes in Figure 7.4. The platform or "monitor" shape, named after the similarly shaped Civil War ironclad ship *Monitor*, has a flat or curved base below a central cylindrical bowl. Clay discs were backing for copper ear

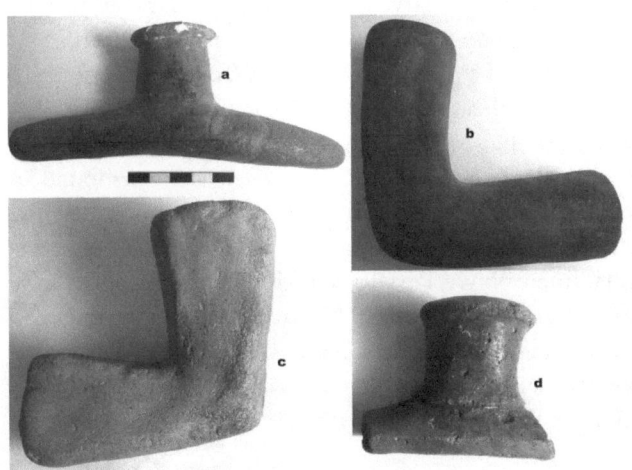

Figure 7.13. Middle Woodland clay pipes: (a) monitor shape from Huckleberry Landing Mound (8Fr12; NMAI#172256); (b) elbow shape also from Huckleberry (NMAI#172257); (c) elbow and (d) (broken) monitor shapes from Mound Below Bristol (8Li3; NMAI#172068). (Nancy Marie White)

decorations (see Plate XIIIb). A clay plummet or pendant came from a Middle Woodland context at the Otis Hare site. Some Middle Woodland clay daub indicates walled structures.

Other Material Culture

Shell Artifacts

As usual, these are of marine shell, lightning whelk and sometimes horse conch and quahog clam. Utilitarian tools are scoops, spatulas, scrapers, celts, hammers, chisels, and awls. The whole whelk shell, either unmodified or with the columella cut out to make a cup, was sometimes put in graves or mound fill. Shell cups were probably for the ceremonial black drink, caffeine-filled yaupon holly tea, important historically for southeastern Native Americans and probably used this early. Other kinds of shell, unmodified, were also grave goods: Moore (1902:228) identified American bittersweet (*Glycymeris americana*) in Pierce Mound A; I saw large oyster shells about 16 to 18 cm long that were grave goods in the Richardson's Hammock Mound. An interesting shell story concerns Burial 30 at Chipola Cutoff Mound (Moore 1903:447), with two skulls and an extremely large lightning whelk, nearly 39 cm long most likely attributable to the Middle Woodland component. Along with all of Moore's other materials from his mound digging, this shell was once housed at the Academy of Natural Sciences in Philadelphia. In 1929 the academy divested itself of all artifacts, wanting to feature natural history only. However, their Malacology Collection online catalog still lists this shell (#ANSP 84614), kept for its outstanding biological value, even though they only have it because it was used by ancient Native Americans and dug out by Moore. Biochemical sourcing might show that this Chipola Cutoff shell and most other whelk artifacts in the region trace to St. Joseph Bay.

Shell pendants or plummets are carved into teardrop or other tapered shapes, sometimes with grooves for suspension. Examples from Green Point Mound (see Figure 2.16) may be Early or Middle Woodland. They could have been everyday objects such as weights, or decorative or sacred items. Near Green Point Mound, in the shell midden associated with it and with the Middle Woodland Porter's Bar Mound about 500 m away, collectors found an unusual pendant labeled a "tabbed circle" (Luer et al. 2015). This is a shell disc with a tab-like projection, a form usually found in Middle Woodland contexts farther south in Florida. Interestingly, Porter's Bar Mound itself may not have produced any shell artifacts, though the earlier Green Point Mound contained several (Knigge 2018). The midden spreads at least 200 m along the bayshore and is domestic refuse associated with both mounds over several centuries, so the temporal association for this tabbed disc is unclear. Also among decorative

Middle Woodland shell artifacts are beads, cylindrical or disc-shaped, from many burial mounds, which may have first appeared in Early Woodland. From Pierce Mounds came dozens of small to large discs (White 2013), and from Richardson's Hammock Mound three dozen beads of multiple shapes and shell species. Pearl beads are also known, such as at Pierce Mound A, one specimen of which is nearly 1 cm long (see Figure 2.10).

Bone, Tooth, and Perishable Artifacts
Both domestic sites and mounds have bone tools that appear utilitarian, including awls and/or hooks, as at Howard Creek (8Gu41; White 1992), Brickyard Creek (8Fr8), and Chipola Cutoff (8Gu5) mounds, and turtle shell from Huckleberry Landing mound (8Fr12). A possible bison bone pendant from Pierce Mound A (Moore 1902:225; White 2013:Figure 26) is an elongated oval, pierced at one end. If it is indeed from a Great Plains animal, it represents quite a long-distance interaction. Animal jaws and teeth, sometimes altered, as found in Hopewellian burial mounds, are known in the region. At Pierce, in the great burned area at Mound A's base, were three carnivore teeth including left lower canines of a wolf and a Florida panther as well as a small rodent's lower jaw. Panther bone was recovered from Waddell's Mill Pond site (Tesar and Jones 2009:693–694), and a panther tooth came from the Yellow Houseboat shell midden (8Gu55; White 1994b), in generic Woodland deposits. These carnivores were probably not food animals but associated with ritual power (Wheeler 2011). In Porter's Bar Mound were three rodent jaws and a deer jaw cut to have a flat bottom (Moore 1902:240–241). Animal teeth and jaws could have been charms or parts of masks or props for shamanistic performances. Turtle shells could have been parts of rattles.

Among all kinds of long-decayed Middle Woodland objects may have been a cane flute in the interior of the copper tube at Pierce; such copper-covered items, flutes or panpipes, were known Middle Woodland grave goods. Copper-covered cane panpipes packed with heavy cordage came from the Mandeville site, far up the lower Chattahoochee (Kellar et al. 1962). We can speculate that other musical instruments or noisemakers probably included drums, rattles, shell horns, and whistles. River cane and bark probably comprised commonplace articles such as mats, baskets, and clothing, and dugout canoes were surely ubiquitous. Masses of burned organic material were above and below burials in mounds, possibly textiles that wrapped the dead. Prestige goods now long gone may have been painted bark, cloth, animal skins, jewelry of wood or seeds, and objects of antler, horn, and hoof. A tradition of fine wood-carving is hypothesized for all of Middle Woodland (Williams and Elliott 1998:10).

Subsistence, Seasonality, and Environmental Shifts

At a time of such complex nondomestic behavior, Middle Woodland societies still obtained wild foods, as their ancestors had done for millennia, continuing established Archaic lifeways. More plants and animals and a wider range of species are known in the research region from Middle Woodland contexts than for earlier times. But data are still limited to the few tested sites whose biotic assemblages have had expert analysis. A few indicators suggest seasonality.

Animal Remains

Middle Woodland faunal assemblages in the South show that people continued to harvest deer, small mammals, turkey, and fish, with aquatic resources most important along coasts (Wright 2017). The Apalachicola–lower Chattahoochee valley region fits this pattern. Archaeologically recovered animal remains show an ample range of taxa including large mammals (deer and bear), small mammals (squirrel, raccoon, opossum, rat, rabbit), birds (turkey, duck), amphibians and reptiles (alligator, turtles), abundant fish (including gar at both inland and coastal sites), and a huge amount of shellfish (freshwater bivalves and snails, estuarine marsh clams, oyster, marine gastropods, and clams). Turkey is present at inland sites but not on the coast so far. Water birds are rare. A problem with understanding Middle Woodland animal use is that many site components are mixed, so ages of specific remains are tentative. For example, in the shell midden at Porter's Bar Mound (8Fr1), five fire pits with remains of cooked turtles were once exposed (Wayne Childers, personal communication 2007), but they could have been from the Early or Middle Woodland or Fort Walton components.

A few sites do have data clear enough to allow specific statements, summarized here moving from the lower Chattahoochee downriver. Bullen (1958) identified bone at J-Y Field (Ja63) as deer, bear, opossum, rabbit, skunk, turtle, and freshwater clams and snails. At the Scholz Steam Plant site, the habitation site near Sampson's Landing Mound (8Ja1), Percy (1976) listed predominantly deer but also box turtle, turkey, and abundant, diverse shellfish, both bivalves and gastropods, collected from the adjacent river. One freshwater clam here was later identified as the Apalachicola ebonyshell, *Reginaia/Fusconaia apalachicola*, now extinct and known only from archaeological contexts (Williams and Fradkin 1999).

From the Otis Hare site, in the middle valley, Shockey (1991) analyzed samples from four Middle Woodland proveniences dating from about AD 400 to 650 (TU1 Levels 13 and 14, and Feature 22, and TU2 F15). The two features were pits for food garbage during the earliest occupation. Then the thick midden piled up over them; maybe people decided that since they were staying longer they should not worry about burying trash but just throw it all over the north end of the site. Fauna represented included 33 identified species and 954 individual animals, even with these tiny samples. No single species predominated, but fish and shellfish were highest in terms of usable meat masses. Aquatic species were far more prominent in the Middle Woodland proveniences as compared with the Late Woodland (TU1 L5) component, in which terrestrial animals dominated. The fish were of diverse sizes, including small ones evidently captured in fine-mesh nets, and species included bottom-feeders, open water fish, and gar, which live in poorly oxygenated waters. They all show fishing everywhere from the main river to backwater streams, and shellfish harvested from the river bottom. Reptiles were alligator and basking turtles, including the Barbour's map turtle, a rare species found only in the Apalachicola basin. Duck bone suggests a winter occupation, as ducks arrive in late October–early November and leave in late spring. This is one of the few indicators of seasonality among faunal assemblages in the region and fits with the meager botanical evidence given further on in this chapter. All these inferences give only a snapshot of a campsite first inhabited early in Middle Woodland times and repeatedly revisited.

Coprolites were recovered at Otis Hare. In the 1990s, Elizabeth Wing at FLMNH examined one Middle Woodland specimen from TU1 L14 and found it contained chewed-up fish-head bones and was either dog or human. Later work on a coprolite from TU1 L13, done by PaleoResearch Institute (Cummings and Kováčik 2018), determined it was from a dog. Their Fourier Transform Infrared Spectroscopy analysis of this specimen suggested both proteins and carbohydrates, but no fats, lipids, or esters. The carbohydrates were probably pectin, not starch, possibly reflecting plant cell wall components in this dog's drinking water or something it ate. The protein indicated that the dog consumed lean meat. University of California, Santa Cruz, Genomics Institute DNA analysis of another coprolite, from TU1 L11, confirmed that it was dog, either domestic or gray wolf or red fox (White 2018). Any of these creatures would probably have loved to scavenge in the midden.

Zooarchaeological remains from the bayshore midden at St. Vincent 5 site (8Fr364) were studied by Marrinan and Parsons (2010) and their FSU paleonutrition class. A 4-liter sample from the deepest 10-cm level of the midden in the meter-square test unit, dated to cal AD 560–660, contained cotton rat, garfish, herring, hardhead catfish, gafftopsail catfish, mullet, black drum, sheepshead, redfish, seatrout, flounder, less-identifiable mammals, birds, ray-finned fishes, and marine catfish within the packed oyster shells of the matrix. Most of the fish were mullet, which seasonally run in huge schools right by the site. As everywhere in the region, Middle Woodland groups here took advantage of local resources. It might be surprising that these sites lack examples of imported food, since the people so much revered the unusual and the exotic.

Plant Remains

Middle Woodland communities in the mid-South and Midwest had already integrated cultivated plants into their diets, and oily and starchy seeds and squash were standard resources. But such native domesticates were evidently not grown in the Deep South, especially on the coastal plain (Gremillion 2002), with the possible exceptions of bottle gourd or tobacco, nonfood crops. Maize reported from the Sycamore site, in the middle Apalachicola (Milanich 1974) is Late Woodland or early Fort Walton in age (see Volume 2). However, people must have been managing useful plants for millennia, for example, planting nut and fruit trees in more convenient places. Few archaeobotanical remains from Middle Woodland sites in the Apalachicola–lower Chattahoochee region have been recovered, and fewer analyzed, but the data are interesting. Wood fragments of pine, beech, tupelo, magnolia, oak, and other hardwoods are common, remnants of fuel, burned structures, or other artifacts. Acorns and hickory nuts are relatively abundant and may have constituted much of the diet, whether as nut meats or processed for oil; nutshells were also fuel. Shrubs, weeds, berries, grasses, and seedy plants include bedstraw, holly, and knotweed. Fruit fragments are gallberry, grape, hackberry, plum/cherry, sparkleberry, sumac, and dried persimmon.

The Otis Hare site dog coprolite microflora consisted of only two pollen grains, of pine and knotweed (*Persica*), which grows in moist or wet sediments, and might have been ingested in the dog's drinking water or anything it ate. This dog's feces had no starch grains but did contain phytoliths of grasses, some sedges and dicots, with signs of phytolith dissolution typical of wet, alkaline environments. The coprolite macrofloral remains were conifer charcoal fragments, probably representing upland pines that burned in campfires or forest fires and were also in something consumed by the dog. One of these tiny charcoal pieces was radiocarbon dated to cal AD 620–690 (Cummings and Kováčik 2018). Another, larger charcoal sample from TU1 L13, the level with the coprolite, was dated cal AD 415–640. Pollen grains of oak, grasses, verbena, and possible torreya tree were also identified in Middle Woodland deposits at Otis Hare (Kiahtipes 2021)

Seasonality, Climate, and Sea Level

Whether Middle Woodland groups lived in the same village year-round and sent out only small parties to collect particular resources, or moved as whole groups to where resources were available, is not yet known, as seasonality evidence is scant. The persimmon fruit and duck bone from Otis Hare imply fall occupation, which makes sense since the riverbank locale would often be inundated in late winter–early spring. Furthermore, the site must have been near the river mussel beds, which were perhaps most accessible during the fall dry period.

The yearly activity cycles of these Indigenous peoples must have responded to seasonal change, but also to climatic conditions and sea-level fluctuations. Though modern sea levels were generally reached by Middle Woodland times, some variations occurred. Periods of increased hurricanes may have happened between 550 BC and AD 150 (Coor 2012), after which less stormy conditions might have brought stability enhancing the emergence of Middle Woodland complexity. Worldwide, a stunning global-scale atmospheric event dating to AD 536 brought about a decade of "years without summer." This substantial cooling period may have lasted until about AD 660 and caused drastic social upheaval, as was well documented in Eurasia (Haldon 2016). Roman historians wrote of drought, cold, dry fog that lessened the sun's brightness, and resulting famine, war, migration, disease, and acute reduction of European populations. Chinese historic records corroborate all this, and northern European tree-ring data indicate radically slowed growth of forests at this time. The cause of this global cooling is unknown, though volcanic eruptions, meteors, comets, and dust storms have all been proposed (Gibbons 2018; Gunn 2000). The archaeological record may reflect this historic climate event and its aftermath. Significantly, the ending dates of this period of colder temperatures are close to the end of the Middle Woodland period.

Mounds and Ritual Practices

Detailed comparison of Middle Woodland mounds in the Apalachicola–lower Chattahoochee region with those across the East is needed. No mounds have been professionally excavated. Data come mostly from Moore's work and collectors' knowledge (Lockman 2020). Burial mound-building begun in the Early Woodland expanded hugely.

Mound Construction Activity

Mound size may not be due to some imagined "monumentality" but dependent on how many people used it or had to be buried in it and over how long, though some find an inverse relationship between size and number of burials (e.g., Charles 1992:177). Ground clearing and preparation, often by fire, was done before initial burials, then later graves were put into existing mounds. No rocks were used in mound fill in the region as they were farther to the north. Mound soils were yellow, brown, black, or white sands, dark midden, and shell midden in coastal areas. At Porter's Bar (8Fr1), an oyster-shell stratum formed the base; a few pockets of shell were with some burials; and shell covered perhaps one-fourth of the mound (Moore 1902:24). At the base of Pierce Mound A, a large fire had left a mass of burned, black organic material and burned sand and shells, with exotic artifacts mixed in. Burials were on top of burned masses or covered by mats of charred material. They could be over or under special sand reddened by hematite or blackened by charcoal, or lenses of hard clay, including red fired clay areas, as at Davis Field Mound (8Ca1), or a red clay basal stratum as at Aspalaga Mound 3 (8Gd1). Some burned materials in graves appear to be redeposited from fires elsewhere, while others seem burned in place. A rare occurrence resembling the bark and log tombs of Midwestern Hopewell appears at Davis Field Mound in the middle Apalachicola. Here, besides burials under charcoal masses, one skeleton was under a layer of unburned bark up to three cm thick, measuring 100 × 60 cm, associated with a log about a meter long and 15 cm thick. Moore (1903:469) recognized these grave elements just before they crumbled to dust as he dug there.

Mound construction materials must have been chosen for their physical properties and color significance (Sherwood and Kidder 2011). Gotier Hammock Mound had contrasting gray, black, white, and yellow strata (see Plate VII). Historic Native Americans in the Southeast associated red, yellow, black, and white with cardinal directions: red signified war, black meant death, and white meant peace and purification (Hudson 1976). Using shell midden fill at coastal mounds seems disrespectful—old garbage covering bodies of presumably honored persons. But this shell might have been repurposed for graves because ancestors had left it. The lime in the shell could have masked odors of decay. In sum, it appears that people sometimes chose special soils but other times just scraped up whatever was nearby. Mounds may have been unplanned, growing accretionally. Burying the dead might have been a seasonal celebration, explaining why some human remains are more "processed" than others, if they were kept until the proper time. In addition to accompanying graves, artifacts were deposited at both specific and seemingly random places in mounds, with ceramic caches most often on the east side.

Mound ritual could have been seasonal, annual, or done at other intervals by villages, kinship units, pilgrims, or unrelated communities. The labor involved was not necessarily what would be needed for a large monument. Partially based on experimental projects, estimates of amounts of soils excavated with a digging stick and brought to a deposition location range from about one to over two cubic meters per 5-hour worker day, or more hours if the ground surface needed preparation (Erasmus 1965; Mainfort 2013:4). Basket loading or piling up different lenses of soils may have been done with baskets or by dragging fill dirt on sheets of fabric or hide. But basket-loads may not be discernible if they are all of the same soil, merged into a layer. In the Midwest and mid-South, building great Middle Woodland earthworks may indeed have been a monumental undertaking. Earthen walls and enclosures are impressive at places such as Pinson in west Tennessee and Marksville in central Louisiana (Mainfort 2013). Such works are so far unknown in the Apalachicola–lower Chattahoochee region.

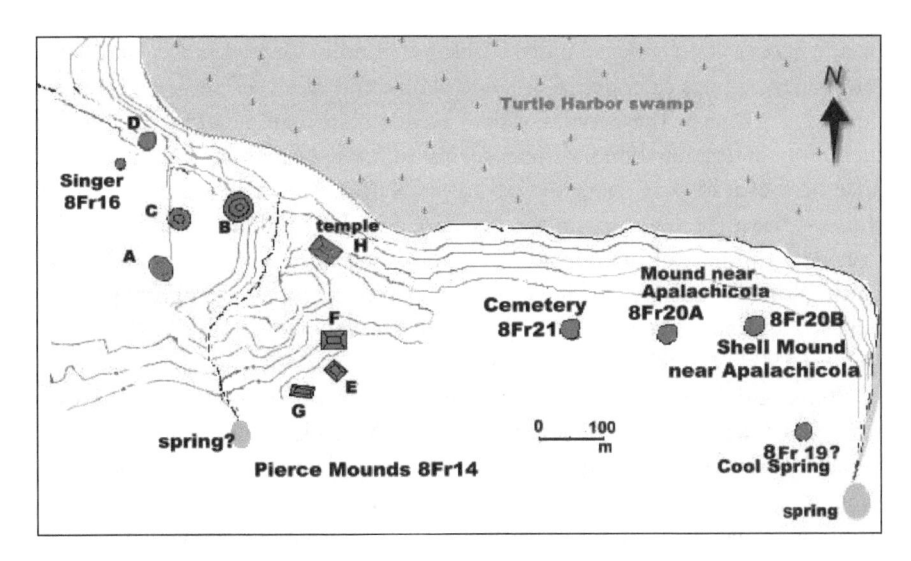

Figure 7.14. Pierce Mounds complex, at the Apalachicola River mouth; Turtle Harbor is old river channel. Mounds Pierce (8Fr14) A, C (?), 8Fr19, Fr20 (A, B) and Fr21 are Middle Woodland. (Nancy Marie White)

That Middle Woodland mounds were always special places is inferred from the number of them that have later components (also see Volume 2). Pierce Mound complex (8Fr14, etc.; Moore 1902; White 2013), at the river mouth, is an example. A schematic map (Figure 7.14) shows its 13 mounds along the old riverbank on a continuous shell midden ridge that runs at least 1 km around the edge of the city of Apalachicola. Seven mounds are aligned in an open oval, but only two of these are Middle Woodland, A and C, which also contained Early Woodland materials. The remaining mounds were apparently deliberately built by later Fort Walton peoples to make the oval. An additional four Middle Woodland mounds are to the east outside the oval: Cemetery (8Fr21); Mound Near Apalachicola (8Fr20A); Shell Mound Near Apalachicola (8Fr20B); and Cool Spring Mound (8Fr19, not relocated). Pierce was at a strategic location for interaction both north–south on the river and east–west along the coast. The river is now shifted eastward, with a marsh named Turtle Harbor in its former channel. Another example of sacred reuse is at Chipola Cutoff mound, where contact-period Fort Walton burials were placed among elaborate Middle Woodland graves (White 2011b, and see Volume 2).

Burial Practices
Data on burial practices in the research region are sometimes better known from Moore's unpublished notes, which might list each grave. The dead were interred extended and supine (on the back); flexed on either side with face up

or down; occasionally flexed on the back; as "bundles" or packages of skull and longbones; as piles of bones; as isolated skulls; and rarely as cremated remains burned elsewhere. These types show considerable manipulation of corpses, including defleshing bones. There seems to have been none of the avoidance of the dead that characterized other Native American cultures beyond the Southeast (such as among the Navajo), and the handling must have been considered respectful treatment. Some graves are in groups, maybe reflecting families or fellowships. At Pierce Mound A were grouped the tightly parallel bundled and flexed Burials 7 to 17 and the parallel extended Burials 42 to 45 (Moore 1902; White 2013:Figure 14).

Some burials that are isolated human skulls or other body parts could be trophies of war or other violence. Decapitation and human heads, real and depicted in stone ceramic, textile, and other media, are known worldwide over thousands of years (Chacon and Dye 2008). I witnessed old trophy skulls still hanging in native longhouses in Borneo, where headhunting was practiced a century ago as a way to earn status. Warfare is not necessarily implicated; indeed, there are no indicators of large-scale conflict during Middle Woodland in the region. Skulls and other bones could have been from honored ancestors placed in graves of relatives. A California study on bone chemistry of Native American burials dating between 4500 and 2500 BP concluded that both extra skulls and headless skeletons in graves represented ancestor veneration rather than trophies since all were of local origin (Eerkens et al. 2016). What different burial treatments reflected is unknown. An early foreigner near the research region, Cabeza de Vaca, noted in 1528 that Texas Indians buried their dead, except for shamans ("physicians" or "medicine men"), whom they burned, and that death ceremonies included dancing and festivities, and mourning involved weeping and wailing at dawn, noon, and sunset for a year (Covey 1961).

Burial practices reflect ideological and social systems. The Middle Woodland obsession with decorative, unusual, and imported objects may have been for appearance and performance but likely was for religion or magic too. However, an important aspect in the research region and throughout the South is that burial goods were not always elaborate, but often everyday items including plain pottery that Moore called "inferior ware." A dichotomy of "sacred versus secular" was set up to explain how mound assemblages differed from those of domestic sites (Sears 1973). Given typical scholarly inertia, this dichotomy is often reiterated as fact rather than a hypothesis to be tested. Most archaeologists now realize that it should be discarded, because the picture is far more complex. While exotics such as copper are usually found in mounds, many ornate objects are at habitation sites, and mundane items are in burials. Besides plain ceramics, grave goods detailed by Moore but less emphasized amid Middle Woodland finery include countless hammerstones, pebbles, hones, unexceptional chert implements and flakes, sandstone and other rocks, masses of clay, shell, and phosphate or lime rock. "Sacred" may not mean the artifacts themselves but their special uses—Catholic holy water looks just like regular water. Items of ritual significance could have been produced and used in nonritual contexts before they were brought to funerals. Separation of spirituality from daily life is really a modern ethnocentric concept (Sahlins 2022). In most traditional societies, and even within our own for some groups, the supernatural is always present. I could not spend a dozen years in Catholic schools without learning this, and modern Buddhism and other religions also do not separate the spiritual, natural, and cultural realms.

The practice of breaking artifacts before burial with the dead implies letting something go, releasing harmful spirits or ending the use of the object along with the ended life of the owner. It included "killing" pots, knocking holes into the bottom. Some West African societies smash pots over graves to create a clean break between the living and dead (Barley 1997:151–152). Or this activity was part of social display or group emotion—but sometimes idiosyncratic: the compound vessel from Chipola Cutoff Mound has holes knocked into all four separate conjoined segments, but the five-chambered one from Gotier Hammock only has one hole punched in the base of the central rectangular chamber. Burials reflected the combined results of different choices. One possibility is the concept of a burial planner, a specialist like event planners today. Such a person, perhaps a shaman, could consult with the grieving family, identify preferences for the mortuary ceremony, and pick themes from what was current but also traditional custom. Each grave may have had some things specific to the deceased, some currently fashionable items, and some pan-regional typical materials, like the requisite clothing, cake, veil, garter, and bouquet-throwing at a modern wedding. As in the saying "something old, something new, something borrowed, something blue," Middle Woodland ritual could have combined "something old, something new, something from far away, something from the dead here today." If funerals were for kin or fellowship groups, some exotic paraphernalia might not necessarily be religious but pertaining to clan totems, team mascots, or other social identifiers.

Ethnographic Examples from Afar
Ethnographic data from a distant part of the world may be useful to examine social aspects of objects from faraway places. During my semesters in Sarawak, East Malaysia, I learned about Indigenous tropical forest peoples in Borneo. Most are farmers, of rice, pepper, now rubber and oil palm, who also still hunt, gather, fish, and retain traditional practices, including long-distance trade. They practice shifting or swidden agriculture, moving every few years

to carve new farm fields out of the jungle as part of the *pindah* or urge to migrate (Walker 2002). These "tribal" peoples have various male and female deities and spirits (Sandin 1968). Women did most labor, including farming. Men hunted and did heavy chores, but also traditionally left for a while and obtained exotic goods to bring back home.

A well-documented group is the Iban (Postil 2006; Sandin 1968), who migrated frequently even after being forced to change somewhat under Muslim Malay influence, then British colonial rule and Christian missionaries. They were competitive but egalitarian, with bilateral kinship (Cramb 2007; Sandin [1968], an ethnographer who was Iban himself, says there were hereditary strata). Chiefs, mostly men, but some women (Hew and Talib 2011), had authority based on leadership qualities. Iban communities still live in longhouses with separate apartments for each of a dozen or two nuclear families but a common porch spanning the whole length of the structure, where socializing, religious ceremonies, and drinking great quantities of tuak (rice wine) take place. Farm huts were near the padi (rice field), and rituals were significant throughout the planting, maintenance, and harvesting. A cherished Iban practice was that young men left home to explore distant lands. They were headhunters, so one quest for a youth traditionally might have been to get a head, but usually it was to seek adventure and return with glory and gifts (now they go to work in timber camps or offshore in the oil and gas industry). This journey, called the *bejalai*, might last for months or years. The men returned with exotic objects obtained during their travels, often huge Chinese ceramic jars that appear too weighty and difficult to carry around for such long times and distances. Like the many tattoos they also acquired, these were items of social status. Every longhouse had some: Chinese big glazed-earthenware jars, or bronze pots or gongs, stored as wealth. The young men's journeys helped them later in leadership positions, especially when it was time for the whole group to migrate.

Other Borneo native cultures also lived in longhouses and moved frequently, even through isolated, rough areas. Bala's (2002) autobiographical ethnography describes the Kelabit people of the highlands, where rugged conditions, with little water travel and steep mountains, did not prevent the exchange of prestige goods. People's ranks ranged from slave to aristocracy, and the ornaments and other imported objects, from jars to glass beads, were insignias of these ranks. Amid the headhunting and warfare done for religious and political prestige and the group migrations, these prized artifacts moved around over centuries. Large, heavy ceramic jars and 40-lb. brass gongs were hauled around the highlands over generations (Harrisson 1959:25). There was amazing interplay between extreme isolation and yet enormous interconnectedness represented by material objects.

The modern Iban are said not to like contemporary western soap operas or other depictions of people flaunting wealth (Postil 2006:107–110). However, they carry on the young male journey tradition and group migrations for periodically clearing new patches of forest. All over Borneo, items such as the now-ancient Chinese jars, gongs, brassware, and beadwork are valuable family assets. They were sometimes used as payments for wrongful deaths or other debts, and thus moved around the landscape, though not rapidly. Large ancient heirloom jars could serve as media for exchange. They were classified into categories based on commonly known value, with the most important type worth a human life in one region (Sandin 1968:124n24). Some of these artifacts were thought to have miraculous properties, and often their value included the genealogy of their ownership. Indigenous academic colleagues in Sarawak told me of some old Chinese jars embodying warrior spirits and thus conveying protection. The jars might be carried long distances to protect a new longhouse settlement for perhaps a year before being returned. I heard of one case of a family jar that purportedly rocks of its own accord, told by a professional anthropologist in that family.

Often the jars and other exotic objects are integrated into funerary practices of past and present Borneo peoples, where procedures done by ritual specialists aim for proper treatment of the dead to insure the safety of the living (e.g., Schiller 2001). Memorial rites can play out over cycles of months or years (Hutchinson and Aragon 2002). I attended a two-day Iban gathering commemorating the death of a woman whose funeral was three months earlier. Whether incorporated into funerals or not, the role of the imported spectacular artifacts was one of respect and possibly magic gained through possession and care, not necessarily religious. In 1996, archaeologists documented a cache of Chinese ceramics uncovered in association with an 1880s Iban longhouse that included jars, dishes, ewers, cups, over half of beautiful celadon, from the Song (AD 960–1279) and Yuan (AD 1271–1369) dynasties. They had been kept all that time, then buried (Ko and Chia 2012). These and other ethnographic examples might help in understanding Middle Woodland valued objects in the southeastern United States.

Economic Interaction and Social Systems

From a modern western viewpoint, the ostentation and opulence of Middle Woodland material culture seem like manifestations of wealth and success (Van Gilder and Charles 2003). However, we cannot explain Middle Woodland in ethnocentric terms, and stylistic trends toward or away from the more complex and ornate occur often in human history. From roughly 1600 through 1800, European Baroque and Rococo architecture, art, and music, heavy with gaudy embellishment, were followed by plain, symmetrical

Classical-period lines, but still supported by affluent patrons. Anthropologists know that style is unpredictable (Kroeber 1957). During Middle Woodland times in the research region, expanding from the already more complex decorative work of Early Woodland complicated-stamped pottery and exotics, craftworkers developed the most elaborate artifacts that had ever been seen before or since. Probably everyone had prestige goods, though elite individuals surely had more. The pervasive ornamentation seems to show a sheer delight in the new and unusual or *neophilia*, an obsession with novelty. Anthropologists have documented this, for example, Margaret Mead (1935:9–13), for the Arapesh people of New Guinea.

Exchange Systems
Middle Woodland exchange amplified or renewed long-distance economic connections that had existed for centuries, adding the obsession with the unusual and perhaps intensifying traffic along waterways. The Chattahoochee-Apalachicola system is the shorter of the only two major passages through the barrier of the Appalachian mountains that connect all the way to the Gulf of Mexico (the other is the Tennessee-Ohio-Mississippi system) that would have facilitated interaction with the Hopewellian Midwest (Brose 1994; Smith 2009:2). With its myriad tributaries and distributaries, it was a conduit for information, materials, and people over a huge area. Gridworks of already ancient overland trails must have existed too. Burying expensive goods took them out of circulation, stimulating the need for more and expanding the "supply chain" network.

Elaborate objects may have been gifts that enhanced a wider exchange of basic commodities such as foods, or the insurance of future assistance. We do not know if a few specialist traders traveled far to get them or if they were passed on from village to village. In a similar fashion to that already described for Borneo, prehistoric Native Americans could have made long journeys for adventure and acquisitions that later became significant to their families and that may have given them political or shamanistic knowledge and influence. These important objects may have been exchanged multiple times, accumulating their own histories that gave added value.

The Middle Woodland "interaction sphere" concept implies circularity and reciprocity. It has been compared with the Kula ring ceremonial exchange of Papua New Guinea famously documented a century ago (Malinowski 1922). Kula participants travel hundreds of miles by canoe across the western Pacific, with great effort and risk, to hand out decorative artifacts: red shell necklaces in a clockwise direction around islands and white shell armbands in a counter-clockwise direction. These objects convey social prestige but also establish mutual relationships, opening the way for transactions in more necessary goods.

While Malinowski, typical for his time, described only important men transporting these objects, Weiner (1992) showed how women also had exchange systems and political power within the Kula. This is one of many examples anthropologists have documented of how ritual exchange in traditional, nonstate societies does not take place apart from everything else but is deeply embedded in economic production, resulting in greater cooperation. Whatever their characteristics, Middle Woodland economic structures probably fluctuated in their intensity, diversity, and acceptance of nonlocal influences (Wright 2017). Nonetheless, it does seem to be a time of less isolationism and more participation in and appreciation of the exceptional and the foreign.

Materials Exchanged
Sourcing studies show how far the exotic artifacts already discussed had to have moved to reach the Apalachicola–lower Chattahoochee region (Figure 7.15). Copper, even from the closest sources in the Appalachian mountains, came from at least 300–500 km to the north; if it was from around Lake Superior, it traveled 2,000 km. Galena was from over 1,000 miles away in Missouri. Greenstone was probably from the north Georgia mountains, though a celt manufacturing center was identified in central Alabama, with grooves in the exposed bedrock from grinding and sharpening (Waselkov and Cottier 2016). The Appalachians were also sources of mica, quartz crystal, and other stones. In exchange for the incoming products, several commodities could have moved north from the Gulf Coastal Plain, including perishables. Williams and Elliott (1998a:11) think carved wood probably moved often along the "Woodland Information Superhighway," which they envision as a network analogous to today's Internet, bringing both knowledge and material goods.

For the Apalachicola–lower Chattahoochee region, a prized trade commodity was likely yaupon holly (*Ilex vomitoria*) leaves to make the black drink, full of caffeine and extremely significant for Native Americans in the Southeast. Dried leaves or seeds are easy to store and carry. Brown (2006) suggests that the shamanic element in Middle Woodland involved strong native tobaccos that could produce hallucinations. Other goods transported might have been palm fronds or parts of other plant or animal species unknown farther north, such as feathers from water birds, ivory-billed woodpeckers, or Carolina parakeets. A Hopewellian mound burial in Illinois included a skeleton of a roseate spoonbill (Parmalee and Perino 1970), a large pink south Florida bird. Other things not available in the Midwest/mid-South might have been smoked or salted marine fish or shellfish. Shark teeth, fossilized or not, sometimes perforated for suspension, as well as alligator teeth and barracuda jaws, are found in Middle Woodland mounds in the Midwest and Northeast; a shark tooth came from the Early Woodland site of Mandeville, far upriver

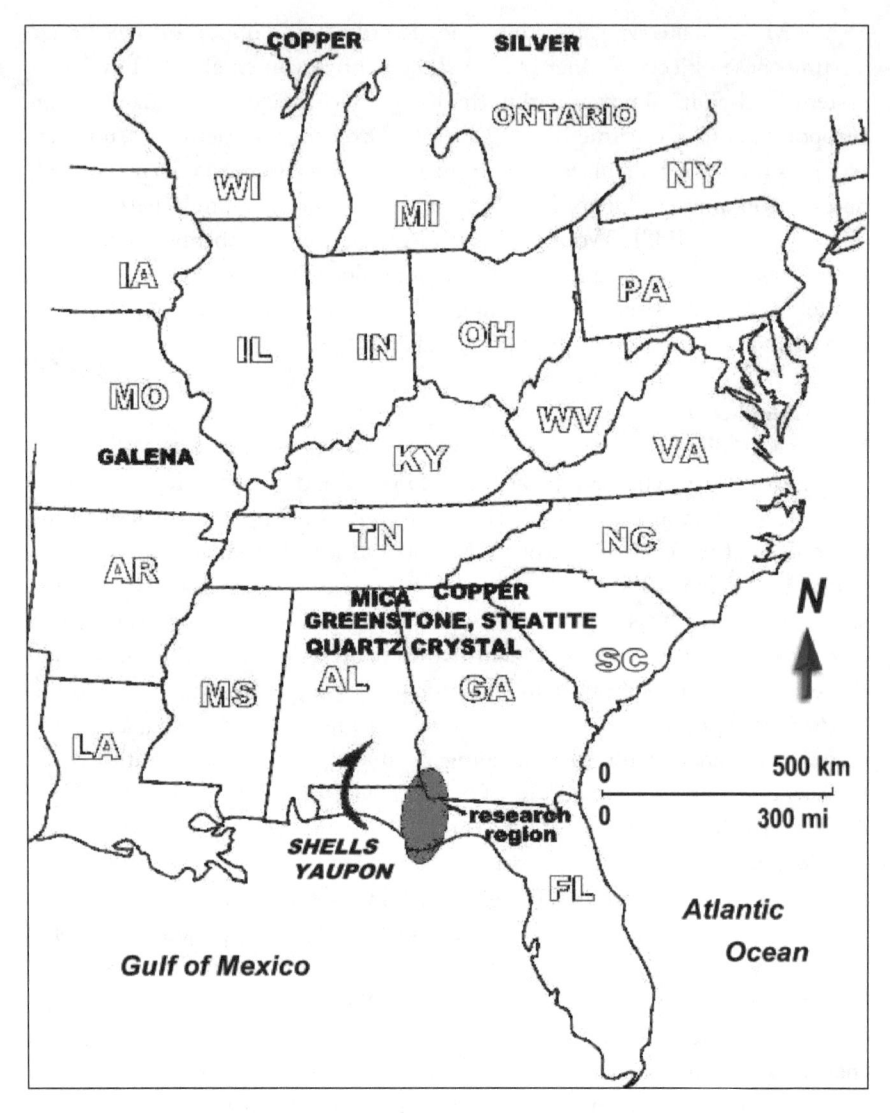

Figure 7.15. Source areas for exotic Middle Woodland materials in the research region (shaded), which may have traded outward the local shells and yaupon holly. (Nancy Marie White)

on the Chattahoochee. At northwest Georgia's Tunacunnhee site, shark vertebrae and teeth were in a mound burial with other exotics (Jefferies 1976). Pearls and pearl beads are common in Midwestern Hopewell mounds; though most are freshwater, some might be from Gulf oysters.

Shells, especially of large gastropods, were seriously meaningful (Milanich

1994:133–134). Gulf whelks and conchs appear at Middle Woodland sites throughout the Deep South, mid-South, and Midwest. In Ohio Hopewell, Carr (2008:210, 281n7) counts 23 people at the Hopewell site, seven at Seip-Pricer Mound, and four at Ater Mound buried with shell cups or dippers. He calls them conchs but photos show lightning whelks (or left-handed whelk, *Busycon perversum*), notable for their exceptional counterclockwise spiral. This atypical direction is thought to have been significant, but other reasons for their desirability may simply have been their hardness, thickness, and durability. Besides cups, shell items in Middle Woodland mounds include beads, spoons, and other things. The shell trade in prehistory surely originated far earlier. Within the research region, unusually salty St. Joseph Bay was full of large gastropods much easier to obtain than those out in the Gulf. Keith (2011:189, Figure 6) mapped probable routes along which exotics moved into the Leake site in northwest Georgia, a possible strategic midpoint between southern Middle Woodland and the Hopewellian region. One route is the Chattahoochee-Apalachicola drainage, but he shows its southbound arms turning east or west before reaching the Gulf of Mexico. This route should be revised to continue all the way down to the Gulf and bays where people got shells and yaupon holly.

Other things to exchange might have been labor, songs, poems, stories, or dances. The mechanisms for movement and development of Middle Woodland ceramic types and traditions in the region, as well as the influx of extralocal artifacts, were probably both trade and the bestowing of presents. In what were likely matrilineal societies with female potters, fancy new Middle Woodland ceramics would not have come from women "marrying in" or "wife-taking" but perhaps from husbands marrying in and bringing gifts—maybe pots from their mothers, with special foods for marriage or courtship offerings. This is a better explanation than physical movement of women for how vessels with similar stamped designs ended up far apart.

Social Systems and Ranking
Well before the emergence of post-processual archaeology there was scientific study of the social dimensions of mortuary practices (Brown 1971; Saxe 1970). One idea was that formal burial places were indicators of kin-group ties to particular territories and resources. As rites of passage, funerals and burials at designated locations could connect group membership with specific land (Morris 1991), but not necessarily within hierarchical systems. Traditional explanations of the Middle Woodland invoke the concept of egalitarian "segmentary tribes" headed by "big men" with special expertise or personal skills (e.g., Walthall 1980:110) and social organization based on community labor and corporate ritual.

However, we can question models hypothesizing single male leaders who controlled valuable goods, gained power over followers, and shifted from achieved to hereditary positions. As discussed in earlier chapters, social-leveling mechanisms probably in effect since the first Native Americans arrived, and still present among some hunter-gatherer groups (e.g., Hoffman 2018; Lee 1969, 2014; Suzman 2017) would be hard to overcome. The "big man" scenario, especially in matrilineal societies, is ethnocentric, sexist, and derived from modern western entrepreneurship values. Interestingly, this model was developed by ethnographic analogy with South Pacific island cultures that were thought to fit, on some idealized cultural-evolutionary scheme, as timeless, ideal types between egalitarian hunter-gatherers and stratified groups. But these cultures were studied in the twentieth century after massive change brought about by western nations in World War II. Before that, as shown actually by archaeological research, they were more highly stratified some 2,000 years ago. However, once the "big man" idea was out there, researchers took it as a given, instead of a hypothesis to test (Torrence 2003).

By contrast with Early Woodland material culture, in Middle Woodland times, types, and numbers of grave goods and their distributions do suggest greater social ranking. Studying the origins of social and economic inequality is important, but difficult. Some proposals invoke rich natural environments in which hierarchy emerged through actions of self-aggrandizing individuals controlling labor and surpluses. Others hypothesize depleted environments in which opportunistic leaders gain power by controlling basic resources, and still others see combinations of both. We have moved from simpler environmental explanations of stress or demographic pressure (e.g., Price and Brown 1985) to a combination of just the right environments and just the right social roles, or just the social roles evolving in themselves. But there is still little clarity about how to correlate ecological and archaeological data with these biased schemes that assume gender disparity and capitalist-type self-promotion. Newer work suggests that inequality takes diverse forms in terms of heredity, time spans, and constraints (e.g., Moreau 2021). In later Fort Walton cultural systems, after AD 1000 in this region and beyond, women are also often buried with rich accoutrements and interpreted to have been important leaders or other revered figures, just as much as men (see Volume 2). Such social positions could have been developing earlier, during Middle Woodland.

The archaeological record shows that small-scale Middle Woodland societies all over the eastern United States had local autonomy and stability for centuries (Lynott 2014:1, 37). Despite the baggage of terminology, they are probably best referred to as egalitarian, complex "tribes" or "middle-range" societies, not yet hierarchical chiefdoms (Wright 2017:56–58). The concept of "tribe" is mostly a recent and artificial construct emerging from neighboring state societies, not from the Indigenous groups themselves (Fried 1975). But it is useful to mean cultures that might award certain individuals higher social standing but still make major decisions and wield power by group consensus. Social inequality must be differentiated from economic inequality, in other words, ranked versus stratified society. Social differentiation may mean having titles, special clothing or jewelry, a bigger house, rights to speak first or use religious paraphernalia. Probably Middle Woodland peoples had all these. But economic differentiation means some people eat better, live healthier, and have all basic needs met, while others do not—things we cannot yet see in the Middle Woodland. One study of skeletal biology of 137 Ohio Hopewell mound burials found no differences in stress, nutrition, infection, trauma, or other status markers among any individuals, male or female, suggesting that status depended on achievement during life, not inheritance (Koot 2012). The picture was probably similar for Middle Woodland peoples in the Apalachicola–lower Chattahoochee valley region.

Middle Woodland People

Most prehistoric human remains known from the research region came from Middle Woodland mounds. Though Moore excavated hundreds of burials, the bones are gone, apparently cruelly discarded. He did give away rare pathological specimens. From Pierce Mound A, Burial 52, a flexed adult skeleton, he sent an unusual femur with a healed fracture (Moore 1902:220) to the Army Medical Museum in Washington, DC. This is now the US Department of Defense Armed Forces Institute of Pathology, National Museum of Health and Medicine, which specializes in elements with unusual anatomy; this bone is still there (personal communication, curator Franklin E. Damann 2013). Moore's unpublished notebook also said that the skull from this mound's Burial 93 was "saved," but not where it went. At Huckleberry Landing Mound (8Fr12), Moore (1902:237) found Burials 1 and 2, flexed skeletons, had "marks of serious inflammation"; Burial 2 had a radius with "an ununited fracture whose rough surface with a certain amount of surrounding callous, showed death to have intervened before the parts could unite." He sent this radius also to the Army Medical Museum, where it remains, labeled as having pseudoarthrosis, an unmended bone fracture.

The bones of Middle Woodland people would likely show that most did a good amount of physical labor: hunting, fishing, gathering, chopping wood, hauling water, processing foods, and making tools. Available data suggest that typical arthritis and accidents of the foraging lifestyle were common, but dental caries were not, as there was no starchy maize yet. Seasonal health hazards or benefits could have been based on types of foods obtained and the work involved. Gut microorganisms, which contribute to health and well-being, were undoubtedly far more diverse than those in modern Americans and varied by season with different foods and other conditions (Peddada 2017). Cranial alteration was typical, at least for elites in mounds. Kelly (1950a:28) said that skeletons he found at the Lake Douglas Mound (9Dr21) had frontal modification, as Moore had also seen often. The frontal bone was flattened, making the forehead slope upward, probably from infancy when the baby was strapped into a cradleboard. The shaping of the malleable infant skull was probably deliberate, for beauty or identity. Later, Kelly (1953:7) noted one adult skull with both frontal and lambdoidal flattening, the latter being a pushed-in upper back of the skull. Crania recovered from looters at Richardson's Hammock Mound that I saw had fronto-occipital (lower back of skull) flattening, which also characterized two other burials from the region: one each at Porter's Bar (8Fr1) and Indian Pass (8Gu1) Mounds. The practice was widespread in native North America, though its health effects are unknown (Cook 2018).

Human effigies from the region (see Figure 7.9) seem to show this head modification and give additional information about Middle Woodland people and bodies. As noted, they feature pierced earlobes, medium-width noses, robust cheeks, and those forehead treatments that resemble a widow's peak. While these figures may represent special people, not everyday folks, they still give an idea of appearance. They resemble depictions of Middle Woodland individuals in clay pots and figurines from nearby regions. For example, the Block-Sterns Mound in Tallahassee produced two Hopewellian-looking kneeling, bare-breasted, wide-belted female figurines. Both have the same widow's peak forehead treatment and are painted red, white, and black (Jones et al. 1998). From the Lewis Place Mound (8Ta1) in Taylor County, Florida, on the Aucilla River, Moore (1902, 1918) obtained an effigy vessel with similar head treatment and also a "breechclout" that protruded in the front like a pack, as well as a possible backpack. To the west on Choctawhatchee Bay, several figurine fragments are known, and also the famous human effigy polychrome jar from Buck Mound (8Ok11), now displayed at the Temple Mound Museum in Fort Walton Beach. It depicts a grimacing person with four legs, a topknot, and pierced earlobes (Lazarus 1979). All these ceramic images suggest that people, at least special ones, wore few clothes but many ornaments and probably also tattoos.

The greater number of Middle Woodland sites in the research region than in earlier times could mean that populations were increasing. Societies may have included many biologically related but also unrelated persons. A study of skeletons of 34 people buried at the Hopewell Mound (33Ro27) in Ohio found that they were indeed descended from Archaic and Early Woodland groups in the area, but were genetically diverse. Their mitochondrial DNA, inherited only through the mother's line, was quite variable, indicating they did not share a recent female ancestor, suggesting burial groups were not based on matrilineal descent (Mills 2003). Another DNA study of 39 individuals in an Illinois Hopewell mound group (Bolnick and Smith 2007) found that people were not buried in matrilineal kin groups, and kinship did not strongly influence burial practices, though the greater mtDNA diversity in men as compared with women did suggest matrilocal residence, men marrying into women's established families.

The Middle Woodland general picture is of people perhaps traveling more often, settling near sparkling waters, delighting in the unusual and exotic, conducting ostentatious rites for the dead, but living in relatively egalitarian, ranked societies that continued to obtain the bountiful wild resources of the springs, stream valleys and bayshores, as their ancestors did. They may have welcomed interesting foreigners, made music and compelling drama amid the recounting of religious beliefs, and dined and danced often around firelight glimmering on their shiny and ornate possessions at occasions honoring the departed and the spirits. I end here with this height of prehistoric elaboration of material culture in the research region. (What happened afterward, from the emergence of food production and late prehistoric chiefdoms through recent historic times, is told in Volume 2.) This fabulous peak of Native American art, craft, socioeconomic and ceremonial accomplishment and ritual complexity that is Middle Woodland is richly demonstrated in the Apalachicola–lower Chattahoochee valley.

References Cited

Adovasio, J. M., Olga Soffer, and Jake Page
2007 *The Invisible Sex: Uncovering the True Roles of Women in Prehistory*. Left Coast Press, Walnut Creek, California.

Ahmad, Shakeel
2011 Barrier Evolution of Cape San Blas, St. Joseph Peninsula, Florida, from Textural Analysis, Ground Penetrating Radar and Organic Matter Isotope Geochemistry. Master's thesis, Department of Geography and Earth Sciences, McMaster University, Ontario.

Allen, Glenn T.
1954 Archaeological Excavations in the Central Northwest Gulf Coast Area. Florida State University Studies, Anthropology, No. 16.

Anderson, David G.
1996 Models of Paleoindian and Early Archaic Settlement in the Lower Southeast. In *The PaleoIndian and Early Archaic Southeast*, edited by David G. Anderson and Kenneth E. Sassaman, pp. 29–57. University of Alabama Press, Tuscaloosa.

2005 Pleistocene Human Occupation of the Southeastern United States: Research Directions for the Early 21st Century. In *Paleoamerican Origins: Beyond Clovis*, edited by R. Bonnichsen, B. Lepper, D. Stanford, and M. Waters, pp. 29–42. Center for the Study of First Americans, College Station, Texas.

2013 Paleoindian Archaeology in Eastern North America. In *The Eastern Fluted Point Tradition*, edited by Joseph A. M. Gingerich, pp. 371–403. University of Utah Press, Salt Lake City.

Anderson, David G., R. Jerald Ledbetter, and Lisa D. O'Steen
1990 Recent Research Results of the Georgia Paleoindian Survey. *The Profile* (Society for Georgia Archaeology News) 68:4–7.

Anderson, David G., D. Shane Miller, Stephen Yerka, and J. Christopher Gillam
2010 PIDBA (Paleoindian Database of the Americas) 2010: Current Status and Findings. *Archaeology of Eastern North America* 38:63–90.

Anderson, Loren C.
1988 Vascular Plant Survey of the Apalachicola Bay Wetlands in Florida. *NOAA Technical Memorandum NOS MEMD 21*. US Department of Commerce, National Oceanic and Atmospheric Administration, Washington, DC.

Andrefsky, William, Jr.
2005 *Lithics*. 2nd ed. Cambridge University Press, New York.

2008 The Analysis of Stone Tool Procurement, Production, and Maintenance. *Journal of Archaeological Research* 17:65–103.

Andrews, Jay D.
1951 Range and Habitat of the Clam *Polymesoda caroliniana* (Bosc) in Virginia (Family Cycladidae). *Ecology* 32(4):758–760.

Archaeological Consultants Inc.
2006 *Cultural Resource Assessment Survey, Jackson Blue Springs Recreation Area, Jackson County, Florida*. Report to the Jackson County Board of Commissioners, Marianna.

Arnold, Dean E.
1993 *Ecology and Ceramic Production in an Andean Community*. Cambridge University Press, Cambridge, England.

Auil-Marchalleck, Stephanie, Colleen Robertson, Angela Sunley, and Lance Robinson
2000 *Preliminary Review of Life History and Abundance of the Atlantic Rangia* (Rangia cuneata) *with Implications for Management in Galveston Bay, Texas*. Management Data Series No. 171, Coastal Fisheries Division, Texas Parks and Wildlife, Austin.

Austin, James S.
2003 Lithic Distribution in the Apalachicola River Valley. Undergraduate honors thesis, Department of Anthropology, University of South Florida, Tampa.

Austin, Robert J, and Angela Matusik
2014 Galena Distribution in Florida: Implications for Prehistoric Trade. Paper presented at the Annual Meeting of the Florida Anthropological Society, Punta Gorda.

Austin, Robert J., Christopher Mickwee, and Joshua M. Torres
2014 *Final Report. Cultural Resources Data Recovery at Bayou Park (8OK898), Eglin Air Force Base, Okaloosa County, Florida*. Report to the Mid-Bay Bridge Authority and 96th Civil Engineering Group, Eglin Air Force Base. Southeastern Archaeological Research, Gainesville, Florida.

Baird, Tom
2020 *A Year on the Bay. St. Joseph Bay, Cape San Blas and the Beaches*. Independently published.

Bala, Poline
2002 *Changing Borders and Identities in the Kelabit Highlands*. Dayak Studies Contemporary Society Series 1. Institute of East Asian Studies, University of Malaysia, Sarawak.

Balsillie, James H., and Joseph F. Donoghue
2004 High Resolution Sea-Level History for the Gulf of Mexico since the Last Glacial Maximum. *Florida Geological Survey Report of Investigations* No. 103, Tallahassee.

Barker, Graeme
2010 The Archaeology of Anthropogenic Environments: Reflections on Environments, Landscape, and Culture. In *The Archaeology of Anthropogenic Environments*, edited by R. Dean. Center for Archaeological Investigations Occasional Paper No. 37. Southern Illinois University, Carbondale.

Barley, Nigel
1997 *Grave Matters: A Lively History of Death around the World*. Henry Holt, New York.

Barnes, Verle
1987 *Portrait of an Estuary*. Helix Press, Corpus Christi, Texas.

Barrett, John C.
2021 *Archaeology and Its Discontents: Why Archaeology Matters*. Routledge, London.

Barrios, Kris, and Angela Chelette
2004 Chipola River Spring Inventory: Jackson and Calhoun Counties, Florida. *Water Resources Special Report* 04-1. Northwest Florida Water Management District, Havana, Florida.

Barsbai, Toman, Dieter Lukas, and Andreas Pondorfer
2021 Local Convergence of Behavior across Species. *Science* 371:292.

Becerra-Valdivia, Lorena, and Thomas Higham
2020 The Timing and Effect of the Earliest Human Arrivals in North America. *Nature* 584:93–97.

Belovich, Stephanie J.
1994 Fractures in the Carlston Annis Shell Mound (Bt-5) Skeletal Population. In *Archaeology of the Middle Green River Region, Kentucky*, edited by William H. Marquardt and Patty Jo Watson, pp. 505–514. University of Florida Institute of Archaeology and Paleoenvironmental Studies Monograph 5, Gainesville.

Belovich, Stephanie J., David S. Brose, Russell M. Weisman, and Nancy Marie White
1982 *Archaeological Survey at George W. Andrews Lake and Chattahoochee River, Alabama and Georgia*. Cleveland Museum of Natural History Archaeological Research Report No. 37.

Binford, Lewis R.
1980 Willow Smoke and Dogs' Tails: Hunter-Gatherer Settlement Systems and Archaeological Site Formation. *American Antiquity* 45:4–20.

Bird, Junius B.
1985 The Preceramic Excavations at the Huaca Prieta, Chicama Valley, Peru. *American Museum of Natural History Anthropological Papers* 62, Part 1. New York.

Blanchard, Charles E.
2000 Canoe Archaeology in Southwest Florida Estuaries. Paper presented at the Annual Meeting of the Florida Anthropological Society, Fort Myers.
2008 Matlacha Pass: Perspectives on Aboriginal Canoe Navigation. *Florida Anthropologist* 61:59–72.

Blanton, Dennis B., and Thomas H. Gresham
2007 An Experimental Perspective on Mississippian Small Pole Structures. In *Architectural Variability in the Southeast*, edited by Cameron H. Lacquement, pp. 32–48. University of Alabama Press, Tuscaloosa.

Blitz, John H., and Karl G. Lorenz
2006 *The Chattahoochee Chiefdoms*. University of Alabama Press, Tuscaloosa.

Blosser, Jack K.
1996 The 1984 Excavation at 12D29s: A Middle Woodland Village in Southeastern Indiana. In *A View from the Core. A Synthesis of Ohio Hopewell Archaeology*, edited by Paul Pacheco, pp. 54–69. Ohio Archaeological Council, Columbus.

Boivin, Nicole, and Alison Crowther
2021 Mobilizing the Past to Shape a Better Anthropocene. *Nature Ecology and Evolution* 5:273–284.

Bolnick, Deborah A., and David Glenn Smith
2007 Migration and Social Structure among the Hopewell: Evidence from Ancient DNA. *American Antiquity* 72:627–644.

Bongiovanni, Rosanne
2017 St. Vincent 5 Site, 8Fr364, Analysis of Skeletal Remains. In *Archaeological Survey and Testing on St. Vincent Island, Northwest Florida*, by Nancy Marie White and Elicia Kimble, pp. 235–242. Report to the Southeast Region, US Fish and Wildlife Service. Department of Anthropology, University of South Florida, Tampa.

Bonnichsen, Robson, and Alan L. Schneider
2001 The Case for a Preclovis People. *American Archaeology* 5(4):35–39.

Bonta, Mark, Robert Gosford, Dick Eussen, Nathan Ferguson, Erana Loveless, and Maxwell Witwer
2017 Intentional Fire-Spreading by "Firehawk" Raptors in Northern Australia. *Journal of Ethnobiology* 37(4):700–718.

Bradbury, Andrew P.
1997 The Bow and Arrow in the Eastern Woodlands: Evidence for an Archaic Origin. *North American Archaeologist* 18:207–233.

Braje, Todd J., Tom D. Dillehay, Jon M. Erlandson, Richard G. Klein, and Torben C. Rick
2017 Finding the First Americans. *Science* 358:592–594.

Braley, Chad O.
1982 *Archaeological Testing and Evaluation of the Paradise Point Site (8Fr91), St. Vincent National Wildlife Refuge, Franklin County, Florida*. Report to the Southeast Region, US Fish and Wildlife Service. Southeastern Wildlife Services, Athens, Georgia.

Bridges, Patricia
1991 Degenerative Joint Disease in Hunter-Gatherers and Agriculturalists from the Southeastern United States. *American Journal of Physical Anthropology* 85:379–391.

Brim Box, Jayne, and James D. Williams
2000 Unionid Mollusks of the Apalachicola Basin in Alabama, Florida, and Georgia. *Alabama Museum of Natural History Bulletin 21*. Tuscaloosa.

Brookes, Samuel O.
2001 Clarence Bloomfield Moore: Some New Perspectives. In *Historical Perspectives on Mid-South Archaeology*, edited by Martha Ann Rolingson. Arkansas Archeological Survey Research Series 58.
2004 Cultural Complexity in the Middle Archaic of Mississippi. In *Signs of Power: The Rise of Cultural Complexity in the Southeast*, edited by Jon L. Gibson and Philip J. Carr, pp. 97–113. University of Alabama Press, Tuscaloosa.

Brooksfilms Limited
1994 *The 2000-Year-Old Man*. Rhino Home Video, Los Angeles, California.

Brooms, McDonald
1995 Amazing and Mysterious Finds. *Stones and Bones* (Alabama Archaeological Society Newsletter) 37(2):3.

Brose, David S.
1994 Trade and Exchange in the Midwestern United States. In *Prehistoric Exchange Systems in North America*, edited by Timothy G. Baugh and Jonathon Ericson, pp. 215–240. Plenum Press, New York.
2002 Museum Paradigms and the History of Southeastern Archaeology. In *Histories of Southeastern Archaeology*, edited by Shannon Tushingham, Jane Hill, and Charles H. McNutt, pp. 13–25. University of Alabama Press, Tuscaloosa.

Brose, David S., and N'omi B. Greber (editors)
1979 *Hopewell Archaeology: The Chillicothe Conference*. Kent State University Press, Kent, Ohio.

Brose, David S., and Nancy Marie White (editors)
1999 *The Northwest Florida Expeditions of Clarence Bloomfield Moore*. University of Alabama Press, Tuscaloosa.

Broughton, Jack M., and Elic M. Weitzel
2018 Population Reconstructions for Humans and Megafauna Suggest Mixed Causes for North American Pleistocene Extinctions. *Nature Communications* 9:5441.

Brown, Fred, and Sherri M. L. Smith
1994 *The Riverkeeper's Guide to the Chattahoochee*. CI Publishing, Atlanta, Georgia.

Brown, Ian W.
1980 *Salt and the Eastern North American Indian, an Archaeological Study*. Bulletin No. 6, Lower Mississippi Survey, Peabody Museum, Harvard University, Cambridge, Massachusetts.
1999 Salt Manufacture and Trade from the Perspective of Avery Island, Louisiana. *Midcontinental Journal of Archaeology* 24:113–151.
2012 *Bottle Creek Reflections. The Personal Side of Archaeology in the Mobile-Tensaw Delta*. Borgo Publishing, Tuscaloosa, Alabama.

Brown, James A.
2006 The Shamanic Element in Hopewellian Period Ritual. In *Recreating Hopewell*, edited by D. Charles and J. Buikstra, pp. 475–488. University Press of Florida, Gainesville.

Brown, James A. (editor)
1971 *Approaches to the Social Dimensions of Mortuary Practices*. Memoirs of the Society for American Archaeology No. 25.

Brown, Kenneth M.
2009 McFaddin Beach. *Texas Beyond History* website.

Brown, Teresa L.
2015 From Dalton to Doulton: The Archaeological Resources of Tyndall Air Force Base, Florida. Paper presented at the Annual Meeting of the Southeastern Archaeological Conference, Nashville.

Broyles, Bettye J.
1968 Reconstructed Designs from Swift Creek Complicated Stamped Sherds. *Southeastern Archaeological Conference Bulletin* 8:49–74.

Broyles, Bettye J., and Clarence Webb
1970 The Poverty Point Culture. *Southeastern Archaeological Conference Bulletin 12*.

Bruhns, Karen. O.
1991 Sexual Activities: Some Thoughts on the Sexual Division of Labor and Archaeological Interpretation. In *The Archaeology of Gender*, edited by D. Walde and N. Willows, pp. 420–429. Chacmool 1991, Archaeological Association of the University of Calgary.

Buckley, Thomas
1988 Menstruation and the Power of Yurok Women. In *Blood Magic: The Anthropology of Menstruation*, edited by Thomas Buckley and Alma Gottlieb, pp. 188–209. University of California Press, Berkeley.

Bullen Ripley P.
1949 Indian Sites at Florida Caverns State Park. *Florida Anthropologist* 2:1–9.
1950 An Archaeological Survey of the Chattahoochee River Valley in Florida. *Journal of the Washington Academy of Sciences* 40:101–125.
1958 Six Sites Near the Chattahoochee River in the Jim Woodruff Reservoir Area, Florida. *River Basin Surveys Papers* No. 14. Bureau of American Ethnology Bulletin 169, pp. 315–358. Smithsonian Institution, Washington, DC.
1959 The Transitional Period of Florida. *Southeastern Archaeological Conference Newsletter* 6(1):43–53.
1975a *A Guide to the Identification of Florida Projectile Points*. Kendall Books, Gainesville.
1975b Suwanee-like Points from Southwestern Georgia. *Florida Anthropologist* 28:52.

Bunzel, Ruth
1929 *The Pueblo Potter: A Study of Creative Imagination in Primitive Art*. AMS Press, New York.

Burke, Ariane, Matthew C. Peros, Colin D. Wren, and Solène Boisard
2021 The Archaeology of Climate Change: The Case for Cultural Diversity. *PNAS* 118(30):e2108537118.

Bush, M. B., A. Rozas-Davila, M. Raczka, M. Nascimento, B. Valencia, R. K. Sales, C. N. H. McMichael, and W. D. Gosling
2022 A Palaeoecological Perspective on the Transformation of the Tropical Andes by Early Human Activity. *Philosophical Transactions of the Royal Society B* 377(1849).

Byers, Anne, and George Willson
1988 Keeping It Wet and Wild. *Nature Conservancy Magazine* 38(4):20–24.

Byrd, Julie C.
2009 The Ragland Foundation Site. A Preform Cache from Northwest Florida. Poster presented at the Annual Meeting of the Southeastern Archaeological Conference, Mobile, Alabama.
2017 Landscape vs. Discontinuous District: Florida Dugout Canoes. Blog, ncptt.nps.gov.

Caldwell, Joseph R.
1958 Trend and Tradition in the Prehistory of the Eastern United States. *American Anthropological Association Scientific Papers* Volume 10. Illinois State Museum, Springfield.

Caldwell, Joseph R., Mark Williams, Karen Y. Smith, Shawn Johns, and Kelly Brown
2014 Archaeological Excavations at Fairchilds Landing and Hares Landing, Seminole County, Georgia. *University of Georgia Laboratory of Archaeology Series Report* Number 82.

Callender, Charles, and Lee M. Kochems
1983 The North American Berdache. *Current Anthropology* 24:433–470.

Cambron, James E., and David C. Hulse
1964 *Handbook of Alabama Archaeology, Part I, Point Types*. Archaeological Research Association of Alabama, University of Alabama, Tuscaloosa.

Carr, Christopher
2008 Social and Ritual Organization. In *The Scioto Hopewell and Their Neighbors: Bioarchaeological Documentation and Cultural Understanding*, edited by Daniel Troy Case and Christopher Carr, pp. 151–299. Springer, New York.

Carr, Christopher, and Daniel Troy Case (editors)
2005 *Gathering Hopewell: Society, Ritual, and Ritual Interaction*. Kluwer Academic/Plenum Publishers, New York.

Carr, Philip J., Andrew P. Bradbury, and Sarah E. Price
2012 Lithic Studies in the Southeast: Retrospective and Future Potential. In *Contemporary Lithic Analysis in the Southeast*, edited by Philip J. Carr, Andrew P. Bradbury, and Sarah E. Price, pp. 1–12. University of Alabama Press, Tuscaloosa.

Carr, Robert S.
2012 *Digging Miami*. University Press of Florida, Gainesville.

Carter, Brinnen C., and James S. Dunbar
2006 Early Archaic Archaeology. In *First Floridians and Last Mastodons*, edited by S. David Webb, pp. 493–515. Springer, New York.

Castelnau, Francis, Comte de
1843 *Essai sur la Floride de Milieu. Nouvelles Annales des Voyages et des Sciences Geographiques* cx, vol. iv: 129–208 (Essay on Middle Florida, translated by A. Seymour). *Florida Historical Quarterly* 26(3):199–255 (1948).

Cerulean, Susan
1992 Delicate Balance. *Florida Wildlife* 46:32.

2015 *Coming to Pass. Florida's Coastal Islands in a Gulf of Change.* University of Georgia Press, Athens.

Chacon, Richard J., and David H. Dye (editors)
2008 *The Taking and Displaying of Human Body Parts as Trophies by Amerindians.* Springer, New York.

Chapais, Bernard
2011 The Deep Social Structure of Humankind. *Science* 331:1276–1277.

Charles, Douglas K.
1992 Woodland Demographic and Social Dynamics in the American Midwest: Analysis of a Burial Mound Survey. *World Archaeology* 24:175–195.

Chase, David W.
1978 Weeden Island–Swift Creek Affinities in the Middle Chattahoochee Valley. *Journal of Alabama Archaeology* 24:60–64.

Chason, H. L.
1987 *Treasures of the Chipola River Valley.* Father and Son Publishing, Tallahassee.

Chilton, Elizabeth S.
2004 Beyond "Big": Gender, Age, and Subsistence Diversity in Paleoindian Societies. In *The Settlement of the American Continents*, edited by C. Michael Barton, Geoffrey A. Clark, David R. Yesner, and Georges A. Pearson, pp. 162–172. University of Arizona Press, Tucson.

Claassen, Cheryl
2008 Shell Symbolism in Pre-Columbian North America. In *Early Human Impact on Megamolluscs*, edited by Andrzej Antczak and Roberty Cipriani, pp. 37–43. British Archaeological Reports S1865, Oxford, England.
2010 *Feasting with Shellfish in the Southern Ohio Valley.* University of Tennessee Press, Knoxville.
2015 *Beliefs and Rituals in Archaic Eastern North America.* University of Alabama Press, Tuscaloosa.

Clausen, C. J., A. D. Cohen, Cesare Emiliani, J. A. Holman, and J. J. Stipp
1979 Little Salt Spring, Florida. *Science* 203:609–614.

Clewell, Andre F.
1977 Geobotany of the Apalachicola River Region. In *Proceedings of the Conference on the Apalachicola Drainage System, 23–24 April 1976*, edited by Robert J. Livingston and Edwin A. Joyce Jr. Florida Marine Research Publications No. 26., pp. 6–20. Florida Department of Natural Resources, Tallahassee.

Codding, Brian F., James F. O'Connell, and Douglas W. Bird
2014 Shellfishing and the Colonization of Sahul: A Multivariate Model Evaluating the Dynamic Effects of Prey Utility, Transport Considerations, and Life-History on Foraging Patterns and Midden Composition. *Journal of Island and Coastal Archaeology* 9:238–252.

Cook, Della Collins
2018 Intentional Cranial Shaping. In *Bioarchaeology of the American Southeast: Approaches to Bridging Health and Identity in the Past*, edited by Shannon Chappell Hodge and Kristrina A. Shuler, pp. 127–144. University of Alabama Press, Tuscaloosa.

Cook, Joe, and Monica Cook
2000 *River Song. A Journey Down the Chattahoochee and Apalachicola Rivers.* University of Alabama Press, Tuscaloosa.

Cook Hale, Jessica W., Nathan L. Hale, and Ervan G. Garrison

2018 What Is Past Is Prologue: Excavations at the Econfina Channel Site, Apalachee Bay, Florida, USA. *Southeastern Archaeology* 38:1–22.

Coor, Jennifer Lynn
2012 Coastal Lake Paleoclimate Records: A Late Holocene Paleostorm Record for the Northeastern Gulf of Mexico Coast. PhD dissertation, Florida State University, Tallahassee.

Couch, Carol A., Evelyn H. Hopkins, and Suzanne Hardy
1996 Influences of Environmental Settings on Aquatic Ecosystems in the Apalachicola-Chattahoochee-Flint River Basin. *Water Resources Investigation Report* Vol. 95, Issue 4278. US Geological Survey, Atlanta.

Covey, Cyclone (translator)
1961 *Cabeza de Vaca's Adventures in the Unknown Interior of America*. Collier Books, New York.

Cramb, R. A.
2007 *Land and Longhouse*. Nordic Institute of Asian Studies Monograph No. 110, NIAS Press, Copenhagen.

Crane, H. R.
1956 University of Michigan Radiocarbon Dates I. *Science* 124:664–672.

Cronk, Lee, and C. Athena Aktipis
2015 The Human Generosity Project. *Anthropology News* 56(7–8):31–32.

Cummings, Linda Scott, and Peter Kováčik
2018 *Pollen, Phytolith, Starch, and Macrofloral Analyses and AMS Radiocarbon Age Determination of a Coprolite Sample from Otis Hare Site (8Li172), Liberty County, Florida*. PaleoResearch Institute Technical Report 2017-093, Golden, Colorado.

Deal, Michael, and Melissa B. Hagstrum
1995 Ceramic Reuse Behavior among the Maya and Wanka. In *Expanding Archaeology*, edited by James M. Skibo, William H. Walker, and Axel E. Nielsen, pp. 111–125. University of Utah Press, Salt Lake City.

Dean, Rebecca M.
2010 The Importance of Anthropogenic Environments. In *The Archaeology of Anthropogenic Environments*, edited by Rebecca Dean, pp. 3–12. Center for Archaeological Investigations, Carbondale, Illinois.

DeBoer, Warren R.
2004 Little Bighorn on the Scioto: The Rocky Mountain Connection to Ohio Hopewell. *American Antiquity* 69:85–107.

DeJarnette, David L.
1975 *Archaeological Salvage in the Walter F. George Basin of the Chattahoochee River in Alabama*. University of Alabama Press, Tuscaloosa.

Delcourt, Paul A., and Hazel R. Delcourt
2008 *Prehistoric Native Americans and Ecological Change*. Cambridge University Press, New York.

Denevan, William M.
1992 *The Native Populations of the Americas in 1492*. University of Wisconsin Press, Madison.

Dengel, Craig
2015 A Mesoscale Approach to the Social Landscape of the St. Andrews Bay Watershed. Paper presented at the Annual Meeting of the Southeastern Archaeological Conference, Nashville.

Denham, James M., and Keith L. Huneycutt (editors)

2004 *Echoes from a Distant Frontier: The Brown Sisters' Correspondence from Antebellum Florida.* University of South Carolina Press, Columbia.

De Vrieze, Jop
2014 Gut Instinct. *Science* 343:241–243.

Dincauze, Dena F.
1996 Large PaleoIndian Sites in the Northeast: Pioneers' Marshalling Camps? *Bulletin of the Massachusetts Archaeological Society* 57(1):3–17.

Dobyns, Henry F.
1983 *Their Number Become Thinned: Native American Population Dynamics in Eastern North America.* University of Tennessee Press, Knoxville.

Donoghue, Joseph F.
1992 Late Quaternary Coastal and Inner Shelf Stratigraphy, Apalachicola Delta Region, Florida. *Sedimentary Geology* 80:293–304.
1993 Late Wisconsinan and Holocene Depositional History, Northeastern Gulf of Mexico. *Marine Geology* 112:185–205.
2011 Sea Level History of the Northern Gulf of Mexico Coast and Sea Level Rise Scenarios for the Near Future. *Climatic Change* 107:17–33.

Donoghue, Joseph F., Demirpolat Suleyman, and William F. Tanner
1990 Recent Shoreline Changes, Northeastern Gulf of Mexico. In *Coastal Sediments and Processes*, edited by William F. Tanner. Proceedings of the Ninth Symposium on Coastal Sedimentology. Department of Geology, Florida State University, Tallahassee.

Donoghue, Joseph F., and Nancy Marie White
1995 Late Holocene Sea Level Change and Delta Migration, Apalachicola River Region, Florida. *Journal of Coastal Research* 11(3):651–663.

Doran, Glen H. (editor)
2002 *Windover: Multidisciplinary Investigations of an Early Archaic Florida Cemetery.* University Press of Florida, Gainesville.

Doran, Glen H., David N. Dickel, and Lee A. Newsom
1990 A 7,290-Year-Old Bottle Gourd from the Windover Site, Florida. *American Antiquity* 55:354–360.

Doucette, Dianna L.
2001 Decoding the Gender Bias: Inferences of Atlatls in Female Mortuary Contexts. In *Gender and the Archaeology of Death*, edited by Bettina Arnold and Nancy L. Wicker, pp. 159–178. AltaMira Press, Walnut Creek, California.

Drechsel, Emmanuel J.
1997 *Mobilian Jargon: Linguistic and Sociohistorical Aspects of a Native American Pidgin.* Clarendon Press, Oxford, England.

Duke, Daron, Eric Wohlgemuth, Karen R. Adams, Angela Armstrong-Ingram, Sarah K. Rice, and D. Craig Young
2021 Earliest Evidence for Human Use of Tobacco in the Pleistocene Americas. *Nature Human Behavior* 6:183–192.

Dunavan, Sandra L., and Volney H. Jones
2011 Tobacco and Smoking in Native North America. In *The Subsistence Economies of Indigenous North American Societies*, edited by Bruce D. Smith, pp. 517–524. Smithsonian Institution Scholarly Press, Washington, DC.

Dunbar, James S.
1991 Resource Orientation of Clovis and Suwanee Age Paleoindian Sites in Florida. In

Clovis: Origins and Adaptations, edited by Robson Bonnichsen and Karen L. Turnmire, pp. 185–213. Center for the Study of the First Americans, Oregon State University, Corvallis.

2006a Pleistocene–Early Holocene Climate Change: Chronostratigraphy and Geoclimate of the Southeast U.S. In *First Floridians and Last Mastodons*, edited by S. David Webb, pp. 103–155. Springer, New York.

2006b Paleoindian Archaeology. In *First Floridians and Last Mastodons*, edited by S. David Webb, pp. 403–445. Springer, Dordrecht, Netherlands.

2012 The Search for Paleoindian Contexts in Florida and the Adjacent Southeast. PhD dissertation, Department of Anthropology, Florida State University.

2016 *Paleoindian Societies of the Coastal Southeast*. University Press of Florida, Gainesville.

Dunbar, James S., C. Andrew Hemmings, Tom Harmon, and Emilee McGann
2022 A Reexamination of the Reexaminations of the Alexon Bison Site (8JE570). *Florida Anthropologist* 75(4):224–250.

Dunbar, James S., S. David Webb, and Michael Faught
1992 Inundated Prehistoric Sites in Apalachee Bay, Florida, and the Search for the Clovis Shoreline. In *Paleoshorelines and Prehistory*, edited by Lucille Lewis Johnson, pp. 117–146. CRC Press, Boca Raton, Florida.

Dycus, Katy
2022 Female Hunters and the Sexual Division of Labor in Early Americas. *Mammoth Trumpet* 37(3):6–9.

Edmiston, H. Lee
2008 *A River Meets the Bay: The Apalachicola Estuarine System*. Apalachicola National Estuarine Research Reserve, Eastpoint, Florida.

Eerkens, Jelmer W., Eric J. Bartelink, Laura Brink, Richart T. Fitzgerald, Ramona Garibay, Gina A. Jorgenson, and Randy S. Wiberg
2016 Trophy Heads or Ancestor Veneration? A Stable Isotope Perspective on Disassociated and Modified Crania in Precontact Central California. *American Antiquity* 81:114–131.

Elias, Scott A.
2010 Advances in Quaternary Entomology. *Developments in Quaternary Sciences* 12. Elsevier, Amsterdam.

Elliott, Daniel T.
2004 *Southwest Georgia Archaeological Survey 2001–2004*. LAMAR Institute Publication Number 60.
2017 *Soapstone in Georgia*. LAMAR Institute Publication Number 112.

Elliott, Daniel T., and Tracy M. Dean
2006 *Flint River Basin Archaeological Survey, Phase 2*. LAMAR Institute Publication Number 77.

Ellis, Erle C., Nicolas Gauthier, Kees Klein Goldewijk, Rebecca Bliege Bird, Nicole Boivin, Sandra Díaz, Dorian Q. Fuller, at al.
2021 People Have Shaped Most of Terrestrial Nature for at Least 12,000 Years. *PNAS* 118 (17):e2023483118.

Emerson, Thomas E.
2003 Materializing Cahokia Shamans. *Southeastern Archaeology* 22:135–154.

Emerson, Thomas E., and Dale L. McElrath
2009 The Eastern Woodlands Archaic and the Tyranny of Theory. In *Archaic Societies*, edited by Thomas E. Emerson, Dale L. McElrath, and Andrew C. Fortier, pp. 23–38. State University of New York Press, Albany.

Endicott, Kirk M., and Karen L. Endicott
2008 *The Headman Was a Woman: The Gender-Egalitarian Batek of Malaysia*. Waveland Press, Long Grove, Illinois.

Erasmus, Charles J.
1965 Monument Building: Some Field Experiments. *Southwestern Journal of Anthropology* 21:277–301.

Erickson, David L., Bruce D. Smith, Andrew C. Clarke, Daniel H. Sandweiss, and Noreen Tuross
2005 An Asian Origin for a 10,000-Year-Old Domesticated Plant in the Americas. *Proceedings of the National Academy of Sciences* 102:18315–18320.

Erlandson, Jon M., and Torben C. Rick
2008 Archaeology, Marine Ecology, and Human Impacts on Marine Environments. In *Human Impacts on Ancient Marine Ecosystems*, edited by Torben C. Rick and Jon M. Erlandson, pp. 1–20. University of California Press, Berkeley.

Estioko-Griffin, Agnes
1986 Daughters of the Forest. *Natural History* 95(5):36–42.

Eyles, Eric
2004 Prehistoric Shell Artifacts from the Apalachicola River Valley Area, Northwest Florida. Master's thesis, Department of Anthropology, University of South Florida, Tampa.

Fairbanks, Charles H.
1971 The Apalachicola River Area of Florida and Discussion. *Newsletter of the Southeastern Archaeological Conference* 10(2):38–40, 63.

Farr, Grayal Earle
2006 Reevaluation of Bullen's Typology for Preceramic Projectile Points. Master's thesis, Department of Anthropology, Florida State University, Tallahassee.

Faught, Michael K.
2004 The Underwater Archaeology of Paleolandscapes, Apalachee Bay, Florida. *American Antiquity* 69:275–289.

2006 Paleoindian Archaeology in Florida and Panama. In *Paleoindian Archaeology. A Hemispheric Perspective*, edited by Juliet E. Morrow and Cristóbal Gnecco, pp. 164–183. University Press of Florida, Gainesville.

Faulkner, Charles H.
1992 The Occurrence of Gar Remains on Tennessee Archaeological Sites. *Tennessee Anthropological Association Newsletter* 17(2):5–8.

Fedje, Daryl, Quentin Mackie, Duncan McLaren, Becky Wigen, and John Southon
2021 Karst Caves in Haida Gwaii: Archaeology and Paleontology at the Pleistocene-Holocene Transition. *Quaternary Science Reviews* 272 (107221).

Ferguson, R. Brian
2018 War May Not Be in Our Nature after All. *Scientific American* 319(3):76–81.

Finch, Bill, Beth Maynor Young, Rhett Johnson, and John C. Hall
2012 *Longleaf, Far as the Eye Can See*. University of North Carolina Press, Chapel Hill.

Flannery, Kent V.
1982 The Golden Marshalltown: A Parable for the Archaeology of the 1980s. *American Anthropologist* 84:265–278.

2006 On the Resilience of Anthropological Theory. *Annual Review of Anthropology* 35:1–13.

Foley, Allen M., Karrie E. Singel, Peter H. Dutton, Tammy M. Summers, Anthony E. Redlow, and Jeannine Lessman

2007   Characteristics of a Green Turtle (*Chelonia mydas*) Assemblage in Northwestern Florida Determined during a Hypothermic Stunning Event. *Gulf of Mexico Science* 2007(2):131–143.

Ford, James A., and Clarence H. Webb
1956   *Poverty Point: A Late Archaic Site in Louisiana*. Anthropological Papers Vol. 46, No. 1, American Museum of Natural History, New York.

Fox, Georgia L.
2015   *The Archaeology of Smoking and Tobacco*. University Press of Florida, Gainesville.

Fradkin, Arlene
1994   *Prehistoric Estuarine Adaptations in the Lower Apalachicola River Valley. The Archaeological Faunal Assemblages from Van Horn Creek and Sam's Cutoff Shell Mounds*. Florida Museum of Natural History, Gainesville, submitted to the Department of Anthropology, University of South Florida, Tampa.

Fretheim, Silje E., Ernesto L. Piana, Hein B. Bjerck, and A. Francisco J. Zangrando
2016   Home By the Sea: Exploring Traditions of Dwelling Reoccupation and Settlement Stability among Marine Foragers in Norway and Tierra del Fuego. In *Marine Ventures: Archaeological Perspectives on Human-Sea Relations*, edited by Hein B. Bjerck, Heidi Mjelva Breibik, Silje E. Fretheim, Ernesto L. Piana, Birgitte Skar, Angélica M. Tivoli, and A. Francisco J. Zangrando, pp. 175–192. Equinox, Sheffield, England.

Fried, Morton H.
1975   The Myth of Tribe. *Natural History* 64(4):12–20.

Frison, George C.
2004   *Survival by Hunting*. University of California Press, Berkeley.

Fritz, Gayle J.
2000   Levels of Native Biodiversity in Eastern North America. In *Biodiversity and Native America*, edited by P. Minnis and W. Elisens, pp. 223–247. University of Oklahoma Press, Norman.

Fry, Douglas P.
2006   *The Human Potential for Peace*. Oxford University Press, New York.

Fry, Douglas P., and Patrick Söderberg
2014   Myths about Hunter-Gatherers Redux. *Journal of Aggression, Conflict, and Peace Research* 6:255–266.

Futato, Eugene M.
2004   The North Alabama Project: An AAS Excavation Scrapbook. *Journal of Alabama Archaeology* 50.

Gadus, E. Frances, Marie E. Blake, Martha Doty Freeman, and Karl Kibler
1999   *National Register Testing of Prehistoric and Historic Sites and Survey of Placement Areas, Channel to Victoria, Calhoun and Victoria Counties, Texas*. Prewitt & Associates Reports of Investigations No. 121, US Army Corps of Engineers, Galveston District.

Gagliano, Sherwood M., Charles E. Pearson, Richard A. Weinstein, Diane E. Wiseman, and Christopher M. McClendon
1982   *Sedimentary Studies of Prehistoric Archaeological Sites*. Coastal Environments, Baton Rouge, Louisiana.

Gardner, William M.
1966   The Waddells Mill Pond Site. *Florida Anthropologist* 19:43–64.

Ghosh, Sanghamitra
2008   Heavy Stable Isotope Investigations in Environmental Science and Archaeology. PhD dissertation, Department of Geological Sciences, Florida State University, Tallahassee.

Gibbons, Ann
2018 Eruption Made 536 "The Worst Year to Be Alive." *Science* 362:733.

Gibson, Jon L.
2000 *The Ancient Mounds of Poverty Point*. University Press of Florida, Gainesville.

Gibson, Jon L., and Philip J. Carr (editors)
2004 *Signs of Power: The Rise of Cultural Complexity in the Southeast*. University of Alabama Press, Tuscaloosa.

Glowacki, Mary
2012 The First Florida "Bling": Paleolithic Beads. *Florida Anthropologist* 65:47–50.

Glowacki, Mary, and James S. Dunbar
2019 Illicit Digging, Illicit Collecting, and Archaeology. A Perspective from Florida. In *New Directions in the Search for the First Floridians*, edited by David K. Thulman and Ervan G. Garrison, pp. 139–159. University Press of Florida, Gainesville.

Gnecco, Cristóbal, and Javier Aceituno
2006 Early Humanized Landscapes in Northern South America. In *Paleoindian Archaeology: A Hemispheric Perspective*, edited by Juliet E. Morrow and Cristóbal Gnecco, pp. 86–104. University Press of Florida, Gainesville.

Goad, Sharon I.
1979 Middle Woodland Exchange in the Prehistoric Southeastern United States. In *Hopewell Archaeology: The Chillicothe Conference*, edited by David S. Brose and N'omi Greber, pp. 239–246. Kent State University Press, Kent, Ohio.

Gore, Robert H.
1992 *The Gulf of Mexico: A Treasury of Resources in the American Mediterranean*. Pineapple Press, Sarasota.

Gould, R. A.
1980 *Living Archaeology*. Cambridge University Press, New York.

Grayson, Donald K., and David J. Meltzer
2015 Revisiting Paleoindian Exploitation of Extinct North American Mammals. *Journal of Archaeological Science* 56:177–193.

Greenman, Emerson
1938 Hopewellian Traits in Florida. *American Antiquity* 3:327–332.

Gremillion, Kristen J.
2002 The Development and Dispersal of Agricultural Systems in the Woodland Period Southeast. In *The Woodland Southeast*, edited by David G. Anderson and Robert C. Mainfort Jr., pp. 483–501. University of Alabama Press, Tuscaloosa.

2011 The Role of Plants in Southeastern Subsistence Economies. In *The Subsistence Economies of Indigenous North American Societies: A Handbook*, edited by Bruce D. Smith, pp. 387–399. Smithsonian Institution Scholarly Press, Washington, DC.

Grimm, David
2016 Dogs May Have Been Domesticated More Than Once. *Science* 352:1153–1154.

Grund, Bridget Sky
2017 Behavioral Ecology, Technology, and the Organization of Labor: How a Shift from Spear Thrower to Self Bow Exacerbates Social Disparities. *American Anthropologist* 119:104–119.

Gunn, Joel D.
2000 A.D. 536 and Its 300-Year Aftermath. In *The Years without Summer: Tracing A.D. 536 and Its Aftermath*, edited by Joel D. Gunn, pp. 5–20. BAR International Series 872. Archaeopress, Oxford, England.

Haas, Randall, James Watson, Tammy Buonasera, John Southon, Jennifer C. Chen, Sarah Noe, Kevin Smith, et al.
2020 Female Hunters of the Early Americas. *Sciences Advances* 6:eabd0310.

Haldon, John
2016 Cooling and Societal Change. *Nature Geoscience* 9:191–192.

Hall, Grant D.
2000 Pecan Food Potential in Prehistoric North America. *Economic Botany* 54:103–112.

Hall, Robert L.
1997 *An Archaeology of the Soul: North American Indian Belief and Ritual*. University of Illinois Press, Urbana.

Halligan, Jessi Jean
2012 Geoarchaeological Investigations into Paleoindian Adaptations on the Aucilla River, Northwest Florida. PhD dissertation, Department of Anthropology, Texas A&M University, College Station.

Halligan, Jessi J., Michael R. Waters, Angelina Perrotti, Ivy J. Owens, Joshua M. Feinberg, Mark D. Bourne, Brendan Fenerty, et al.
2016 Pre-Clovis Occupation 14,550 Years Ago at the Page-Ladson Site, Florida, and the Peopling of the Americas. *Science Advances* 2(5).

Hand, Eric
2018 Ice Age Impact. *Science* 362:1346.

Harrisson, Tom
1959 *A World Within: A Borneo Story*. Cresset Press, London.

Hasty, A. H., Earl D. Fowler, R. T. Avon Burke, W. H. Buckhannan, Z. C. Foster, and G. L. Fuller
1939 *Soil Survey of Decatur County, Georgia*. US Department of Agriculture, Washington, DC.

Hayden, Brian
1995 Pathways to Power: Principles for Creating Socioeconomic Inequalities. In *Foundations of Social Inequality*, edited by T. Douglas Price and Gary M. Feinman, pp. 15–86. Plenum Press, New York.

Hays, Christopher T., Richard A. Weinstein, and James B. Stoltman
2016 Poverty Point Objects Reconsidered. *Southeastern Archaeology* 35:213–236.

Heckenberger, Michael J.
2005 *The Ecology of Power: Culture, Place, and Personhood in the Southern Amazon, A.D. 1000–2000*. Routledge, New York.

Heimlich, Marion Dunlevy
1952 *Guntersville Basin Pottery*. Geological Survey of Alabama, University of Alabama, Tuscaloosa.

Hemmings, C. Andrew, James S. Dunbar, and S. David Webb
2004 Florida's Early-Paleoindian Bone and Ivory Tools. In *New Perspectives on the First Americans*, edited by B. Lepper and R. Bonnichsen, pp. 87–92. Center for the Study of First Americans, College Station, Texas.

Hendry, Charles W., Jr., and J. William Yon
1958 *Geology of the Area in and around the Jim Woodruff Reservoir*. Miscellaneous Studies, Report of Investigations No. 16. Florida Geological Survey, Tallahassee.

Heuvelmans, Martin
1974 *The River Killers*. Stackpole Books, Harrisburg, Pennsylvania.

Hew, Cheng Sim, and Rokiah Talib

2011 *Tra Lehnder: Iban Woman Patriot of Sarawak*. Universiti Malaysia Sarawak, Kuching.

Hill, Kim, and Robert Boyd
2021 Behavioral Convergence in Humans and Animals. *Science* 371:235.

Hill, Kim R., Robert S. Walker, Miran Božičević, James Eder, Thomas Headland, Barry Hewlett, A. Magdalena Hurtado, et al.
2011 Co-Residence Patterns in Hunter-Gatherer Societies Show Unique Human Structure. *Science* 331:1286–1289.

Hine, Albert C.
2013 *Geologic History of Florida*. University Press of Florida, Gainesville.

Hobbes, Thomas
1996 [1651] *Leviathan, or the Matter, Forme, & Power of a Commonwealth Ecclesiasticall and Civill*. Edited with an Introduction and Notes by J. C. A. Gaskin. Oxford University Press, New York.

Hoffman, Carl
2018 *The Last Wild Men of Borneo*. William Morrow, New York.

Holden, Constance
2006 Long-Ago Peoples May Have Been Long in the Tooth. *Science* 312:1867.

Hollenbach, Kandice D.
2009 *Foraging in the Tennessee River Valley, 12,500 to 8000 Years Ago*. University of Alabama Press, Tuscaloosa.

Hollimon, Sandra E.
2001 The Gendered Peopling of North America: Addressing the Antiquity of Systems of Multiple Genders. In *The Archaeology of Shamanism*, edited by Neil S. Price, pp. 123–134. Routledge, London.

Hoopes, J., and W. Barnett
1995 The Shape of Early Pottery Studies. In *The Emergence of Pottery*, edited by W. Barnett and J. Hoopes, pp. 1–10. Smithsonian Institution Press, Washington, DC.

Hopkins, Sewell Hepburn, Jack W. Anderson, and Kalman Horvath
1973 *The Brackish Water Clam* Rangia cuneata *as Indicator of Ecological Effects of Salinity Changes in Coastal Waters*. Department of Biology, Texas A&M University, College Station, Texas.

Hubbell, T. H., A. M. Laessle, and J. C. Dickinson
1956 *The Flint-Chattahoochee-Apalachicola Region and Its Environments*. Bulletin of the Florida State Museum, Biological Sciences 1(1). University of Florida, Gainesville.
1976 *The Southeastern Indians*. University of Tennessee Press, Knoxville.

Hudson, Charles (editor)
1979 *Black Drink: A Native American Tea*. University of Georgia Press, Athens.

Huffman, Jean
2006 Historical Fire Regimes in Southeastern Pine Savannas. PhD dissertation, Department of Biology, Louisiana State University, Baton Rouge.

Hunt, Ron
1975 Problematical Stone Find. *Florida Anthropologist* 28:72.

Hunter, Donald G.
1975 Functional Analysis of Poverty Point Clay Objects. *Florida Anthropologist* 28:57–71.

Hurt, Wesley R.
1947 The Preliminary Archaeological Survey of the Chattahoochee Valley Area in Alabama. In *Archaeological Salvage in the Walter F. George Basin of the Chattahoochee River in*

Alabama, by David L. DeJarnette, pp. 6–86. University of Alabama Press, University, Alabama (1975).

Huscher, Harold A.
1959a *Appraisal of the Archaeological Resources of the Columbia Dam and Lock Area, Chattahoochee River, Alabama and Georgia*. River Basin Surveys, Smithsonian Institution, Washington, DC.
1959b *Appraisal of the Archaeological Resources of the Walter F. George Reservoir Area, Chattahoochee River, Alabama and Georgia*. River Basin Surveys, Smithsonian Institution, Washington, DC.
1964 The Standing Boy Flint Industry. *Southern Indian Studies* 16:3–20.
1967 Post Pleistocene Climatic Change in the Southeastern United States. *Southeastern Archaeological Conference Bulletin* 5:3–10.

Hutchinson, Dale L.
2004 *Bioarchaeology of the Florida Gulf Coast*. University Press of Florida, Gainesville.

Hutchinson, Dale L., and Lorraine V. Aragon
2002 Collective Burials and Community Memories: Interpreting the Placement of the Dead in the Southeastern and Mid-Atlantic United States with Reference to Ethnographic Cases from Indonesia. In *The Space and Place of Death*, edited by Helaine Silverman and David B. Small, pp. 27–54. Archaeological Papers of the American Anthropological Association No. 11.

Hutchinson, Lee, Terrance Simpson, Nancy White, and Michael McDaniel
1991 Public Archaeology and Middle Woodland Research in the Middle Apalachicola Valley. Paper presented at the Annual Meeting of the Florida Anthropological Society, Pensacola.

Ingle, Robert M., and Charles E. Dawson Jr.
1953 *A Survey of Apalachicola Bay*. Technical Series No. 10, State of Florida Board of Conservation, Tallahassee.

Isphording, Wayne C.
1985 *Sedimentological Investigation of the Apalachicola Bay, Florida, Estuarine System*. Sea Grant Report to the US Army Corps of Engineers, Mobile District. Department of Geology, University of South Alabama, Mobile.

Jackson, H. Edwin
1991 The Trade Fair in Hunter-Gatherer Interaction: The Role of Intersocial Trade in the Evolution of Poverty Point Culture. In *Between Bands and States*, edited by Susan A. Gregg, pp. 265–280. Occasional Paper No. 9, Center for Archaeological Investigations, Southern Illinois University, Carbondale.

Jackson, Lawrence J.
2006 Fluted and Fishtail Points from Southern Coastal Chile. In *Paleoindian Archaeology: A Hemispheric Perspective*, edited by Juliet E. Morrow and Cristóbal Gnecco, pp. 105–122. University Press of Florida, Gainesville.

Jahn, Otto L., and Ripley P. Bullen
1978 The Tick Island Site, St. Johns River, Florida. *Florida Anthropological Society Publications* 10.

Jahoda, Gloria
1967 *The Other Florida*. Charles Scribner's Sons, New York.

Jefferies, Richard W.
1976 *The Tunnacunnhee Site: Evidence of Hopewell Interaction in Northwest Georgia*. Anthropological Paper No. 1, University of Georgia, Athens.

Jenkins, Ned J.
1978 Prehistoric Chronology of the Lower Chattahoochee Valley. *Journal of Alabama Archaeology* 24:73–91.

Jenkins, Ned J., and Craig T. Sheldon
2014 Ceramic Chronology, Social Identity, and Social Boundaries: Central Alabama and Neighbors 100 B.C.–A.D. 1350. *Journal of Alabama Archaeology* 60:61–117.

Jennings, Matthew H.
2011 *New Worlds of Violence: Cultures and Conquests in the Early American Southeast*. University of Tennessee Press, Knoxville.

Johnson, David M.
2017 *Alabama's Prehistoric Indians and Artifacts*. Borgo Publishing, Tuscaloosa.

Johnson, Valerie
1993 Apalachicola Bay: Endangered Estuary. *Florida Water* 2(1):14–24.

Jones, B. Calvin
1993 The Late Archaic Elliott's Point Complex in Northwest Florida. Paper presented at the Annual Meeting of the Florida Anthropological Society, Clearwater.

Jones, B. Calvin, Daniel T. Penton, and Louis D. Tesar
1998 1973 and 1994 Excavations at the Block-Sterns Site, Leon County, Florida. In *A World Engraved. Archaeology of the Swift Creek Culture*, edited by Mark Williams and Daniel T. Elliott, pp. 222–246. University of Alabama Press, Tuscaloosa.

Jones, Mary Katherine
1974 Archaeological Survey and Excavation in the Upper Sweetwater Creek Drainage of Liberty County, Florida. Master's thesis. Department of Anthropology, Florida State University, Tallahassee.

Jones, S. E., H. Barton, C. O. Hunt, M. Janowski, L. Lloyd-Smith, and G. Barker
2016 The Cultural Antiquity of Rainforests: Human-Plant Associations during the Mid–Late Holocene in the Interior Highlands of Sarawak, Malaysian Borneo. *Quaternary International* 416:80–94.

Kassabaum, Megan C.
2018 Early Platforms, Early Plazas: Exploring the Precursors to Mississippian Mound-and-Plaza Centers. *Journal of Archaeological Research* 27:187–247.

Kaufman, Wallace, and Orrin Pilkey
1979 *The Beaches Are Moving*. Anchor Press, Garden City, New York.

Keck, Gayle
2021 Collaboration with Collectors. *American Archaeology* 25(1):12–18.

Keffer, Kaitlyn
2015 Northwest Florida Prehistoric Materials from the Cauthen Collection. Undergraduate honors thesis, Department of Anthropology, University of South Florida, Tampa.

Keith, Scot J.
2011 The Leake Complex: A Middle Woodland Hopewellian Ceremonial Center and Gateway Community. *Early Georgia* 39(2):173–200.

Kellar, James H., A. R. Kelly, and Edward V. McMichael
1962 The Mandeville Site in Southwest Georgia. *American Antiquity* 27:336–355.

Kelley, Caitlin
2013 Ten Thousand Years of Prehistory on Ocheesee Pond, Northwest Florida. Master's thesis, Department of Anthropology, University of South Florida, Tampa.

Kelly, A. R.

1938 *A Preliminary Report on Archaeological Explorations at Macon, Georgia.* Anthropological Papers No. 1, Bureau of American Ethnology Bulletin 119:1–68. Washington, DC.

1950a Survey of the Lower Flint and Chattahoochee Rivers. *Early Georgia* 1(1):26–33.

1950b *An Early Flint Industry in Southwest Georgia.* Georgia Department of Mines, Mining, and Geology; the Geological Survey Bulletin 56:146–153. University of Georgia Laboratory of Archaeology Manuscript No. 53. Athens.

1950c The Hornsby's Bluff Site, 9Se7 [now 9Dr22] and Other Notes from the Jim Woodruff Reservoir Survey, 1948–1953. On file at the University of Georgia Laboratory of Archaeology, Athens.

1953 *A Weeden Island Burial Mound in Decatur County, Georgia, and Related Sites on the Lower Flint River.* University of Georgia Laboratory of Archaeology Series, Report No. 1. Athens (reprinted 1960).

2010 *WPA Archaeological Excavations at the Macon North Plateau.* LAMAR Institute Publication 150.

Kelly, L. T., and L. Brotons
2017 Using Fire to Promote Biodiversity. *Science* 355:1264–1265.

Kelly, Robert L.
1995 *The Foraging Spectrum.* Smithsonian Institution Press, Washington, DC.
2003 Colonization of New Land by Hunter-Gatherers. In *Colonization of Unfamiliar Landscapes*, edited by Marcy Rockman and James Steele, pp. 44–58. Routledge, London.

Kiahtipes, C. A.
2021 *Otis Hare (8Li172) and Sunstroke (8Li217) Palynological Assessment.* Report by the USF Institute for the Advanced Study of Culture and the Environment for the Anthropology Department, University of South Florida, Tampa.

Kidder, Tristram R.
2006 Climate Change and the Archaic to Woodland Transition (3000–2500 cal B.P.) in the Mississippi River Basin. *American Antiquity* 71:195–231.

Kimbrough, Rhonda Majors
1999 A Norwood Simple Stamped Vessel from the Apalachicola National Forest, Florida. Paper presented at the Annual Meeting of the Florida Anthropological Society, Fort Walton Beach.

Kingsland, Kaitlyn
2017 New Data from Early Woodland Materials: Depot Creek Shell Mound, Northwest Florida. Undergraduate honors thesis, Department of Anthropology, University of South Florida, Tampa.

Kinsella, Larry
2013 The Bannerstone: A Prehistoric Prey-Specific Artifact Designed for Use in the Eastern Woodlands of North America. *Ethnoarchaeology* 5(1):24–55.

Kiple, Kenneth F.
2000 The Question of Paleolithic Nutrition and Modern Health. In *Cambridge World History of Food*, edited by Kenneth F. Kiple and Kriemhild Coneè Ornelas, pp. 1704–1709. Cambridge University Press, New York.

Kistler, Logan, Álvaro Montenegro, Bruce D. Smith, John A. Gifford, Richard E. Greene, Lee A. Newsom, and Beth Shapiro
2014 Transoceanic Drift and the Domestication of African Bottle Gourds in the Americas. *Proceedings of the National Academy of Sciences* 111:2937–2941.

Knigge, Kerri

2018 Porter's Bar: A Coastal Middle Woodland Burial Mound and Shell Midden in Northwest Florida. Master's thesis, Department of Anthropology, University of South Florida, Tampa.

Knight, Vernon James Jr., and Tim S. Mistovich
1984 *Walter F. George Lake: Archaeological Survey of Fee Owned Lands, Alabama and Georgia.* Report to the US Army Corps of Engineers; Report of Investigations No. 42, Office of Archaeological Research, University of Alabama, Tuscaloosa.

Knight, Vernon James Jr., and Frank T. Schnell
2004 Silence over Kolomoki: A Curious Episode in the History of Southeastern Archaeology. *Southeastern Archaeology* 23(1):1–11.

Knudson, Ruthann
2015 We Are All One: Anzick Children Reburied. *Mammoth Trumpet* 30(2):11–20.

Ko, Jonathan, and Stephen Chia
2012 Classification of Ceramics Discovered in Kampung Senengeh, Samarahan, Sarawak. *The Sarawak Museum Journal* 70(91 New Series):183–198.

Koldehoff, Brad, and Julie A. Bukowski
2010 Modified Pebbles as "Medicine Stones": A Case Study from the American Bottom. *Illinois Archaeology* 22(2):690–704.

Koot, Michael G.
2012 Ohio Hopewell Leadership and Biological Status: Interregional and Intraregional Variation. PhD dissertation, Department of Anthropology, Michigan State University, East Lansing.

Koppe, Martin
2010 Étude de Céramiques de la Vallée de l'Apalachicola en Floride par Spectrométrie Portable de Fluorescence X. Master's thesis, Université Michel de Montaigne, Bordeaux 3, France.

Krech, Shepard, III
1999 *The Ecological Indian.* W. W. Norton, New York.

Kreiser, Kelsey
2018 Collecting the Past: Using a Private Collection of Artifacts to Assess Prehistoric Occupation of the Chipola River Valley in Northwest Florida. Master's thesis, Department of Anthropology, University of South Florida, Tampa.

Kwas, Mary L.
1982 Bannerstones: A Historical Overview. *Journal of Alabama Archaeology* 28:154–178.

Kroeber, Alfred Louis
1957 *Style and Civilizations.* Cornell University Press, Ithaca, New York.

Lauro, James
1982 The Edgefield Scraper and Waller Knife, Early Archaic Tools from the Pearl River Drainage, Central Mississippi. *Journal of Alabama Archaeology* 28:147–154.

Lacquement, Cameron H. (editor)
2007 *Architectural Variability in the Southeast.* University of Alabama Press, Tuscaloosa.

Lane, Philip, Jeffrey P. Donnelly, Jonathan D. Woodruff, and Andrea D. Hawkes
2011 A Decadally-Resolved Paleohurricane Record Archived in Late Holocene Sediments of a Florida Sinkhole. *Marine Geology* 287:14–30.

Langlands, Alexander
2018 *Craeft: An Inquiry into the Origins and True Meaning of Traditional Crafts.* W. W. Norton, New York.

Lapham, Heather A.
2011 Animals in Southeastern Native American Subsistence Economies. In *The Subsistence Economies of Indigenous North American Societies*, edited by Bruce D. Smith, pp. 401–429. Smithsonian Institution Scholarly Press, Washington, DC.

Largent, Floyd
2004 Diving into Florida Prehistory. *Mammoth Trumpet* 19(4):18–20.

Larson, Ron
1995 *Swamp Song: A Natural History of Florida's Swamps*. University Press of Florida, Gainesville.

Lauro, James
1982 The Edgefield Scraper and Waller Knife, Early Archaic Tools from the Pearl River Drainage, Central Mississippi. *Journal of Alabama Archaeology* 28:147–154.

Lazarus, William C.
1958 A Poverty Point Complex in Florida. *Florida Anthropologist* 11:23–32.
1965 Significance of Dimensions of Big Sandy I-Like Projectile Points in Northwest Florida. *Florida Anthropologist* 18(3, pt. 1):187–199.

Lazarus, Yulee W.
1971 Clay Balls from Northwest Florida. *University of South Carolina Institute of Archaeology and Anthropology Notebook* 3:47–49.
1979 *The Buck Burial Mound*. Temple Mound Museum, Fort Walton Beach, Florida.

Lee, Richard B.
1969 Eating Christmas in the Kalahari. *Natural History* 78:10. Reprinted in *Applying Anthropology*, edited by Aaron Podolefsky and Peter J. Brown, pp. 201–211. Mayfield Publishing, Mountain View, California.
1992 Art, Science, or Politics? The Crisis in Hunter-Gatherer Studies. *American Anthropologist* 94:31–48.
2014 Hunter-Gatherers on the Best-Seller List: Steven Pinker and the "Bellicose School's" Treatment of Forager Violence. *Journal of Aggression, Conflict, and Peace Research* 6:216–228.

Lee, Richard B., and Irven Devore (editors)
1968 *Man the Hunter*. Aldine, Chicago.

Lepper, Bradley T.
2016 Who Were the People That Peopled America? *Mammoth Trumpet* 31:4–14.
2019 Along the Coast or Down the Ice-Free Corridor—How Did the First Americans Get Here? *Mammoth Trumpet* 34:13–20.

Light, Helen M., Melanie R. Darst, and J. W. Grubbs
1998 *Aquatic Habitats in Relation to River Flow in the Apalachicola River Floodplain, Florida*. US Geological Survey Professional Paper 1594. US Department of the Interior, Washington, DC.

Light, Helen M., Kirk R. Vincent, Melanie R. Darst, and Franklin D. Price
2006 *Water-Level Decline in the Apalachicola River, Florida*. US Geological Survey Science Investigations Report 2006-5173. US Department of the Interior, Reston, Virginia.

Liu, Kam-biu, Houyuan Lu, and Caiming Shen
2007 A 1200-Year Proxy Record of Hurricanes and Fires from the Gulf of Mexico Coast: Testing the Hypothesis of Hurricane-Fire Interactions. *Quaternary Research* 69:29–41.

Lively, Matthew
1965 The Lively Complex: Announcing a Pebble Tool Industry in Alabama. *Journal of Alabama Archaeology* 11(2).

Livingston, Robert J.
1983 *Resource Atlas of the Apalachicola Estuary*. Florida Sea Grant College Report No. 55, Florida State University, Tallahassee.
1984 *The Ecology of the Apalachicola Bay System: An Estuarine Profile*. Report to the National Coastal Ecosystems Team, Fish and Wildlife Service, US Department of the Interior, Washington, DC.

Livingston, Robert J., and Edwin A. Joyce (editors)
1977 *Proceedings of the Conference on the Apalachicola Drainage System, 23–24 April 1976*, Gainesville, Florida. Florida Marine Research Publications No. 26. Florida Department of Natural Resources Marine Research Laboratory, St. Petersburg.

Lloyd, Janet R., Judith A. Bense, and Jesse L. Davis Jr.
1983 Tallahatta Quartzite Quarries in the Escambia River Drainage. *Journal of Alabama Archaeology* 29:126–142.

Lockman, Michael
2020 Middle Woodland Mounds of the Lower Chattahoochee, Lower Flint, and Apalachicola River Basin. Master's thesis, Department of Anthropology, University of South Florida, Tampa.

Loponte, Daniel, Mirian Carbonera, and Romina Silvestre
2015 Fishtail Projectile Points from South America: The Brazilian Record. *Archaeological Discovery* 3:85–103.

Luer, George M., Todd Lumley, and April Lumley
2015 A Tabbed Circle Artifact from the Florida Panhandle. *Florida Anthropologist* 68:65–74.

Lynott, Mark
2014 *Hopewell Ceremonial Landscapes of Ohio*. Oxbow Books, Haverton, Pennsylvania.

Mainfort, Robert C., Jr.
2013 *Pinson Mounds*. University of Arkansas Press, Fayetteville.

Malinowski, Bronislaw
1922 *Argonauts of the Western Pacific*. Routledge and Kegan Paul, London.

Mann, Jason
2016 The Thrash Site: A Poverty Point Related Site in Southeast Alabama. Presentation at the Annual Meeting of the Southeastern Archaeological Conference, Athens, Georgia.

Marquardt, William H.
2010 Shell Mounds in the Southeast: Middens, Monuments, Temple Mounds, Rings, or Works? *American Antiquity* 75:551–570.

Marquardt, William H., and Laura Kozuch
2016 The Lightning Whelk: An Enduring Icon of Southeastern North American Spirituality. *Journal of Anthropological Archaeology* 42:1–26.

Marrinan, Rochelle A., and Alexandra L. Parsons
2010 *Faunal Remains from St. Vincent 5 (Pickalene Midden), 8Fr364*. Report to the University of South Florida, Tampa. Department of Anthropology, Florida State University, Tallahassee.

Mayo, Karen L.
2003 Archaeological Investigations on Black's Island, Gulf County, Florida. Master's thesis, Department of Anthropology, University of South Florida, Tampa.

McClellan, Jim
2014 *Life along the Apalachicola River*. The History Press, Charleston, South Carolina.

McClenachan, Loren, and John N. Kittinger
2013 Multicentury Trends and the Sustainability of Coral Reef Fisheries in Hawai'i and Florida. *Fish and Fisheries* 14:239–255.

McKnight, Matthew David
2007 The Copper Cache in Early and Middle Woodland North America. PhD dissertation, Department of Anthropology, Pennsylvania State University.

McMichael, Edward V., and James Kellar
1960 *Archaeological Salvage in the Oliver Basin.* University of Georgia Laboratory of Archaeology Series No. 2. Athens.

McNabb, Tyler
2012 Developing Proxies for Late Holocene Sea-Level and Climate Change along the Northeastern Gulf of Mexico Coast. Master's thesis, Department of Geology, Oklahoma State University, Stillwater.

McWeeney, Lucinda, and Douglas C. Kellogg
2001 Early and Middle Holocene Climate Changes and Settlement Patterns along the Eastern Coast of North America. *Archaeology of Eastern North America* 29:187–212.

Mead, Margaret
1935 *Sex and Temperament in Three Primitive Societies.* William Morrow, New York.

Means, D. Bruce
1977 Aspects of the Significance to Terrestrial Vertebrates of the Apalachicola River Drainage Basin, Florida. In *Proceedings of the Conference on the Apalachicola Drainage System, 23–24 April 1976,* edited by Robert J. Livingston and Edwin A. Joyce Jr., pp. 37–57. Florida Marine Research Publications No. 26. Florida Department of Natural Resources, Tallahassee.

1985 The Canyonlands of Florida. *Nature Conservancy News,* September/October:13–17.

1994 Temperate Hardwood Hammocks. *Florida Wildlife* 48(6):20–21.

Meehan, Betty
1982 *Shell Bed to Shell Midden.* Australian Institute of Aboriginal Studies, Canberra.

Meredith, Steven M.
2009 A Study of Early Paleoindian Settlement in the Coastal Plain of Alabama. *Current Research in the Pleistocene* 26:89–91.

Mikell, Gregory A., and Rebecca Saunders
2007 Terminal Middle to Late Archaic Settlement in Coastal Northwest Florida. *Southeastern Archaeology* 26:169–195.

Milanich, Jerald T.
1974 *Life in a Ninth Century Household: A Weeden Island Fall Winter Site in the Upper Apalachicola River, Florida.* Bureau of Historic Sites and Properties Bulletin No. 4, Florida Department of State, Tallahassee.

1994 *Archaeology of Precolumbian Florida.* University Press of Florida, Gainesville.

2007 Gordon R. Willey and the Archaeology of the Florida Gulf Coast. In *Gordon R. Willey and American Archaeology,* edited by Jeremy A. Sabloff and William L. Fash, pp. 15–25. University of Oklahoma Press, Norman.

Milanich, Jerald T., Ann S. Cordell, Vernon J. Knight Jr., Timothy A. Kohler, and Brenda J. Sigler-Lavelle
1984 *McKeithen Weeden Island.* Academic Press, New York. (Republished 1997 as *Archaeology of Northern Florida A.D. 200–900.*) University Press of Florida, Gainesville.

Milanich, Jerald T., and Charles H. Fairbanks
1980 *Florida Archaeology.* Academic Press, New York.

Miller, D. Shane, Ashley M. Smallwood, and Jesse W. Tune (editors)
2022 *The American Southeast at the End of the Ice Age.* University of Alabama Press, Tuscaloosa.

Mills, Lisa A.
2003 Mitochondrial DNA Analysis of the Ohio Hopewell of the Hopewell Mound Group. PhD dissertation, Department of Anthropology, Ohio State University, Columbus.

Milner, George R.
1999 Warfare in Prehistoric and Early Historic Eastern North America. *Journal of Archaeological Research* 7:105–151.

Minar, C. Jill
2000 Spinning and Plying: Anthropological Directions. In *Beyond Cloth and Cordage*, edited by Penelope Ballard Drooker and Laurie D. Webster, pp. 85–99. University of Utah Press, Salt Lake City.

Moon, Steven Elliott
1999 Patterns of Paleoindian Land Use on the Eastern Gulf Coastal Plain of Southeastern Alabama: New Evidence from the Artifact Collector Community. Master's thesis, Department of Anthropology, Iowa State University, Ames.

Mooney, Charles N., and A. L. Patrick
1915 *Soil Survey of Franklin County, Florida*. US Department of Agriculture, Washington DC.

Moore, Clarence B.
1902 Certain Aboriginal Remains of the Northwest Florida Coast, Part II. *Journal of the Academy of Natural Sciences* 12:123–355.
1903 Certain Aboriginal Mounds of the Apalachicola River. *Journal of the Academy of Natural Sciences* 12:440–492.
1907 Mounds of the Lower Chattahoochee and Lower Flint Rivers. *Journal of the Academy of Natural Sciences* 13:427–456.
1918 The Northwestern Florida Coast Revisited. *Journal of the Academy of Natural Sciences* (2nd Series) 16:514–581.

Moore, Wayne E.
1955 *Geology of Jackson County, Florida*. Geological Bulletin No. 37, Florida Geological Survey, Tallahassee.

Moreau, Luc
2021 More Than Meets the Eye: Inequality in Hunter-Gatherer-Fisher Societies in the Past. *The SAA Archaeological Record* 21(1):13–16.

Morris, Ian
1991 The Archaeology of Ancestors: The Saxe/Goldstein Hypothesis Revisited. *Cambridge Archaeological Journal* 1:147–169.

Morse, Dan F.
1997 *Sloan: A Paleoindian Dalton Cemetery in Arkansas*. Smithsonian Institution Press, Washington, DC.

Mueller, Tom
2016 Plundering the Past. *National Geographic* 229(6):58–81.

Nature Conservancy
2000 Large-Scale Conservation Areas, 2. Apalachicola River and Bay. *Nature Conservancy Florida Chapter News* Winter:8.
2014 Florida's Forests: Restoring the "Trees of Life." *Nature Conservancy* Magazine October–November:insert before page 1.

Neely, Paula
2020 Reassessing the Age of Clovis. *American Archaeology* 24(4):8.

Newsom, Lee A.

2002 The Paleoethnobotany of the Archaic Mortuary Pond. In *Windover: Multidisciplinary Investigations of an Early Archaic Florida Cemetery*, edited by Glen H. Doran, pp. 191–210. University Press of Florida, Gainesville.

Newsom, Lee A., and Matthew C. Mihlbachler
2006 Mastodons (*Mammut americanum*) Diet Foraging Patterns Based on Analysis of Dung Deposits. In *First Floridians and Last Mastodons*, edited by S. David Webb, pp. 263–331. Springer, New York.

Noss, Reed F.
2013 *Forgotten Grasslands of the South*. Island Press, Washington, DC.

O'Donnell, Peter
1969 *A Taste for Death*. Fawcett Publications, Greenwich, Connecticut.

Odell, George H.
2004 *Lithic Analysis*. Kluwer Academic, New York.

Oliver, José R.
2008 The Archaeology of Agriculture in Ancient Amazonia. In *Handbook of South American Archaeology*, edited by Helaine Silverman and William H. Isbell, pp. 185–216. Springer, New York.

Orlando Sentinel
1994 Adding Up Storm's Casualty Count. *Orlando Sentinel*, September 7.

Osterman, Lisa E., David C. Twichell, and Richard Z. Poore
2009 Holocene Evolution of Apalachicola Bay, Florida. *Geo-Marine Letters* 29:395–404.

Outland, Robert B., III
2004 *Tapping the Pines. The Naval Stores Industry in the American South*. Louisiana State University Press, Baton Rouge.

Parker, Brian Thomas
1994 Archaeological Investigations of the Thank-You-Ma'am Creek Site, Northwest Florida. Master's thesis, Department of Anthropology, University of South Florida, Tampa.

Parker, Brian, and Nancy Marie White
1992 *Archaeological Test Excavations at the Lost Dog Sites, 8Fr820, 8Fr820A, and 8Fr820B, in the Apalachicola National Forest, Northwest Florida*. Report to the US Forest Service, Tallahassee. Department of Anthropology, University of South Florida, Tampa.

Parmalee, Paul W., and Gregory Perino
1970 A Prehistoric Archaeological Record of the Roseate Spoonbill in Illinois. *Transactions of the Illinois State Academy of Science* 63:254–258.

Patterson, Leland W.
2004 Current Data on Gar Scale Arrow Points in Southeast Texas. *Houston Archaeological Society Journal* 127:7–8.

Pawlowicz, Leszek M., and Christian E. Downum
2021 Applications of Deep Learning to Decorated Ceramic Typology and Classification: A Case Study Using Tusayan White Ware from Northeast Arizona. *Journal of Archaeological Science* 130:105375.

Pearson, Charles E., Richard A. Weinstein, Sherwood M. Gagliano, and David B. Kelley
2014 Prehistoric Site Discovery on the Outer Continental Shelf, Gulf of Mexico, United States of America. In *Prehistoric Archaeology on the Continental Shelf*, edited by Amanda M. Evans, Joe Flatman, and Nic Fleming, pp. 53–71. Springer Press, New York.

Peck, Robert McCracken, and Patricia Tyson Stroud
2012 *A Glorious Enterprise: The Academy of Natural Sciences of Philadelphia and the Making of American Science*. University of Pennsylvania Press, Philadelphia.

Peddada, Shyamal
2017 Seasonal Change in the Gut. *Science* 357:754–755.

Penton, Daniel T.
2001 Cultural Prisms Distort. *FHC Forum* 24(3):34–35. Florida Humanities Council, St. Petersburg.

Percy, George W.
1971 *Preliminary Report to the Division of Recreation and Parks, Department of Natural Resources, State of Florida, on Archaeological Work in Torreya State Park during the year 1971 by the Department of Anthropology at Florida State University*. On file at the Florida Division of Historical Resources, Tallahassee.

1974 A Review of Evidence for Prehistoric Indian Use of Animals in Northwest Florida. *Bulletin of Historic Sites and Properties* No. 4. Florida Department of State, Tallahassee.

1976 *Salvage Investigations at the Scholz Steam Plant Site, A Middle Weeden Island Habitation Site in Jackson County, Florida*. Bureau of Historic Sites and Properties Miscellaneous Project Report Series 35, Florida Department of State, Tallahassee.

Percy, George W., and David S. Brose
1974 Weeden Island Ecology, Subsistence, and Village Life in Northwest Florida. Paper presented at the 39th Annual Meeting of the Society for American Archaeology, Washington, DC.

Percy, George W., and M. Katherine Jones
1976 An Archaeological Survey of Upland Locales in Gadsden and Liberty Counties, Florida. *Florida Anthropologist* 29:105–125.

Peres, Tanya M.
2017 Foodways Archaeology: A Decade of Research from the Southeastern United States. *Journal of Archaeological Research* 25:421–460.

Perri, Angela R., Tatiana R. Feuerborn, Laurent A. F. Frantz, Greger Larson, Ripan S. Malhi, David J. Meltzer, and Kelsey E. Witt
2021 Dog Domestication and the Dual Dispersal of People and Dogs into the Americas. *PNAS* 118(6):e2010083118.

Pettigrew, Devin, John C. Whittaker, Justin Garnett, and Patrick Hashman
2015 How Atlatl Darts Behave: Beveled Points and the Relevance of Controlled Experiments. *American Antiquity* 80:590–601.

Phelps, David S.
1965 The Norwood Series of Fiber-Tempered Ceramics. *Southeastern Archaeological Conference Bulletin* 2:65–69.

Pitblado, Bonnie L.
2014 An Argument for Ethical, Proactive, Archaeologist-Artifact Collector Collaboration. *American Antiquity* 79:401–424.

Pitblado, Bonnie L., Matthew J. Rowe, Bryon Schroeder, Suzie Thomas, and Anna Wessman (editors)
2022 Special Issue, Professional-Collector Collaboration: Moving beyond Debate to Best Practice. *Advances in Archaeological Practice* 10(1):1–121.

Pitblado, Bonnie L., and Michael Shott
2015 The Present and Future of Archaeologist-Collector Collaboration. *SAA Archaeological Record* 15(5):36–39.

Pluckhahn, Thomas J.
2003 *Kolomoki: Settlement, Ceremony, and Status in the Deep South, A.D. 350 to 750*. University of Alabama Press, Tuscaloosa.

Porter, Louise M.
1975 *The Chronological History of the Lives of St. Joseph.* St. Joseph Historical Society, Port St. Joe, Florida.

Postil, John
2006 *Media and Nation Building: How the Iban Became Malaysian.* Berghahn Books, New York.

Prendergast, Eric
2015 The Archaeology of the McKinnie Site (8JA1869), Apalachicola River Valley, Northwest Florida: Four Thousand Years in the Backswamp. Master's thesis, Department of Anthropology, University of South Florida, Tampa.

Prendergast, Eric, and Nancy Marie White
2014 Mounds at Turtle Harbor (Video). Vimeo.
2017 Apalachicola River Valley Archaeology. apalacharchaeology.blog.

Price, Mark
2019 Mysterious Stone Structures in North Carolina's Rivers Linked to Prehistoric People. *News & Observer*, December 5.

Price, Sarah E.
2008 *Phase III Archaeology at Plash Island, Archaeological Site 1BA134, in Baldwin County, Alabama.* Center for Archaeological Studies, University of South Alabama, Mobile.

Price, T. Douglas, and James A. Brown (editors)
1985 *Prehistoric Hunter-Gatherers: The Emergence of Cultural Complexity.* Academic Press, New York.

Prufer, Olaf H.
1962 Prehistoric Hopewell Meteorite Collecting: Further Evidence. *Ohio Journal of Science* 62(6):314–316.

Puglisi, Melany
2008 Crassostrea virginica: *Smithsonian Marine Station at Fort Pierce Species Inventory.* Smithsonian Institution, Washington, DC.

Quinn, Rhonda L., Bryan D. Tucker, and John Krigbaum
2008 Diet and Mobility in Middle Archaic Florida: Stable Isotopic and Faunal Evidence from the Harris Creek Archaeological Site (8Vo24), Tick Island. *Journal of Archaeological Science* 35:2346–2356.

Quitmyer, Irv
2013 Precolumbian Site Seasonality and Harvest of Estuarine Resources at Pineland Site Complex. In *The Archaeology of Pineland: A Coastal Southwest Florida Site Complex, A.D. 50–1750*, edited by William H. Marquardt and Karen J. Walker, pp. 349–372. University of Florida Institute of Archaeology and Paleoenvironmental Studies Monograph 4, Gainesville.

Rafferty, Sean
2021 *Native Intoxicants of North America.* University of Tennessee Press, Knoxville.

Randazzo, Anthony F., and Douglas S. Jones
1997 *The Geology of Florida.* University Press of Florida, Gainesville.

Reich, David
2018 *Who We Are and How We Got Here: Ancient DNA and the New Science of the Human Past.* Pantheon, New York.

Reiger, John F.
1999 Artistry, Status, and Power: How "Plummet"-Pendants Probably Functioned in Pre-Columbian Florida—and Beyond. *Florida Anthropologist* 52:227–240.

Reinhard, Karl J., Sergio M. Chaves, John G. Jones, and Alena M. Iñiguez
2008 Evaluating Chloroplast DNA in Prehistoric Texas Coprolites: Medicinal, Dietary, or Ambient Ancient DNA? *Journal of Archaeological Science* 35:1748–1755.

Reitz, Elizabeth J., Barnet Pavao-Zuckerman, Daniel C. Weinand, and Gwyneth A. Duncan
2010 *Mission and Pueblo Santa Catalina de Guale, St. Catherine's Island, Georgia: A Comparative Zooarchaeological Analysis*. Anthropological Papers of the American Museum of Natural History No. 91.

Rizk, Felix F.
1991 The Late Holocene Development of St. Joseph Spit. PhD dissertation, Department of Geology, Florida State University, Tallahassee.

Roberts, Patrick, Chris Hunt, Manuel Arroyo-Kalin, Damian Evans, and Nicole Boivin
2017 The Deep Human Prehistory of Global Tropical Forests and Its Relevance for Modern Conservation. *Nature Plants* 3:17093.

Robertson, Gail, Val Attenbrow, and Peter Hiscock
2009 Multiple Uses for Australian Backed Artefacts. *Antiquity* 83:296–308.

Rockman, Marcy, and James Steele (editors)
2003 *Colonization of Unfamiliar Landscapes. The Archaeology of Adaptation*. Routledge, London.

Roksandic, Mirjana, Sheila Mendonça de Souza, Sabine Eggers, Meghan Burchell, and Daniela Klokler (editors)
2014 *The Cultural Dynamics of Shell Middens and Shell Mounds: A Worldwide Perspective*. University of New Mexico Press, Albuquerque.

Rosenau, Jack C., Glen L. Faulkner, Charles W. Hendry, and Robert W. Hull
1977 *Springs of Florida*. Florida Geological Survey Bulletin No. 42, Tallahassee.

Rupert, Frank R.
1990a *Geology of Gadsden County, Florida*. Florida Geological Survey Bulletin No. 62, Tallahassee.

1990b *The Geomorphology and Geology of Calhoun County, Florida*. Florida Geological Survey Open File Report No. 32, Tallahassee.

1991 *The Geomorphology and Geology of Liberty County, Florida*. Florida Geological Survey Open File Report No. 43, Tallahassee.

Russell, Dale A., Frederick J. Rich, Vincent Schneider, and Jean Lynch-Stieglitz
2009 A Warm Thermal Enclave in the Late Pleistocene of the Southeastern United States. *Biological Reviews* 84:173–202.

Russo, Michael
1991 Archaic Sedentism on the Florida Coast: A Case Study from Horr's Island. PhD dissertation, Department of Anthropology, University of Florida, Gainesville.

1994 Why We Don't Believe in Archaic Ceremonial Mounds and Why We Should: The Case from Florida. *Southeastern Archaeology* 13:93–109.

Sahlins, Marshall
1972 *Stone Age Economics*. Aldine-Atherton, Chicago.

2022 *The New Science of the Enchanted Universe: An Anthropology of Most of Humanity*. Princeton University Press, Princeton, New Jersey.

Sandin, Benedict
1968 *The Sea Dayaks of Borneo*. Michigan State University Press, East Lansing.

Sankar, Ravi Darwin
2015 Quantifying the Effects of Increased Storminess and Sea-Level Change on the Morphology of Sandy Barrier Islands along the Northwestern and Atlantic Coasts of

Florida. PhD dissertation, Department of Earth, Ocean, and Atmospheric Science, Florida State University, Tallahassee.

Sasser, Leland D., Ken L. Monroe, and Joseph L. Schuster
1994 *Soil Survey of Franklin County, Florida*. US Department of Agriculture, Washington, DC.

Saunders, Joe W., Rolfe D. Mandel, C. Garth Sampson, Charles M. Allen, E. Thurman Allen, Daniel A. Bush, James K. Feathers, et al.
2005 Watson Brake, a Middle Archaic Mound Complex in Northeast Louisiana. *American Antiquity* 70:631–668.

Saunders, Rebecca, and Christopher T. Hays (editors)
2004 *Early Pottery Technology, Function, Style, and Interaction in the Lower Southeast*. University of Alabama Press, Tuscaloosa.

Saunders, Rebecca, and Michael Russo
2011 Coastal Shell Middens in Florida: A View from the Archaic. *Quaternary International* 239:38–50.

Saxe Arthur A.
1970 The Social Dimensions of Mortuary Practices. PhD dissertation, Department of Anthropology, University of Michigan, Ann Arbor.

Scarry, John F.
1975 *The Sassafrass Site (8Gd12), a Multicomponent Site on the Apalachicola River*. Report on file, Florida Division of Historical Resources, Tallahassee.

Schieffer, Adam M.
2013 Archaeological Site Distribution in the Apalachicola/Lower Chattahoochee River Valley of Northwest Florida, Southwest Georgia, and Southeast Alabama. Master's thesis, Department of Anthropology, University of South Florida.

Schiller, Anne
2001 Mortuary Monuments and Social Change among the Ngaju. In *Social Memory, Identity, and Death: Anthropological Perspectives on Mortuary Rituals*, edited by Meredith S. Chesson, pp. 70–79. Archeological Papers of the American Anthropological Association No. 10.

Schnable, Jon E., and H. Grant Goodell
1968 *Pleistocene-Recent Stratigraphy, Evolution, and Development of the Apalachicola Coast, Florida*. Special Paper No. 112, Geological Society of America. Boulder, Colorado.

Schnell, Frank T., Jr.
1969 Archaeological Resurvey: A Relatively Unexplored Potential. *Southeastern Archaeological Conference Bulletin* 11:55–57.
1973 *A Preliminary Assessment of Archaeology Resources Remaining in the Walter F. George Lake Area*. Report to the National Park Service, Washington, DC.
1975 An Archaeological Survey of Lake Blackshear. *Southeastern Archaeological Conference Bulletin* 18:117–122.

Schoolcraft, Henry Rowe
1847 *Notices of Some Antique Earthen Vessels Found in the Low Tumuli of Florida, and in the Caves and Burial Places of the Indian Tribes North of Those Latitudes*. Read at the Monthly Meeting of the New York Historical Society, June 1846. W. Van Norden, New York.

Scott, Thomas M., Guy H. Means, Rebecca P. Meegan, Ryan C. Means, Sam B. Upchurch, R. E. Copeland, James Jones, et al.
2004 *Springs of Florida*. Florida Geological Survey Bulletin No. 66, Tallahassee.

Sears, William H.

1956 *Excavations at Kolomoki: Final Report.* University of Georgia Series in Anthropology No. 5. University of Georgia Press, Athens.

1959 *NSF G-5019. An Investigation of Prehistoric Processes on the Gulf Coastal Plain.* Final Report to the National Science Foundation. Washington, DC.

1973 The Sacred and the Secular in Prehistoric Ceramics. In *Variations in Anthropology: Essays in Honor of John C. McGregor*, edited by Donald Lathrap and Jody Douglas, pp. 31–42. Illinois Archaeological Survey Publications, Urbana.

1992 Mea Culpa. *Southeastern Archaeology* 11:66–71.

Shannon, George Ward, Jr.

1987 A Reconsideration of Formative Cultural Development in the Southeastern United States. PhD dissertation, Department of Anthropology, Michigan State University. University Microfilms International, Ann Arbor.

Sharon, Don W., and Thomas. C. Watson

1971 The Two Egg Quarry Site. *Florida Anthropologist* 24:77–80.

Sherwood, Sarah C., and Tristram R. Kidder

2011 The DaVincis of Dirt: Geoarchaeological Perspectives on Native American Mound Building in the Mississippi River Basin. *Journal of Anthropological Archaeology* 30:69–87.

Shockey, Bruce J.

1991 *Faunal Material from the Otis Hare Site (8Li172).* Report to the University of South Florida. Zooarchaeology, Florida Museum of Natural History, Gainesville.

Shott, Michael J.

2017 Estimating the Magnitude of Private Collection of Points and Its Effects on Professional Survey Results. A Michigan Case Study. *Advances in Archaeological Practice* 5(2):125–137.

Simpkins, Daniel L., and Dorothy J. Allard

1986 Isolation and Identification of Spanish Moss Fiber from a Sample of Stallings and Orange Series Ceramics. *American Antiquity* 51:102–117.

Simpson, J. Clarence

1956 *Florida Place Names of Indian Derivation.* Florida Geological Survey Special Publication No. 1.

Simpson, Terrance Lane

1996 *Prehistoric Settlement Patterns in the Apalachicola River Valley: A GIS Approach.* Master's thesis, Department of Anthropology, University of South Florida, Tampa.

Skibo, James M., Michael B. Schiffer, and Kenneth C. Reid

1989 Organic-Tempered Pottery: An Experimental Study. *American Antiquity* 54:122–146.

Smith, Betty A. (editor)

1978 Report of the Excavations at Fairchild's Landing and Hare's Landing, Seminole County, Georgia, by Joseph R. Caldwell. Prepared for the National Park Service, Purchase Order #PX589070204.

Smith, Brent W.

1991 The Late Archaic–Poverty Point Trade Network. In *The Poverty Point Culture*, edited by K. M. Byrd, pp. 173–180. Geoscience and Man 29. Louisiana State University, Baton Rouge.

Smith, Bruce D.

2011 General Patterns of Niche Construction and the Management of "Wild" Plant and Animal Resources by Small-Scale Pre-Industrial Societies. *Philosophical Transactions of the Royal Society B* 366:836–848.

Smith, Bruce D., and Melinda A. Zeder
2013 The Onset of the Anthropocene. *Anthropocene* 4:8–13.

Smith, Karen Y.
2009 Middle and Late Woodland Period Cultural Transmission, Residential Mobility, and Aggregation in the Deep South. PhD dissertation, University of Missouri–Columbia.

Smith, Karen Y., and Vernon J. Knight
2014 Core Elements and Layout Classes in Swift Creek Paddle Art. *Southeastern Archaeology* 33:42–54.

2017 Swift Creek Paddle Designs and the Imperative to Be Unique. *Southeastern Archaeology* 36:122–130.

Smith, Karen Y., and Keith Stephenson
2017 The Spatial Dimension of the Woodland Period. *Southeastern Archaeology* 37:112–128.

Smith, Maria Ostendorf
1996 Biocultural Inquiry into Archaic Period Populations of the Southeast. In *Archaeology of the Mid-Holocene Southeast*, edited by Kenneth E. Sassaman and David G. Anderson, pp. 134–154. University Press of Florida, Gainesville.

1997 Osteological Indications of Warfare in the Archaic Period of the Western Tennessee Valley. In *Troubled Times: Violence and Warfare in the Past*, edited by D. L. Martin and D. W. Frayer, pp. 241–265. Gordon and Breach, Amsterdam.

Snow, Frankie
2007 *Swift Creek Design Catalog*. South Georgia College, Douglas, Georgia.

Snyder, Lynn M., and Jennifer A. Leonard
2011 The Diversity and Origin of American Dogs. In *The Subsistence Economies of Indigenous North American Societies*, edited by Bruce D. Smith, pp. 525–541. Smithsonian Institution Scholarly Press, Washington, DC.

Somerville, Andrew D., Isabel Casar, and Joaquín Arroyo-Cabrales
2021 New AMS Radiocarbon Ages from the Preceramic Levels of Coxcatlan Cave, Puebla, Mexico: A Pleistocene Occupation of the Tehuacan Valley? *Latin American Antiquity* 32(3):612–626.

Southern Environmental Law Center
2016 *Tri-State Water Wars (AL, GA, FL)*. Website.

Spence, Michael W., and Brian J. Fryer
2005 Hopewellian Silver and Silver Artifacts from Eastern North America. In *Gathering Hopewell: Society, Ritual, and Ritual Interaction*, edited by Christopher Carr and D. Troy Case, pp. 714–733. Kluwer Academic/Plenum, New York.

Speth, John D., Khori Newlander, Andrew A. White, Ashley K. Lemke, and Lars E. Anderson
2013 Early Paleoindian Big-Game Hunting in North America: Provisioning or Politics? *Quaternary International* 285:111–139.

Staedter, Tracy
2017 Neil deGrasse Tyson Warns Science Denial Could "Dismantle" Democracy. *Live Science*, April 20.

Ste. Claire, Dana
1996 A Technological and Functional Analysis of Hernando Projectile Points. *Florida Anthropologist* 49:189–200.

Steere, Benjamin A.
2017 *The Archaeology of Houses and Households in the Native Southeast*. University of Alabama Press, Tuscaloosa.

Stewart, Tamara
2011 Ninety-Four Hundred Year-Old Dog Bone Identified. *American Archaeology* 15(1):9.
2020 Researchers Say Volcanic Eruptions Cause Ice Age 13,000 Years Ago. *American Archaeology* 24(3):11.
2022 Sacred Objects from the Heavens. *American Archaeology* 26(1):40–46.

Struever, Stuart, and Gail L. Houart
1972 An Analysis of the Hopewell Interaction Sphere. In *Social Exchange and Interaction*, edited by E. Wilmsen, pp. 47–80. University of Michigan Museum of Anthropology Papers No. 46, Ann Arbor.

Suzman, James
2017 *Affluence without Abundance: The Disappearing World of the Bushmen*. Bloomsbury, New York.

Swanton, John R.
1934 Review of *Florida Place-Names of Indian Origin and Seminole Personal Names*, by William A. Read. *American Speech* 9 (3):218–220.
1946 *The Indians of the Southeastern United States*. Bureau of American Ethnology Bulletin 137. Smithsonian Institution, Washington, DC.

Tesar, Louis D., and B. Calvin Jones
2009 *The Waddell's Mill Pond Site (8JA65): 1973–74 Test Excavation Results*. Florida Bureau of Archaeological Research, Tallahassee.

Tesar, Louis D., and Jeff Whitfield
2002 A Reduction Deduction: A Clovis-like Fluted Point Base from the Chipola River. *Florida Anthropologist* 55(2):89–102.

Thomas, B. P., H. H. Weeks, and M. W. Hazen Jr.
1961 *Soil Survey of Gadsden County, Florida*. US Department of Agriculture Soil Conservation Service, Washington, DC.

Thomas, David Hurst
2014 The Shellfishers of St. Catherines Island: Hardscrabble Foragers or Farming Beachcombers? *Journal of Island and Coastal Archaeology* 9:169–182.

Thompson, Victor D., William H. Marquardt, Alexander Cherkinsky, Amanda D. Roberts Thompson, Karen J. Walker, Lee A. Newsom, and Michael Savarese
2016 From Shell Midden to Midden Mound: The Geoarchaeology of Mound Key, an Anthropogenic Island in Southwest Florida, USA. *PLoS ONE* 11(4):1–22.

Thulman, David K.
2007 A Typology of Fluted Points from Florida. *Florida Anthropologist* 60:63–75.

Tiffany, William J., III, Robert E. Pelham, and Frank W. Howell
1980 Hyperostosis in Florida Fossil Fishes. *Florida Scientist* 43:44–49.

Toner, Mike
2016a People of the White Earth. *Archaeology* 69(3):55–62.
2016b The Story of Holy Ground. *American Archaeology* 20(2):32–37.

Torrence, Robin
2002 Thinking Big about Small Tools. In *Thinking Small: Global Perspectives on Microlithization*, edited by Robert G. Elston and Steven L. Juhn, pp. 179–189. Archaeological Papers of the American Anthropological Association 12(1).
2003 "Like Everywhere You've Never Been": Archaeological Fables from Papua New Guinea. In *Theory, Method, and Practice in Modern Archaeology*, edited by Robert J. Jeske and Douglas K. Charles, pp. 287–300. Praeger, Westport, Connecticut.

Trinkaus, E.
1987 Bodies, Brawn, Brains, and Noses: Human Ancestors and Human Predation. In *The Evolution of Human Hunting*, edited by M. H. Nitecki and D. V. Nitecki, pp. 107–145. Springer, Boston.

Trowell, Chris
1998 A Kolomoki Chronicle: The History of a Plantation, a State Park, and the Archaeological Search for Kolomoki's Prehistory. *Early Georgia* 26(1):12–81.

Truncer, James
2004 Steatite Vessel Manufacture in Eastern North America. *BAR International Series* 1326. Archaeopress, Oxford, England.

Tsutaya, Takumi, and Minoru Yoneda
2013 Quantitative Reconstruction of Weaning Ages in Archaeological Human Populations Using Bone Collagen Nitrogen Isotope Ratios and Approximate Bayesian Computation. *PLoS ONE* 8(8):e72327.doi:10.1371.

Tullos, Rosie B.
2018 *Analysis of Skeletal Remains from the Burial Mound, Richardson's Hammock Site (8Gu10), Northwest Florida*. Report on file, University of South Florida, Tampa.

Tuross, Noreen, Marilyn L. Fogel, Lee Newsom, and Glen H. Doran
1994 Subsistence in the Florida Archaic: The Stable Isotope and Archaeobotanical Evidence from the Windover Site. *American Antiquity* 59:288–303.

Twichell, David C., L. Edmiston, B. Andrews, W. Stevenson, J. Donoghue, R. Poore, and L. Osterman
2010 Geologic Controls on the Recent Evolution of Oyster Reefs in Apalachicola Bay and St. George Sound, Florida. *Estuarine, Coastal, and Shelf Science* 88:385–394.

Twichell, David C.; James G. Flocks, Elizabeth A. Pendleton, and Wayne E. Baldwin
2013 Geologic Controls on Regional and Local Erosion Rates of Three Northern Gulf of Mexico Barrier–Island Systems. *Journal of Coastal Research* 63:32–45.

Tykot, R. H., N. M. White, J. P. Du Vernay, J. S. Freeman, C. T. Hays, M. Koppe, C. N. Hunt, et al.
2013 Advantages and Disadvantages of pXRF for Archaeological Ceramic Analysis: Prehistoric Pottery Distribution and Trade in NW Florida. In *Archaeological Chemistry VIII*, edited by R. Armitage et al., pp. 233–244. ACS Symposium Series, American Chemical Society, Washington, DC.

Tyler, William D.
2008 The Paleoindian Chipola: A Site Distribution Analysis and Review of Collector Contributions in the Apalachicola River Valley, Northwest Florida. Master's thesis, Department of Anthropology, University of South Florida, Tampa.

Ubelaker, Douglas H.
1988 North American Indian Population Size, A.D. 1500 to 1985. *American Journal of Physical Anthropology* 77:289–294.

University of South Alabama
2004a Ocala Chert. *Geoarchaeology at South Alabama*.
2004b Tallahatta Sandstone. *Geoarchaeology at South Alabama*.

University of South Carolina
2017 Fingerprints to the Past. Website.

Upchurch, Sam B., Richard N. Strom, and Mark G. Nuckels
1982 *Methods of Provenance Determination of Florida Cherts*. Report to the Florida Department of State, Tallahassee.

US Army Corps of Engineers (USACOE)
1978 *Apalachicola, Chattahoochee, and Flint Rivers, Alabama, Florida, and Georgia, Navigation Charts*. USACOE District Engineer, Mobile, Alabama.
2015 *Draft Environmental Impact Statement. Update of the Water Control Manual for the Apalachicola-Chattahoochee-Flint River Basin in Alabama, Florida, and Georgia and a Water Supply Storage Assessment*. US Army Corps of Engineers, Mobile District.
n.d. *Flood of July 1994, Apalachicola-Chattahoochee-Flint River Basin*. US Army Engineer District, Mobile, Alabama.

US Fish and Wildlife Service
2018 *Gulf Sturgeon*. Website.

Van de Noort, Robert
2011 *North Sea Archaeologies: A Maritime Biography, 10,000 BC–AD 1500*. Oxford University Press, Oxford, England.

Van Gilder, Cynthia, and Douglas K. Charles
2003 Archaeology as Cultural Encounter: The Legacy of Hopewell. In *Theory, Method, and Practice in Modern Archaeology*, edited by Robert J. Jeske and Douglas K. Charles, pp. 114–129. Praeger, Westport, Connecticut.

VanDerwarker, Amber M., C. Margaret Scarry, and Jane M. Eastman
2007 Menus for Families and Feasts: Household and Community Consumption of Plants at Upper Saratown, North Carolina. In *The Archaeology of Food and Identity*, edited by K. Twiss, pp. 16–49. Center for Archaeological Investigations, Occasional Paper No. 34. Southern Illinois University, Carbondale.

Vernon, Robert O.
1942 Tributary Valley Lakes of Western Florida. *Journal of Geomorphology* V:302–311.

Voorhies, Barbara, G.
2000 Reconstructing Mobility Patterns of Late Hunter-Gatherers in Coastal Chiapas, Mexico: The View from the Shellmounds. *Anais do IX Congresso da Sociedade de Arqueologia Brasiliera*.

Voosen, Paul
2018 Ice Age Impact. *Science* 362:738–743.
2022 Impact Crater under Greenland's Ice Is Surprisingly Ancient. *Science* 375(6585):1076–1077.

Wade, Lizzie
2017 Relics of the First Americans? *Science* 356:13.
2021 Footprints Support Claim of Early Arrival in the Americas. *Science* 373(6562):1426.

Wakida-Kusunoki, Armando T., and Clyde L. MacKenzie Jr.
2004 Rangia and Marsh Clams, *Rangia cuneata, R. flexuosa*, and *Polymesoda caroliniana*, in Eastern México: Distribution, Biology, and Ecology, and Historical Fisheries. *Marine Fisheries Review* 66(3):13–20.

Walker, John H.
2002 *Power and Prowess. The Origins of Brooke Kingship in Sarawak*. Allen and Unwin and University of Hawai'i Press, Honolulu.

Walker, Karen J.
1988 Faunal Remains from Five Apalachicola River Sites. Appendix 1. In *Archaeological Investigations at Six Sites in the Apalachicola River Valley, Northwest Florida*, by Nancy Marie White, pp. 227–257. National Oceanic and Atmospheric Administration Technical Memorandum, NOSSRD 26. Washington, DC (1994).

2000 The Material Culture of Precolumbian Fishing: Artifacts and Fish Remains from Coastal Southwest Florida. *Southeastern Archaeology* 19:24–45.

Walker, Karen J., Frank W. Stapor Jr., and William H. Marquardt
1995 Archaeological Evidence for a 1750–1450 BP Higher-Than-Present Sea Level along Florida's Gulf Coast. In *Holocene Cycles. Climate, Sea Levels, and Sedimentation*, edited by Charles W. Finkl Jr., pp. 205–218. Coastal Education and Research Foundation, Charlottesville, Virginia.

Walker, Renee B., and Boyce N. Driskell (editors)
2007 *Foragers of the Terminal Pleistocene in North America*. University of Nebraska Press, Lincoln.

Waller, Ben I.
1971 Hafted Flake Knives. *Florida Anthropologist* 24:173–174.

Walthall, John A.
1980 *Prehistoric Indians of the Southeast: Archaeology of Alabama and the Middle South*. University of Alabama Press, Tuscaloosa.
1981 Galena and Aboriginal Trade in Eastern North America. *Illinois State Museum Scientific Papers*, Vol. 17. Springfield, Illinois.

Wardle, Harriet Newell
1929 Wreck of the Archaeological Department of the Academy of Natural Sciences of Philadelphia. *Science* 70(1805):119–121.

Warren, Lyman O.
1963 Horse's Hoof Core-Planes from Pinellas and Pasco Counties, Florida, and the Oaxaca Valley. *Florida Anthropologist* 16:133–136.

Waselkov, Gregory A.
1987 Shellfish Gathering and Shell Midden Archaeology. *Advances in Archaeological Method and Theory* 10:93–210.

Waselkov, Gregory A., and John W. Cottier
2016 Celt Production and Resharpening: Some Indirect Evidence from Central Alabama. *Journal of Alabama Archaeology* 62:1–10.

Waselkov, Gregory A., Donald A. Beebe, Howard Cyr, Elizabeth L. Chamberlain, Jayur Madhusudan Mehta, and Erin S. Nelson
2022 History and Hydrology: Engineering Canoe Canals in the Estuaries of the Gulf of Mexico. *Journal of Field Archaeology* 47:7, 486–500.

Waters, Michael R.
2019 Late Pleistocene Exploration and Settlement of the Americas by Modern Humans. *Science* 365:6449.

Waters, Michael R., and Thomas W. Stafford Jr.
2007 Redefining the Age of Clovis: Implications for the Peopling of the Americas. *Science* 315:1122–1126.

Watson, Patty Jo
2012 Forty Years' Pursuit of Human Prehistory in the World Underground. In *Sacred Darkness: A Global Perspective on the Ritual Use of Caves*, edited by Holley Moyes, pp. 185–194. University of Colorado Press, Boulder.

Watts, Betty M.
1975 *The Watery Wilderness of Apalach*. Apalach Books, Tallahassee, Florida.

Watts, W. A., B. C. S. Hansen, and E. C. Grimm
1992 Camel Lake: A 40,000-yr Record of Vegetational and Forest History from Northwest Florida. *Ecology* 73(3):1056–1066.

Wauchope, Robert
1966 *Archaeological Survey of Northern Georgia.* Memoirs of the Society for American Archaeology No. 21.

Webb, S. David (editor)
2006 *First Floridians and Last Mastodons: The Page-Ladson Site in the Aucilla River.* Springer, New York.

Webb, S. David, Jerald T. Milanich, Roger Alexon, and James S. Dunbar
1984 A *Bison antiquus* Kill Site, Wacissa River, Jefferson County, Florida. *American Antiquity* 49:384–392.

Webb, William S.
1957 *The Development of the Spearthrower.* University of Kentucky Department of Anthropology Occasional Papers in Anthropology No. 2. Lexington.

Weinberg, Bennett Alan, and Bonnie K. Bealer
2001 *The World of Caffeine.* Routledge, New York.

Weiner, Annette
1992 *Inalienable Possessions. The Paradox of Keeping-While-Giving.* University of California Press, Berkeley.

Weiner, Annette B., and Jane Schneider (editors)
1989 *Cloth and Human Experience.* Smithsonian Institution Press, Washington, DC.

Wharton, Charles H.
1978 *The Natural Environments of Georgia.* Georgia Department of Natural Resources, Atlanta.

Whatley, John S.
2002 An Overview of Georgia Projectile Points and Selected Cutting Tools. *Early Georgia* 30(1):7–133.

Wheeler, Ryan J.
1994 Early Florida Decorated Bone Artifacts: Style and Aesthetics from Paleo-Indian through Archaic. *Florida Anthropologist* 47:47–60.
1998 Walker's Canal: An Aboriginal Canal in the Florida Panhandle. *Southeastern Archaeology* 17(2):174–181.
2011 On the Trail of the Panther in Ancient Florida. *Florida Anthropologist* 64:139–162.

Wheeler, Ryan J., and Ray M. McGee
1994 Technology of Mount Taylor Period Occupation, Groves' Orange Midden (8VO2601), Volusia County, Florida. *Florida Anthropologist* 47:350–379.

Wheeler, Ryan J., James J. Miller, Ray M. McGee, Donna Ruhl, Brenda Swann, and Melissa Memory
2003 Archaic Period Canoes from Newnans Lake, Florida. *American Antiquity* 68:533–551.

White, Anta M., Lewis R. Binford, and Mark L. Papworth
1963 *Miscellaneous Studies in Typology and Classification.* Museum of Anthropology, University of Michigan Anthropological Paper No. 19, Ann Arbor.

White, Nancy Marie
1981 *Archaeological Survey at Lake Seminole.* Cleveland Museum of Natural History Archaeological Research Report No. 29.
1982 The Curlee Site (8Ja7) and Fort Walton Development in the Apalachicola Lower Chattahoochee Valley, Northwest Florida. PhD dissertation, Department of Anthropology, Case Western Reserve University, Cleveland. Xerox University Microfilms, Ann Arbor, Michigan.

1992 The Overgrown Road Site (8Gu38), a Swift Creek Camp in the Lower Apalachicola Valley. *Florida Anthropologist* 45:18–38.

1994a Commentary: Gordon Willey; The Novel. *AAA Anthropology Newsletter* 35(3):16–17.

1994b *Archaeological Investigations at Six Sites in the Apalachicola River Valley, Northwest Florida*. National Oceanic and Atmospheric Administration Technical Memorandum, NOSSRD 26, Washington, DC.

1996 *Archaeological Investigations of the 1994 Record Flood Impacts in the Apalachicola Valley, Northwest Florida*. Report to the Florida Division of Historical Resources, Tallahassee. University of South Florida, Department of Anthropology, Tampa.

1999 *Apalachicola Valley Remote Areas Archaeological Survey, Northwest Florida*, Volume 1: The Survey and Sites Located. Report to the Florida Division of Historical Resources, Tallahassee. University of South Florida, Department of Anthropology, Tampa.

2003a Testing Partially Submerged Shell Middens in the Apalachicola Estuarine Wetlands, Franklin County, Florida. *Florida Anthropologist* 56(1):15–45.

2003b Late Archaic in the Apalachicola/Lower Chattahoochee Valley of Northwest Florida, Southwest Georgia, Southeast Alabama. *Florida Anthropologist* 56(2):69–90.

2004 Late Archaic Fisher-Foragers in the Apalachicola–Lower Chattahoochee Valley, Northwest Florida–South Georgia/Alabama. In *Signs of Power: The Rise of Cultural Complexity in the Southeast*, edited by Jon L. Gibson and Philip J. Carr, pp. 10–25. University of Alabama Press, Tuscaloosa

2005 *Archaeological Survey of the St. Joseph Bay State Buffer Preserve, Gulf County, Florida*. Report to the Apalachicola National Estuarine Research Reserve, Eastpoint, Florida, and the Division of Historical Resources, Tallahassee. Department of Anthropology, University of South Florida.

2008 *Archaeology for Dummies*. Wiley Publishing, Hoboken, New Jersey.

2010 Gotier Hammock Mound and Midden on St. Joseph Bay, Northwest Florida. *Florida Anthropologist* 63(3–4):150–182.

2011a *Archaeology at Chattahoochee Landing, Gadsden County, Northwest Florida*. Report to the Florida Fish and Wildlife Conservation Commission and the Division of Historical Resources, Tallahassee. Department of Anthropology, University of South Florida, Tampa.

2011b Middle Woodland and Protohistoric Fort Walton at The Lost Chipola Cutoff Mound, Northwest Florida. *Florida Anthropologist* 64(3–4):241–273.

2013 *Pierce Mounds Complex. An Ancient Capital in Northwest Florida*. Report on file at the Florida Division of Historical Resources, Tallahassee.

2014a What I Believe about the Useful Diversity of Theory in Southeastern Archaeology. *Southeastern Archaeology* 33:255–268.

2014b Apalachicola Valley Riverine, Estuarine, Bayshore, and Saltwater Shell Middens. *Florida Anthropologist* 67:77–104.

2018 *Apalachicola Valley Archaeological Survey and Synthesis, Northwest Florida*. Report to the Division of Historical Resources, Florida Department of State, Tallahassee.

2019 The Montgomery Fields Site on the Lower Flint River. *Early Georgia* 47(1 and 2):27–42.

2021a Chattahoochee Landing Mound Complex (8Gd4) at the Apalachicola River Forks, Northwest Florida. *Florida Anthropologist* 74(4):193–226.

2021b Native American Archaeology of St. Vincent Island, Northwest Florida. *Adventures in Florida Archaeology* 2021:8–13. Florida Historical Society Archaeological Institute, Cocoa.

2023 University of South Florida Digital Commons website for the Apalachicola Valley Archaeology Supporting Data.

White, Nancy Marie, and Richard W. Estabrook
1994 Sam's Cutoff Shell Mound and Late Archaic Elliott's Point in the Apalachicola Delta, Northwest Florida. *Florida Anthropologist* 47(1):61–78.

White, Nancy Marie, and Elicia Kimble
2017 *Archaeological Survey and Testing on St. Vincent Island, Northwest Florida*. Report to the Regional Historic Preservation Office, Southeast Region, US Fish and Wildlife Service, Hardeville, SC. Department of Anthropology, University of South Florida, Tampa.

White, Nancy Marie, Terrance Simpson, and Suella McMillan
1992 *Apalachicola Valley Archaeology* (booklet). W. T. Neal Civic Center, Blountstown, Florida. Reprinted 1998 by the Neal Center and the Apalachicola National Estuarine Research Reserve.

White, Nancy Marie, Nelson D. Rodriguez, Christopher Smith, and Mary Beth Fitts
2002 *St. Joseph Bay Shell Middens Test Excavations, Gulf County, Florida, 2000–2002*. Report to the Division of Historical Resources, Tallahassee. Department of Anthropology, University of South Florida, Tampa.

White, Nancy Marie, Keith D. Ryder, Scott M. Grammar, and Karen L. Mayo
1995 *Archaeological Survey of Dog Island, Franklin County, Florida*. Report to the Barrier Island Trust, Tallahassee. Department of Anthropology, University of South Florida, Tampa.

White, Nancy Marie, and Audrey Trauner
1987 *Archaeological Survey in the Chipola River Valley, Northwest Florida*. Report to the Division of Historical Resources, Tallahassee. Department of Anthropology, University of South Florida, Tampa.

White, Nancy Marie, and Richard A. Weinstein
2008 The Mexican Connection and the Far West of the Southeast. *American Antiquity* 73:227–277.

White Deer, Gary
1997 Return of the Sacred: Spirituality and the Scientific Imperative. In *Native Americans and Archaeologists: Stepping Stones to Common Ground*, edited by Nina Swidler, Kurt E. Dongoske, Roger Anyon, and Alan S. Downer, pp. 37–43. AltaMira Press, Walnut Creek, California.

Whitford, A. C.
1941 Textile Fibers Used in Eastern Aboriginal North America. *Anthropological Papers XXXVIII*, Part 1, American Museum of Natural History, New York.

Whitmarsh, Tim
2015 *Battling the Gods. Atheism in the Ancient World*. Alfred A. Knopf, New York.

Whittaker, John
2010 Weapon Trials: The Atlatl and Experiments in Hunting Technology. In *Designing Experimental Research in Archaeology*, edited by Jeffrey R. Ferguson, pp. 195–222. University Press of Colorado, Boulder.

Wide Open Spaces
2017 Impressive 7-Year-Old Hunter Kills Deer with Atlatl on Video. wideopenspaces.com.

Wilk, Richard R.
1985 The Ancient Maya and the Political Present. *Journal of Anthropological Research* 41:307–326.

Willey, Gordon R.
1949 *Archeology of the Florida Gulf Coast*. Smithsonian Miscellaneous Collections 113. Washington, DC.

1985 Comments on the Archaeology of Northwest Florida in 1984. *Florida Anthropologist* 38:178–183.

1988 *Portraits in American Archaeology*. University of New Mexico Press, Albuquerque.

1993 *Selena*. Walker, New York.

1999 Inconsequent Thoughts and Other Reflections on Florida Archaeology. *Florida Anthropologist* 52:201–204.

Willey, Gordon R., and Richard B. Woodbury
1942 A Chronological Outline for the Northwest Florida Coast. *American Antiquity* 7:232–254.

Williams, James D., Arthur E. Bogan, and Jeffrey T. Garner
2008 *The Freshwater Mussels of Alabama and the Mobile Basin of Georgia, Mississippi, and Tennessee*. University of Alabama Press, Tuscaloosa.

Williams, James D., Robert S. Butler, Garly L. Warren, and Nathan A. Johnson
2014 *Freshwater Mussels of Florida*. University of Alabama Press, Tuscaloosa.

Williams, James D., and Arlene Fradkin
1999 *Fusconaia apalachicola*, a New Species of Freshwater Mussel (Bivalvia: Unionidae) from Precolumbian Archaeological Sites in the Apalachicola Basin of Alabama, Florida, and Georgia. *Tulane Studies in Zoology and Botany* 3(1):51–62.

Williams, Mark
2003 Introduction to the 2003 Edition. In *Archaeology of the Funeral Mound, Ocmulgee National Monument, Georgia*, pp. vii–xii. US National Park Service, Washington, DC.

Williams, Mark, and Daniel T. Elliott (editors)
1998 *A World Engraved: Archaeology of the Swift Creek Culture*. University of Alabama Press, Tuscaloosa.

Williams, Mark, and Victor Thompson
1999 A Guide to Georgia Indian Pottery Types. *Early Georgia* 27(1):1–14.

Williams, Ted
2000 False Forests. *Mother Jones* 25(3):72–79.

Williams, Thomas J., Michael B. Collins, Kathleen Rodrigues, William Jack Rink, Nancy Velchoff, Amanda Keen-Zebert, Anastasia Gilmer, et al.
2018 Evidence of an Early Projectile Point Technology in North America at the Gault Site, Texas, USA. *Science Advances* 4(7).

Wilson, Bee
2012 *Consider the Fork: A History of How We Cook and Eat*. Basic Books, New York.

Wing, Elizabeth S., and Antoinette B. Brown
1979 *Paleonutrition*. Academic Press, New York.

Witherington, Blair, and Dawn Witherington
2007 *Florida's Living Beaches*. Pineapple Press, Sarasota.

Wolf, Eric R.
1982 *Europe and the People without History*. University of California Press, Berkeley.

Woodward, Deena S.
2012 Paleo-Indian to Spanish Occupation around Choctawhatchee Bay, Northwest Florida, as Documented in a Private Artifact Collection. Master's thesis, Department of Anthropology, University of South Florida, Tampa.

Worth, John E.
1988 Archaeological Investigation of a Mississippian Fall-Line Chiefdom on the Middle

Flint River. Paper presented at the Annual Meeting of the Southeastern Archaeological Conference, New Orleans.

Worthington, Brian E.
2008 An Osteometric Analysis of Southeastern Prehistoric Domestic Dogs. Master's thesis, Department of Anthropology, Florida State University, Tallahassee.

Wright, Alice P.
2017 Local and "Global" Perspectives on the Middle Woodland Southeast. *Journal of Archaeological Research* 25:37–83.

Yates, William Brian
2000 Implications to Late Archaic Exchange Networks in the Southeast as Indicated by the Archaeological Evidence of Prehistoric Soapstone Vessels throughout Florida. Master's thesis, Department of Anthropology, Florida State University, Tallahassee.

Yerger, Ralph W.
1977 Fishes of the Apalachicola River. In *Proceedings of the Conference on the Apalachicola Drainage System, 23–24 April 1976*, edited by Robert J. Livingston and Edwin A. Joyce Jr., pp. 22–33. Florida Marine Research Publications No. 26. Florida Department of Natural Resources, Tallahassee.

Index

Page numbers in italics refer to illustrations and tables.

Academy of Natural Sciences of Philadelphia, 7, 83, 252
Adena culture, 198, 225, 236; mound ceremonialism, 198, 222
Africa, x, 89; human origins, 192. *See also* ethnographic analogies
African Americans, 7
agriculture, 85; fertility rates, 161; historic, 18, 26, 100; skeletal indicators, 87, 216
American Indians. *See* Native Americans
Andrews Dam. *See* George W. Andrews Dam and Reservoir
ANERR. *See* Apalachicola National Estuarine Reseach Reserve (ANERR)
animals, 66–79; amphibians, 32, 69, 123, 183, 254; crustaceans, 32, 36, 38, 67, 74, 183; endangered species, 69, 70, 77; insects, 36, 66, 70, 164. *See also* bivalve mollusks; fish; gastropods; mammals; reptiles; shellfish
antler, 66, 92, 117, 145, 159, 182, 253; tools, 124, 148, 152–154, *153*
Apalachee Bay, 80, 95, 143–44, 150–51
Apalachee Wildlife Management Area, 29
Apalachicola Bay, 4, 24, 34, *35*, 36, 38–40, 53, 72, 75, 77, 95, 105, 106, 134, *147*, *149*, 165, 200, 231, 240; formation, 43; oysters, 78; paleochannels, 39, 43
Apalachicola National Estuarine Research Reserve (ANERR), xiv, 34
Apalachicola National Forest, 34, 140, 201
Apalachicola River, 1, *2*, 5, 8, 10, 12, 24–27, 30, 31–40, 43, 47, 72, 74–75, 76, 78, 99–101, 104, 143, 147, *147*, 199, 218, 234, *259*; delta, 4, 33, 35, *35*, 43, 63, 77–79, 80, *93*, 95, 107, 143, 151, 163, 167, 184, 189; distributaries, 34–35, 44, *129*; middle, 11, 55, 77, 97, 165, 223, 225, 251; migration, 32, 33, 35–36, 39, 43, 78–79, 89, 99, 101, 142, 151, 163–64, 184, 259; paleochannels, 39, 89, 96–97, 106, 167, 169; tributaries, 27, 32, 33–35, 44, 97, 99; upper, 3, 11, 18, 30, 32, 47, 100, *127*, 155, 165, 174, 199, 203, 219
Apalachicola–Chattahoochee–Flint Rivers (ACF), *2*, *9*; "water wars," 5, 31
Apalachicola–lower Chattahoochee valley region, *2*, *3*, *9*, 25, *26*, 96; animal resources, 66–83; bone and shell artifacts, 81–83; chipped stone resources, 48–51; clay and ceramics, 57–58; early interest and investigations, 5–7; early professional archaeology, 7–8, 10–11; environments, 23–43; geographic locations, 9; ground stone and other rocks, 51–56; karst and caves, 45–46; landscape manipulation, 70–71; latest professional work, 11–14; metals, 56–57; people, 85–88; plants, 58–66; seasonality and climate, 84–85; shell middens, 77–81; shellfish, 76–79; soil and features, 46–48; subbasins, *26*; time periods/cultures, *16*; waterways and transport, 44–45
archaeology, 2, 10, 12, 19, 86; classification, 19, 95; curation, 10, 12, 21, 87; early

professional, 7–8, 10–11; early regional investigation, 5–7; ethics, 21–22, 103, 105; experimental, 64, 120, 152, 155, 179, 181, 258; interpretations, 10, 19–20, 138, 191–92, 225; latest regional work, 11–14; methods, 14, 16–21; models, 14–15, 76, 118–19, 125, 159, 163, 187, 222, 267–68; practical applications, 68, 75, 77, 84, 86; preservation, 45, 66–67, 81, 97, 163, 183, 185; public, ix, 4, 13, 18, 21–22; reconstructions, 15, 89, 118, 120, 186; site formation processes, 13, 28, 79, 107; temporal and cultural constructs, 15–16, *16*, 225; terminology, xi, 225; theory, 14–16, 138; typologies, 13, 20, 138, 144–45, 149, 151, 152, 203, 209; underwater, 92, 94–95, 144

archaeological sites: 41CL9 (TX), 184; 8Gd338, 99; 9Er57, 97; Agate Basin (WY), 120; Alexon Bison, 94; Anzick (MT), 124; Arnold Soybean Field (8Ja204), 229, *230*; Ater, 267; Baby Oak (8Gu126), 82; Baggett (8Ja442), *100*, 103; Banpo (China), 58; Bayou Park site (8Ok898), 167, 181, 184; Bell (8Ok19), 209; Bevis (8Ja502), *100*, 103–4, *140*; Bird Field (9Se13), 183; Bird/Byrd Hammock (8Wa30), 80; Black's Island (8Gu11), 42; Block-Sterns site (8Le148), 198, 223, 270; Blue Hole Spring (8Ja112), 55, 232; Brickyard Creek (8Fr8), 253; Buck Mound (8Ok11), 270; Bullpen (1Ho22), 177; Cahokia, 62; Cemetery Mound (8Fr21), 135, 231, 234, 259; Conch Island (8Gu20), 42; Cool Spring Mound (8Fr19), 259; Corbin Tucker (8Ca142), 202; Cypress Ridge (8Gu58), *140*; Dan Gray (8Ja520), *149*; Davis Field Mound (8Ca1), 256; Dudley (8Ja450), *140*; Duncan McMillan (8Ca193), *169*, 170; Econfina Channel, 151; Eight Mile (8Fr55), *147*, 148, *149*; El Inga (Chile), 115; Estiffanulga Dump (8Li207), *140*; Fairchild's Landing (9Se14), 10, 50, 223, 229, 239, 249, 251; Fell's Cave (Chile), 114–15; For Sale (8Ja513), *100*, 104; Four-Hole Pond (8Ca185), *102*, 103, 114; Gaston Spivey (8Ca114), 243; Gault (TX), 91; Gigger Point, 233; Gotier Hammock, *82*, *Plate VII*, 223, 226, 245, *246*, 258, 261; Hardnut Landing (Mound near, 9Dr18), 235, *237*, *241*, 245; Hare Hammock, 233; Harrell/3 Rivers State Park (8Ja39), 98, *98*; Helena Crossing (AR), 242; HJ-A (8Ja2069), *153*, 242; HJ-AU Rocky Creek (8Ja2040), 147, *147*; HJ-BJ (8Ca293), *169*; Homer Sims 3 (8Ja448), *140*; Hopewell Mound (33Ro27), 267; Indian Pass (8Gu1), 222, 270; Isabel Landing Mound (8Gu4), *210*; Jackson Blue Springs (8Ja68), 101, 142; Jackson Mound (8Fr15), 57, 222, 232, 234, 237, 245; J. B. Young, (8Ca99), *140*; Keene (8Ja1847), 100, 142, 151, *204*; Kemp's Landing (8Ja2), 222; Kerr's Landing Mound (9Dr14), 198; Leake, 267; Lewis Place Mound (8Ta1), 270; Lightning (8Ca101), *140*; Lime Sink (8Ja28 or J-26), 48; Little Redfish Creek (8Fr1367), 53, *141*, 143, 231; Log Landing Mound (9Dr27), 232, *232*; Lonice (8Ja522), *140*; Lost Crew (8Gu130), *82*; Lost Dog (8Fr820), 201; McFaddin Beach, 108; McKeithen, 224; Magnolia Bridge (8Ja437), *169*; Malloy (8Ja124), 103; Marksville, 240, 258; McFaddin Beach (TX), 108; Montgomery Fields (9Dr10), 10, 98, 183; Mound Near Apalachicola (8Fr20A), *74*, 259; Mound Below Bristol (8Li3), 199, 212, 251; Mound near Estiffanulga (8Li7), 199; Mound Near Rock Bluff Landing (8Li5), 237, 243, 244, *244*; Mounds at Eleven Mile Point (8Fr10), 43; Nameless Creek (8Li195), *140*, 143; numbering, 10; OK Landing Mound (8Ca2), 57, 234; Omussee Creek (1Ho27/101), 202; Omussee Creek Park (1Ho26), 76–77; Overgrown Road (8Gu38), 231; Parish Lake (8Ca10), 223; Parrish Lake Road (8Ca90), *98*, 100; Peacock Bridge (8Ja433), 147, *153*; Pharr, 240; Pinson Mounds, 258; Ragland Foundation (8Ja1846), 145–46; Reddie Point, 233;

Ring Jaw Island (8Ca92), *169*; Robinson 4 (8Ja275), 142; Rock Hill (8Ja21 or J-19), 48; Rozar (9Dr91), 50; Ryan-Harley, 124; Sampson's Landing (8Ja1), 254; Sassafras (8Gd12), 47; Saul's Creek Road East (8Gu33), *140*; Scholz Steam Plant site (8Ja104), 76, 254; Sealy Plantation (9Se11), 55, *56*, 233; Seip-Pricer, 267; Shell Mound Near Apalachicola (8Fr20B), 259; Shoemake Landing Mound (9Er1/87), 245; Sloan (AR), 124; Spivey Road Borrow Pit (8Ca128), *140*; St. Stephen's Church (8Li76), 76; St. Vincent Point (8Fr354), 106; St. Vincent 6 (8Fr365), *232*; Stuck Truck (8Li221), 100, *100*; Sunstroke (8Li217), 77; Swift Creek (9Bi3), 238; Sycamore (8Gd13), 11, 76, 177, 256; Tan Vat (8Ja20 [J-18]), 154, 232; Ten Mile Creek Overlook (8Ca108), *140*; Tick Island, 161; Torreya Ranger (8Li8), 77; Tunnacunnhee, 234, 265; Two Egg Quarry (8Ja1126), 48; Tyler CF1 (8Ja2077), 98, 100; Tyler TM1 (8Ja2081), *116*; Tyler TM2 (8Gd1990), 100; Underwater Indian Mound (9Se27), 31, 55, 232, 234, 241, 243; Wakulla Springs Lodge, 124; Warm Mineral Springs, 145; Warrior River Mound, 230–31; Watson Brake, 160; Welch, (8Ja537), *140*; Whaley's Mill (9Se10), 183; Windover (8Br246), 63, 124, 145, 148, 157–58, 161; X-156-1 (8Le2105), 145; Yellow Flower (8Gu132), 82; Yent, 233; Yon Mound (8Li2), 11. *See also* Aspalaga Landing Mounds (8Gd1); Bristol Mound (8Li4); Chattahoochee Landing Mound complex (8Gd4); Clark Creek (8Gu60); Hare's Landing (9Se33); Howard Creek Mound (8Gu41); Huckleberry Landing (8Fr12); J-Y Field (8Ja63); Keene Dog Pond (8Ja1848); Kolomoki (9Er1); Lake Douglas Mound (9Dr21); Lane Springs (9Dr5); Mandeville; Marksville; McKinnie (8Ja1869); Otis Hare (8Li172); Paradise Point (8Fr71); Pierce Mounds (8Fr14); Porter's Bar (8Fr1); Richardson's Hammock (8Gu10); Sam's Cutoff (8Fr754); St. Vincent 3 (8Fr362); St. Vincent 5 (8Fr364 Pickalene Bar); Thank-You-Ma'am Creek (8Fr755); Trestle Bridge (8Ja186); Waddell's Mill Pond (8Ja65)

Archaic period, *16*, *133*, 137–93; bow and arrow, 152; burials, 79, 191; ceramics, 20, 138; chipped stone tools, 37; dates, 137–38; earthworks, 160; environment, 79, 138, 140; ethnographic analogies, 158; features, 47, 52; ground stone, 146; habitation patterns, 105, 137; human remains, 160; ideological systems, 137; interpretations, 20; Kentucky, 190; material culture, 63, 160; mobility, 137–38, 156; population density, 156; projectile points, 95, 104, 109, 116–17, 137–38, 140, 143–44, 147; settlement patterns, 39, 138 141–42; shell middens, 79; Shell-Mound-Archaic, 154; sociopolitical systems, 137; subsistence, 68, 75–76, 137–39, 158–59, 215, 254; violence and warfare, 159. *See also* Early Archaic; Middle Archaic; Late Archaic

art, 59, 124, 179, 239; 213

Aspalaga Landing Mounds (8Gd1), 86, 199, 221, 230, 233, 243, 258; 243.

Aspalaga, FL, 28

Atlantic Coast, 73, 75–76, 79, 145, 160, 174, 177, 205; shell middens, 78–80

atlatl, 64, 112, 148, 152–55, 159; proficiency of use, 154

Aucilla River, 37, 48, 92–95, *93*, 104, 109, 115, 117–18, 120, 144, 146, 270

Australia, 90, 152; microlith technology, 191

avocational archaeologists, 21–22, 48, 63, 98–100, 103, 105, 115, 146, 155

bannerstone, 51, 137, 152–55, *153*, 158, 232

BAR. *See* Bureau of Archaeological Research (BAR)

barrier formations, 34, *35*, 38, 41, 143; age, 41, 167; islands, 3, 4, 24, 33, 35, 38–42, 47, 62, 105–7, 167, 174, 202; peninsulas, 42, 143. *See also names of islands*

Barry, Dave, x

beaches, 4, 40–42, 108, *Plate V*; relict

ridges, 37, 40, 41, 42; St. Joseph Peninsula, 42
beads, 187; bone, 159; chert, 124; cylindrical, 253; disc, 124, *134*, 174, 198, 200, 212, 253; garfish scale, 73; ivory preform, 118, 124; jasper, 51, *Plate XI*, 174, 188–89; pearl, *67*, 253; quartz, 124; seed, 118, 159; shell, 6, 82, 83, 159, 189–190, 198, 200, 212–13, *213*, 249, 253, 267; stone, 160, 181, 188
belief systems, 14–15, 186, 217, 224, 231, 239, 270–71; cardinal directions, 119, 257; Late Archaic, 162; left-handed whelk/lightning whelk, 267; sacred items, 66, 144, 156, 252, 261; sacred places, 46, 104, 215, 222; shamanism, 63, 253, 265; spiritualism, 36, 42, 44, 59, 63, 66, 109, 155, 247, 261; supernatural, 44, 63, 126, 261; totems, 261
biases, 14–15, 33, 59, 64, 66–67, 72, 76, 123, 185; ceramics, 177, 197, 219; Middle Woodland, 227–29, 268; Pleistocene, 122; preservation, 5, 60, 63; sampling, 17, 31, 36, 77, 91, 108, 151, 163, 164–65, 219; site distribution, 17–18; warfare, 191
birds, 41, 66, 69–70, 72, 123–24, 146, 183, 214, 254, 255, 265; bone tubes, 148; Carolina parakeet, 265; ducks, 70, 254, 255, 256; geese, 31; preservation, 67; roseate spoonbill, 265; snow goose, turkey, 70–71, 243, 254; woodpecker, 32, 34, 66, 69, 265. *See also* iconography; seasonality
bison/buffalo, 68, 93, 94, 101, 117, 121, 253; horn core, 107; kill sites, 91, 120
bivalve mollusks, 31, 76–78, 254; American bittersweet, 252; cockle, 79; mussels, 76–77, 183, 214; scallop, 79
black drink tea (asi). *See* yaupon holly
Black's Island, 42, 75; spring on, 40
Blakely, GA, 30, 97
Blountstown, FL, 11, 32, 33
body modifications, cranial, 88, 215–16, 270; pierced earlobes, 86, 205, 234, 243, 270; tattoos, 65, 117, 270; teeth, 88. *See also* human remains; iconography
bola stones. *See* ground stone: bola stones

bone, 65, 66, 68, 74, 81, 88, 92, 93, 94, 117, 120, 159, 171, 182, 186, 256; beads, 159; bison pendant, 253; dating, 20; deer, 253; Florida panther, 253; jaw, 145, 253 ornament, 68; pneumatized, 73, *74*, 213; preservation, 64, 162; South America, 73; "tilly" (pneumatized), 73; tools, 74, 75, 81, 94, 117, 118, 145, 148, 155,159, 182, *182*, 213; tubes, 148; tusks, 118; worked skull, 145
bone chemistry, 86, 87, 158, 161, 260; stable isotope analysis, 161, 189–90
Borneo, x, 261; *See* ethnographic analogies
Bridges, Jeff, 115
Bridges, Lloyd, 115
Bristol Mound (8Li4), *136*, 233, 240, 247, *247*
Brooks, Mel (*The 2000-Year-Old-Man*), 173, 217
Brose, David S., ix, xiv, 11, 15, 223, 250. *See also* ceramics: Percy-Brose model and revisions
Broyles, Bettye, 239
Bullen, Ripley P., 8, 10, 12, 46, 48, 97, 112–13, 142, 146, 153, 168–69, 172, 175, 178, 214, 226–28, 232, 254
burials (human), 6, 145, 155, 159, 187, 190–91, 198, 199–200, 202, 205, 219, 222, 234, 243, 253, 257–58, 260, 267, 271; adult, 124; bark and log tombs, 258; bundles, 260; children, 73, 124, 154, 159; cremations, 201, 260; dog, 71; extended, 259; flexed, 159, 189, 215, 259, 269; group, 260, 271; wrapped, 48; isolated skulls, 260; log-lined, 224; men, 159, 191, 215; Ohio Hopewell, 269; pits, 215; secondary, 88, 215; shell midden, 79; Shell-Mound-Archaic, 154; South America, 122; supine, 259; wet environments, 148; women, 122, 145, 154, 159, 189. *See also* cemeteries

caches, 186, 249; biface, 146, 229–30; celts/axes, 231; ceramic, 198, 258, 260; Clovis, 124; point, 105, 114; Poverty Point-type objects, 179
Caldwell, Joseph R., 8, 10, 208, 227–29, 239, 249

California: aboriginal population, 85; bone chemistry study, 260; Yurok hunter-gatherers, 122
Canada, 113–14; British Columbia, 70, 91; Ontario, 56, 234
cane (river cane), 63, 66, 117, 148, 154, 157, 182, 232, 253; flutes or panpipes, 234, 253; uses, 66
canoe (prehistoric), 45
Cape San Blas, 39–40, *141*, 143; erosion, 42
Cat Point, FL, 105, 106
caves, 11, 29, 37, 46, 91, 101, *Plate I*, 142; Coxcatlan (Mexico), 91; Dry Hinds (TX), 185; fauna, 46; Fell's (Chile), 114–15; preservation, 118
celt. *See* ground stone: celts/axes; chipped stone tools: celts/axes
cemeteries, 86; Early Archaic, 145, 148; Fort Walton, 202; Late Archaic, 188, 190; Middle Archaic, 145; Paleoindian, 124; Windover site (8Br246), 157–59, 161
Central America, 92; Mexico, 32, 59, 63, 79, 91, 110, 157, 162
ceramics, 6, 15, 21, 46, 47, 57–58, 66, 69, 97, 103, *Plates XIV–XVI*, 131, 138, 160, 173, 176, 187, 194–97, 214, 224, 226, 228, 235–252; adornos, 236, 240, 243, *244*, 245; Alachua Cob Marked, 20; Alligator Bayou Stamped, 239–240; Alligator Stamped, 436, 240; Basin Bayou Incised, 226, 245, *246*; basketry impressed, 175; biases, 219; Carrabelle Incised, 246, 251; Carrabelle Punctated, 246, 249, 251; "ceramic distances," 250; check-stamped, 196–97, 198, 199–200, 201, 206, 207–8, *207*, 211, 226, 236, 246–47, *247*, 249–51; Chinese, 58; cob-marked, 20, 250, 251; coil method, 175, 194–95, 205; complicated-stamped, 195, 198, 199, 201, 202, 207, 208–11, 224, 226, 227, 235–40, 247–51, 264; cord-marked, 64, 198, 202, 208, 211, 246; Crooked River Complicated-Stamped, 209, 236, 238; cutouts, 245, 249; dentate stamping, 177; Deptford Check-Stamped, 194, 200, 201–2, 203, *207*, 208–9, 251; Deptford Fabric-Marked, 194–95, 201, 203, *206*, 208; Deptford Linear Check-Stamped, 194–95, 200, 201, 203, *207*, 208; Deptford Plain, 194; Deptford series, 178, 197, 201, 203, 205, 210–11, 219, 225, 246; Deptford Simple-Stamped, 194–95, 201–2, *207*, 249; design and morphology, 20, 195; disc, *Plate XIII*, 199, 205, 212, 251; discoidals/diskc, 58; early Weeden Island series, 198, 199, 211, 219, 221, 224–28, 235–36, 240–245, *244*, 247–51, fabric-marked, 64, 65, 206, 207, 208, 246, 251; fiber-tempered, 20, 38, 47, 58, 59, 142, 162–64, 165, 167, 168, 170, 172, 174–78, *175*, 181, 182, 184, 190, 192, 194–95, 205–7; fired-clay lumps/irregular chunks, 58, 181; French Fork Incised, 245; function, 246, 247; griddle, 184; grit and grog-tempered, 195, 206; grit-tempered, 20, 58, 195, 206, 236; grog-tempered, 20, 58, 178, 195, 201, 206, 236; Gulf Check-Stamped, 200, 246, 251; incised, 177; indeterminate ceramic, 197; Indian Pass Incised, 246; Keith Incised, 246, 251; "killing", 261; late Weeden Island series, 236, 249; linear check-stamped, 198; Marksville, 236, 245; mobility, 176; net-marked, 65, 65, 211, 246, 251, 251; New River Complicated-Stamped, 209, 210, 211, 236; nomenclature, 177; Norwood, 177; Orange wares, 177; origins, 58, 174, 176; paddles, 198, 208, 209, 236, 238–39, 246, 250; painted, 58, *Plates XIV–XVI*, 198, 240, *244*, 249; palmetto-fiber temper, 177; Percy-Brose model, 250–51; plainwares, 20, 168, 195, 196, 198, 199, 200, 201, 206, 207, 226, 236, 249, 251, 260; polychrome, 270; production, 177, 208; punch-and-drag technique, 240; punctate, 177, 240; radiocarbon dates, 58, 174–75; rim treatment, 20, 195, 206, 208, 209, 210, *210*, 211, 236, 237, 240, 243, 246, 247; ritual, 245; rocker-stamped, 211, 240; roller stamp, 198, 208; salt pans, 56; sand-tempered, 20, 58, 178, 195, 206, 236, 249; sand- and grog-tempered, 245;

Santa Rosa series, 211, 239–40; Santa Rosa Stamped, 211, 239–40; semi-fiber tempered, 163; shell-tempered, 20, 58; simple-stamped fiber-tempered, 175–78, 207; slab method, 175–76; sourcing studies, 58; spatial distribution, 209, 239; sponge-spicule-tempered, 178; St. Andrews Complicated-Stamped, 209, *210*, 236, 238, 249; St. John's, 178; St. Simons Plain, 177; Stallings, 177; Stallings Island, 177; Stallings Punctate, 177; structural perspective pattern study, 239; surface obliteration, 13; surface treatment, 58, 206, 207–9, 211, 239; Swift Creek Complicated-Stamped, 194–95, 198, 199, 200, 202, 206, 209, *210*, 211, 218, 225, 226, 235–38, *237*, *238*, 249, 250; Swift Creek–early Weeden Island, 236; Swift-Creek series, 198, 201, 208, 210–11, 219, 224, 227–28, 235, 236–40, 249–50; Swift-Creek type site, 235; symbolism, 247–48; temper, 20, 58, 174, 177–78, 194–95, 206, 236; temporal markers, 7, 178, 197; Tucker Ridge Pinched, 246; "type-variety" system, 20; type frequency, 225, 249, 251; typologies, 20, 58, 205, 235–36; use wear, 20, 58; USF sorting guide, 58; Wakulla Check-Stamped, 250–51; Weeden Island Cutout, *Plate XVI*, 235; Weeden Island excised, 235; Weeden Island I, 236, 240, 249; Weeden Island II, 246, 249; Weeden Island Incised, x, *Plates XIV*, *XV*, 240, *241*, 243, *244*, 245, 247, 249–51; Weeden Island modeled, 235; Weeden Island Plain, *Plate XVI*, 240, *241*, *242*; Weeden Island Punctated, 235, 240, 243–44, *244*, 250–51; Weeden Island Red, 235, 240, 251; Weeden Island series, 219, 236, 240, 246–47, 250; Weeden Island type site, 235; Weeden Island Zoned-Red, Plates *XIV*, *XV*, 240, 250; Wheeler, 177–78; Wheeler Plain, 178. *See also* effigies/figurines; food: preparation; pipes; portable X-ray fluorescence (pXRF); trace element analysis; SnowVision/World Engraved project; Swift Creek design database

Chason, Hub, 21, *54*, 102–3, *102*, 111, 112, 115, *117*, 117, 142, 146, 151, 154
Chattahoochee Landing mound complex (8Gd4), 6, *207*, 226
Chattahoochee River, *2*, *3*, 5, 7–8, 10–13, 25–29, *25*, *26*, 27, *27*, 30, 32, 37, 46, 72, 98, 142, 200, 212, 234; lower, 10, 11–12, 24, 37, 48, 50, 51, 95, 97, *Plate I*, 183, 222, 223, 226, 229, 239, 245, 253, 254; manipulation, 29; migration, 99; paleochannels, 97
Chattahoochee River 1 site (8Ja8 [J-5]), 12, 97, 142, 168, 178, 182, 183. 188, 197, 214–15
chert, 6, 29, 48–50, *49*, 89, 104, 108–10, *Plates VIII–X*, 143, 145, 162, 164, 170, 199, 218, 229; Albany, 48; Chipola basin, 37; Flint River, 48; formations, 48; Gulf Coastal Plain, 110; Marianna Quarry Cluster, 48; "quarry cluster" approach, 48; Wacissa Cluster, 48. *See also* lithics; Tallahatta quartzite/Tallahatta sandstone.
children, 15, 76, 122–23, 126, 161, 180; burials, 73, 154, 159; cranial alteration, 270; grave goods, 155; human remains, 190; infants, 148, 155
Chipola Archaeology Society, 103
Chipola Cutoff Mound (8Gu5), 21, 83, 253, 261; burials, 252; ceramics, 245; grave goods, 74, 252
Chipola River, *2*, *3*, 8, *9*, 12, 24, *25*, 27, 33, 37–38, 49, *54*, 89, 95, 99, 101–5, 111, 114, 115, 117, *Plates III*, *IX*, 142, 146, *147*, 147, 149, 151, 152, *153*, 154, 164, *169*, 173, 174, 232, 259; basin, *26*, 37, 103–4, 119, 142, 198; Cutoff, 33; lower, 38; Paleoindian site density, 101-5; Pleistocene, 99; relict beach ridges, 37; tributaries, 37, 101; upper, 48, 101, 147
chipped stone. *See* chert; coral; quartz; silicified wood; Tallahatta quartzite/Tallahatta sandstone
chipped stone tools, 37, 48, 50–51, 91, 110, 117, 124, 144–45, 151–52, 156, 199, 203, 224; adze, 117, *117*, 145, 172; Aucilla adze, 117, *117*, 146; biface, 94, 104, 110–11, *Plate IX*, 145, 146, 203,

229; celts/axes, 229; chisel, 107, *Plate VIII*; chopper, 110; core, 109, 111, 124, 146; drill, 152; Edgefield scraper, 115–16; expedient, 51, 115; flake knife, 94; graver, 107, 114, *Plate VIII*; hammerstone, 168; prismatic blade, 229; Hopewellian-type flake knife, 211; "horse-hoof core-plane," 110, 111, *111*, 146; knife, 112, 142, 159, 168; Lively Complex; microlithic industries, 171–72; preforms, 124, 145; scraper, 6, 104, 110–11, 114, 117, 142, 145, 146, 168; uniface, 104, 110–11, 114, 124, 203. *See also* microtools; projectile points; Waller knife

Choctawhatchee Bay, *2*, 79, 107, 151, 167, 172, 181, 188, 209, 270

clams, 21, 36, 76–78, 176; Apalachicola ebonyshell, 76–77, 254; freshwater, 160, 254; marine, 254; marsh (general), 35, 67, 76, 77–78, 254; marsh (*Polymesoda*), 35, 67, 78, 183, 214; marsh (*Rangia*), 35–36, 67, 78, 151, 164, 168, 182, 183, 184, 197, 199, 214; quahog, 79, 212, 214, 252; sunray venus, 79

Clark Creek site (8Gu60), 36, 47, 53, 70, 80, *Plate VI*, 164, *165*, 170, 174, 178, 179, 183, 188, 190, 197, 203, 211–13, *212*, 216, *238*, 238; radiocarbon date, 167

climate, 19, 43, 84–85, 160; Anthropocene, 84; atmospheric event (AD 536), 257; change, 84, 105, 110, 114, 123, 138, 140; El Niño, 19; glacial maximum, 92; global warming, 14, 28, 30, 114, 123, 138; Holocene, 29,30, 92, 138, 148, 156, 194; Hypsithermal/Holocene Climate Optimum, 148; Pleistocene, 29, 37, 84, 89, 92, 97, 105, 114, 123; Younger Dryas, 92, 113–14, 139

Clovis, 91, *93*; biases, 119, *Plate VIII*; burial, 124; horizon, 91–92, 94, 113; linguistic-based migration hypothesis, 92; Middle Paleoindian chronology and environment, 113–14; outrepassé flaking. *See also* burials: Clovis; caches: Clovis; Page Ladson site; Paleoindian; projectile points: Clovis; projectile points: fluted; projectile points: unfluted Clovis; Younger Dryas.

CMNH. *See* museums: Cleveland Museum of Natural History (CMNH)

coastal sites, 10, 72, 74–75, 77–79, 83, 89, 143, 150, 162–63, 170, 172, 181, 187, 197–98, 211, 214, 232, 233, 254; faunal remains, 72, 75, 183; Poverty Point-type objects, 179

collectors, xi, 8, 10, 11, 17, 18, 21–22, 51, 53, 68, 87, 89, 92, 95, 97, 99, 103, 105, 108, 117, 137, 143, 154, 156, 165, 166, 179, 252, 257. *See also* archaeology: ethics; looters

color, 59, 66; black, 234. 240, 257, 258; brown, 257; cardinal directions, 258; gray, 258; greenstone, 53; mound construction, *Plate VII*, 257, 258; red, 90, *Plate X*, 155, 156, 174, 201, 231, 240, 243, 258, 270; significance, 258; silver, 234–35; soil, 47; symbolism, 47; white, *Plate VII*, 234, 257, 258; yellow, *Plates VI*, *VII*, 156, 201, 257, 258

Columbia Reservoir. *See* lakes: Andrews Lake; George W. Andrews Dam and Reservoir

Columbus, GA, 12, 24, 25

Conch Island, 42

copper, 56, 201, 211, 218; body adornments, 56, *Plate XIII*, 199, 202, 205, 212, 234, 251; sources, 56, 234, 265, *266*; tubes, 56, 234, 253

coprolites: dog, 59, 70, 226, 255, 256; human, 70

coral, 43; agatized, 50, 152

craft, 44, 124; specialization, 65, 155, 188, 238, 245, 248, 264; woodworking, 117, 145, 146, 152

Creek Indian names: "àsi-àpi-laiki", 28; Aspalaga, 28; Estiffanulga, 28; "Thlonotiska", 48; Wewahitchka, 28

creeks, 34, 46, 95, 101, 104; Cowart's (AL), 24, 37, 97, 101; Cowart's (FL), 103, 104; Davis Mill (FL), 104; Depot (FL), 39, 203; Marshall (AL), 24, 37, 97, 101; Merrit's Mill/Spring (FL), 101; Mosquito (FL), 99; Omussee (AL), 1, 24, 97; Spring (FL), 102,; Spring (GA),

24, 30, 48, 97, 146; Standing Boy (GA), 110; Van Horn (FL), *Plate IV*
CWRU. *See* universities: Case Western Reserve University (CWRU)

dams and reservoirs, 5, 7–8, 10, 28–30, 31, 38, 72, 98–99, 183. *See also* George W. Andrews Dam and Reservoir; Jim Woodruff Dam and Reservoir; Walter F. George Dam and Reservoir
dance, 124, 126, 260, 267, 271
Darwin, Charles, 152
daub, 57, 64, 181, 252. *See also* structures: wattle and daub
DeBaillou, Clemens, 8
Depot Creek site (8Gu56), 75, 80, *164*, 164, 175; *182*, 183, 190, 201–2, 210, 211, 212; radiocarbon dates, 201–2
diet, 59, 87, 123, 146, 156–58, 161, 189, 216, 256. *See also* subsistence
Dog Island, 41, 151; bay side, 143; canoe, 45
dogs, 70–71, 89, 91, 93, 124, 157, 184, 214; as food, 70, 160, 183; coprolites, 59, 71, 226, 255, 256; teeth, 148
domestication, 184; dogs, 124; plant, 59, 157, 215. *See also* bottle gourd
Donoghue, Joe, xvi, 36, 107
drugs, 62–63; caffeine, 63, 252, 265; datura or jimson weed, 62; nicotine, 63. *See also* tobacco; yaupon holly
Dunbar, Jim, 108, 112, 114

Early Archaic, 110, 124, 137–48, 151; Aucilla River sites, 144–46; bola stones, 51, *139*, 146–48; burials, 145; caches, 145–46; cemeteries, 145, 157; chipped stone tools, 117; chronometric dating, 138; coastlines, 93, 143; complexity, 158; dates, 139, 142; dogs, 157; earthworks, 158; environment, 138, 140; exchange networks, 158; forager models, 159; ground stone, 146–48; habitation, 145, 156; human remains, 160; material culture, 140–48; mobility, 158; people, 160–61; perishables, 145, 148; population, 140, 159; projectile points, 104, 108, 110, 114, 116, 137–46, *140–41*,

155, 159, 202; ritual, 79; settlement patterns, 137, 141–44; site distribution, *139*, 140–42; subsistence, 124, 137, 156–58; Windover site (8Br246), 63, 157. *See also* mounds; radiocarbon dates; Younger Dryas
Early Woodland, 86, Plate VI, 194–217, 223, 224; adaptations, 194; Adena mound ceremonialism, 198, 222; belief systems, 217; bone artifacts, 75, 213; burial mounds, 195, 198–201, 211, 257; burials, 73, 87, 198, 199, 216; ceramics, 20, 97, 178, 190, 194–201, 202, 205–12, 206, 214, 217, 218, 219, 238, 246, 249–50; ceremonial systems, 216–217; chronometric dates, 194–95; coastal vs. inland adaptation, 196; dates,; environment, 214–15; exchange networks, 217; faunal remains, 70, 214; floral remains, 214–15; geomorphological time, 202–3; ground stone, 51, 52, 203, 205; habitation sites, 47, 197–98, 201, 202–3, 212, 215; human biology, 87, 215–16; human remains, 87, 215–16; lithics, 203–5; material culture, 194, 264; mica, 55; mounds, 53, 54, 63, 198–201, 212, 216, 222, 225, 249; pendants/plummets, 53; projectile points, 195, 197, 203, *204*, *205*; Santa Rosa–Swift Creek, 211; sea levels, 195, 202; seasonality, 202, 214–215; settlement patterns, 194–97; shell artifacts, 82, 212–13, 253; site distribution, *196*; social systems, 216–17; steatite, 54; subsistence, 194, 202, 214–15; temporal markers, 197; terminology, 217; warfare, 217. *See also* Mandeville site (9Cy1 or Cla1); radiocarbon dates; storms: Early Woodland
earthworks, 47, 71, 79, 160, 186, 219, 222, 258; Hopewell, 222; Kolomoki, 224; Late Archaic, 186; Middle Archaic, 160, 162; Poverty Point site, 186. *See also* mounds; mound centers/complexes
economic systems, 14, 15, 45; distinctions, 125; Early/Middle Archaic, 159; Early Woodland, 216; inequality, 159, 215, 269; Late Woodland, 59; production, 265; stratification, 218; wealth, 160

effigies/figurines, 58, 86, 212, 236, 249; animal, 218, 240, 245, 247; bird, 66, *Plate XVI*, 240, 245; human, 179, 212, *212*, 216, 218, 240, *242*, 243, 270. *See also* fiber arts and crafts: figurines
El Niño–Southern Oscillation (ENSO), 19, 160
ENSO. *See* El Niño–Southern Oscillation (ENSO)
Estiffanulga, FL, 28
ethnographic analogies, 15, 75–76, 118, 123, 138, 158, 214, 260; Agta of the Philippines, 158; American Indian potters, 248; Arapesh of New Guinea, 264; Australian throwing sticks, 152; Borneo (East Malaysia) indigenous lifeways, 260–61; Central and South American Indian ceramics, 58; East African hunter-gatherers, 161; European stylistic trends, 263; foragers, 161, 173, 216–17; hunter-gatherers, 123, 125; hunter-gatherer-fishers, 15, 192; Iban lifeways, 262; Iban rituals and object veneration, 263; Kelabit exchange networks, 262; Laguna artisan, 248; modern Zimbabwe hunters, 121; Navajo, 260; New Guinea middens, 81; nonwarring cultures, 192; Norwegian marine foragers, 167; Papua New Guinea foragers, 217; Papua New Guinea Kula ring, 264; Pueblo potters, 248; shellfish collection in Australia and New Guinea, 76; shellfish-collectors, 76; South Africa hunters and gatherers, 120, 122, 125; South African foragers, 161; South Pacific island cultures and "big man" scenario, 268; Tierra del Fuego marine foragers, 167; West African pot smashing, 261; Xingu, Amazon, 217
ethnohistoric accounts, 15, 64, 9, 181; Texas indigenous burial practices (16th century), 260
Europeans, 2, 45, 90, 121, 192–93; British, 6; invasion, 85; Spanish, 45, 90, 121
exchange networks, 158, 189, 211, 217; Middle Woodland, 218, 224, 242, 264–67; Poverty Point, 186; shell, 266–67; steatite, 172; Woodland Information Superhighway, 265; yaupon holly, 63, 267

Fairbanks, Charles, 227–28
fall line, 2, 12, 24, 25, 110, 118, 224, 249
farming, x, 2, 59, 62, 75, 139; skeletal indicators, 161. *See also* agriculture
faunal remains, 20, 42, 66–70, 72–76, 78–79, 93, 114, 145, 183–84, 190, 195, 214, 254–55; analysis, 66–67, 70, 76, 161
features, 47–48, Plates *VI*, *VII*, *X*; 151; 159, 181, 198, 223, 226; basin, 201; earth oven, 179; hearth, 47, 58, 145, 179, 223; living surface, 223; pit, 46, 47, 52, 131, 133, 156, 174, 179, 199, 201, 223–24, 226, 254; postmold, 47, 81, 167, 223; unusual Middle/Late Archaic, 155–56, 174, 188. *See also* midden
fiber arts and crafts, 64–66, 117, 151; bags, 76, 118, 148; basketry, 64, 66, 118, 175, 179, 183, 253, 258; clothing, 64–65, 73, 183, 253; cordage, 64, 118, 183, 231, 247, 253; fabric/textiles, 64, 118, 148, 159, 208, 253; figurines, 148; footwear, 118, 148; Malay fishing crafts, 65; mats, 64, 118, 148, 183, 253; *See also* nets, ceramics: net-marked, ceramics: cord-marked
figurines. *See* effigies/figurines; fiber arts and crafts: figurines
fired-clay balls/nodules. *See* Poverty Point objects (PPOs); Poverty Point–type objects
fish, 39, 42, 71–76, 78, 124, 137, 146, 158, 159, 160, 185, 202, 214, 254, 255; catfish, 72–73, 183, freshwater, 42, 72–73; garfish, 21, 67, 72, 73, 183, 214, 254, 255; preservation bias, 67; saltwater, 29, 36, 72, 73, 183, 184, 255, 265
fishing, 38, 42, 65, 66, 71–76, 87, 185, 214, 231, 255; fish throat gouges, 182; gigs, 183; hooks, 213; microtools, 172; spear, 72; traps, 65; weirs, 65–66, 71, 158
Flint River, *2*, 3, *3*, 5, 7–8, *9*, 10, 11–13, 24–26, *26*, *27*, 29–31, 32, 37, 48, 50, 72, 97, 98, 99, 110, 177, 183, 198, 232, 233, 235, 249; Creek name, 48; tributaries, 30, 97

Index

Flint River valley, lower, *27*, 29–31, 146, 219
Flint-Chattahoochee confluence, *2, 3*, 6, 7, *9*, 24, *25-27*, 30–32, 48, 50, 55, 97–99, 111, 142, 146, 183, 222, 226
floral remains, 19, 20, 59–61, 64, 97, 124, 157–59, 162; 183–85, 256; botanical analysis, 59–60, 162; phytoliths, 256; pollen, 59, 97, 140, 256
Florida Bureau of Archaeological Research (BAR), 11; Isolated Finds Program, 95, 103
Florida Geological Survey, 13
Florida Park Service, 8
Florida State Museum. *See* museums: Florida Museum of Natural History (FLMNH)
food: preparation, 58, 173, 176, 179–81, 183, 187; production, 59, 62, 125, 186, 215, 219, 250–51; storage, 176, 215
foragers, x, 71, 76, 87, 118, 119, 123, 125–26, 159, 167, 176, 187, 189, 191, 250; central place model, 119; health, 159, 161; Late Archaic, 202–3; Mexico, 157; settlement/subsistence models, 159; 5. *See also* ethnographic analogies
forks. *See* Flint-Chattahoochee confluence
Fort Gaines, GA, *2*, 8, 11, 25, 28, 201
Fort Walton culture/period, 18, 53, 155, 184, 197, 199, 200, 222, 225; burials, 199, 200, 259, 268; cemetery, 202; ceramics, 202; maize, 256; mounds, 259; radiocarbon dates, 200
fossils, 33, 37, 48, 49, 68, 74, 89, 92, 94, 99, 100, 101–2, 108
Frison, George, 120–21
FSU. *See* universities: Florida State University (FSU)

Gardner, William, 11
gastropods, 43, 78, *82*, 83, 254, 266-67; crown conch, 214; freshwater snail, 77, 160, 254; horse conch, 42, 78, 82, 182, 252; marine, 183, 254; snails, 76–78, 214; terrestrial snails, 67, 183, 214; tulip snail, 83, 214; whelk, 82, 82, 83, 201, 252, 267. *See also* left-handed whelk

gender, 15, 76, 122–23, 126, 268. *See* kinship, men, matrilineality, women
Geographic Information Systems (GIS), 13
George W. Andrews Dam/Reservoir, 7, 10, 28, 110. *See also* lakes: Andrews Lake; Columbia Reservoir
GIS. *See* Geographic Information Systems (GIS)
gorgets, 53–55, *54*, 173–74, 230, 231; distribution, 173; greenstone, 53, 54, 174; sandstone, 53, 55; shell, 82, 83; slate, 53
Gotier Hammock Mound/Gotier Hammock (8Gu2), *82*, *Plate VII*, 223, 245, *246*, 258, 261; radiocarbon dates, 226
Grady, H. L., 6
Green Point Mound (8Fr11), 15, 79, 82, 83, *Plate XV*, 200, 210, *210*, 212, 240, 252
greenstone, 53–54, 218, 231; celt manufacturing center, 265; celts/axes, 52, 53, 231; gorgets, 53–54, 54, 174; pendants/plummets, *Plate XII*, 174, 203; ring, 53; sources, 265; symbolism, 53. *See also* ground stone
ground stone, 6, 51–54, 104, 172–74; abraders, 145, 146; batons, 230–31; bola stones, 51, 137, *139*, 145–48, *147*; bowls, 162, 164, 173; celts/axes, 51, 52, 53. 229, 231, 265; charms, 146; cobbles, 29, 51, 117, 14, 146, 155, 173, 203, 230; disk, 234; gaming stones /chunkey, 146, 230; grinding stones/metates, 51, *52*, 205; hammerstones, 142, 261; hemisphere, 231; hones, 146, 173, 199, 230, 233, 261; "kaolin clay" cylinder, 230; Middle Archaic, 52; necklace, 155; net sinkers, 146; pebbles/pebble tools, 155, 199, 203, 230; pendants, 51, 52, 53, 55, 231; pendants/plummets, 53, *Plate XII*, 174, 231; pipes, 54, 173, 231, *232*; ring, 53; "rubbing stones," 110, wedges, 145. *See also* bannerstone; beads; gorgets
Gulf Coast, 41, 47, 50, 61, 69, 81, 84, 91, 92, 96, *Plate V*, 143, 146–47, 160, 161, 163, 179, 181, 188, 222; Mexican, 78
Gulf of Mexico, *2, 3*, 11, 21, 23, 24, 28, 32, 39–40, 42, 43, 45, 75, 83, 89, 94–95, 107, 108, 195, 238, 249, 264; paleochannels, 39, 93, 95

habitation sites, 81, 138, 160, 201, 212, 232, 233, 234, 260; coastal, 187; Early/Middle Archaic, 145; Middle Woodland, 219, 223–24, 253, 254; villages, 60, 187, 197, 201, 218, 222, 223, 239, 249, 256

Hare's Landing (9Se33), 10, 222, 223, 229, 234, 239, 241, 242, 243, 245, 249

hematite, 124, *Plate X*, 155–56, 174, 231, 233; pigment, 231, 258

historic period, 68, 71, 75, 231; agriculture, 34, 100; American settlers, 6; apiaries, 36, 164; black drink, 252; burials, 179, 215; canals, 34; color significance, 258; contact, 193, 259; ethnocentric accounts, 90; farming, 103; illnesses, 90; language families, 126; matrilineality, 154; Native American food preparation, 181; transegalitarian societies, 125; warfare, 193

Holocene/Recent Era, 37, 43, 68, 123, 156, 161; burials, 122; climate, 29, 92, 138, 148; Early, 29, 42, 146, 158; environment, 139–40; extinctions, 138; Middle, 184

Hopewell Culture, 218, 222, 225–226, 228, 231, 236; bark and log tombs, 256; earthworks, 222; exchange networks, 264, 266; flake knives, 211; faunal remains, 265; human remains, 269; "interaction sphere," 227; mica cutouts, 233; mounds, 225, 253; Ohio, 267

Howard Creek Mound (8Gu41), 199, 205, 210, 211, 233, 234, 253, 270

Huckleberry Landing Mounds (8Fr12), 54, 135, 199, 205, 211, 230, 234, 251, 253, 269

human remains, 86–88, 145, 160, 189, 215–16, 226, 252, 269–70; adult, 191, 269–70; children, 190; cranial modification, 88; DNA, 59, 86, 90, 255, 270–71; flexed, 269; infants, 148; Ohio Hopewell, 269–70; preservation, 86; status markers, 269; study of, 86; teeth, 189

Hunt, Ron, 98

hunter-gatherer-fishers, x, 62, 89, 122–23, 138, 156, 158, 162, 187, 193, 194, 216, 268

hunters, 68, 120, 122, 154, 160; overkill, 123

Hurt, Wesley R., 10

Huscher, Harold A., 10, 97, 110. 177

Hutchinson, Lee, xvi

hydrology, 17, 19, 31, 33, 37, 92, 164; fluvial migration, 43; fluvial processes, 36, 202–3; Late Archaic shift, 79

Ice Age. *See* Pleistocene

iconography, 209, 247; animal, 55, 66, 232, 233, 236, 239, *241*, 243, 245, 247; arrowhead, 56, 233; bird, 66, 69, 70, *Plate XVI*, 236, 237, 240, *241*, 243, *243*, 245, 247; human, 86, 216, 236, 240, *242*, 243, *244*, 270; rattlesnake, 55, 70, 232

ideology, 15, 36, 45, 64–65, 119, 122, 124, 137, 211, 217, 218; ancestor veneration, 15, 88, 260; burial practices, 260; Early/Middle Archaic, 159–60; landscapes, 15; Late Archaic, 186, 188–89; magic, 15, 70, 124, 146, 186, 231, 234, 253, 260; Mesoamerican, 46; religion, 114, 124, 260; world sectors, 247

IF. *See* isolated artifact finds (IFs)

Indian Pass, 106

indigenous peoples. *See* Native Americans

interaction networks, 14, 27, 45, 54, 108, 174, 192, 226, 253, 259, 264

isolated artifact finds (IFs), 95, *96*, *139*, 143, *150*, *153*

ivory, 93, 118; bead preform, 118, 124; foreshaft, 94, 115, 117–18; harpoon, 118; point, 94, 117–18; workshop area, 94

Jaketown complex, 171

jasper: beads, 51, *Plate XI*, 174, 188–89; raw material, 174

Jenkins, Ned, 11, 50

jewelry. *See* body adornments

Jim Woodruff Dam and Reservoir, 7–8, 27–28, 30, 31, 110, *127*. *See also* Lake Seminole

Johnny Boy Landing, FL, 103

Jones, Calvin, xv, 11, 57, 189

J-Y Field site (8Ja63), 232, 254; radiocarbon date, 226, 228

Keene Dog Pond site (8Ja1848), 100, *140*, 142–143, 151, *204*, 226; radiocarbon date, 202

Kelly, A. R., 7, 8, 10, 48, 97, 110–11, 146, 198, 212, 227, 233, 247, 249, 269

kinship, 125, 187, 192, 258, 260. *See also* matrilineality, patrilineality

Kolomoki Mounds (9Er1), 12, 219, 224, 233; "Kolomoki problem," 227–29; ceramics, 224, 239, 249; radiocarbon dates, 228, 249

Kroeber, Alfred, 14

Kula ring ceremonial exchange, 265-65

labor, 76, 79, 87, 125, 154, 160, 173, 186, 187, 258, 267; communal, 187, 216; divisions of, 15, 123, 126, 154, 158, 216; skeletal evidence, 216, 269

lakes: Andrews Lake, 11, 28, 110; Camel Lake, 97, 140; Dead Lakes, 33, 38, 104; Lake Blackshear, 13; Lake Eufaula, 7–8; Lake Seminole, *3*, 7, 11, 12, 17, 28, 31, 99, 127; Lake Wimico, 34, 35, *35*, 36, 40, 43, 97, 143, 202–3, 215; Outside Lake, 101

Lake Douglas Mound (9Dr21), 198, 212, 215, 231, 247, 249, 269

Lake Superior region, copper, 56, 234, 265, *266*

Lane Springs site (9Dr5), 48, 97; "early flint industry," 110

Late Archaic, 77, 79, 156, 162–93, 195, 197, 201, 203, 211, 226, 233; adaptations, 163; baked-clay objects, 162; beads, 51, *Plate XI*, 174; belief systems, 162; bone artifacts, 182, *182*; burials, 187, 189–91; cemeteries, 188; "ceramic Late Archaic", 177; ceramics, 138, 162, 175–76, 178, 187, 205, 207; dates, 162; diet, 189–90; earthworks, 186–88; economy, 189; Elliott's Point complex, 163, 189; environment, 162, 167; faunal remains, 68, 184; fired clay lumps/irregular chunks, 181; floral remains, 183, 184–85; gorgets, 53; ground stone, 53, 172–74; Gulf Coast adaptations, 180–81; Gulf Formational stage, 163; habitation patterns, 167, 187; human remains, 87, 189–91; independant adoption rates, 181; interaction networks, 162, 174, 188–89; "lobes and fishes" hypothesis, 79; mobility, 162, 173, 176; mounds, 188; Norwood phase, 177; people, 188–91; plant domestication, 59; preceramic, 142, 162, 167–69, 182; projectile points, 143, 149, 162, 164, 169, *169*, 203; seasonality and diet, 185–86; sedentism, 173, 188; settlement patterns, 163–67; shell artifacts and perishables, 81, 182–83; shell middens, 35–36, 77–79, *80*, 162, 183, 188; shell rings, 187; site distribution, 162, 164–65, *166*, 188; social and ideological systems, 186–88; social networks, 192; southwest Florida, 187; stable isotope analysis, 189–90; steatite bowls, 54, 55, 172–73, *173*; structures, 167, 187; subsistence, 162, 183–86, 190, 214; terminology, 163; models, 163; "Transitional Period," 163; underwater sites, 163; unusual pit features, 174, 188; violence and warfare, 190–93. *See also* ceramics: fiber-tempered; microtools; Jaketown complex; Poverty Point complex; Poverty Point objects (PPOs); radiocarbon dates

Late Woodland, 222, 225, 250; ceramics, 196, 208. 224, 235–36, 240, 246, 248–51; maize, 256; faunal remains, 74; habitation sites, 223; terminology, 250. *See also* food production; radiocarbon dates, subsistence

left-handed whelk, 42, 78, 82–83, 182, 212, 252, 267; beads, 213; nomenclature, 82; gorgets, 83

lidar (Light Detection and Ranging), 17, 24, *25*, *164*, 165

lightning whelk. *See* left-handed whelk

limestone, *Plates III, XIII*, 43, 45–46, 48, 55–56, 101, 128, 146, 230; abrader, 145; bannerstone, 153; bola stones, 146; discs, *Plate XIII*, 234; gorget, 230; ground stone, 52, 54, 173, 205; pendants/plummets, 231

lithics, 20, 48–51, 97, 101, 156, 168, 172, 201; debitage, 12, 20, 51, 94, 95, 104, 110, 115, 124, *Plate X*, 142, 145, 146,

Index

151, 156, 168, 170, 172, 199, 203, 261; hafting, 148; Macon Plateau Flint Industry, 110; "non projectile-point" assemblages, 109; Standing Boy Flint Industry, 110; thermal alteration/heat-treating, 49, 152, 229; typologies, 20, 51; use wear, 53, 146, 155, 171, 173, 230, 231; patina/weathering, 48–50, 98, 107, 110, 146. *See also* chipped stone tools; ground stone; projectile points

Little Salt Spring, FL, 92

Little St. George Island (Cape St. George), 35, 40–41, 97

looters, 22, 43, 86, 87, 88, 200, 219, 221, 226, 233

Louisiana, 76, 151. 160, 162, 171, 174, 179, 181, 186, 240, 258; ceramics, 236, 245. *See also* Poverty Point complex

lower Chattahoochee valley, 3, *3*, 9, 17, 25, *25*, *26*, 31, 33, 47, 48, 50, *Plate I*, 142, 145, 208, 219, 224, 249; chert, 48; defined, 12, 25; environment, 28–29; Paleoindian, 96, 97–99; sites, 29, 96, 110

LSU. *See* universities: Louisiana State University (LSU)

mammals, 123, 160, 214, 254, 255; bats, 46; bear, 66, 68, 120–21, 254; beaver, 69, 183; bobcat, 68, 120, 145, 183; Caribbean monk seal, 75; coyote, 120; deer, 68, 75, 139, 145, 160, 182–83, 213, 254; dolphin, 72, 74–75; elk, 101; Florida panther, 66, 68, 121; horse,; manatee, 41, 75; muskrat, 183; opossum, 69, 183, 254; otters, 29, 74; rabbit, 69, 183, 254; raccoon, 69, 183, 254; red fox, 255; rodents, 69, 183, 254, 255; skunk, 254; whales, 74, 75; wolf, 66, 68, 253, 255. *See also* bone; faunal remains

Mandeville site (9Cy1 or Cla1), 200–201, 211, 212, 215, 233, 234, 253, 265; radiocarbon dates, 201

Marianna, FL, 37, 101, 103, 113

Marrinan, Rochelle, xv, 67, 255

matrilineality, 15, 125, 154, 248, 267–68, 271

McKinnie site (8Ja1869), 47, 52, 133, 155, 165, 169–70, 169, 174, 176, 188; radiocarbon dates, 167–68, 174

Mead, Margaret, 264

megafauna, 68, 93–94, 114, 120, 122–23, 137; camelids, 93, 101, 121; dire wolves, 121; giant armadillo, 68, 101, 121; giant sloth, 68, 101–2, 121; horse, 68, 101, 121; mammoth, 68, 91, 101, 112, 118, 121–22, 138; mastodon, 68, 93, 94, 99, 101–2, 117, 118, 121–22, 138; saber-toothed cats, 121; tapir, 121

men, 122, 125, 159, 160–61, 191, 192, 265; grave goods, 155; labor, 158; Late Archaic health, 190; stereotypes, 122, 154. *See also* burials: men; human remains

metals, 56–57, 234–35; galena, 56–57, 57, 201, 211, 218, 234–35, 265; silver, 56, 218, 234. *See also* copper

methods: field, 16–19; lab, 19–21, 51; online descriptions, 4

mica, 25–26, 47, 54–55, 57, 199, 206, 211, 218, 230, 232–33; cutouts, 54, *56*, 232–33; sources, 265

microtools, 162, 164, 170–72, *170*, *171*, 181, 188, 189, 195. *See also* Poverty Point complex; Jaketown complex

midden, 19, 38, 42, 47, 67, 69, 70, 73, 77, 80, *81*, 82–84, 156, 160–61, 167, 181, 183, 184, 188, 201, 222 249, 250, 252, 254, 255, 257; burials in, 79; clamshell, 36, 87, *Plate VI*, 143, 151, 163, *164*, *165*, 168, 184, 197; coastal, 78–79, 83; construction, 76, 216; curved, 80; deposition, 77, 79, 195, 223; estuarine, 77–79, 80, *Plate VI*, *164*, *165*, *170*, 176, *182*, 214, 215; freshwater, 31, 163, 183, 214, 223, 225, 229, 233, 249, 251; function, 79, 187; linear, 36, 80; mounded or ridged vs. mounds, 216; oyster, 36, 39, 78–79, 105, 163–64, 168, 184, 197, 202, 214, 233, 255; ridge, 36–37, 39, 81, 166, 259; ring-shaped, 80, 187; riverine, 77, 78, 79; shell, 21, 31, 32, 35–36, 39, 42, 47–48, 55, 67, 69, 70, 73, 75–76, 79–81, 87, 105–6, *Plate VI*, 143, 148, 150, 151, 160, 162–64, 167–68, 170, *170*, 173, 176, 179, 182–84, *182*, 187, 189, 194, 197–98, 199, 202, 203. 209–13, 214, 215–16, 223, 225, 226, 229, 231, 232, 233, 234, 238, 249, 251, 252, 253, 254, 257, 259; types, 78

Middle Archaic, 137, 138, 148–57; atlatl and bannerstone, 51, 152–55, 158; biases, 151; burials, 159; cemeteries, 145; complexity, 158; dates, 148, 151; earthworks, 158, 160, 186; exchange networks, 158; forager models, 159; group size, 159; habitation, 145, 156; human remains, 160–61; Hypsithermal, 148; migration, 161; mobility, 158; mounds, 138, 160; people, 155–56, 160–61; projectile points, *133*, 137, 143, 148–49, *149*, 151–52, 155–56, 169, 170 settlement patterns, 151; site distribution, *150*; steatite bowls, *55*, 172; subsistence, 151, 152, 156–58, 161. See also mounds; radiocarbon dates

Middle Woodland, 11, 50, 53, 56, 197, 200, 205, 214, 218–271; bone and teeth artifacts, 253; burial mound ceremonialism, 200, 218; burial practices, 88; 218, 259–61, 271; ceramics, 15, 86, 199, 200, 208–11, 218, 219, 224, 226, 227, 235–252, 267; climate and sea levels, 256–57; dates, 218, 226; dog coprolites, 59, 71; early Weeden Island ceramic series, 198, 219, 240–45; environment and social change, 250, 257; ethnographic analogies, 261–63; exchange networks, 224, 235, 242, 264; exotics, 265–66, 266; faunal remains, 74, 254–55, 265; floral remains, 256 ground stone and other rock, 52, *52*, *53*, Plates XII, XIII, 230–34, 232; habitation sites, 219, 223–24, 233; human remains, 88, 269–70; ideology, 218, 260; "interaction sphere," 264; interpretive constraints, 219–20, 224; Kolomoki Mounds, 226; metals, 57, 234–35; mica, 232–33; mound construction activity and ritual, 222, 257–59; mounds, 52, 53, 63, 198, 200, 218–19, *221*, 200–23, 225–26, 234–235, 252, 267; people, 270–71; Percy-Brose model and revisions, 250–51; perishables, 253; projectile points, 203, 229, *230*; research biases and errors, 227–29; "Santa Rosa-Swift Creek," 240; seasonality, 256; settlement patterns, 218–20, 256; shamanism, 63; shell artifacts, 82, 252–53, 267; site distribution, 220, *220*, 222; social systems and ranking, 218, 268–69; steatite, 54, *55*, *232*; structures, 223; subsistence, 215, 218, 254–56; Swift-Creek ceramic series, 218, 219, 236–40; Swift Creek-early Weeden Island (proper terminology), 227, 236; warfare/conflicts, 260. See also radiocarbon dates

migration, 161, 194–95, 235; explanations, 119; *pindah*, 262

Milanich, Jerald T., xv, 4, 11. 177, 228

Millender, Pat, xiv

Miller, Carl, 8, 10, 227

Mississippi Valley, 33, 85; ceramics, 7, 236, 245; raw materials, 51, 235

Mississippian culture, 201, 227, 230; ceramics, 20, 224; mounds, 198; sea level, 40

mobility, 122, 138, 158, 161–62, 173, 176, 187; logistical, 138; residential, 138; sedentism, 156, 158, 173

Moore, C. B., 6–7, 21, 43, 83, 87, 199–200, 219, 222, 226, 230–31, 233, 234, 240, 243, 249, 252, 259–60, ceramics, 260; excavations, 269–70; *Gopher*, 7

Moses, Jimmy, xiv

mounds, 6, 11, 17, 79, 83, 88, 138, 160, 186, 212, 218, *221*, 222–23, 228 229, 230, 231, 233, 235, 240, 243, 245, 247, 249, 254; Adena, 198, 239; Brazilian *sambaquis*, 79; burial, 2, 6, 14, 47, 52, 53, 55, 74, 79, 87, 160, 194–95, 198, 199, 211, 215–217, 218–22, 224, 225, 226, 231, 233, 234, 240, 243, 249, 253, 257; color symbolism, 47; conical, 199, 201, 216, 222; construction, 47, 79, 138, 158, 160, 186, 187, 198, 200, 201, 216, 219, 224, 227, 249, 250, 258–59; early investigations, 5–7; Hopewellian, 233; interpretations, 162; Mexican Pacific coast, 79; platform/flat-topped pyramid, 198, 201, 216, 222, 227; sand, 79, 160, 199, 216, 222; shell, 47, 76, 79, 160, 199; temple, 6; Woodland period, 46, 87

mound centers/complexes, 6, 54, 56, 66, 68, 160, 199–200, 218, 221, 222, 224, 226; See also Aspalaga Landing (8Gd1);

Chattahoochee Landing (8Gd4); Mandeville site (9Cy1 or Cla1); Pierce Mounds complex (8Fr14); Poverty Point complex
mountains: Appalachian, 54, 119, 172, 265; Blue Ridge, 23
museums: Army Medical Museum (US Department of Defense Armed Forces Institute of Pathology, National Museum of Health and Medicine), 269; British Museum, 6, 147, *147*; Brunei Technological Museum, 65; Cleveland Museum of Natural History (CMNH), 11, 50; Columbus Museum (GA), 10; Daytona Museum of Arts and Sciences, 121; Florida Museum of Natural History (FLMNH), 6, 11, 12, 13, 67, 243, 255; National Museum of Natural History, 6; National Museum of the American Indian (NMAI), 7, 230; Fort Walton Beach Temple Mound Museum, 209, 270
music, 69, 126, 271; musical instruments, 157, 234, 253; songs, 124

NAGPRA. *See* Native American Graves Protection and Repatriation Act
National Geographic Society, 22
National Park Service, 10
Native American Graves Protection and Repatriation Act (NAGPRA), 86
Native Americans, 2, 5, 6, 15, 28, 31, 34, 56, 62, 64, 71, 83, 86, 90, 181, 252; "balance between spirit and matter" beliefs, 44, 119; black drink, 265; blood types, 90; color significance, 258; genders, 126; genetic diversity, 90; historic, 231; ideologies, 247; languages, 90, 92, 126; Late Archaic, 193; matrilineality, 154; plant domestication, 59; populations, 85; potters, 248; prehistoric life expectancy, 87; racist myths, 90; resistance to illnesses, 90; stereotypes, 126; symbolism, 247; terminology, xi; tobacco cultivation, 63; tobacco ritual, 63
Nature Conservancy, 27, 34
nets, 65, 72, 74, 111, 118, 120, 122, 158, 185, 255; bags, 65; weights, 53, 146, 179, 231, 252. *See also* ceramics: net-marked; fishing; ground stone: pendants/plummets
New York Historical Society, 6
NMAI. *See* museums: National Museum of the American Indian (NMAI)
nuts, 60, 121, 124, 146, 157, 160, 173, 183, 184, 214, 215, 256; acorns, 256

Ocheesee Pond, FL, 100
ocher/iron oxide, 55, 124, 133, 156, 174; *See also* pigment
Otis Hare site (8Li172), 55, *56*, 59, *65*, 69, 71, 223, 225, 226, 231, 233, 237, 238, 238, 251, 252, 255, 256; radiocarbon dates, 225–26
oyster, 21, 29, 35–36, 38, 39, 42, 67, 76, 77–78, 106, 144, 150, 163, 167, 176, 183, 184, 214, 234, 252, 254, 255, 257

Page-Ladson site, 93–94, 109, 121, 144, 146; radiocarbon dates, 94
paint, 65, 270; black, 240; on ceramics, 240; red, 240, 243. *See also* pigment
Paleoindian period, 89–126, 142, 148, 187; Agate Basin site (WY), 120; Alabama, 95, 97; ancient riverbank/island formation hypothesis, 107; Apalachicola River valley, 99–101; atlatl, 152; Aucilla River sites, 93–95, 104, 115, 117–18, 120, 124, 145; biases, 119, 122; big game hunting, 121–23; burials, 124–25; cemetery, 124; Chipola Valley concentration, 95, 101–5; chipped stone tools, 37, 152; coastal evidence, 105–8; diet, 123; dogs, 157; Early/pre-Clovis, 94, 113; Edgefield scraper, 115; extinctions, 123; Gault site, 91; Georgia, 95, 97; interaction networks, 108; Late, 94, 114, 115, 124; linguistic branches, 90; "Lively Complex," 109; lower Chattahoochee and Flint valleys, 97–99; Middle/Clovis horizon, 94, 113–15; other chipped stone tools and ground stone, 117; other plant and animal resources, 123–24; perishables and other organic artifacts, 117–18; population, 87, 90, 101, 114, 125; pre-projectile points/pre-Clovis,

92, 94, 109–11; projectile points, 89, 91–92, 94, 95, 97–108, *98*, *100*, *102*, *106*, 111–15, 117, *Plate VIII*, 142, 144, 147; settlement models, 97, 99, 105; settlement patterns, 39, 46, 101, 118, 138; site distribution, 91, *93*, 94, *96*, 97, 104–5, 108–9; sociopolitical systems, 125–26; South America, 114; St. Vincent Island, 105; subsistence, 37, 68, 89, 104; Tennessee Valley, 97. *See also* Page-Ladson site; sea levels, Sloth Hole site; Younger Dryas

Paradise Point site (8Fr71), 105–7, 146, 229–30; radiocarbon dates, 202

Parker, Brian, xvi, 67, 181

parks: Florida Caverns State Park, 37, 46; Seminole State Park, 29, 30; Three Rivers State Park, 50

pathology: anemias, 161; arthritis, 160; broken bones, 160; decapitation, 191; degenerative joint disease, 160; dental, 87, 88, 160–61, 189, 269; dismemberment, 191; fractures,; labor, 158, 160, 269; neural tube defects, 161; nutritional stress, 161; physiological stress, 161, 189–90; scalping, 191; trauma, 87, 159, 161, 190

patrilineality, 125

pearl, 66, 266; beads, *67*, 253, 266

pebbles. *See* chipped stone tools; ground stone; stone

pendants/plummets, *Plate XII*, 203; bone, 253; clay, 252; greenstone, 53; quartz, 52, 53; sandstone, 55; shell, 252; "tabbed circle," 252

Pensacola, FL, *2*, 211, 240

Penton, Dan, xv, 11

Percy, George, xiv, 11, 68, 77, 223, 250, 254. *See also* ceramics: Percy-Brose model

perishables, 63–66, 65, 117–18, 148, 152, 182–83, 205, 213, 242, 253, 257, 258, 265; feathers, 64, 66, 69, 182, 265

Pierce Mounds complex (8Fr14), x, 6, 7, 79, *Plates XIII*, *XIV*, 147, 199–200, 218, 221, 231, 232, 252, *259*, 259; bola stone, *147*; bone, 68, 253; burials, 200, 234, 240, 243, 260, 269; ceramics, *Plate XIV*, 206, 207, 240, *242*, 243, 244, 245, 247; copper, 56, *Plate XIII*, 253; grave goods, 66, *67*; human remains, 269; mounds, 56, 66, 199–200, 213, 234, 240, 243, 245, 252–53, 259, 260, 269; pipe, *232*; shell artifacts, *213*, 253; silver, 234. *See also* archaeological sites: Cemetery Mound (8Fr21), Mound Near Apalachicola (8Fr20A), Shell Mound Near Apalachicola (8Fr20B), Cool Spring Mound (8Fr19); Singer Mound (8Fr16), 200, *259*

pigment, 55, 57, 90, 124, 155, 156, 174, 231; 234–35, 258

pipes, 63, 231; ceramic, 6, 199, 251; elbow, 63, 251; platform ("monitor"), 251; steatite, 54, 231, *232*, 251; tubular, 63

plants, 29, 35, 36, 41, 58–66, 89, 121, 123–24, 137–38, 146, 157–58, 182, 184–85, 215, 256; amaranths, 60, 157; bottle gourd, 59, 64, 89, 124, 157, 184, 215, 256; chenopods, 60, 157, 184; cultivation, 63, 256; Curcurbita pepo pumpkin, 157; datura (jimson weed), 62; fruit, 60–62, 120, 157–58, 176, 184–85, 215, 256; gourds, 121; grasses, 36, 60, 174, 184, 256; maize, 59, 87, 184, 190, 256, 269; management, 59, 60, 62, 157, 215, 256; prickly pear, 157, 159 rush, 39; saw palmetto, 61, 148, 174; seeds, 60–61, 65, 123, 157, 159–60, 176, 256; squash, 157, 184, 256; tubers, 62, 215; use, 58–59, 61–62, 66, 157; vines, 60, 64. *See also* Spanish moss

Pleistocene, 1, 28, 30, 35, 40–41, 46, 101, 137, 157, 163; barrier formations, 107; Beringia, 90; burials, 122; coastlines, 89, 92, *93*; environment, 114, 120, 123, 138, 140; first inhabitants,43; fossils, 37, 89, 92, 99, 108; landmasses, 92, 93; Late, 29, 43, 92; paleochannels, 97, 99; population migrations, 90; post-, 77, 78, 116, 143; sea levels, 89–90, 92; shorelines, 91, 93; sinkholes, 104; site distribution, 91, 109. *See also* megafauna

population; black, 86; demographics, 85–86, 101, 118, 156; Early Archaic, 140; Early Woodland, 197; ethnicity,

90, 235; groups, 235–36; growth, 189; interpretive models, 197; Middle Woodland, 218, 270; Paleoindian, 119; pressure, 119
portable X-ray fluorescence (pXRF), 20, 57, 176, 211
Porter's Bar mound and village (8Fr1), 79, 134, 179, 180, 200, 222, 230–31, 234, 240, *242*, 243, 244, *244*, 245, 252, 253, 254, 257, 270
Poverty Point complex, 174, 179, 186–87; clay effigies/figurines, 179; exchange networks, 189; lapidary industry, 174, 188; microtools, 171; related sites, 187; site, 181, 186–87, 188; trade fair model, 189
Poverty Point objects ("PPOs"), 57, 162, 179–81, *180*, 184, 186–88, 195; distribution, 179; trace element analysis, 181, 188
pre–projectile point culture. *See* Paleoindian period: pre-projectile point/pre-Clovis
projectile points, 21–22, 39, 48, 50, 52, 93, 103, 111, 118, 122, *Plates VII, VIII*, *149*, 152, 155, 156, 160, 167–68, 187, 203, 229; Abbey, 148, *149*; Adena, 203; Alachua, 149, 152; Baker's Creek, 229, *230*; Beaver Lake, 103, 107, *Plate VIII*, 132; Benton, 137, 148, *149*; beveled, 110, 144–45, 146; Big Sandy, 110, 137, *140*, 142, 144; Boggy Branch, 148; Bolen, 137, 140, *141*, 142, 144–45, 146, 155, 226; Bolen Beveled, 110, *140–41*, 142–45, 159, 226; Bolen Plain, 145; Broward Subtype 1, *140*, 229; Chipola, 100, 107, 113, *Plate VIII*, 147; Clay, 168, *169*; Clovis, 91–92, 94, 98–100, 98, *100*, *102*, 103, 105, *106*, 107–8, 112–15, 124, *Plate VIII*, 147; Clovis/Suwannee, 103; Clovis/Suwannee/Beaver Lake, 103; corner-notched, 137, 140, 145; Cotaco Creek, 168; Cottonbridge, 148; Cumberland, 113; Dalton, 100, *100*, 103, 104, 105, 107, 113–15, 124, 146; Dalton/Hardaway,103; Duval, *140*; Ecusta, 110; Elora, 148; Eva, 137, 140, 148; "fishtail," 114–15; Florida Adena, *204*; Florida Archaic Stemmed, 109, 145, 149, 152, 168; Florida Hamilton, *Plate X*, 148; fluted, 91, 94, 97, 100, 107, 112–13, 118; garfish scales, 73; Gary, 168; Gilchrist, 103, 113, *141*; Greenbriar, 100, 103, 113; Greenville, 203; guides, 20, 51, 203; Halifax, 148; Hamilton, *Plate IX*, 156, 169, 229; Hardaway Side-Notched, *140*; Hardee, *141*; Hardee Beveled, 143–44; Hernando, 203, *204*; Hillsborough, 148; Kirk, 143, 155; Kirk Corner-Notched, 137, 140, *140*, 142, 143, 144; Kirk Serrated, 137, *149*; Kirk Serrated/Stemmed, 149; Lafayette, 140; lanceolate, 89, 91, 114, 137, 144; Ledbetter, 149, *149*, 168, *169*, 170; Leon, *140*; Levy, 149, 152, *169*, 170; Lost Lake, 140, *141*, 144; Marianna, 100, 103, 112, 113; Marion, 149, *149*, 152; Morrow Mountain, 137, *140*, 149, 151, 156; notched, 116, 137, 161, 168, 170, 203; O'Leno, 100; Ottare, *169*, 170; outrepassé flaking, 112; Paris Island, 170; Pickwick, 149, 168, *169*, 170; Putnam, 149, 151, 152; Quad, 103; Redstone, 103, 112; Santa Fe, 113–14, *Plate VIII*; Savannah River, 149; side-notched, 137, 140, 144–45; Simpson, 92, 98, 100, *102*, 103, 107, 112–15, *Plate VIII*; South America, 92, 114–15; spear and arrow points, 152; St. Albans, 149; stemmed, 91, 114, 137, 148, 151, 161, 168, 170, 229; Sumter, 149, *149*, 155; Suwannee, 92, 94, 97, 98, *98*, *102*, 103, 107, 109, 110, 112–14, 124; Swannanoa, 203, *204*; Sykes, 137, 149; Tallahassee, 100, 107, 115; Taylor, *140*; Thonotosassa, 149, 156; typologies, 112, 144, 149, 151, 152, 164, 168, 203; unfluted Clovis, 99, 100, *100*, *102*, *106*, 107, 113–14, *Plate VIII*; unfluted lanceolate, 91, 94; Wacissa, *141* 143–44; Wade, 168; Westo, 140, 168, *169*; Wheeler, 103; White Springs, 149. *See also* isolated finds (IFs)
pXRF. *See* portable X-ray fluorescence (pXRF)

quartz, 29, 46, 50, 224, 229, 231, 233; bead, 124; crystals, 211, 218, 265; microtools, 171; pebbles, 233; pendant, 52, 53, *Plate*

XII, 231; projectile point, 229, *230*; sand, 47

quartzite, 20, 51, *52*, 146, 156, 231, 233; bannerstone, 153; cobbles, 155, 203, 230; discoidal, 230; pebbles, 174; pendants/plummets, 231

radiocarbon dates, 20–21, 58, 197, 200, 251; earliest in research region, 156; Early Archaic, 144–45; Early Woodland, 143, 197, 199, 201–2, 215, 226, 228; Kolomoki, 228, 249, 450; Late Archaic, 156, 162, 167–68, 170, 172, 174; Middle Archaic, 151, 156, 172; Middle Woodland, 143, 225–28, 237, 245, 255, 256; Page-Ladson site, 94; Poverty Point-type objects, 181

Raiders of the Lost Ark, 21

reptiles, 32, 123; alligator, 66, 68–69, 121, 183, 214, 254, 255, 265; gopher tortoise, 69; snakes, 32, 66, 70, 121, 124, 183; tortoise, 69. *See also* turtle

residue, 172–73, 226; analysis, 20, 173, 184

Richardson's Hammock site (8Gu10), 42, 52, 52, 79, 88, *210*, 214, 231, 233, 243, *244*, 252, 253, 269; radiocarbon dates, 226

ritual, 44, 52, 63, 69, 70, 88, 112, 124, 156, 160, 187, 188, 192, 216, 218. 225, 245, 253, 261; animals, 66, 68; burial, 79; corporate, 267; death, 191; exchange, 265; mounds, 258; shell, 80, 82, 83

River Basin Surveys (RBS), 7, 10

rock art, 46, 186

Sam's Cutoff site (8Fr754), 36, 78–79, 80, 87, 163, *170*, 183–84, 189–90; radiocarbon dates, 168

sandstone, 55–56, 146, 174, 231, 233, 261; bannerstone, 153; bowl, 173; gorgets, 53, 55; hones, 55, 173, 230; pendants, 55

Schnell, Frank T., Jr., 10, 85

Schoolcraft, Henry, 6

sea levels, 36, 38, 39, 43, 77–78, 89–90, 92–93, 95, 108, 114, 143, 148, 163; Early Woodland, 195; Archaic, 78, 156; fluctuation, 40, 194, 202, 257; Holocene, 29, 35, 39–40; 78, 138, 140, 163, 167, 184; Pleistocene, 106, 108, 114, 119; Middle Woodland, 256; stands, 150

Sears, William, 11, 227–229; Kolomoki, 227–29

seasonality, 1, 13, 31, 34, 60, 61, 71, 72–73, 76, 78, 84, 119, 120–21, 138, 159, 161, 162, 185–86, 214, 253, 256–57; faunal assemblages, 255;

sedentism, 187–88, 219, 250

settlement patterns, 35, 42, 45, 60, 71, 81, 108, 138, 158; Archaic, 39, 159; barrier formations, 41; Early Archaic, 137, 141–44; Early Woodland, 194; Late Archaic, 163–67; Middle Archaic, 151; Middle Woodland, 218–20, 250; Paleo, 39, 97, 99, 105, 108, 118

shell, 31, 43, 47, 65, 66, 79, 80, 81, 83, 162–63, 189, 218, 261; awls, 82, *82*, 83, 182, 252; beads, 6, 82, 159, 189, 190, 198, 200, 212–13, *213*, 249, 253, 267; celts, 252; ceramic rocker, 211; chisels, 82, 252; columella tools, 82, 182, 212; cups, 63, 82, 252, 267; dates, 202; debitage, 79, 182, 212; dippers, 267; engraved, 69, 83; gorget, 82, 83; "gouges", 212; hammers, 82, 212, 252; lime, 79, 258; marginella, 83; olive, 83; oyster, 252; pendants/plummets, 82, 212, 252; perforators, 82; picks, 182; quahog triangle, 79; ridges, 6, 199; right-angle pointed tool, 82, *82*; "reservoir effect," 20; rings, 80, 197; rocker stamp,; scoops, 182, 212, 252; scrapers, 82, *82*, 252; spatulas, 82, 182, 212, 252; spoons, 267; symbolism, 83; tools, 43, 79, 82, *82*, *83*, 214. *See also* midden; mound

shellfish, 20, 21, 29, 31, 32, 35–36, 38, 42, 66, 71, 74, 76–79, 137, 148, 151, 158, 176, 179, 184–85, 202, 203, 254, 255; environmental indicators, 67; preservation bias, 67; sea urchin, 75. *See also* bivalve mollusks; clams; gastropods

Silver Lake Wildlife Management Area, 30

slate: bannerstones, 153; gorgets, 53, 231

Sloth Hole site, 145; Paleoindian, 94, 115, 118, 124

Smithsonian Institution, 10, 48, 227, *See*

also museums: National Museum of Natural History, National Museum of the American Indian (NMAI); River Basin Surveys (RBS)

Snow, Frankie, xiii, 237; stamped design database, 209

SnowVision/World Engraved project, 239; machine learning, 20, 239

sociopolitical systems, 14, 45, 112, 122, 137, 159, 192, 215, 248, 271; big man model, 267–68; burial practices, 260; clan, 154, 160, 187 239; chiefdoms, ix, 268; Early/Middle Archaic,160; Early Woodland, 216–17; egalitarian, 125, 137, 154, 158, 162, 187, 188, 192, 217, 267; hereditary leadership, 125, 216, 268; hierarchy, 216, 267; identity markers, 80, 154, 179–80, 206, 270; inequality, 14, 57, 160, 186, 215, 268–69; inherited ranks, 160; Late Archaic, 162,186–88; matrilocal residence, 248, 271; "middle-range" societies, 268; past models, 268; prestige, 122, 264; "prestige technologies", 187; ranked, 125, 159, 187; ranked versus stratified, 269; social-leveling mechanisms, 268; status, 88, 144, 154–55, 160, 217, 260, 269–70; stratification, 268; transegalitarian, 125, 187; tribes, 268

South America,63, 73, 89–90, 92; Brazil, 79, 115; Chile, 114–15; projectile points, 91–92, 114–15; shell mounds (sambaquis), 79; women hunters, 122

Southwestern US, 58, 63, 71; Pueblo potters, 248

Spanish moss, 58, 59, 174, 175, 178, 184; radiocarbon date, 174. *See also* ceramics: fiber-tempered; temper

springs, 29–30, 32, 37, 40, 44, 89, 92, 94, 101, 104, 106, 151; Blue Spring, 33, *Plate II*; Jackson Blue Springs, 101; Little Salt, 92; salt, 56

St. Andrews Bay, 107, 233

St. George Island, *3, 35,* 40–41, 71, 98, 107, 141, 143, 153, 153; sites, 41; State Park, *Plate V*

St. Joseph Bay, *3,* 18, 24, 35, *35,* 40, 75, 78, 82, 83, 131, 164, 214, 223, 226, 252; environment, 42–43, 71; gastropods, 267; material culture, 43; salinity, 42; shell middens, 69, 78–79, 82

St. Joseph Bay State Buffer Preserve, xiv, 34, 143

St. Joseph Peninsula, *3*, 24, *35,* 40, 42, 151; Richardson's Hammock, 42

St. Vincent 3 site (8Fr362), 105, 107, *111, Plate VIII, 140,* 143, 203, *204, 230,* 247

St. Vincent 5 site (8Fr364 Pickalene Bar), 53, 53, 57, 72, 74, 74, 79, 105–6, 106, 134, 140–41, 143, 149, 171, 171, 174, 231, 232, 233, 238, 255; radiocarbon date, 226

St. Vincent Island, 40, 52, 53, 67, 72, 74, 87, 143, 146, 151, 165, 166, 175, 188, 202, 231, 232, 234; Paleoindian, 105–8, 111

St. Vincent Sound, 43, 106, 222–23

steatite/soapstone, 54, *55,* 188–189, 218, 232; bannerstone, 154, 232; bowls, *55*, 162, 164, 168, 172–73, *173*, 176, 188; exchange networks, 188, 192; pipes, 54, *55,* 231, *232*; quarries, 172; residue radiocarbon dates, 172; technology, 172–73

stone, 186; bitumen/natural asphalt,; granite, 134, 231, 233; lapidary industry, 188; obsidian, 108; pebbles, *Plate X*, 261; plumbago/mineral graphite, 233. *See also* chert; quartz; quartzite; steatite; Tallahatta quartzite/Tallahatta sandstone

stone tools. *See* lithics; chipped stone tools; ground stone

storms, 38, 39–41, 43, 46, 84–85, 143, 167; Early Woodland, 194–95; hurricanes, 84, 195, 257; Hurricane Katrina, 186; Hurricane Michael, 32, 42, 84; secondary deposition, 108; Tropical Storm Alberto, 84; Tropical Storm Beryl, 84. *See also* barrier formations

structures, 64, 66, 70, 81, *81,* 187, 197, 223, 252; patterns, 19; wattle and daub, 64

submerged sites, 89–90, 108, 202, 222

subsistence, 14, 35–36, 37, 39, 60–61, 68–79, 83, 87, 89–90, 119, 125, 137, 146, 160–62, 165; Amazon, 72; aquaculture, 71; aquatic resources, 38, 42, 71–79,

148, 158, 167, 254; Archaic, 137–39; catchment area, 45, 186; deer, 68; dogs, 70; Early and Middle Archaic, 156–158; Early Woodland, 194, 202, 215; farming, 59; foraging, 59, 77, 158, 160, 218; hunting, 37, 65, 68–69, 72, 75–76, 87, 89, 93, 109, 112, 119–25, 137, 138, 146, 151, 154–55, 158–59, 183, 214, 218; Late Archaic, 162, 183–86; Late Woodland, 255; Middle Archaic, 151, 152, 161; Middle Woodland, 218; Paleo, 89, 119–24, 254–56; water, 45. *See also* ethnographic analogies; fishing
Swift Creek design database, 209, 235, 237
symbolism, 15, 83, 179, 247–48; clan totems, 247; Middle Woodland ceramics, 247

Tallahatta quartzite/Tallahatta sandstone, 50
Tate's Hell State Forest/Tate's Hell Swamp, 34
teeth: animal, 117, 148, 159, 253, 265; human, 160–61, 189–90
Tesar, Louis D., xv, 11, 112
Thank-You-Ma'am Creek site (8Fr755), 78, 80, 172-73, *173*, 178, 181, 183; radiocarbon date, 168, 172
tobacco, 59, 62–63, 70, 256; nicotine, 63; reactions, 63, 265; Southwest, 63; uses, 63, 231
topography, 26–27, 29–30; bluffs, 12, 29–30, 32–34, 47, 99, 100, 142, 165, 219; coastlines, 90–92, 93, 106, 156, 167; dunes, 4, 38, 40–41, 42, 47, 143, 167; elevations, 33, 34; floodplains, 28, 32–33, 34, 219; karst, 29, 30, 32 45–46, 101; marine terraces, 33, 46; ponds, 3, 29, 50, 104; ravines, 3, 30, 32, 99; ridges, 32; sinkhole, 29, 44, 92, 94, 104, 114, 145, 186; terraces, 98, 103, 155, 232
Torreya State Park/Torreya Ravines and Bluffs, 32, 43, 219
trace element analysis, 20, 57, 176, 181, 188, 248
trees: beech, 97, 140, 256; cedar, 4, 39, 61–62; cypress, 3, 36, 38, 61, 121, 145; elm, 157; Florida soapberry (Sapindus marginatus), 39; Florida yew, 30; hackberry, 157; hardwoods, 29, 32, 59–60, 140, 151, 214, 256; hickory, 60, 97, 140, 157, 214; magnolia (Magnolia grandiflora), 3, 62, 157, 256; maple, 62; oak, 3, 4, 27, 41, 60, 140, 157, 184, 214, 256; pecan, 60; sabal or cabbage palm (Sabal palmetto), 4, 27, 61, 174; pine, 3, 27, 29-30, 32, 34-35, 41, 60–61, 97, 140, 152, 157, 184, 214, 256; spruce, 97, 140; sweetgum, 62; sycamore, 62; torreya, 30–31, 32, 33, 256; tupelo, 36, 62, 164, 256
Trestle Bridge site (8Ja186), 51, 52, 203, 205, *205*, *206*, 207–8, *209*
turtle, 39, 42, 69, 124, 160, 183, 185, *241*, 254, 255; Barbour's map, 30, 69, 255; freshwater, 69, 254; rattles, 69; sea, 69, 214; shells, 69, 145, 148, 199, 253. *See also* seasonality

UF. *See* universities: University of Florida (UF)
UGA. *See* universities: University of Georgia (UGA)
underwater sites, 91, 93, 93, 95, 118, 143, 144–45, 151, 163, 164
United States Department of Agriculture (USDA): soil surveys, 17
United States Geological Survey (USGS), 17
universities: Case Western Reserve University (CWRU), 11; Florida State University (FSU), 10, 11, 219, 255; Louisiana State University (LSU), 11; Tulane, 11; University of Florida (UF), 11; University of Georgia (UGA), 8, 10, 48, 227, 233; University of New Orleans, 11. *See also* University of South Florida (USF)
University of South Florida (USF), 19, 21, 129; archaeology lab, 17, 67; Digital Commons website, x–xi
US Army Corps of Engineers, 7, 10, 29, 31
USDA. *See* United States Department of Agriculture (USDA)
USF. *See* University of South Florida (USF)
USGS. *See* United States Geological Survey (USGS)

Van Horn Creek site (8Fr744), 74, 78, *80*, 178, 181, 182, *182*, 183–84

Waddell's Mill Pond site (8Ja65), 11, 46, 198, 211, 222, 253; radiocarbon date, 199
Waller knife, 95, 98, 100, 108, 115–17, *116*
Walter F. George Dam and Reservoir, 7–8, 10, 12, 25, 28, 200. *See also* lakes: Lake Eufaula
warfare, 14, 159, 191–93; Mayan studies, 191; trophies, 200; Woodland, 217, 260
watercraft, xi, 45, 46; canoes, 45, 157, 182, 253
waterways, *2*, 26, 39, 43, 44–45, 104, 109, 140, 151, 164, 217, 219; exchange, 264; Tennessee-Ohio-Mississippi system, 264. *See also* Apalachicola-Chattahoochee system
weapons, 154; bow and arrow, 112 144, 152, 154; clubs, 111, 183; darts, 112, 144, 152, 203; harpoons, 183; spears, 112, 118, 144, 152, 154–55, 183, 203. *See also* atlatl; projectile points
Wewahitchka, FL, *3*, 21, 28, 38, 101
Whitfield, Jeff, xiii–xiv, 38, 49, 100, 103, 112
Willey, Gordon R., xv, 7–8, 14, 20, 162, 174, 208–9, 220–1, 226, 235–36, 238, 246, 248, 250; *Archeology of the Florida Gulf Coast*, 7; ceramic typology, 209, 211, 236–37, 240; *Selena*, 7, 8
Wingate, Jack, 99
women, 76, 122–23, 125, 158–61, 192, 216, 248, 267, 271; fertility rates, 161; grave goods, 155; labor, 158; Late Archaic health, 190; menstrual cycles, 84, 122; Pueblo potters, 248; stereotypes, 154; weapon use, 154. *See also* burials: women; effigies/figurines; kinship; matrilineality
wood, 92, 117, 171–72, 182; ash, 47; atlatl, 152; bowls, 157, 179; charcoal, 20, 60, 133, 143, 156, 167, 184, 199, 201, 202, 226, 228, 256, 258; floats, 183; paddles, 208, 239; pestle, 148; point, 155; preservation, 64, 214; shafts, 148; silicified/petrified, 50, 233; stakes, 145, 148, 159; vessels,; Woodland Information Superhighway, 265

yaupon holly, 63, 157; "àsi-àpi-laiki", 28; black drink tea (asi), 28, 63, 252, 265; trade, 265, 266–67
Yellow Houseboat site (8Gu55), *80*, 87, *140*, 143, 171, 183, 215, 253
Younger Dryas, 92, 113–14